The Modern World

1914 to 1980

A NEW CERTIFICATE APPROACH

Philip Sauvain

Stanley Thornes (Publishers) Ltd

First published in 1989 by:
Stanley Thornes (Publishers) Ltd
Old Station Drive
Leckhampton
CHELTENHAM GL53 0DN
England

British Library Cataloguing in Publication Data
Sauvain, Philip, *1933–*
    The modern world, 1914 to 1980: a new certificate
    approach.
    1. World, 1900–
    I. Title
    909.82

    ISBN 0–7487–0049–8

Cover illustration: the lunar module, *Eagle*, which landed on the moon on 20 July 1969, reproduced by kind permission of NASA.

Typeset by Tech-Set, Gateshead, Tyne & Wear.
Printed and bound in Great Britain at The Bath Press, Avon.

Contents

Chapter One

The First World War

INTRODUCTION

Source A   London – August 1914

Was awakened by loud noises. Great crowds are parading the streets, exulting in the anticipation of war . . . I cannot sleep. They are going mad. Have they no imagination?

The Private Diaries of Sydney Moseley, Max Parrish, 1960

Source B   Berlin – August 1914

Up and down the wide road of Unter den Linden crowds paced incessantly by day and night singing the German war songs . . . The most mighty storm of cheering was reserved for the Crown Prince . . . Him the people cheered for they had never known war.

Henry W. Nevinson, *More Changes More Chances,* James Nisbet, 1925

Source C   Munich

The Odeonsplatz, Munich, 2 August 1914

1 What were the similarities in the way in which people greeted the war in Britain and Germany?

2 Does the photograph support or contradict the written sources? Which famous leader was among those who welcomed the outbreak of war?

3 What reservations about the coming war are expressed in these sources?

4 Look at each of the three Sources A, B and C in turn. Are they primary or secondary sources? Give reasons for your answer.

Despite the euphoria in the streets, many politicians feared the worst. According to Walter H. Page, the American ambassador in London, the German ambassador was distraught, the British foreign secretary and the Austrian ambassador both wept, and King George V threw up his hands and exclaimed: 'My God, Mr Page, what else could we do?'

Their anguish was justified. They knew better than the public what tragedy the war would bring. In the end it cost the lives of about 1.5 million French, 1 million British, 2 million Russian, 0.5 million Italian and 3 million Austrian and German soldiers.

OUTBREAK OF WAR

Causes

BERLIN, 9 August 1914

Exactly what was the real cause of the war no one seems to know, although it is discussed night and day. One thing grows clearer to me every day: neither the people here nor there wished for war, but here they are now being carried off their legs with patriotism, at seeing so many enemies on every side.

To me it seems that Europe was thirsting for war, and that the armies and navies were no longer to be restrained.

Evelyn, Princess Blücher, *An English Wife in Berlin*, Constable, 1921

Even today, over 70 years later, it is far from clear 'exactly what was the real cause of the war' or who was to blame. In 1919 (as you can see in Chapter 3), the Allies made Germany take all the blame for starting the War. Modern experts agree that the German military were, indeed, 'thirsting for war and no longer to be restrained'. But, as you have seen, the celebrations at the outbreak of war were not confined to Berlin or Munich. Nor were the Serbians, Russians, French and British entirely free from blame either. The general atmosphere in 1914 was tense. The reasons why are not hard to find.

1 The Alliance System France and Germany hated each other. The French bitterly resented the fact that Alsace and Lorraine had been taken by Germany after her defeat in the Franco–Prussian War in 1871. This is why both countries sought alliances with friendly nations. Germany was particularly concerned about the threat from her colossal eastern neighbour, Russia. As a consequence, Europe separated into two armed camps. On the one hand, Germany, Austria-Hungary and Italy – the Central or Triple Alliance powers. On the other hand, France, Russia and Britain – the Triple *Entente* powers.

2 Balkan Nationalism Russian and Austrian rivalry in the Balkans was another potential cause of war. The Austro-Hungarian empire was already in decline. It was further weakened when Russia encouraged the Slav nationalists who wanted to create a Pan-Slav union of all the Slav peoples under the protection of Russia. Since many Slavs lived in Austria-Hungary, the Austrians saw Slav nationalism, especially in Serbia (now part of Yugoslavia), as a serious threat to their empire and a potential cause of war.

Launching the battleship Dreadnought *at Portsmouth in 1906*

3 The Arms Race Every major continental power had a huge conscript army which could be mobilised at a moment's notice. Guns, shells and bullets had been stockpiled in case of war. This arms race made the prospect of war more rather than less likely, since commanders on both sides were keen to use their new weapons and to try out their new armies. British and German rivalry in building dreadnought battleships also contributed to the arms race. Although Britain had only a small professional army, she did have the most powerful navy in the world to defend her islands and empire overseas. By 1909, Britain had eight dreadnoughts and Germany had seven. Influential voices in Britain urged the Government to build more. By 1914, Britain had 29 and Germany had 17.

4 Colonial Rivalry Germany wanted a colonial empire to rival the British and French empires. Since most of the world's surface had already been claimed by the colonial powers, any growth in the size of the German Empire could only be made at the expense of existing empires, such as those of France or Britain.

5 The Schlieffen Plan Germany feared an attack on two fronts – from France in the west and from Russia in the east. The Kaiser regarded it as essential to find a way of meeting this threat without splitting the German forces in two. However, General von Schlieffen had calculated that it would take Russia, with her primitive railway system, at least six weeks to mobilise her armies and prepare for war. This would give Germany enough time to knock France quickly out of the war, if the German army made a surprise attack through neutral Belgium where the French least expected it.

The acceptance of the Schlieffen Plan meant that Germany would always have to start a war with France and Russia, since it would defeat the object of the plan to wait until they had mobilised their armies and were ready to fight. The main snag was that Britain guaranteed Belgium's neutrality. Would Britain enter a war if Belgium was attacked?

6 German Militarism Many high-ranking German commanders believed that fighting a major war now, sooner than later, was essential. Russia was already modernising and expanding her armies and her railway system. She would soon be a formidable enemy. At a secret meeting on 8 December 1912, the Kaiser,

> predicted that if the Austrians did not now face up to the Serbian menace, they would have considerable trouble from the Slav minorities within the Austro-Hungarian monarchy: the fleet must henceforth look on England as an enemy. Moltke [the Army chief] regarded war as unavoidable, 'the sooner the better': Tirpitz [the Navy chief] still wanted another eighteen months before the navy was ready.
>
> Alan Palmer, *The Kaiser,* Weidenfeld and Nicolson, 1978

1 *What type of historical source is this?*
2 *How do we know it is almost certainly based on actual eyewitness accounts or documentary records of the meeting?*
3 *Why were the problems of Austria-Hungary a reason for treating England as an enemy?*
4 *Why do you think this meeting has been used to prove that Germany started the First World War?*

Sarajevo

*28 June 1914.
Austrian Archduke
Ferdinand and his
wife leave Sarajevo
Town Hall. Minutes
later they are dead*

On Sunday, 28 June 1914, R.D. Blumenfeld, editor of the *Daily Express,* noted in his diary:

> H.G. Wells came over to tea. While we were talking news came that Austria's Crown Prince and his wife have been assassinated by a Serbian. That will mean war. Wells says it will mean more than that. It will set the world alight. I don't see why the world should fight over the act of a lunatic.

The news of the assassination shocked the world. But an official at the Austrian Legation in Belgrade (capital of Serbia) reported to Vienna that,

> The accounts of eyewitnesses say that people fell into one another's arms in delight, and remarks were heard, such as: 'It serves them right, we have been expecting this for a long time '

The reaction of the Austrian Government to the outrage was delayed. No one could doubt the gravity of the situation. After all it was the heir to the Austro-Hungarian throne who had been killed. But there was a problem. If war was declared against Serbia, would Russia come to Serbia's aid? Could the war be localised? If not, would Germany come to Austria's aid when Russia mobilised her forces? The Austrians had to find out the answer first before committing their army to a war with Serbia. They got their answer on 5 July when the Austrian ambassador met the Kaiser at Potsdam near Berlin.

Yes! Germany would support Austria. Indeed, so positive was the reply, it gave the Austrians complete freedom of action for their next move. The Kaiser's advice was 'It is now or never. Deal with the Serbs. Straight away.' He thought that the Czar was unlikely to intervene but if he did, then 'Germany would stand at Austria's side.'

So, on 23 July, the Austrians dealt with Serbia. They delivered an ultimatum to Serbia which they knew the Serbs could not accept in its entirety, since Austria demanded the right to send officials into Serbia to hunt for the Archduke's killers.

On 28 July, Austria declared war on Serbia. On 29 July Russia reacted by mobilising her forces. Two days later, Germany gave Russia an ultimatum, warning that German mobilisation, 'is bound to follow if Russia does not stop every measure of war against us and against Austria-Hungary within 12 hours'.

Meanwhile the German ambassador in Paris was told,

Please ask French Government whether it intends to remain neutral in a Russo–German war. Reply must be made in 18 hours.

On 1 August the German ambassador in Paris reported back to Berlin,

Upon my repeated definite inquiry whether France would remain neutral in the event of a Russo–German war, the Prime Minister declared that France would do that which her interests dictated.

Since no 'satisfactory' reply had come from St. Petersburg either, Germany mobilised her forces at 5.15 p.m. and declared war on Russia at 7.30 p.m. On the same day her forces invaded Luxembourg. France immediately ordered a general mobilisation from midnight. Italy, the third partner in the Triple Alliance, declared she would be neutral.

On 3 August Germany declared war on France and began to invade Belgium. This violated the neutrality of Belgium, which had been guaranteed by Britain over 80 years earlier. When the British ambassador told the German chancellor, Bethmann Hollweg, that failure to withdraw from Belgium would mean war, he got the incredulous reply,

Just for a word – 'neutrality', a word which in wartime had so often been disregarded – just for a scrap of paper Great Britain is going to make war on a kindred nation who desired nothing better than to be friends with her.

---

1 *Why did the Germans assume that Russia's mobilisation must mean that armies were being mustered to fight them as well as Austria-Hungary?*

2 *What might have happened had Russia agreed to the terms proposed in the German ultimatum?*

3 *Why did Germany take France's response as meaning 'No'?*

4 *Write one or two sentences commenting on the way in which the artist has depicted Germany in the cartoon below? What was the point of the cartoon?*

5 *Compare the picture of Germany with the one of Belgium. What effect did the cartoonist want to convey?*

Punch, *12 August 1914*

BRAVO, BELGIUM!

Although there was no formal requirement that Britain should go to war in support of her Triple *Entente* partners, there was a moral obligation. Germany had declared war on both Russia and France. The British Government felt it had no option. On 4 August 1914, Britain declared war. The following day, Wednesday 5 August 1914, the *Daily Express* headline was:

England Expects That Every Man Will Do His Duty

World War

These were the crucial decisions. Others followed later. Italy never did come to the aid of her Triple Alliance partners – despite their attempts to persuade her to do so. Instead, she joined the *Entente* powers in 1915, hoping to make sweeping gains at Austria's expense at the end of the war. Germany and Austria-Hungary were joined by Turkey in November 1914 and by Bulgaria in October 1915. Because they were situated in Central Europe, they were called the Central powers. Turkey had turned to the Germans for help after the Balkan Wars and Germany was helping to build the Baghdad Railway through the Ottoman Empire. But it was a foolish decision, since it meant that the Allies could seize what remained of the Ottoman Empire in the Middle East (Palestine, Syria, Iraq). As for Bulgaria, she wanted to regain some of the territories she had lost as a result of the Second Balkan War in 1913.

Japan fulfilled her treaty obligations to Britain by declaring war on Germany on 23 August 1914. China also joined in on 14 August 1917. By that time the United States had entered the conflict as well.

HOW THE WAR WAS FOUGHT

The Battle of the Marne

The German armies swept into Belgium but the Schlieffen Plan started to go wrong when the Belgian army stubbornly held up the German advance at Liège, giving enough time for a small British Expeditionary Force of 90 000 men (the BEF), led by General French, to assemble in Flanders. It also gave the much larger French armies, led by Marshal Joffre, time to prepare as well. On 19 August 1914, the Kaiser issued an order to the German army, 'to exterminate first the treacherous English and to walk over General French's contemptible little army'.

The Schlieffen Plan called for the encirclement of Paris. But the German First Army, led by General von Kluck, which should have passed to the west of Paris, advanced towards the north-east of the city instead. This meant that the flank (or southern side) of the advancing army was vulnerable when the French Sixth Army mounted a counter-attack from the south. The German armies had already reached the fringes of Paris when they were driven back to the River Marne in September. Joffre was hailed as the 'Saviour of France', although his victory was due more to good luck than good judgement. The German generals made many serious mistakes and the army commander, General von Moltke, resigned after accepting that the German army had failed to achieve its target – to knock France out of the war in six weeks. The Princess Blücher wrote in her diary,

BERLIN, October 12, 1914

It is being whispered here that this defeat on the Marne may prove the decisive turning of the war, and the greatest misfortune for Germany, in spite of her successes everywhere else.

At this stage, French, British and German generals still assumed that the war would be one of rapid movement. It was not. Instead it was stalemate. Both sides were immensely strong in defence and poor in attack. Machine guns easily commanded the low-lying lands of northern France and Flanders. The armies dug in and the remaining period of the war was primarily one of trench warfare on the Western Front.

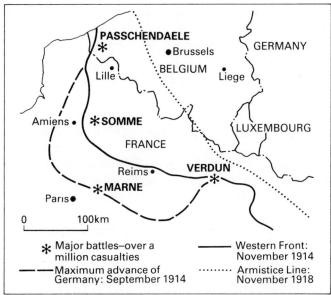

Map showing the Western Front in 1914 and in 1918

Map of the Eastern Front in 1914

Things were different in the east, where the *Entente* forces were aided at first by the advance of Russian armies into East Prussia. The Russian armies had mobilised much earlier than the Germans had expected them to do when the Schlieffen Plan was drawn up. The threat from Russia drew off a substantial German army, which might otherwise have helped the Western Front armies to break through at the battle of the Marne. The Russian initiative was not held for long, however, and they were massively defeated by Hindenburg at the battle of Tannenberg in late August.

The Russians had greater success against the forces of Austria-Hungary in the south where they captured much of Galicia.

1 *What was the furthest distance penetrated by German forces into enemy territory during the fighting on the Western Front? What was the shortest distance?*

2 *How far did the Allied armies advance into German territory in 1918?*

3 *Why did the BEF survivors call themselves 'the Old Contemptibles'?*

Trench Warfare

At first the war was fought in a spirit of duty, chivalry and honour, as if there was something noble in going to the front to kill enemy soldiers. The poet Rupert Brooke, (who died on his way to Gallipoli in 1915) wrote:

> Now, God be thanked Who has matched us with His hour,
> And caught our youth, and wakened us from sleeping

In Germany, the Princess Blücher said young officers went to war with 'a sort of reckless joy in the certainty of the near death awaiting them'. This madness soon changed to reality in the mud of Flanders. The war became one of a stalemate. There were numerous offensives and long drawn-out battles, such as Verdun and the battle of the Somme in 1916. But rarely did either side capture more than a few kilometres of territory after the initial phase of the war.

The reasons were simple: shell-fire, barbed wire, poison gas and machine guns. The no-man's land between the trenches was usually barren of cover and swept by machine-gun fire. The toll of life was horrendous. On the first day of the battle of the Somme, 19 000 British soldiers were killed in what became a three-month battle. At Verdun, in the spring and summer of 1916, there were over a million French and German casualties.

By early 1915, the Germans had built an elaborate network of trenches on the Western Front. From now on, German tactics were primarily defensive. The Allied forces tried to break through the German lines but without success and with heavy losses.

It is almost impossible to find a personal diary of the War, by anyone living in Europe at that time which does not contain harrowing tales of the loss of close relatives. Diaries, letters, memoirs, poems, newspapers, novels, magazines and many other historical sources help us to picture the conditions in which the soldiers on both sides had to fight.

Source A   A British attack on the Somme

On the fourth morning at 7.30, dazed by the shelling which had begun at dawn, warm and sleepy with rum, Horden stumbled forward blindly across No Man's Land. It seemed to him that he was alone in a pelting storm of machine-gun bullets, shell fragments, and clods of earth. Alone, because the other men were like figures on a cinematograph screen – an old film that flickered violently – everybody in a desperate hurry – the air full of black rain. He could recognize some of the figures in an uninterested way. Some of them stopped and fell down slowly. The fact that they had been killed did not penetrate to his intelligence . . . They were unreal to him. His mind was numbed by noise, the smoke, the dust – unable to apprehend anything but the necessity for hurrying frantically on – on, on – out of the storm . . . They must go on. On, on! They dared not stop. The earth spouted everywhere. Hadn't the barrage lifted?

. . . He raised his head slightly . . . There seemed queerly few other men. He squinted to left and right. 'Don't bunch,' they had been told. They weren't bunching . . .

Daniel George (Queen's Westminster Rifles), *Gommecourt,* quoted in *Vain Glory,* edited by Guy Chapman, Cassell, 1937

Source B British casualties, 1 July 1916

	Killed or died from wounds	Wounded	Missing	Taken prisoner	Total
Officers	993	1 367	96	12	2 468
Other Ranks	18 247	34 156	2 056	573	55 032
Total	19 240	35 523	2 152	585	57 500

Vain Glory, edited by Guy Chapman, Cassell, 1937

Source C The German defence

The next morning the English attack began and the guns were not silent for two hours during the day. At dawn I looked around me: what a ghastly picture! Not a trace of a trench left; nothing but shell holes as far as the eye could reach – holes which had been filled by fresh explosions, blown up again and again filled. In them we lay as flat on the ground as if we were dead, for already flocks of enemy aeroplanes were humming over us. We were absolutely at their mercy, and with remorseless accuracy they directed the English heavy guns, shell after shell, into our line, and themselves fired with machine guns at anybody who made the slightest movement below.

Hour after hour passed. The wounded lie helplessly groaning. The supply of water runs out . . . Our mouths are full of earth; three times buried and three times dug up again, we wait – wait for night or the enemy! . . .

Suddenly the barrage lifts – the shells are falling behind us – and there, close in front, is the first wave of the enemy! Release at last! Everyone who is not wounded, everyone who can raise an arm, is up, and like a shower of hailstones our bombs pelt upon the attacking foe! . . . Anyone who reaches our line is at once polished off in a hand-to-hand bayonet fight.

Such is the battle of the Somme – Germany's bloody struggle for victory. This week represents the utmost limit of human endurance – it was hell!

Private Karl Gorzel quoted in *German Students' War Letters,* Methuen

Source D **A French attack in 1917**

'A brilliant trench-raid by our Allies in Champagne: a French raiding party leaving their own trenches.' The Illustrated London News, *20 October 1917*

1 What facts can you deduce from Source B?

2 What types of historical source are A, B, C and D?

3 Why did the Germans long for a British attack by the infantry?

4 What did Private Gorzel mean by, a) 'first wave', and b) 'three times buried and three times dug up again'?

5 What did Daniel George mean when he wrote, a) 'the other men were like figures on a cinematograph screen', b) 'They weren't bunching', and c) 'No Man's Land'?

6 What weapons were used by, a) the British aircraft, and b) the Germans?

7 What was one of the jobs of a pilot during the battle of the Somme?

8 How had the British troops been fortified for their ordeal?

9 Write a diary entry for 1 July 1916 for a soldier who shared Rupert Brooke's enthusiasm for the War (see page 10) only two years earlier.

10 Imagine you are one of the French soldiers shown in Source D. Use the photograph to help you write two or three sentences describing your raid on the German trenches.

The only remarkable thing about the battle of the Somme was the first use of tanks in warfare on 15 September 1916. Bert Chaney recalled

> We heard strange throbbing noises, and lumbering slowly toward us came three huge mechanical monsters . . . they looked ready to topple on their noses, but their tails and the two little wheels at the back held them down and kept them level.

Quoted in *People at War 1914–1918*, edited by Michael Moynihan, David and Charles, 1973

A British tank in difficulties in the trenches

The War at Sea

Trench warfare was less relevant on the Eastern Front. There the German armies advanced towards Russia. This was one reason why the Allies attempted a breakthrough using naval power to land troops in Turkey in the Dardanelles (Gallipoli). If it had been successful, this attack on the underbelly of the Central powers could have knocked the Turks out of the War and opened up a supply route to the Russians. It might also have frightened Bulgaria and inhibited her from joining the Central powers. In practice, the Gallipoli campaign was badly planned and executed. The Allied forces, many of them from Australia and New Zealand (the ANZAC forces), met unexpectedly tough resistance from the Turkish defenders. They were forced to withdraw after sustaining heavy casualties.

Although the Royal Navy prevented the main German navy from leaving the North Sea, it was powerless at first to prevent German submarines, U-boats, from harassing and sinking merchant ships in the Atlantic. These naval tactics had their effect on both sides. The Royal Navy stopped food and supplies reaching Germany while German U-boats stopped them reaching Britain. As a result, food rationing had to be introduced. In May 1915, German U-boats sank the liner *Lusitania* off the coast of Ireland, killing many United States citizens as well as those from Britain. Some Americans wanted an immediate declaration of war but President Wilson calmed them down, since Germany promised to restrict the activities of her submarines in future. Wilson, meanwhile, took steps to make America ready for war.

The only major naval battle of the war was fought off the coast of Jutland in 1916. The Royal Navy suffered heavier losses there (3 battleships, 11 other ships, 6000 dead) than the German navy (11 smaller ships, 2500 dead) and the German admirals acclaimed it as a great victory. But so, too, did the British. In any case, it had little effect. The German Navy was still unable to leave the North Sea ports. It had failed to relieve the British blockade.

At the end of January 1917, German U-boats resumed unrestricted warfare on merchant shipping in the Atlantic. By sinking United States ships, they helped to push President Wilson into declaring war on Germany in April. This was a turning point in the War, since it meant that America's unlimited men and resources could now be put into the battle against Germany and the other Central powers.

The War at Home and in the Air

Bombing the enemy's trenches. 'The machines dive on their target pouring out a storm of machine-gun bullets, and at intervals releasing a bomb, which falls with tremendous effect on the men below. The work is dangerous, and our machines frequently return with their frames and fabrics riddled with bullets.'

The Sphere, 5 October 1918

For the first time in world history, people at home shared some, at least, of the dangers of modern warfare. Air raids damaged buildings but caused relatively few deaths. Many of these raids were carried out by powered airships or Zeppelins (named after their inventor, Count Zeppelin). Air aces fought each other in the skies. The best known became heroes, such as Baron von Richthofen (who shot down over 80 Allied aeroplanes before being killed in action) and another young German pilot called Hermann Göring. By the end of the War it was clear that air forces would make a major contribution in succeeding conflicts in the twentieth century.

Women's work was vital to the war effort, since large numbers of young men had volunteered for the armed services. Wartime production lines were highly mechanised. But in Germany and in Britain, there were many complaints about the profits being made by wealthy industrialists from the sale of armaments and munitions.

Defeat for Germany

By the start of 1918, the Germans had every reason to think the tide was turning in their favour. There were mutinies in the French army. The British had suffered heavy losses at Passchendaele in Flanders, while the Italians had been heavily defeated at Caporetto in the south. People in France and Britain were calling for peace while the Americans had yet to make an impact on the War. Meanwhile, the Russians had already pulled out (see page 30). Yet all was not well in Germany, either. The Allied blockade of the German ports caused massive food shortages which led to serious unrest (see page 76).

In the spring of 1918, the Germans launched one last effort to win the War, before American troops could reinforce the tired and jaded Allied armies. This German spring offensive began on 21 March 1918 and was so successful it pushed the Allies back to the Marne again.

But by now the German armies and the German people were exhausted. They could not withstand the onslaught when the Allies launched a counter-offensive in July and August, aided by tanks and massive reinforcements of fresh American troops. In September, the Germans recognised the inevitability of defeat. They began talks to try to negotiate an armistice.

Meanwhile the Italians won a decisive victory over the Austrians at Vittorio Veneto. The retreat of the demoralised Austrian army hastened the end of the Dual Monarchy. The Austria-Hungary empire split up. Czechoslovakia proclaimed its independence on 21 October, Yugoslavia a week later, and Hungary on 1 November (see page 44). In Germany itself there was massive unrest. Socialists marched through the streets. Speakers advocated a revolution on Russian lines. The German navy mutinied at Kiel at the end of October. On 9 November 1918, the Kaiser abdicated. Two days later, at 11.00 a.m., on 11 November 1918, the armistice came into being. The War was over.

FURTHER QUESTIONS AND EXERCISES

1 *See if you can find an elderly relative or some other person who was alive during the First World War. Ask them what they can remember about the War. Did it affect them in any way?*

2 *What was the significance of this instruction?*

   'Let the last man on the right touch the Channel with his sleeve'

   Who wrote it? When, why and how was it important in 1914? To whom or what does it refer?

Source A

Monday: Out for first time. Strange sensation. Worse than being in a submarine. At first unable to see anything, but imagined a lot . . . Suddenly we gave a terrible lurch. Lookout said we were astride an enemy trench. 'Give them hell,' was the order. We gave them it. Our guns raked and swept trenches right and left.

From a soldier's diary, *The Manchester Guardian*, November 1916

Source B

Coming towards us were a troop of French cavalry. I should say a hundred and fifty or two hundred strong. Gosh but they looked splendid . . . They laughed and waved their lances at us, shouting 'Le Bosch fini.' . . . Over the top of the hill they charged, lances at the ready. There was not a sound from us. Then, only a few seconds after they disappeared, the hellish noise of machine-guns broke out. We just looked at each other. The only words I heard spoken were 'Bloody Hell . . .' That's what it must have been over that hill, for not one man came back.

Incident on 26 March 1918, recalled by William Pressey in *People at War 1914–1918*, edited by Michael Moynihan, David and Charles, 1973

3 a) *What 'strange sensation' was the soldier describing in Source A?*

   b) *What did the French cavalry troopers mean by 'Le Bosch fini'? Why were they wrong?*

   c) *Why do you think cavalry were still being used in war in 1918?*

   d) *What conclusion do you think an intelligent person would have come to after reading Sources A and B? Why do you think the Allied commanders were late in coming to that conclusion?*

4 *Write a reasoned essay explaining why war broke out in 1914.*

Chapter Two
The Russian Revolution

INTRODUCTION

*Fighting on the
Russian Front*

Patriotism, love of 'Mother Russia' and the 'Little Father' (the Czar), were the dominant emotions in Russia in August 1914. But by the end of the month (26–31 August 1914) the Russian army had been soundly beaten by General Hindenburg at the battle of Tannenberg. German armies marched into Russian territory, occupying Poland and Lithuania. By the end of 1915 they were inside Russia itself. The loss of life was appalling. To make matters worse, there were inadequate hospitals, nurses, drugs and medicines for the wounded. The railways could not cope with the movement of men and supplies. The Russian war industry lagged behind Germany's.

Russia's armies were badly led and inadequately armed, clothed and fed. Deserters left the army in droves and there were frequent mutinies. This should have warned the Czar and his advisers that, if a revolution came, there might be no effective army or police force left to suppress it. But the Czar only made matters worse by taking personal command of the armed forces in September 1915.

---

1 *Why did this make matters worse?*

2 *Who would be blamed for Russia's defeats in the future?*

THE FEBRUARY REVOLUTION 1917

Grievances

The Russian people had many grievances against the Czar. The peasants wanted land and freedom from oppression. Opponents of the regime feared the Okhrana (the Czar's secret police). Political prisoners were exiled to Siberia. Newspapers were censored. National groups within the Russian empire (such as the Poles) were governed by Russian officials and made to speak Russian. Many opponents of the Czar, such as Lenin (a Bolshevik Communist), had fled to other countries.

Russia's ruling classes were also critical of the Czar when the Czarina Alexandra put her trust in a Siberian peasant-priest called Grigori Rasputin, who alone seemed able to alleviate the haemophilia (incessant bleeding) suffered by her son. Rasputin's influence over the Czarina (and therefore over the weak-minded Czar as well) was envied and feared by the nobles at court. There were even rumours that he was a German spy, and that the Czarina, a German princess, was also working for the Germans! In despair, a group of nobles murdered Rasputin on 30 December 1916. By then, however, many people in Russia no longer respected the Czar as they had before the War.

Rasputin

Protest

Poor harvests (because many peasants were fighting at the front) and the grossly inefficient railway system helped to cause disastrous shortages of food and fuel. To the underpaid and the poor the twin discomforts of hunger and biting cold were intolerable. Millions of wretched Russians despaired of a solution or an end to the war. Yet they could see that the well-to-do flourished. A lady-in-waiting said she had never seen finer diamonds and gowns as those worn during the 1915–16 winter season.

With the onset of winter in 1916, further food and fuel shortages sharpened the discontent already felt by many urban workers. There were frequent strikes and demonstrations. But the Czar ignored these ominous warnings. On 7 March 1917 he left Petrograd for the front.

Bread and Peace

The following day, Thursday, 8 March 1917, shortages of bread brought people on to the streets of Petrograd to complain. Workers downed tools in factories to join the demonstrations. As the day drew on, more and more people joined the protests. The police did little to prevent these demonstrations and some soldiers even joined the mobs. By Saturday 10 March 1917, over 250 000 striking workers demonstrated in the streets of the capital. Many called openly for the downfall of the Czar. The situation was rapidly getting out of control.

Source A

On February 25 (March 10) the whole of working-class Petrograd had joined the revolutionary movement. The political strikes in the districts merged into a general political strike of the whole city. Demonstrations and clashes with the police took place everywhere. Over the masses of workers floated red banners bearing the slogans: 'Down with the Czar!' 'Down with the war!' 'We want bread!'

History of the Communist Party of the Soviet Union (Bolsheviks),
edited by a Commission of the Central Committee of the Communist
Party, Foreign Languages Publishing House, Moscow, 1939

[NB The Russians used the old Julian, not the Gregorian, calendar in 1917. This is why two dates are shown in Source A – February 25 and March 10.]

Crowds demonstrating in Petrograd, March 1917

Source B

On Saturday the 25th Petersburg seethed in an atmosphere of extraordinary events from the morning on. The streets, even where there was no concentration of people, were a picture of extreme excitement. I was reminded of the 1905 Moscow insurrection. The entire civil population felt itself to be in one camp united against the enemy – the police and the military. Khabalov's proclamations were quite openly torn down from the walls. Policemen suddenly vanished from their posts. Factories were at a standstill. No trams were running. I don't remember whether any newspapers appeared that day, but in any case events had far outstripped anything the half-stifled press of the day could have conveyed to the people.

The Russian Revolution 1917, A Personal Record by N.N. Sukhanov,
(written in June–August 1921, and first published in Moscow in 1922),
edited, abridged and translated by Joel Carmichael, Oxford, 1955

Source C

On February 25, the Cossack detachments and infantry went over to the people. The Nevsky Prospekt and adjoining streets were invaded by milling crowds. A meeting attended by thousands of people was held at the Nicholayevsky Station near the statue of Alexander III, but the Cossack troops made no attempt to interfere and even fraternized with the crowds. Suddenly a detachment of mounted police arrived, led by an officer. He gave orders for the warning bugle to be sounded but at that very moment there was a shot from a Cossack rifle and the police officer fell dead. The police immediately fired a salvo into the crowd and people fled into the adjoining streets.

Alexander Kerensky (Russian prime minister in July 1917),
The Kerensky Memoirs, Cassell, 1965

Source D

It is, as he assures us repeatedly, by no means a history, but merely his own personal reminiscences, written down shortly after the events it describes.

Source E

I have only tried to set down my record of that period in the history of my country to which I was a witness or in which I was a participant . . . I have arrived at these conclusions, not as a historian, but as an eyewitness.

Source F

The study of the history of the C.P.S.U.(B) strengthens our certainty of the ultimate victory of the great cause of the Party of Lenin–Stalin, the victory of Communism throughout the world.

1 *Look at the photograph on page 19. Which source tells us what these demorㅡⴰⴰtors wanted?*

2 *What was significant about the incident described in Source C?*

3 *How does Source C appear to contradict Source B?*

4 *Each of the sources D, E and F comes from the preface to one of the three books from which sources A, B, and C have been taken. Match up each pair of sources, so the comments in the preface relate to the description of the events which took place on February 25 (March 10).*

5 *Which of the three sources A, B or C, a) is a primary source, b) is a secondary source, c) may be biased in support of one particular view?*

6 *British textbooks give 7 November as the starting date of the October Revolution in 1917. Why was it called the October Revolution?*

7 *Write your own account of the events of February 25 (March 10) using evidence from the photograph and from all three sources A, B, and C.*

Two days later, on Monday 12 March, demonstrators set fire to public buildings and attacked police stations and army barracks. Police and soldiers openly supported the demonstrators. Few army units in Petrograd could be relied on. Soldiers refused to fire on the crowds and some shot their officers instead.

Abdication of the Czar

That same day, the Czar issued an edict dissolving the Duma (the Russian parliament). But the representatives refused to accept this and formed a Liberal Provisional Government instead. The President of the Duma sent a telegram to the Czar saying, 'Nothing can be hoped from the troops of the garrison'. At the same time, in another part of Petrograd a Soviet of Workers' and Soldiers' Deputies was being formed. It was elected by the army units and factories taking part in the demonstrations. Two weeks later it issued the famous war cry, 'Workers of the World, unite!'

The Czar had little choice. He faced a disastrous war against Germany on the one hand and the collapse of his authority in Petrograd on the other. He abdicated on 15 March 1917. The 'February' Revolution – a spontaneous leaderless movement by the discontented workers of Petrograd – was over.

THE PROVISIONAL GOVERNMENT

Kerensky

The Provisional Government was led initially by the liberal politician Prince Lvov and later by a brilliant young left-wing lawyer, called Alexander Kerensky, one of the leaders of the Social Revolutionary Party.

Alexander Kerensky

The new Government issued a statement on 16 March 1917 announcing various measures which they had agreed with the Petrograd Soviet of Workers' and Soldiers' Deputies. These included:

- a political amnesty for all political prisoners
- free speech and freedom to strike and join a trade union
- equality for all, irrespective of class, religion or nationality
- a Constituent Assembly, elected by universal suffrage and a secret ballot, to be called to determine the new constitution.

These alone were tremendous gains when compared with the rights enjoyed by a Russian citizen under the autocratic Czar. However, a serious problem for the Provisional Government arose in April, when Lenin and many other exiled Bolsheviks (Communists) returned home to Russia.

The April Theses

Lenin was greeted in Petrograd, on 3 April 1917, by cheering crowds. He immediately announced that the time for the Bolshevik revolution had arrived. On the following day he announced his April theses. These were:

- that the armed forces were engaged in an imperialist war, which could only be ended if the capitalist society was overthrown. [A capitalist society is one in which the ownership of farms and factories (the means of production) and of the means of distribution (railways, ports, shops, banks) are in private hands.]
- that the real revolution was yet to come. The second stage would come next – the seizure of power by the peasants and workers.
- that the Provisional Government should not be supported.
- that the Soviet of Workers' and Peasants' Deputies was 'the only possible form of revolutionary government' in Russia. The Communist Party should do its best to strengthen the Soviets.
- that the police, army and bureaucracy should be abolished.
- that all land and all the banks should be owned by the State.
- that the Soviet of Workers' and Peasants' Deputies should control the means of production and distribution.

Lenin states his April Theses in Petrograd, April 1917

1 *What were the 'April Theses'?*

2 *Who did Lenin want to put in the place of the Provisional Government?*

3 *Why did he say the real revolution had yet to come?*

4 *What reasons can be used to back up Lenin's view that the 1914–18 conflict was an 'imperialist war'? Do you agree?*

5 *Why did Lenin urge Russians not to support the Provisional Government, even though it had carried out a number of much-needed reforms?*

Lenin ruled out immediately any hope that the Bolsheviks and their supporters would co-operate with the Provisional Government. There was to be no government of national unity. The Bolsheviks were committed to overthrow the regime, however liberal. These views were supported at the next Party Conference. Lenin said the Russian soldiers wanted *peace*. The Russian peasants wanted *land*. The industrial workers wanted a decent wage and adequate supplies of food and *bread*. He satisfied them all with the slogan, '*Peace – Land – Bread*'.

Treason

The Provisional Government's most pressing problem, however, was the War, since it was this which lay at the back of the unrest at the time of the February Revolution. However, the liberal ministers of Russia were clearly reluctant to put Russia at the mercy of an illiberal, autocratic Germany ruled by the Kaiser, a German Czar. The War would continue, even though it was unpopular. When Kerensky became minister of war in the summer, he had to overcome the effect of Bolshevik propaganda against the War, such as Lenin's appeal to working-class soldiers,

> We summon you to a social revolution. We appeal to you not to die for others, but to destroy others – to destroy your class enemies on the home front!

In his *Memoirs,* Kerensky said

> My words to the soldiers were: 'It's easy to appeal to exhausted men to throw down their arms and go home, where a new life had begun. But I summon you to battle, to feats of heroism – I summon you not to festivity, but to death; to sacrifice yourself; to sacrifice yourselves to save your country!'

Alexander Kerensky, *The Kerensky Memoirs,* Cassell, 1965

> **1** *Was Lenin a pacifist? What was his aim? What did he offer the soldiers? What did Kerensky offer?*
>
> **2** *Imagine you are a Russian peasant drafted into the Russian army in 1914. After three years of bitter suffering and privation, you welcome the February Revolution and the appeals of demonstrators for peace and 'Down with the war!'. What is your reaction to the words of Lenin and Kerensky, three months later?*

Kerensky began a new offensive in June in Galicia, in southern Poland. Initial victories soon turned into defeats and thousands of Russian soldiers took Lenin's advice and fled or deserted the army.

The July Uprising

Trotsky

On 2 July, 1917, Lenin and Trotsky tried to arouse support for an uprising against the Government but the attempt was premature and badly organised. It failed. Many Bolsheviks, including Trotsky, were put in prison. Lenin escaped to Finland. Others, not so lucky, were shot. The Provisional Government closed down *Pravda*, the Bolshevik newspaper. For the moment the Bolshevik threat had been successfully crushed.

Alexander Kerensky became the prime minister and continued the policies of the previous government. He sustained the war effort (he thought) by appointing General Kornilov as supreme commander. But Kornilov had other ideas. He led a right-wing revolt against Kerensky which collapsed dismally. Kerensky called on the Petrograd Soviet for help and released the Bolsheviks in gaol to muster support against Kornilov.

From this time (September) onwards the Bolsheviks began to gain thousands of new recruits. They also gained a majority in the Soviet of Workers' Deputies in Petrograd, where Trotsky was the chairman.

THE OCTOBER REVOLUTION

Growing Unrest

Strikes and protests grew more numerous in the cities and towns, since workers were still faced with food and fuel shortages. By now, Russia was fed up with the War. In the countryside peasants began to seize land from the estates of the nobles. In many rural areas there was complete anarchy. Thousands of peasant soldiers deserted the army to return home to take a share in the estates which were being dismantled.

*Red Guards storming
the Winter Palace in
Petrograd, on 7
November 1917,
during the October
Revolution*

Lenin, Trotsky and other Bolshevik leaders made the decision to strike
now and take over the government. On Wednesday 7 November they seized
power in a brilliantly organised revolution. Trotsky did much of the planning.
For weeks the Bolsheviks built up their support among the industrial
workers and soldiers of Petrograd. They set three main targets:

- The main bridges across the River Neva and the channels of its delta.
These, and the telegraph station, were seized early in the morning of
Wednesday 7 November 1917.
- The four main railway stations to the south of the Winter Palace, the State
Bank, the electricity power station and the two bridges immediately to the
west of the Winter Palace, were taken later in the day on Wednesday 7
November.
- The Winter Palace, the main prison and the railway stations north of the
Neva were captured on Wednesday night or on Thursday 8 November.

---

1 *Why did they choose these targets?*

2 *Why did they set out to capture them in this order? Why not try to
take them all at the same time?*

Remarkably, this epoch-making Revolution, which had incalculable
consequences for the history of the modern world, was achieved with very
little bloodshed and little immediate reaction or opposition from the Russian
people. The newspapers even appeared on the next day as usual!

Source A

But no resistance was shown. Beginning at 2 in the morning the stations, bridges, lighting installations, telegraphs, and telegraphic agency were gradually occupied by small forces brought from the barracks . . . From evening on there were rumours of shootings and of armed cars racing round the city attacking Government pickets. But these were manifestly fancies. In any case the decisive operations that had begun were quite bloodless; not one casualty was recorded. The city was absolutely calm.

The Russian Revolution 1917, A Personal Record by N.N. Sukhanov,
(written in June–August 1921 and first published in Moscow in 1922),
edited, abridged and translated by Joel Carmichael, Oxford, 1955

Source B

Proclamation Issued by the Military Revolutionary Committee
10.00 a.m., 25 October [7 November] 1917

To the citizens of Russia: The Provisional Government is overthrown. The state power has passed into the hands of the organ of the Petersburg Soviet of Workers' and Soldiers' Deputies, the Military Revolutionary Committee, which stands at the head of the Petersburg garrison and proletariat. The cause the people have been fighting for – the immediate proposal of a democratic peace, the elimination of private property in land, workers' control of production, and the formation of a Soviet Government – is assured. Long live the revolution of the workers, soldiers, and peasants!

Quoted in *The Russian Revolution 1917, A Personal Record* by N.N. Sukhanov

Soviet artist's impression of the storming of the Winter Palace, 7 November 1917

Source C

When I arrived at the Palace on the morning of November 7 I found that its food supplies had been stopped, so that the guards had left, being unable to get food. Kerensky had set out on a dangerous mission to bring loyal troops from outside the city . . .

The next room to mine was that of Konovaloff. The Ministers gathered from time to time in his room or mine, and through the window watched the crowds on the bridges. The situation grew more and more critical. Five thousand sailors arrived from Kronstadt, and the cruiser *Aurora* entered the Neva and lay with guns directed upon the Winter Palace. The Fortress of SS. Peter and Paul was now in the hands of the Bolsheviks, and its guns were also turned upon the Palace. The Government offices on the other side of the square were gradually surrendering to the Bolsheviks, whose troops were little by little surrounding the Palace itself.

[The author left the Winter Palace unmolested by Bolshevik soldiers.]

During the night the booming of guns began. I knew they were the guns of the *Aurora* bombarding the Palace. An ultimatum was sent to the Ministers to surrender. They refused. Bolsheviks began to penetrate into the Palace . . . A battle ensued, during which there were some hundred casualties on either side . . . The Palace was pillaged and devastated from top to bottom by the Bolshevik armed mob, as though by a horde of barbarians.

Dr David Soskice in the *Manchester Guardian,* Thursday, December 27 1917.
Quoted in *The Guardian Omnibus,* edited by David Ayerst, Collins, 1973

---

1 *Was the announcement in Source B strictly accurate?*

2 *Use the evidence in these sources to explain why the Bolsheviks achieved victory so quickly and with so little shedding of blood.*

3 *What were the Bolsheviks fighting for?*

4 *Why was the storming of the Winter Palace left to the last?*

5 *How did the Soviet artist see the storming of the Winter Palace? In what ways do Source C and the photograph on page 25, confirm or contradict that impression?*

6 *Write an account of the day's events using information you can derive from the picture and from the written sources.*

In another part of Petrograd, the Second All-Russia Soviet Congress was meeting in the Smolny Institute. It was addressed by Lenin and Trotsky. The delegates were told by Lenin that a Council of People's Commissars had been set up and that decrees were to be issued, firstly to claim the land for the peasants, secondly to give workers control of the factories, and, thirdly, to start negotiations with the Germans to end the War.

These momentous events were taken calmly by the people of Petrograd. Workers, peasants, students, soldiers, clerks and teachers alike had little criticism to make of Lenin's Bolsheviks. They were prepared to see them try (where Kerensky and the Czar before him had failed) to bring the War to an end and give them the food they desperately needed.

Kerensky's Failure

The Provisional Government collapsed for a number of reasons. It had failed:

- to end the War
- to solve the food and fuel shortages
- to call the Constituent Assembly, promised in March
- to recognise and appreciate the real nature of the threat presented by the Petrograd Soviet and later the Bolsheviks under Lenin (a superb organiser and dynamic leader) and Trotsky (a brilliant planner and thrilling speaker). Kerensky could have crushed the Bolsheviks in the summer, had he wished.
- to solve the problem of what to do about the peasants and their seizure of the great landed estates
- to convince the Russian people that they had gained anything from the February Revolution.

CONSOLIDATING THE REVOLUTION

Lenin's immediate task after seizing power was to fulfil the promises he had made: Peace – Land – Bread – Freedom.

The Constituent Assembly

The Bolsheviks did not immediately dispense with the idea of democratic elections. Lenin's Decree on Land (see opposite) specifically promised that decisions about the great estates would be made by the Constituent Assembly when it met. But when the new Constituent Assembly was actually elected the Bolsheviks found they were in a minority, the Social Revolutionary Party (which had formerly supported Kerensky) getting twice as many seats as Lenin's supporters (370 to 175).

Accordingly the ruling Bolsheviks found an excuse for closing the Assembly. They said it had been elected on the basis of lists of voters drawn up 'before the October Revolution' and that the 'Party of Right-Wing Socialist-Revolutionaries' (who were in a majority) refused to co-operate with the 'supreme body of Soviet power, the Central Executive Committee of the Soviets'.

Lenin's Promises – Land

Lenin

On the day after the October Revolution, Lenin began to fulfil his promises with the issue of the Land Decree. This officially abolished ownership in land without compensation. The estates of the Czar, the nobility and the Church were to be put at the disposal of local Soviets (councils) until the Constituent Assembly met. In future the right to use the land would belong to those who worked on it but *ownership* was in the hands of the people – in other words, the State. This was not what some peasants thought Lenin meant when he said that the Bolsheviks would give the people land!

A decree signed by Lenin as Chairman of the Council of People's Commissars on 27 November 1917 gave workers control over the running of their factories. But the Communists did not want to ruin the economy, so there were no drastic changes at first. They did not nationalise industries straight away. One month later the Bolshevik Government nationalised the banks but promised to protect the savings of people who had deposited money there.

Lenin's Promises – Freedom

The Declaration of the Rights of the Peoples of Russia, which was signed on 15 November 1917 by Stalin as People's Commissar for Nationalities and by Lenin, fulfilled the Bolshevik promise that the Russian peoples would be given their freedom. It declared that henceforth the peasants were freed from the rule of the landowners, since all ownership in land had been abolished. It freed the factory workers from the 'tyranny of capitalists' since the workers now had control of works and factories.

From this time onwards all the peoples of Russia (i.e. the different national groups, such as the Kazakhs) were free and equal. The Declaration said they had the right to self-determination, even to the extent of leaving Russia and forming an independent state.

But, as you have seen, Lenin didn't abide by the results of the free elections to the Constituent Assembly. Nor did Freedom extend to the newspapers. A Decree published on 9 November 1917 laid down that a publication could be suppressed by the Council of People's Commissars, if it called for 'open resistance or insubordination to the Workers' and Peasants' Government'. Yet one of the early calls of the Petrograd Soviet in March 1917 had been for freedom of speech and freedom of the press!

Nonetheless, the decision to allow free self-determination led to the breaking away of a number of the minority national groups on the Russian frontiers who had been, until then, part of the Russian Empire. These national groups included the peoples living in Latvia, Estonia and Bessarabia (all re-occupied by Soviet troops at the start of the Second World War). Some countries which eventually became independent, like Poland and Lithuania, were still in German hands at the time of the October Revolution.

A meeting of the Council of Commissars in 1917.
Can you pick out Lenin and Trotsky in this picture?

Lenin's Promises – Bread

This promise, made in the light of the food shortages before the Revolution, was more difficult to keep. As you will see on pages 116–17, food shortages during the civil war which followed the October Revolution, resulted in a terrible famine. Lenin's policy of War Communism penalised peasants and actually discouraged them from producing the surplus corn needed by the Red Army and the Russian workers who lived in the towns.

Lenin's Promises – Peace

Peace was something that Lenin could bring about promptly and on the day after the seizure of Petrograd, the new Russian Government called on all the warring nations to start peace talks. The Bolsheviks wanted a 'just and democratic peace' in which there would be no territorial gains without a free vote by the peoples concerned.

This proved to be the stumbling block to the successful conclusion of the peace talks between Russia and the Central powers, which began a month later in the town of Brest-Litovsk (December 1917). An armistice (stop to the fighting) was agreed on 15 December but the Russians could not agree to Germany's territorial demands.

Lenin wanted peace at any price and was prepared to accept the German demands immediately. Other Communist leaders, including Trotsky, objected that a humiliating peace agreement with Germany would destroy the prestige and strength of the Bolshevik Revolution. Trotsky proposed that they should announce the end of the fighting but not actually conclude a peace agreement with the Central powers. 'Neither peace nor war' he said. But when the German armies started to march on Russia once more, resistance to the German peace terms collapsed.

Punch, *20 February 1918*

THE LIBERATORS

1 *What was the point of this cartoon?*

2 *Did the cartoonist approve or disapprove of the Bolshevik Revolution?*

3 *Which of the Russian leaders is depicted in this cartoon?*

4 *Is a cartoon like this a primary or a secondary source?*

5 *Why did Lenin go back on his earlier promise to allow the Russians to elect a Constituent Assembly?*

Brest-Litovsk

The Treaty of Brest-Litovsk was signed, reluctantly, on 3 March 1918. By its terms Russia agreed that Latvia, Lithuania, Estonia, Finland and Poland should all become independent. Even more reluctantly, Russia had to agree to the creation of an independent state in the Ukraine. She also agreed to pay a large sum of money in reparations for war damage.

As a result Russia lost about a third of her population, a third of her agricultural land (including much of the rich grain-growing region of the Ukraine), and about two-thirds of her heavy industry.

The Germans were well satisfied. They had eliminated one of their major enemies and could now send troops from the Russian front to reinforce those fighting on the Western Front and in Italy. They could also send troops into the newly-independent nations recognised by the Treaty, to ensure they stayed within Germany's sphere of influence.

The harsh terms imposed by the Germans were counter-productive, however, since they made a mockery of their own claims in 1919, that the terms of the Treaty of Versailles were harsh and unfair.

FURTHER QUESTIONS AND EXERCISES

'Workers of the world unite! Year of the Proletarian dictatorship. October 1917 to October 1918'

1   *It is 1917. You live in Petrograd as a factory worker, teacher, soldier, policeman, shop assistant, or princess. What is your attitude to the War, the food shortages, the Czar, the authorities, and the strikers in the streets? Write entries for your diary saying what you saw and did, a) on Saturday 10 March 1917 (25 February), and b) on Wednesday 7 November 1917 (25 October).*

2   *Study the poster opposite carefully and write down what it tells you about Bolshevik Russia in 1918. What message did the Russians want to convey? What was their aim? What were the benefits of Communism?*

3   *Why was the Czar overthrown in March 1917? Why was the February Revolution closely followed by the October Revolution? How did Lenin manage to seize power with such ease? Write a reasoned essay explaining the causes and results of the Russian Revolution in 1917?*

4   *What lessons for the future did the October Revolution offer, a) revolutionaries in other countries, and b) foreign governments?*

Chapter Three
The Paris Peace Treaties

INTRODUCTION

Source A

Trafalgar Square in London on Armistice Day 1918. The front cover of The Sphere, 16 November 1918

Source B Armistice Day in the American Trenches in France

Eleven o'clock! The war ended! It would make a better story if I could tell of men cheering, yelling, laughing, and weeping with joy, throwing their tin hats in the air, embracing one another, dancing with delight. But they didn't. Nothing happened. The war just ended . . . The men stood talking in groups.

Webb Miller, *I Found No Peace*, Gollancz, 1937

> **1** *Compare the information in the picture with the extract. Why do you think there was such a difference in the way in which news of the Armistice was received in London compared with the trenches in France?*
>
> **2** *What sort of journalist was Webb Miller?*

At the time, people used to call it 'the Great War', because no other war in history had involved so many soldiers, from so many countries, on so massive a scale. Over 8.5 million soldiers had been killed out of a total of over 70 million who fought in the War. Many people throughout the world had been affected in some way or other. All were soon to be affected by the peace settlement in Paris, and its consequences.

THE PEACE SETTLEMENT

Fourteen Points

Early in 1918, the American President, Woodrow Wilson, announced the terms which he thought could bring the War to a successful end.

1. Open covenants of peace and no secret diplomacy in future.
2. Absolute freedom of navigation.
3. Removal as far as possible of all economic barriers.
4. Adequate guarantees for the reduction of national armaments.
5. An absolutely impartial adjustment of colonial claims in the interests of the peoples concerned.
6. All Russian territory to be evacuated.
7. Complete restoration of Belgium in full and free sovereignty.
8. All French territory freed, and the wrong done by Prussia in 1871 in the matter of Alsace–Lorraine righted.
9. Readjustment of Italian frontiers on lines of nationality.
10. Peoples of Austria-Hungary accorded an opportunity of autonomous development.

11. Romania, Serbia and Montenegro evacuated. Serbia given access to the sea, and relations of Balkan States settled on lines of allegiance and nationality.
12. Non-Turkish nationalities in the Ottoman Empire assured of autonomous development and the Dardanelles to be permanently free to all ships.
13. An independent Polish State.
14. An Association of Nations affording guarantees of political and territorial independence for all States.

The *Evening News*, London, Wednesday 9 January 1918

---

1 *What did he mean by: 'no secret diplomacy in future', 'on lines of allegiance and nationality', and 'autonomous development'?*

2 *Which of the causes of the First World War (see pages 2–4) do you think Wilson had in mind when he drew up this list?*

3 *What did the following countries stand to lose or gain under Wilson's Fourteen Points: a) France, b) Belgium, c) Austria, d) Germany, e) Serbia, f) Russia, g) UK, h) Turkey, i) Italy, j) USA?*

4 *Which new countries were likely to be created, or given their independence, under these Fourteen Points?*

Lloyd George (UK) and Clemenceau (France) on left, Wilson (USA) on right at the Versailles Peace Conference 1919

When the Germans agreed to the Armistice, they assumed that Wilson's Fourteen Points would provide the substance of the eventual peace treaty. They were soon to be proved wrong.

A Dictated Peace

The peace conferences which ended the War were held in and around Paris in 1919–20. A separate peace treaty was drawn up for each of the five Central powers. The peace settlement with Germany, which followed the Armistice, was signed six months later, on 28 June 1919, at Versailles. It was drawn up by the great powers, chiefly Britain, France, Italy, and the United States. But many other countries were also represented at Versailles, notably Japan, China, and the Commonwealth countries.

Germany was not consulted, so it was not a negotiated treaty. It was forced on the Germans, as were the other treaties on Austria, Hungary, Bulgaria and Turkey. This imposition of the Treaty by threat of force, infuriated many Germans, such as Adolf Hitler. It lit a fuse which later led to the crises which exploded in the years immediately before the outbreak of the Second World War in 1939. A final straw was the Allied insistence that the Germans acknowledge that they alone were guilty of starting the War. They did not even let Germany keep the gains she took from Russia at Brest-Litovsk (see page 31). On the other hand, the Allies did not invite Russia, either, to take part in the peace talks.

A Revengeful Peace

For much of the time, the conference delegates argued among themselves. Much of the fighting during the War had been on the Western Front in northern France. By contrast British and American soldiers fought on foreign soil, as did the Italians for most of the War. Many French towns and villages had been reduced to rubble during four years of heavy fighting. Fields and woods were pitted with craters and shell-holes. Hundreds of thousands of French people were homeless. One and a half million French soldiers had been killed in action. Clemenceau spoke for the French people as a whole when he demanded peace terms which would use German money to help restore and rebuild France. The French wanted revenge. They wanted to punish Germany and weaken the country so much, that the German people would never again be strong enough to wage war against France. They even argued strongly that the River Rhine should be made the new frontier between the two countries. This would have given France a large portion of Germany.

A Just and Lasting Peace

The Americans were more concerned about getting a just and lasting peace. President Wilson did not want the European powers enlarging their own frontiers and empires at the expense of the Central powers. On the other hand, he had no intention of letting the Germans escape without paying some form of penalty. Lloyd George also sought a satisfactory peace settlement which would hold. He wanted a peace treaty that would exact fair compensation from the Central powers without reducing them to poverty and anarchy. The British had no desire to see Germany, or the countries of the former Austro-Hungarian empire, succumb to a new Bolshevik Revolution. By then danger signals were already being sounded in different parts of Europe. They threatened the fragile peace. There had been left-wing uprisings in several countries following the earlier Bolshevik Revolution in Russia in November 1917 (see pages 24–8). The Spartacist uprising had taken place in Berlin in January 1919 (see page 48). Communists led by Bela Kun had already taken over in Hungary in March 1919 (see page 47).

1 *Why was it easier for Lloyd George and Woodrow Wilson to talk about a 'just and lasting peace' than it was for the French delegates?*

2 *What* ism *was Lloyd George afraid of? Why? What* ism *was Woodrow Wilson afraid of? Why?*

In the end the peace settlement was something of a compromise. It was neither as tough as that demanded by the French, nor as fair as that for which the British and Americans had argued. Only one Allied delegate, from China, refused to sign (see page 190). Some delegates, such as Orlando of Italy, walked out of the Conference in disgust. Others, like Japan, expressed dissatisfaction with the terms of the agreement. To Wilson's disappointment, the US Senate later refused to ratify the Treaty because it would have meant joining the League of Nations (see page 154).

THE TREATY OF VERSAILLES

Effects of the Treaty

You can see the effects of the boundary changes imposed by the Paris Peace Treaties on the maps on the following pages. A summary of the principal terms of the Treaty of Versailles can be seen in the paragraphs which follow. The net effect of the Treaty was:

- to 'rob' Germany of about one tenth of its territory in Europe
- to take away all of Germany's colonies abroad
- to impose severe restrictions on the composition, dispersal and future development of the German armed forces
- to hinder German relations with neighbouring countries (such as Austria). The two German-speaking nations were expressly forbidden from forming a union or *Anschluss*
- to burden future generations of the German people with a huge bill for the damage and destruction caused by the War. The Germans had to agree to pay the Allies a vast sum of money, called *reparations*, even though many Germans were desperately poor and close to starvation.

One of the most promising features of the Treaty, however, was the Covenant which all the participating nations signed, agreeing to form and join the League of Nations (see pages 206–8).

'The Signing of the Peace Treaty in the Hall of Mirrors, Versailles'. Painting by Sir William Orpen. Exhibited in the Royal Academy in 1920

Military Provisions

German army: to be reduced to only 100 000 men. Conscription not permitted. The number of guns to be strictly limited. Germany not allowed to station armed forces in the Rhineland. This is to act as a neutral buffer area separating Germany from her neighbours France, Belgium and the Netherlands.

German navy: to be reduced to only 15 000 sailors, 6 battleships, 6 light cruisers, 12 destroyers and 12 torpedo boats. German navy not allowed to have any submarines.

German air force: to be abolished. By October 1920, Germany will not be allowed to have an air force.

Reparations

Germany to pay a large sum in compensation, much of it in the form of goods, such as 40 million tonnes of coal to France and the Low Countries. The Treaty fixed a temporary sum, pending the calculation of the full amount of reparations claimed by the Allies. This was eventually settled at $32 000 million – a huge sum of money, even by today's standards. It was obviously far beyond the means of the Germans to pay, since they too had been drastically affected by the War. It was later a chief cause of the catastrophic inflation of the German mark in 1923 (see page 78).

Territorial Adjustments

- Alsace and Lorraine to be given back to France, Eupen and Malmedy to Belgium, Hultschin to Czechoslovakia, Memel to Lithuania.

- The Saar coalfield to go to France; but the people to vote by plebiscite in 1935 on whether to stay in France or not (when the time came, they voted for a return to Germany).

- Plebiscites also to be held in Allenstein (East Prussia or Poland), Schleswig (Germany or Denmark) and Upper Silesia (Germany or Poland), to determine whether the people there want to be German or part of the neighbouring state.

- Poland, formerly part of the Russian empire and now a separate nation, to be given part of West Prussia – as a corridor between East Prussia and Germany, to give her access to the free port of Danzig.

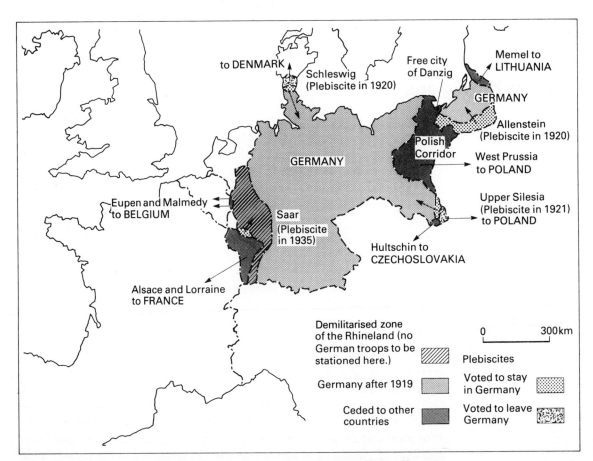

Map showing the territorial adjustments imposed by the Paris Peace Treaties.

The German Empire

German overseas possessions to be governed by the great powers as mandates of the new League of Nations:

- Tanganyika to Britain
- Cameroons and Togoland to Britain and France
- German South West Africa to South Africa
- Ruanda-Urundi to Belgium
- Samoa to New Zealand
- New Guinea to Australia
- Mariana, Marshall and Caroline Islands in the Pacific, and the German concessions in Shantung Province (in China), to Japan.

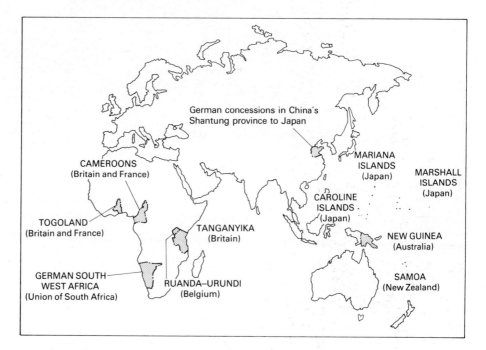

Germany's Guarantees

Article 43   'In the area defined above [the left bank of the Rhine] the maintenance and the assembly of armed forces . . . are forbidden'

Article 80   'Germany acknowledges and will respect strictly the independence of Austria'

Article 81   'Germany . . . recognizes the complete independence of the Czechoslovak State [and its] frontiers'

Article 82   'The old frontier as it existed on August 3, 1914, between Austria–Hungary and the German Empire will constitute the frontier between Germany and the Czechoslovak State'

Article 87   'Germany . . . recognizes the complete independence of Poland'

Signing the Treaty

A vast crowd in Berlin in June 1919 protesting against the terms of the Treaty of Versailles

The German signatures on the Treaty of Versailles

'Faites entrer les Allemands,' says Clemenceau in the ensuing silence. His voice is distant but harshly penetrating. A hush follows. Through the door at the end appear two huissiers with silver chains. They march in single file. After them come four officers of France, Great Britain, America and Italy. And then, isolated and pitiable, come the two German delegates. Dr Müller, Dr Bell. The silence is terrifying. . . . They keep their eyes fixed away from those two thousand staring eyes, fixed upon the ceiling. They are deathly pale. They do not appear as representatives of a brutal militarism. . . . It is all most painful.

They are conducted to their chairs. Clemenceau at once breaks the silence. 'Messieurs', he rasps, 'la séance est ouverte'. He adds a few ill-chosen words. 'We are here to sign a Treaty of Peace.'

Harold Nicolson, *Peacemaking, 1919*, Constable, 1933

---

1 *What impression did the German delegates create?*

2 *Why was it 'all most painful'? What do you think the ceremony reminded Harold Nicolson of? Quote words and phrases from his account which tell you this.*

3 *Why did Harold Nicolson think Clemenceau's opening words, 'We are here to sign a Treaty of Peace', were 'ill-chosen'?*

4 *Do you think the detailed terms of the Treaty of Versailles were fair to Germany? Were they fair to France?*

5 *Examine the different parts of the Treaty and compare them with the causes of the War outlined on pages 2–4. How did the Allies hope to prevent the outbreak of a Second World War? What did they have to ensure, if this was to be achieved?*

6 *Who should have had a say in the carving up of Germany's overseas possessions? What was Wilson's original intention in the Fourteen Points (see page 35)? How did Wilson try (at Versailles) to prevent these possessions from becoming colonies of the great powers?*

7 *The rich Saar coalfield was undeniably German. Yet it was given to France for 15 years as compensation for the damage done to French coal mines during the War. France was short of coal, so this was an effective way of making sure she got compensation but it also enlarged her frontiers at Germany's expense. Was this fair? Was this sensible? Discuss the reasons for and against.*

8 *Were the Allies right to insist that the Germans acknowledge that they alone were guilty of starting the War?*

9 *Why do you think the Allies insisted on the War Guilt clause? What could they justify doing as a result of this clause?*

10 *The large banner, shown in the photograph of Berlin in June 1919, reads 'Nothing but the 14 Points'. Why were the defeated Germans so incensed by the terms of the Treaty? Compare the terms of the Treaty of Versailles with President Wilson's Fourteen Points (see page 35). Was the British Socialist writer, Beatrice Webb, correct when she wrote in her diary, 'Wilson's fourteen points, upon which Germany surrendered, have been, in the spirit and in the letter, repudiated.'?*

OTHER TREATIES

Treaty of St Germain (with Austria)

By this time the old Austro-Hungarian empire had disintegrated. During the last months of the war soldiers from the different nations, who formed part of the empire, began to desert from the army and some fought for the Allies. Uprisings led to the creation of national councils in exile. In the summer of 1918 the Allies recognised Czechoslovakia as an independent state and on

21 October the Czechs and Slovaks officially proclaimed their independence. The Serbians followed suit a week later when they founded Yugoslavia. Hungary did likewise on 1 November. Austria, too, became a republic on 13 November.

The Austrian government resented the fact that their new republic was held responsible for the misdeeds of the old Habsburg empire. But this argument carried little weight and the Austrians were made to pay reparations and to limit the size of their army. New boundary changes also meant that substantial numbers of German-speaking peoples were transferred from Austria to neighbouring countries as part of the peace settlement.

This is why part of the Austrian Tyrol was given to Italy, while German-speaking lands in Bohemia and Moravia were incorporated in the newly-created nation state of Czechoslovakia. Other territorial changes affected some of the peoples of Slovenia and Croatia, who now became Italians, rather than citizens of Yugoslavia.

> **1** *How did Czechoslovakia get its name?*
> **2** *What did Italy gain from the War?*

The Austro–Hungarian empire after 1919

Austria–Hungary in 1914

Treaty of Trianon (with Hungary)

This treaty was similar to the other Paris peace agreements. Reparations were agreed, the army was limited in size, and large portions of the old kingdom of Hungary were dispersed. These went mainly to Romania, Czechoslovakia and Yugoslavia. By this time the new republic had been replaced by a monarchy, headed by Admiral Horthy as regent. But Hungary was only a shadow of its former self – about a quarter of the area and only a third of the population.

Treaty of Neuilly (with Bulgaria)

Its main provisions also included reparations, reduction in the size of the armed forces and loss of territory (chiefly Thrace to Greece).

Treaty of Sèvres (with Turkey)

This treaty redistributed Turkish territory in Europe (e.g. Eastern Thrace and part of the Aegean Islands to Greece). It placed a number of Turkey's Middle Eastern possessions in the care of Britain (Palestine and Mesopotamia), and France (Syria and the Lebanon), as mandates of the League of Nations. In addition the existence of the independent kingdom of Hejaz (later Saudi Arabia) was confirmed by the treaty.

The terms of the treaty were denounced by Mustafa Kemal, leader of a successful revolution which overthrew the Sultan. After Turkey went to war with Greece, he negotiated a new treaty at Lausanne in 1923.

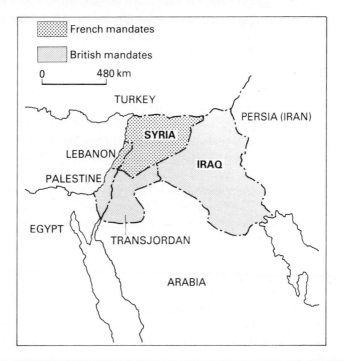

Map showing how the Ottoman Empire was allocated by the Treaty of Sèvres

The Treaty of Sèvres had a dramatic effect on the geography of the Middle East, since it broke up the old Ottoman Empire. Turkey had long been regarded as the 'sick man of Europe'. Her grip on the outlying territories of her empire had been loosened in the years before the War. Now she paid the penalty. So, too, did the rest of the world. The creation of new nation states (such as the Lebanon, Syria, Iraq and Jordan) did not create stability. Nor did it confer peace.

1 *What term do we use today to describe the region formerly part of the Ottoman Empire (shown on the map)?*

2 *Which new country has been created in this area from which old country? Which government was given responsibility for that area after the First World War?*

3 *Is there any historical reason to explain why the major Western powers still have an interest in this area?*

EUROPE AFTER THE WAR

Empires and Republics

In 1914 Britain, Germany, Russia, Turkey and Austria-Hungary all had large empires ruled by an emperor or sultan. By 1923 only the British Empire remained intact. Indeed it had been substantially augmented with the addition of territories once ruled by Turkey and Germany – the Middle Eastern and African mandates (which you can see on the maps).

- Czar Nicholas II of Russia abdicated in 1917 and was murdered by the Bolsheviks in 1918.
- Kaiser William II of Germany fled to exile in the Netherlands which had been neutral during the First World War.
- The Emperor Francis Joseph of the Austro–Hungarian Habsburg empire died in 1916. His successor, Charles, was unable to hold the empire together when it split into a number of independent republics in 1918.
- The Sultanate of Mohammed V of Turkey was replaced in 1923 by a Republican government led by Mustafa Kemal, who was known as Kemal Ataturk.

Seeds of Totalitarianism

The new republics, among them the USSR, Germany, Poland, and Czechoslovakia, faced many problems in the next 20 years. Having rid themselves of one form of dictatorship (that of the monarchies), most soon acquired new forms of dictatorship and totalitarian systems of government. Totalitarianism is government in the hands of a dictator and a single political party. Total control is exercised over the people. There are no opposition parties. No opportunity is given to the people to let them choose an alternative government. Totalitarian governments often maintain control through terror, propaganda and control of the media.

As you will see in Chapter 6, many European countries attempted to intervene in the civil war which followed the Bolshevik Revolution in Russia in 1917. Fear of Communism and its consequences also led other European governments to take repressive measures to make sure there was no Bolshevik Revolution in their own countries. This reaction, and the fears that inspired it, were fertile grounds for the development of right-wing dictatorships and the establishment of totalitarian systems of government. Josef Pilsudski became the dictator of Poland. Admiral Horthy controlled Hungary. Right-wing governments dominated the countries of eastern Europe, with the exception of Czechoslovakia. One-party systems of government were normal. In no sense of the word were they democracies.

Revolution

The Bolshevik Revolution in Russia was a very potent force after the War. It was an example to workers throughout Europe. It showed that ordinary working people could seize power and transfer ownership of land and property from the rich to the poor.

Many of the soldiers who returned from the War were now unemployed. Welfare benefits were meagre. Some people came close to starvation. Why had the War been fought? What benefits had it brought the working class? Wealthy factory owners and industrialists made profits from wartime production. There was no such gain for the worker or the peasant. Much talk in wartime had been made about heroes fighting for their country. What did the country offer its heroes when the fighting stopped? Many discontented and disenchanted soldiers and workers saw a return to the old pre-war way of life, where everyone knew his place and the life style of the rich continued to contrast sharply with that of the poor.

It is not surprising, then, that politicians like Hitler, Mussolini and Lenin, who offered new and different solutions to these problems, soon found ready listeners and willing supporters. Europe was fertile ground for the fanatic. Hitler's Nazis, Mussolini's Fascists and like-minded extremist groups on the far right promised people a better life (see the poster on page 51), as did the Communists of Russia, the European Marxists, and other extreme left-wing groups, throughout Europe.

In Hungary, a communist leader, called Bela Kun, led a successful rebellion in March 1919. Kun had been captured by the Russians during the War and returned to Hungary after the Bolshevik Revolution. For several months Hungary became Europe's second Soviet, until overthrown by the right-wing leader, Admiral Horthy, with Romanian help, in November that same year.

The Spartacists

Rosa Luxemburg in 1919

In Germany the Spartacists, a group of Marxists led by Rosa Luxemburg and Karl Liebknecht, opposed the moderate socialism of the new German government, led by Friedrich Ebert. As Marxists they believed in a class struggle between poor and rich, between worker and factory owner, between peasant and farmer, and between the working class and the middle/upper classes. Revolution was inevitable. The workers would take power and govern the country – the dictatorship of the proletariat.

The Spartacists urged the workers of Germany to overthrow the government of Ebert and the moderate socialists. In January 1919 they took to the streets. On 15 January 1919, the Princess Blücher described the rebellion in her diary, after talking to an English officer who had just come from Berlin,

> He gave me a graphic description of the scenes in the streets during the Spartacus 'Putsch'. There were machine-guns at every corner, and more than once the people in the street threatened to shoot him, and one day smashed the window of the taxi he was in with a hand-grenade. He witnessed himself no less than three murders in the streets. . . . The lack of food, the high prices, the universal demoralization amongst the German people is the best soil possible for the spread of Bolshevism . . . In the prevailing disorder, Spartacus reigns supreme, and as the Government have not as yet gained the upper hand over the 'freed slaves', the streets are often stained with blood. . . . The method in this madness is the wish of the Spartacus group to prevent the National Assembly being constituted and to introduce the Commune, or dictatorship of the Proletariat. Rosa Luxemburg and Liebknecht are still at large, although a high price has been set on their heads and there are men enough willing to shoot them.
>
> Evelyn, Princess Blücher, *An English Wife in Berlin*, Constable, 1921

1 *Why were they called Spartacists? What was their aim?*

2 *To what did the Princess Blücher attribute their initial success?*

3 *How was her own attitude to violence somewhat one-sided?*

The *Freikorps*

In fact, Rosa Luxemburg and Karl Liebknecht were both murdered by the *Freikorps* – a volunteer army of right-wing and extremist ex-soldiers. This 'Free Corps', consisting of ex-servicemen led by discontented ex-officers, posed a threat of its own to the legitimate government in Germany. They linked up with other Nationalist groups who bitterly resented the terms of the Treaty of Versailles. In March 1920 they attempted to seize power in Berlin with soldiers commanded by General von Luttwitz. Wolfgang Kapp was named chancellor but German workers, opposed to the *Freikorps*, called a general strike. The *putsch* (attempted takeover of the government) failed. Many of the *Freikorps* nationalists later became Nazis. One infamous group, the Erhardt Brigade, already wore swastikas on their uniforms.

FURTHER QUESTIONS AND EXERCISES

PEACE AND FUTURE CANNON FODDER

'Peace and Future Cannon Fodder'. Cartoon by Dyson in The Daily Herald, 1919

The Tiger: "Curious! I seem to hear a child weeping!"

1 *Look at the cartoon on page 49. Identify Lloyd George of Britain, Wilson of the USA, Clemenceau of France and Orlando of Italy. Which of these was 'The Tiger'? What was the point of the cartoon? What justification did the cartoonist have for making this judgement? How accurate was it?*

2 *What is nationalism? Why is Czechoslovakia said to be an example of a nation state? What do you think gives people a national identity? Is it a common language, religion, heritage, or political belief?*

3 *Write brief notes explaining the significance of the following:*

   a) the Spartacist riots   *d) Totalitarianism*
   b) the Freikorps   *e) the downfall of the emperors*
   c) Bela Kun   *f) the League of Nations mandates*

4 *Look at the maps on pages 40, 44 and 45. Which countries gained most from the Paris Peace Treaties? Which of the leading Allies gained least?*

5 *Write a short reasoned essay summing up the effects of the First World War. How successful were the Paris Peace Treaties in resolving the problems which led to the outbreak of war in 1914?*

Chapter Four

Fascist Italy

INTRODUCTION

1919 ~Bolscevismo~   1923 ~Fascismo~

Fascist propaganda poster in 1923

> **1** *How has the artist shown the difference between life under Bolshevism and life under Fascism? What is the advantage of living under a Fascist government? What does Bolshevism bring?*
>
> **2** *Is propaganda like this any different from normal advertising?*

Fascism grew fast in Italy in the early 1920s because Mussolini and Italians like him were alarmed at the speed with which Bolshevism (Communism) was taking root in Italy at the end of the First World War. Benito Mussolini, socialist and pacifist before the War, changed his mind after serving in the Italian army. Hatred of Communism, fury at the terms of the Paris Peace Settlement, and scorn for Italy's weak politicians, gave him a burning desire to lead Italy to a glorious future. He founded the Fascist Party in 1919 and came to power only three years later. By 1926, he was dictator of Italy and acclaimed as *Il Duce* – the Leader.

THE FIRST WORLD WAR

The Treaty of London

Italy remained neutral in 1914. Germany and Austria-Hungary both tried to persuade Italy to fight, or at worst remain neutral, but, by the terms of the secret Treaty of London (26 April 1915), the Italians agreed to fight with the Allies in return for a number of territories after the War. Italy was also promised enlarged colonies in Africa if the Allies took possession of Germany's overseas empire after the War.

However, the Italian army made little progress in the war against Austria. When Russian resistance collapsed in 1917, German reinforcements helped to break through the Italian lines at Caporetto. Many Italian soldiers were killed, wounded, captured or deserted. Mussolini admitted,

> Never in my life as an Italian and as a politician have I experienced a sorrow equal to that which I suffered after news of Caporetto.

Only at the end of the war did the Italians redeem their self esteem at the battle of Vittorio Veneto. By then over 650 000 Italian soldiers had been killed but with little military gain to make up for their sacrifice.

The Paris Peace Agreements

The Italian failure to contribute decisively to the Allied war effort may have told against them at the peace talks. The other Allies, notably the Americans, were not inclined to honour in full the terms of the Treaty of London, which had been agreed before the United States declared war.

Italy gained the South Tyrol, Trieste and a small part of the Dalmatian coastline but not the Adriatic port of Fiume whose population was part-Yugoslav and part-Italian. Italy wasn't even given a German colony as a mandate. Nor was she able to expand her African colonies of Libya, Eritrea and Somaliland as promised in 1915. Mussolini wrote

> For Italy . . . it was a complete shattering of ideals. We had won the War; we were utterly defeated in the diplomatic battle.

One Italian hothead decided to act before the League of Nations even came into existence. On 12 September 1919, Gabriele d'Annunzio and a group of 5000 like-minded adventurers, seized Fiume for Italy without the support of the Government. They proved to Mussolini that direct action could work.

THE RISE OF MUSSOLINI

The Communists

Italy faced many problems. She had huge, crippling debts as a result of her war effort. Prices of some goods rose fourfold between 1915 and 1921. The rapid rise in the cost of living led to a high rate of unemployment. The general perception, that the Italian delegates in Paris had failed, led to a lack of confidence in the Italian political system. When the Fascists took power in 1922 they claimed that the enemies of Italy were the 'political class of weak and defective men who in four long years knew not how to give a Government to the nation'.

In 1919, these problems led to unrest. Communist factory workers in the northern industrial towns, such as Milan and Turin, took Bolshevism as their model. There were many strikes and demonstrations. Matters came to a head in August 1920 when many workers in heavy industry were locked out by their employers. The workers retaliated by occupying their factories and places of work.

> The trade marks and factory signs were taken away, while upon the roofs and the doors of the factories the Red banners with the sickle and hammer, symbol of the Soviets, were hoisted with cheers . . .
>
> The occupation of the factories in several Italian towns was merely an opportunity for violent demonstrations. There were dead at Monfalcone, there were dead in Milan, and there were dead in other towns on the peninsula.
>
> Benito Mussolini, *My Autobiography*, translated by Richard Washburn Child, Hutchinson, 1928

---

1 *What did the factory workers do to alarm Mussolini? What was he afraid of?*

2 *What type of historical source is this? Is it likely to be a reliable and accurate statement of what actually occurred at the time? Give reasons for your answer.*

3 *Which parts of the account could be checked to see if they are true? Which parts of the account are Mussolini's own opinions?*

The Fasci

These first moves towards Communism led Mussolini and other Nationalists to start the first of the Fascist Party groups in Milan on 23 March 1919. They called themselves the *Fasci Italiani del combattimento* or 'groups of fighters for Italy'. In particular, they pledged themselves

- to support the claims of ex-soldiers from the First World War
- to oppose any countries which threatened to harm Italy's interests abroad – notably Italy's claim to Fiume and Dalmatia.

Mussolini standing in front of a Roman monument

In ancient Rome the _fasces_ were the symbols of authority carried by magistrates. They consisted of bundles of rods bunched around an axe. Mussolini's Italian Fascists used the same symbol as a sign of their authority and power. They chose a symbol from ancient Rome because that was the time when Italy had last acquired a great empire – when Rome ruled the Western world.

The Fascists hoped to see Italy take her rightful place once more, as one of the most powerful countries on earth. This is why Mussolini liked to stand in front of Roman buildings, statues and monuments when he addressed crowds. His followers adopted the Roman salute as well, the upraised arm, which they had copied from Gabriele d'Annunzio, and which Hitler, in turn, later borrowed from the Fascists.

The Fascists said democracy had failed Italy. What was needed was strong government. They were ashamed, as Nationalists, by the humbling of the Italian armed forces during the war and by the alleged humiliation of the Italian delegates at the Paris Peace Conference. Yet for all its high ideals, Fascism appealed most to ex-soldiers and thugs who relished the opportunity to wear a uniform, carry a weapon, and strut around with other Fascists looking for trouble. These Fascist uniformed gangs soon became known and feared throughout Italy as the Blackshirts.

Confrontation

There were numerous opportunities for Fascists to engage Communists and their sympathisers in street fighting in the industrial towns of northern Italy in 1920–2. Like the *Freikorps* in Germany (see page 48) these bully boys of Fascism sought to avenge the failures of their leaders after the War.

Source A

'THE TRAGEDY OF THE BOMB IN MILAN. By a bomb explosion at the Diana Theatre at Milan last week nine persons were killed – some reports give a larger total – and about a hundred injured. The outrage is one of many disorders which have occurred in Italy in the effort to cause a general strike by way of protest against the imprisonment of the Anarchist Malatesta.' The Graphic, *2 April 1921*

Source B

On the 23rd of March [1921] ... the Communists caused a bomb to explode at the Diana Theatre in Milan. It was crowded with peaceful citizens attending an opera. The bomb instantly killed twenty people. Fifty others were injured. All Milan gave up to anguish and anger and vengeance ... The action squads turned their activity into the suburbs firmly held both by Communists and Socialists ... and put to flight the subverters of civil order. The political authority was powerless; it could not control the disorders and disturbances. On the 26th March I concentrated all the Fascists of Lombardy. They filed off, marching compactly in columns through the principal streets of Milan. It was a demonstration of strength not to be forgotten. At last I had brought defenders of civil life, protectors of order and citizenship ... From that day on began the progressive crashing down and crumbling of the whole structure of Italian subversive elements. Now these elements were driven like rats to their holes and were barricaded in the few forts of the Workers' Chambers and of the district clubs.

Benito Mussolini, *My Autobiography*, translated by Richard Washburn Child, Hutchinson, 1928

---

1 *Who were the 'Italian subversive elements' according to Mussolini? Who were the 'action squads'?*

2 *What happened in Milan from 23–6 March 1921? How did the Fascists react after the explosion at the Diana Theatre?*

3 *What was the significance of this incident in the history of Fascism according to Mussolini?*

4 *Why did Mussolini march his Fascist supporters through the streets of Milan? What did he hope to demonstrate or prove?*

Mussolini

In 1921, the Fascists gained 35 seats in the Italian parliament after their gangs of thugs intimidated voters and opponents alike during the run-up to the election. Thereafter they took the name *Partito Nazionale Fascista* (National Fascist Party).

Their money and support came at first from farmers, shopkeepers, landowners and factory owners. These were the people who had most to lose if the Communists seized power in Italy. As the movement grew it widened its appeal, even to members of the police force and the armed services. The growth in Fascist popularity accelerated despite the fact that they were as much to blame as the Communists and Socialists for the vicious street fights which disfigured Italy's cities at this time.

The Fascists, however, always took good care to make it seem as if they were the victims of unprovoked attacks by the Bolsheviks. Mussolini claimed that Fascism stood for law and order and that many Fascists had been killed or beaten because they supported justice and fair play. In fact, many Liberals, Socialists, and Communists were themselves beaten up by Fascist street gangs armed with clubs.

In February 1921, there were serious riots in Florence, when Fascists and Communists fought in the streets. Two months later, at the time of the elections to the Italian parliament, over 500 people were killed or wounded in clashes between the Fascists and their opponents.

Backing for Fascism

Despite the bloodshed, the Fascist Party was also gaining respectability where it mattered most, among the rich and powerful families of Italy. Soon it had the financial backing of some of the most distinguished financiers and industrialists in Italy. Bankers and industrial magnates like Alberto Pirelli, the tyre manufacturer, Giovanni Agnelli of Fiat and Count Giuseppi Volpi di Misurati, a multi-millionaire, gave them the necessary financial backing and support they needed to build a major political party. These people of wealth and influence pinned their hopes for the future on the militant, uniformed Fascists in their black shirts. Big and small businesses alike wanted a stable, disciplined Italy. They welcomed the promise of strong government,not the indecision and near-anarchy they got under the existing political system. Politicians seemed unable to give Italy the strong democratic government it needed to solve the problems left over from the War.

The March on Rome

By the summer of 1922, the Italian government seemed incapable, or unwilling, to stop the spread of Fascist violence and to protect the rights of all its citizens. The majority parties in the Italian parliament were then the Liberals and Democrats. They held well over twice as many seats as the Socialists and eight times as many as the Fascists. But the prime minister, Luigi Facta, was slow to act in the face of the Fascist threat.

In August 1922 the trade unions called a general strike in protest at the way in which the authorities (police, army and government) turned a blind eye to the violent strike-breaking methods of the Fascists. In turn, Mussolini – with only 35 Fascist seats in parliament – demanded that Luigi Facta should resign in favour of the Fascist Party. The government refused to take him seriously. But by now, Mussolini had the support and approval of most of the leading figures in industry and of the Italian Establishment. His supporters included many senior police officers and Army commanders. More importantly, he had even convinced the King that his Fascist Party could form an effective government.

In October, Mussolini decided to take direct action. He planned to 'March on Rome' and appointed a military command to carry out his plans.

The Fascist generals assembled about 25 000 of Mussolini's Blackshirts, the *squadristi*, in strategic locations to the north and east of Rome. Many were armed but they were neither trained nor equipped to fight a modern army. General Badoglio thought that 'five minutes of fire' would be enough to disperse them if they marched on Rome.

Despite this threat to democracy, the King refused to impose martial law. Instead, the threat of civil war and the backing Mussolini got from powerful figures in the Establishment, persuaded the King to ask Mussolini to form a government instead.

> His Majesty the King asks you to come immediately to Rome, for he wishes to offer you the responsibility of forming a Ministry.

Some of the *squadristi* did actually march on Rome but Mussolini himself came by train. He arrived on 30 October in time for the victory parade on the 31st!

Source A

Mussolini with other Fascist leaders after the 'March on Rome' in 1922

Source B

Monday 21 October 1922 Noon ROME

The Fascist revolution is triumphant today all over Italy. The Fascisti this morning, when marching into Rome, were acclaimed by tens of thousands of people, and Signor Mussolini, called by special telegram from the King, has come to undertake the task of forming a new government.

Italy is thus on the threshold of a new period in its history, which it is hoped, will lead her on to greater destinies. Mussolini, the man of iron nerve, of dauntless courage, of striking initiative and patriotic ardour, has imposed his will and personality upon the entire nation. Hundreds of thousands obey his beck and call.

His army of Fascisti, with their black shirts and strict military discipline, recall the red shirts of the days of Garibaldi and Mussolini himself is like a second edition of the great hero of Italy's *risorgimento*.

The *Daily Telegraph*, 21 October 1922

Source C

Italian State Drama

The Fascisti have respected the Constitution no more than the Bolsheviks. Unopposed by the Army and the Police, their highly-disciplined and well-armed host of 300 000 Black Shirts took the law into their own hands. Railways, telegraphs and posts were seized; the control of towns and provinces was wrested from the authorities; and there was a concentration on Rome, where all concerned were informed that the Fascisti 'want power and will have it'. The Government wanted to proclaim martial law; the King refused to sign the decree, and the Government resigned.

What the upshot may be remains to be seen. It is bound to affect not only Italy, but foreign countries, including our own, as well, for the Fascisti want the Mediterranean for the Mediterraneans, the conversion of the Adriatic into an Italian lake, and the re-opening of the Dalmatian question.

The Graphic, 4 November 1922

Source D

Fascisti! Italians! The day of decisive battle has struck. Four years ago this day the National Army launched a supreme offensive that led to victory! Today the Army of Blackshirts seizes again the mutilated victory, and pointing desperately towards Rome, carries it back to the glories of the Capitol. The martial law of the *Fascismo* goes into full effect . . .

Fascisti of all Italy! We must and shall win! Long live Italy! Long live *Fascismo!*

Mussolini's *Fascisti* Proclamation in Milan, October 1922

---

1 What part did the Blackshirts play in 'the Fascist revolution'? Was it a genuine revolution?

2 Why did Mussolini make sure that photographs were taken showing him marching with his generals, even though he took a train to Rome?

3 What did the writer of Source C think might be the effects on Britain and other countries of a Fascist victory?

4 How do the two newspaper accounts differ from each other?

5 Why do you think Mussolini and the Italian Fascists later gloried in the myth that they seized power as the result of a 'March on Rome'? How did Mussolini actually come to power in 1922?

Benito Mussolini (1883–1945)

Benito Mussolini was born in 1883, the son of a blacksmith. In his youth he was a pacifist (against war), an atheist (not believing in the existence of a God) and a republican (wanting a president rather than a king). He was also a revolutionary socialist and served a prison sentence in 1908. He left the socialists during the First World War because they wanted Italy to stay neutral. Mussolini thought that Italy stood to gain from the War. He served in the army himself, being invalided out in 1917.

After the War he started the Fascist Party and became prime minister in 1922 and leader (*Il Duce*) until the surrender of Italy in 1943.

At the peak of his power he was idolised by the majority of Italians and regarded by many as 'Italy's greatest son'. In appearance he was stocky, plump and bull-necked. Like Hitler, he was a brilliant speaker, able to whip up a crowd to a frenzy of excitement. He had a mastery of short telling phrases which could later be used as slogans. After an assassination attempt he told the Italian people

If I advance, follow me: if I retreat, kill me; if I die, avenge me.

Arrogant and dramatic gestures were used to make his points, stabbing the air with his hands and arms. He told the crowds

Fascism wants men to be active and to engage in activity with all their energy

He lived up to this ideal himself – in public. Italian newsreel films show him stripped to the waist, harvesting corn, playing sports, acting the part of the model member of a Fascist State. Italian children were taught to repeat the Fascist Creed: 'I believe in the genius of Mussolini'.

The British publishers of his autobiography, in 1928, called him,

a man, who whatever may be said of his political ideology, is undoubtedly great and whom history will record as the saviour of post-war Italy.

His biggest mistake was to enter the Second World War in June 1940 as an ally of Hitler. When the Allies invaded Italy in 1943 he was imprisoned but later rescued by the Germans and made leader of German-occupied Italy. But in 1945, attempting to flee to safety, he was captured and executed by Italian partisans. His body was later strung up like a meat carcase in the streets of Milan.

MUSSOLINI'S ITALY

Holding on to Power

As soon as he came to power, Mussolini took steps to ensure that his Fascist government would be long-lasting, unlike those of his democratically elected predecessors. He reorganised the voting system for parliament. He wanted to ensure that the Fascists would always have a decisive majority. So, instead of proportional representation, the Acerbo Law, which was passed in November 1923, gave a substantial majority of the seats in parliament to the party which received the greatest number of votes at an election. It sounded democratic but, in practice, Fascist thugs used violence to intimidate the opposition parties and to frighten the more reluctant voters in the polling booths. Not surprisingly, Mussolini won a convincing victory at the April 1924 election, gaining 405 seats out of a total of 535 in parliament.

> From the ballot boxes of April 6th there overflowed a full, irrevocable, decisive victory for the National [Fascist] list. It obtained five million votes against two million represented by all the other lists put together. My policy and our regime were supported by the people.
>
> Benito Mussolini, *My Autobiography*, translated by Richard Washburn Child, Hutchinson, 1928

The Fascist Party now dominated Parliament. Giacomo Matteotti, a respected Socialist politician, was incensed by Mussolini's election tactics and spoke openly about Fascist methods. He had already written a book entitled *The Fascisti Exposed*. In May 1924 he attacked Mussolini in a speech in parliament. Mussolini called it 'outrageously provocative' and said it deserved 'some more concrete reply' than a speech in return. Ten days later Fascist thugs took Mussolini at his word. They seized Matteotti in a street in Rome and bundled him into a car. Two months later his body was found under a hedge. Mussolini denied having anything to do with the murder but the scandal even threatened his position as *Il Duce*. In his autobiography Mussolini claimed

> By my orders we began the most anxious and complete investigations . . . Very soon it was possible to identify the guilty . . . They came from the Fascist group, but they were completely outside our responsible elements . . . All this should have stilled the storm.

In fact, the murderers were extreme right-wing Fascists. It seems likely that Mussolini was probably telling the truth when he claimed that he had nothing to do with Matteotti's murderers. Nonetheless, although Matteotti's murderers were arrested and sent to prison, they were released only a year or so later. Mussolini complained that, instead of 'the storm' dying down, the murder was blown up out of all proportion,

> solely from hate for Fascism . . . The Press, the meetings, the subversive and anti-Fascist Parties of any quality, the false intellectuals, the defeated candidates, the brain-soft cowards, the rabble, the parasites, threw themselves like ravens on a corpse.

1 *Why did Mussolini's 'complete investigations' fail to still 'the storm'? How do we know he did not disapprove of the actions of Matteotti's murderers?*

2 *Why do you think he described his investigations into Matteotti's murder as being 'most anxious'? What was he anxious about?*

3 *What does the murder of Matteotti tell you about the grip Mussolini had on the country in 1924? Was Italy still a democracy at this time?*

4 *Write a short reasoned account explaining the circumstances which led to the murder of Matteotti.*

The shock of Matteotti's murder caused the non-Fascist members to shun parliament. This was called the 'Aventine secession'. The opposition parties hoped that their absence would bring down Mussolini and his government. The refusal of the opposition parties to take part in legislative work in the Chamber of Deputies, however, was a mistake. Instead of bringing down Mussolini, it had the opposite effect. It allowed Mussolini and the Fascists to pass the necessary legislation through parliament turning Italy into a one-party state and banning all other political parties.

On Christmas Eve, 1925, the Fascist-dominated parliament gave Mussolini the powers of a dictator when they passed the Decree Law. In future, only the King could dismiss the head of the government, not parliament. No future legislation could be discussed by parliament unless first approved by *Il Duce*. Henceforth, all power and authority in Italy came from Mussolini, instead of from the votes of the people, as in a democracy.

Repression

The Fascist Government quickly introduced measures to set up machinery to deal with enemies of the State. As in most totalitarian systems of government, the press was censored. A secret police force called OVRA was formed in 1926 to instil fear among people opposed to the regime. The gangs of Fascist thugs were incorporated into a State Militia to prevent them becoming an unruly, ill-disciplined, armed mob. Mussolini was very proud of this particular achievement. Meanwhile, a special judicial tribunal was also established in 1926 to try people accused of crimes against the Fascist State. It had power to sentence people to death for treason. Concentration camps or penal settlements were also built on islands off the coast of Italy to house the political prisoners – the enemies of the State. The treatment of these prisoners was harsh and often brutal.

Despite the emphasis placed on law and order, however, justice was only implemented for the Fascists and their supporters. Crimes against opponents and opposition politicians went unpunished. In 1925, Giovalli Amendola, editor of *Il Mondo* was attacked by Fascist thugs. They smashed the windows of his car and inflicted injuries from which he later died. Nonetheless, Fascist Italy was less repressive than many of the other totalitarian regimes of that time, or since. The crackdown on opposition parties and other opponents of the regime by the Fascists was less sweeping than it was in Nazi Germany or the Soviet Union. In the 18 years between 1922 and 1940, only ten people were actually executed and five of those were convicted terrorists. At most, something like 4000 people were imprisoned in the concentration camps. This would have been intolerable in a democratic country. But it was minute compared with the millions who died in Nazi concentration camps or the million Russians who were executed on Stalin's orders during the Purges of 1936–8.

The persecution of the Jews in Italy from 1938 onwards was probably the gravest crime of the last years of Fascism. Even this was more at Hitler's prompting than from Mussolini's natural instincts. Indeed, he told a fellow Fascist that he didn't 'believe in the least in this stupid anti-Semitic theory'.

The Race Law of 10 November 1938 classified a Jew as anyone with a Jewish parent. Jews were banned from owning businesses employing more than 100 people. They could not own substantial buildings or estates in the country. They were banned from joining the Fascist Party, couldn't fight in the Italian army, and were also barred from working for the Government.

---

1 *How did Mussolini become a dictator?*

2 *How did the Fascists deal with their opponents?*

3 *Why do you think Mussolini introduced the Race Law in 1938?*

Fascism

'Fascist' today is a term of abuse, levelled against anyone, or any government, thought to be dictatorial or too right wing. In Mussolini's Italy it meant something different.

- Fascists were fiercely anti-Communist. This made them popular with farmers and factory owners.
- Fascists were passionate nationalists, believing fervently in their country right or wrong.
- Fascists supported compulsory military service (conscription) and relished impressive military parades and ceremonies.
- Fascists used propaganda and indoctrinated the young with militaristic and nationalistic ideals.
- Above all, Fascists believed in a one-party state with one leader – *Il Duce*. They wanted a totalitarian state (see page 46). The State was all. It was the reason for living. The interests of the individual had to be subordinated to, and if necessary, sacrificed in the interests of the State. If a choice had to be made then the State must always come first.

Mussolini in uniform

1 Describe the appearance of Mussolini. How would his bearing and his clothes lead you to suspect he was a dictator?

2 What is a one-party state? Give a modern example of such a state.

3 What arguments did the Fascists use to justify the one-party state?

4 Why was Government control of education and propaganda essential?

Reforms

Despite the fact that newspaper articles prove that the actions of Mussolini's Fascists were well known in Britain, visitors, such as Winston Churchill were impressed by the progress made by the Italians under Mussolini's rule. These reforms included the following:

- In 1932–3 a large team of engineers drained the Pontine Marshes, an area of malarial swamp which lay between Rome and Naples. This was one of a number of projects designed to combat unemployment during the Depression and to modernise Italy. Other schemes included the construction of hydroelectric dams, hospitals, schools, government offices and other public buildings.

- Mussolini transformed the Italian transport system by insisting that the railways be run efficiently. He was much admired for his ability to get the trains to run on time! The building of bridges, canals and fast roads, called *autostrada*, were among other public works which improved internal communications in Italy.

- Mussolini wanted to make Italy self-sufficient, so that she could produce all her own food and manufactured goods. He declared war on low productivity. There was to be a 'battle of the births', to increase the population of Italy and provide the extra hands needed by expanding industry and a growing army. The 'battle' for wheat doubled grain production between 1922 and 1939. Effective too was the 'battle' for steel, with a similar doubling of output. Farmers were encouraged to mechanise their farms and to use up-to-date methods. Industrialists were stimulated to expand and modernise.

The bus station in the new town of Littoria in the newly-drained Pontine marshes

- Mussolini insisted that industry be organised on corporate lines. Workers and management were to work together for the good of their industry and ultimately for the State – the highest ideal in a Fascist society. The individual worked for the benefit of everyone, the whole of society and not just for self and personal gain. This is why trade unions were banned in 1925. Striking was prohibited by the Fascist Labour Law in 1926. In return, workers were given many benefits, such as paid holidays and social insurance. The Fascists claimed that trade unions were unnecessary in a system where the aims of management and workers were said to be identical. Both were represented on the councils and syndicates set up to organise the State economy and to ease co-operation between all sides of industry. In practice there were many disputes. The tribunals, which assessed these cases, often took the side of the workers rather than that of the employers. On major issues they usually favoured management.
- Mussolini's government improved educational standards in Italy, by raising the school-leaving age and making it more difficult for pupils to avoid going to school. They built new schools and set higher standards of attainment. Between 1922 and 1939 the number of pupils in secondary schools increased by 120 per cent.

  There was another reason, however, for this interest in education. The Fascists knew that they could use education to indoctrinate the young to become good Fascists themselves through propaganda and military training. Sports and keeping fit were stressed. Slogans and memorable phrases were used to drive home the message, for example

Nothing has ever been won in history without bloodshed!
The Young must know how to obey.
Credere! Obbedire! Combattere! ('Believe! Obey! Fight!')

Italian children were encouraged, but not forced, to join the Militia of the *Avanguardisti* (14 years and over) and the *Balila* (under 14). These were intended to give moral and physical training to the young, in order to make them worthy of the new standard of Italian life . . . they are destined to become Fascist men of the future, from whose ranks national leaders will be selected.

Benito Mussolini, Fascism, Ardita, 1935

Young girls parading in Fascist uniforms

- Mussolini expanded, equipped, and trained the Italian armed forces in preparation for his conquests. The Fascists used the semi-military training of Italian children to good advantage to do this. When a Fascist officer was interviewed by a British newspaper correspondent in 1936, he was asked

'Then do you think that the Italian soldier has improved under the Fascist regime?'
'Yes, he has. The men are already half-trained on joining their regiment. They need a shorter period of instruction than before; there is a sporting atmosphere in the army which has its utility. Gymnastics and athletic games are the rule.'

The same officer was less enthusiastic about Mussolini's Militia.

'Storm troops indeed! They are police troops, a political police, and the men are ne'er-do-wells whose one idea is not to risk their skin but to let others do the work. . . . The Blackshirts are a mass of good-for-nothings whose one idea is theft and worse.'

The Manchester Guardian, Friday, July 10 1936,
quoted in The Guardian Omnibus 1821–1971, edited by David Ayerst, Collins, 1973

- Mussolini also took credit for dealing effectively with the Sicilian Mafia. On a visit to Sicily he had suffered the humiliation of travelling round the island under the protection of a local Mafia boss rather than under the protection of the police! The ruthless methods of the Fascists curbed the powers of the Mafia for a number of years. Many gangsters emigrated to America instead.

---

1 *Why were the boys and girls of the* Avanguardisti *and the young children in the* Balila *made to wear uniforms? What was the point of making them march up and down in parades? How did Mussolini expect training like this to make them into good Fascists? What benefits did the Fascist State derive from this type of youth training?*

2 *Who were the members of the Militia? Why do you think the Fascist army officer had such a low opinion of them?*

3 *Write several sentences giving a number of reasons which you think may explain why foreign visitors were so impressed by the progress made by Italy under the Fascist dictatorship.*

4 *Which of these reforms do you think would have been welcomed by, a) a farmer, b) an unemployed building worker, c) a high taxpayer, d) a shopkeeper, e) a trade unionist, f) a factory owner, g) a teacher?*

Foreign Policy

Mussolini wanted to make Italy great once more. He said 'I will make Italy great, respected, feared'.

He proposed to do this in international affairs by showing that he brooked no interference in Italy's spheres of influence, in particular, the Mediterranean and Adriatic regions. Within a year of taking office he took belligerent action over the Corfu Incident (see page 212). Four Italian soldiers had been ambushed by Greek bandits in Albania. Mussolini demanded apologies and a sum in compensation from the Greek Government.

> Greece gave us a deaf ear. . . . Without hesitation I sent units of our naval squadron to the Greek island of Corfu. There the Italian marines landed.

In January 1924 he concluded an agreement with Yugoslavia, which officially made Fiume Italian. But he lost Dalmatia. In 1926 he signed a treaty with Albania. It virtually turned that small Adriatic nation into an Italian protectorate. He eventually annexed Albania in April 1939, less than six months before the outbreak of the Second World War.

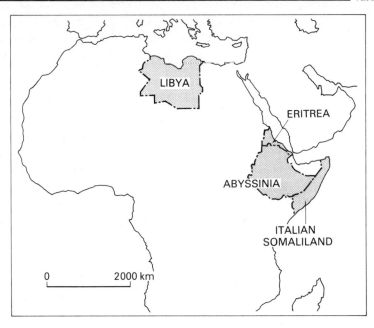

Italy's African empire

The Paris Peace Treaties left Italy without the colonies she wanted. In 1934, Mussolini combined Italy's North African colonies of Cyrenaica and Tripolitania to form Libya. In the following year, 1935, he used a minor incident on the Abyssinian border with Italian Somaliland to justify a full-scale invasion of Abyssinia which shocked the world (see page 221). Mussolini hailed this victory as a great conquest. Abyssinia, together with Eritrea and Italian Somaliland, was later renamed Italian East Africa.

---

1 *Why did Mussolini attack Abyssinia rather than a British colony, such as Kenya, or a French colony like Senegal?*

2 *Why do you think Mussolini later sent the Italian Army to attack the British and Commonwealth forces defending Egypt and North Africa in 1940? What do you think he hoped to achieve by this?*

3 *What has happened to Mussolini's Italian colonies today?*

Mussolini liked to couple the role of belligerent with that of statesman. In 1933 he engineered and signed a pact with England, France and Germany. In 1934 he moved troops to the border to deter Hitler from seizing Austria after the assassination of Dollfuss, the Austrian dictator. In 1935 he joined with Britain and France in denouncing German rearmament at a meeting at Stresa in northern Italy. In 1938 he played a leading part in negotiating the Munich agreement (see page 242).

Despite his earlier friendship with France and Britain, however, their disapproval of his Abyssinian war only moved Mussolini closer to his fellow dictator, Adolf Hitler. Mussolini resented the fact that France and Britain both had large colonial empires already. What was wrong with an Italian empire acquired by conquest like those of the other European powers?

By the end of 1936 another conflict erupted much nearer home. Both Germany and Italy gave General Franco of Spain and his rebels substantial military support in the Spanish Civil War (see page 228). These actions resulted in a pact of friendship with Germany in October 1936. Mussolini tried to reassure the world with the words,

> This Berlin–Rome connection is not so much a diaphragm as an axis, around which can revolve all those states of Europe with a will towards collaboration and peace.

In 1937 he agreed the Anti-Comintern Pact (against Communism) with Germany and Japan (see page 227) and, in 1939, signed the Pact of Steel with Hitler.

Hitler with Mussolini in 1938

1 *Why were Germany and Italy called the Axis Powers in the Second World War? In which years did Mussolini change from being a supporter of peace to a man of war?*

2 *What benefits at home in Italy could a dictator like Mussolini expect to gain from conquering a poor African country like Abyssinia? How would such a war affect, a) unemployment in Italy, b) Mussolini's standing in Italy as Il Duce, c) Mussolini's position in relation to other world leaders, such as Hitler?*

3 *Why did Mussolini become the ally of Nazi Germany? What could he hope to gain from such an alliance?*

Making Peace with the Pope

Ever since the unification of Italy in the middle of the nineteenth century, the Pope had been a 'prisoner within the Vatican' – a small patch, or enclave, of land in the middle of Rome. Each new Pope had been unwilling to step on to Italian soil surrounding the Vatican City because Rome had once been part of a much larger Papal State governed by the Pope. The Catholic Church had received no adequate compensation for the loss of this land in 1870. So, for 60 years, the Catholic Church and the Italian government had been in a state of disagreement.

In February 1929 Mussolini gained one of his greatest achievements, therefore, when he signed an agreement with the Pope. He ended the ill-feeling which existed between Church and State in Italy.

This was all the more surprising since Mussolini had originally been an atheist opposed to Church influence in Italy. But the Lateran Treaty and Concordat with the Pope provided an amicable settlement of the 60-year-old dispute. The main terms of the Lateran Treaty were as follows:

- The Pope recognised the Italian State. In return the Italian government acknowledged the Pope's authority as independent sovereign ruler of the Vatican City State inside Italy.
- The Italian government agreed to pay 750 million lire in cash and the interest on 1000 million lire worth of Italian government bonds, as compensation for the loss of the Papal territories in 1870.

The Italian government also agreed that in future:

- Catholicism would be the State religion
- marriages in the Catholic church would be recognised by Italian law
- there would be religious instruction in school
- the Church would be exempted from the payment of taxes
- Catholic organisations would be allowed to operate in Italy without hindrance from the State.

---

1 *Why do you think Italy's peasants and workers welcomed the agreement with the Pope? How did it help to consolidate Mussolini's position with the people of Italy?*

2 *What possible disadvantages were there in the Concordat with the Pope?*

3 *Was it a good thing for the Pope to come to an agreement with a Fascist dictator like Mussolini?*

The Depression Years

The Great Depression of the 1930s hit Italy hard and over a million Italians were thrown out of work, despite the Fascist Government's programme of public works and the Corporate State with its emphasis on harmony between employer and employee.

Mussolini tried to lessen the effects of the Depression by shortening working hours, providing welfare benefits and imposing tariffs (taxes) on foreign goods. But he was less successful in this than Hitler was in Germany. To make matters worse, the invasion of Abyssinia and the Italian supply of military aid to General Franco in Spain meant that taxes had to be increased to pay for these foreign adventures. By 1939 many Italians were having second thoughts about their Fascist State.

FURTHER QUESTIONS AND EXERCISES

1   a) *Who are the three people depicted in this cartoon?*

     b) *How do we know the middle figure is Mussolini? What is he carrying over his right shoulder?*

     c) *Which is Italy? Who is looking after Italy?*

     d) *What was the point of the cartoon?*

2 Why were Italians, like Gabriele d'Annunzio and Benito Mussolini, dissatisfied with the peace agreements made at the end of the First World War? Do you think their complaints were justified?

3 Write brief notes on each of the following:

a) the March on Rome   c) the Blackshirts

b) Giacomo Matteotti   d) the Concordat with the Vatican

4 What do you think were Mussolini's greatest achievements? What were his biggest failures?

Chapter Five

Nazi Germany

INTRODUCTION

Source A

Adolf Hitler addressing a rally in pre-war Germany

Source B

Adolf Hitler (extreme left) in Landsberg Prison after the failure of the Munich putsch on 8–9 November 1923 when the Nazis and their band of Storm Troopers – the Sturmabteilung or SA – and other supporters were fired on by the police. Sixteen Nazis were killed and Hitler was arrested. Hitler wrote Mein Kampf, the bible of the Nazi Party, during the nine months he spent in prison here.

Source C

An unknown soldier in the World War was temporarily blinded as a result of mustard gas poisoning on November 8, 1918, and confined to the military hospital in Pasewalk. Because of his reaction to the horrendous Stock Exchange uprising, he made the decision to become a politician and to take action himself in the destiny of his deluded and humiliated Nation. Nobody could have anticipated that this same man little more than 14 years later, as Führer and Reich Chancellor, would stand at the head of the entire German Nation.

Only Adolf Hitler himself, with the infallible confidence in the genius of his own power, knew the way to take.

Philipp Bouhler in *Adolf Hitler: Pictures from the Life of the Führer 1931–35*,
(published in Germany in 1936), translated by Carl Underhill Quinn, Peebles Press, 1978

Source D

Herr Adolf Hitler's National Socialist German Workers' Party had its beginning in 1919, when he with others founded a 'German Workers' Party' in Munich. It was 'a group of six people, with no fixed aims, no programme, only the desire somehow to struggle out of the muddle of those days' – a description not inapplicable to the present party, except that the six people have become 6 millions.

The Times, 18 September 1930

Source E

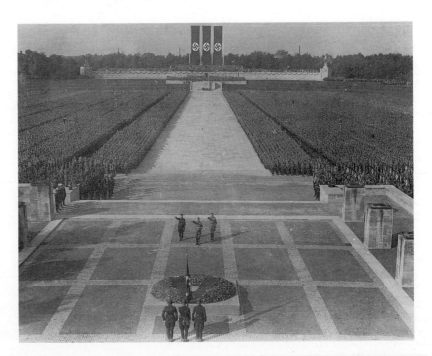

Hitler taking the salute as German Chancellor on Party Day at Nuremberg in September 1934

1 *Make a list of the facts, not opinions, which you can derive from the written extracts and from the photographs. Write a short account of Hitler's career to 1934 based only on these facts.*

2 *Look at Source E. Why do you think the photographer chose that particular viewpoint?*

3 *What is very unusual about the scene depicted in Source B? What details suggest that it was deliberately taken to impress the people who might see the photograph?*

4 *Is there any reason to think that there may be bias in either or both of the two written sources? Can you find any bias?*

5 *Do you think Source C is a primary or a secondary historical source? Back up your answer with evidence from the extract.*

It was on 12 September 1919, that Adolf Hitler, a rather nondescript ex-corporal in the German army, first attended a meeting of the newly-founded German Workers' Party in Munich. It was the beginning of a dramatic and startling epoch in German history and a fateful step for Europe and the world.

Hitler was then 30 years old and remarkable neither for his appearance nor his personality. He had already seen thirty years of his life go by without achieving any particular distinction, apart from the Iron Cross awarded for bravery during the War.

In 1918, recovering from a gas attack in a field hospital, he learned the news of the Armistice and the German capitulation. Hitler was horrified. To make matters worse, Germany now had a Socialist President, instead of the Kaiser who had abdicated. Even a Communist Germany seemed a possibility during the Spartacist uprising in January 1919. Hitler, like many other Germans, felt that Germany had been betrayed by its leaders.

Four years after his attendance at the meeting of the German Workers' Party, ex-corporal Hitler was marching, as an equal, next to General Erich Ludendorff, the brilliant chief of staff who had jointly led the German army during the War. But their attempt to seize power in the 1923 Munich *putsch* failed.

Yet incredibly, it only took another ten years for Hitler to become dictator of Germany at the age of 43. By the time he was 50 he had transformed Germany and was about to launch a war which would extend his authority from Jersey to Moscow, and from Arctic Norway to the deserts of the Middle East.

THE WEIMAR REPUBLIC

Revolution

A speaker makes a violent revolutionary speech at the funeral procession of rioters killed during disturbances on 24 December 1918

Even before the end of the First World War, on 11 November 1918, Germany looked as if it might slide into anarchy and chaos. Socialist revolutionaries seized power in Bavaria, declaring it a republic; sailors mutinied at Kiel; and members of the Reichstag (the German parliament) called for peace and an end to the war. Bethmann-Hollweg, Michaelis, von Hertling and Prince Max of Baden were all chancellors (prime ministers) of Germany in the short space of 15 months from July 1917 to October 1918 – a crucial period for the German war effort.

The final straw came with the announcement on 9 November, that the Kaiser had abdicated and had left Germany to go into exile in the neighbouring, neutral Netherlands. Germany was proclaimed a republic. Within two months of the Armistice there was an uprising, the Spartacist revolt in Berlin (see page 48). Although this was put down by the *Freikorps*, it was only a foretaste of things to come, since the *Freikorps* themselves tried to seize power in the Kapp *putsch* of March 1920.

BERLIN, Evening, November 9, 1918

Gebhardt and I were sitting quietly reading our papers, when at about two o'clock a perfect avalanche of humanity began to stream by our windows, walking quietly enough, many of them carrying red flags. . . . There, evidently no one sorrowed at the loss of an emperor. There could hardly have been a greater air of rejoicing had Germany gained a great victory. More and more people came hurrying by, thousands of them densely packed together – men, women, soldiers, sailors.

Evelyn, Princess Blücher, An English Wife in Berlin, Constable, 1921

> **1** *Why were the Berliners rejoicing? Suggest reasons based on the information given in the extract.*
>
> **2** *How do we know that some of the demonstrators were Socialists?*
>
> **3** *What type of historical evidence is this? How far do you think you can rely on a source like this to be accurate and reliable?*

In the meantime the politicians thrashed out the details of a constitution for the new republic. They did this at the small German town of Weimar, because it was well away from the riots and street fighting now disrupting life in Berlin. It was at Weimar that the new National Assembly met for the first time in February 1919. Soon afterwards its members elected Friedrich Ebert as the first president of the new German republic.

The new constitution laid down rules for the system of government, now that the Emperor had gone. The president was to stay in office for seven years and would appoint the chancellor (equivalent to a prime minister in many countries) from those politicians best able to get the support of the representatives in the Reichstag. The first of these postwar chancellors was Gustav Bauer. Almost immediately he had the unpleasant task of having to accept the terms of the peace agreement imposed at Versailles.

Problems Facing the Weimar Republic

The task facing the new German chancellor was hardly an enviable one.

- In the first place, as you have seen, Germany was a hotbed of revolution. Marxist groups, armed ex-soldiers and nationalists made trouble. The humiliation of defeat hit Germany hard. The old way of life had gone. In this vacuum the Germans needed strong and decisive but democratic government, to replace the autocratic system of government they had been used to under the Kaiser.

- The new constitution, which has been described as 'perfect' and 'ideal', provided an electoral system based on proportional representation. This had the virtue of allowing smaller political parties to be represented in the Reichstag. But it also meant that none of the bigger political parties in Germany was ever likely to get a majority of the seats in parliament. The most likely result was that coalition governments would have to be formed from two or more of the parties. This only worked if they agreed a common policy.

The Occupation of the Ruhr

The Treaty of Versailles imposed a huge burden of reparations on the German people. Yet after their defeat in the War there was little chance that Germany would ever be able to meet this debt. When she fell behind with her

payments at the end of 1922 the French and Belgian governments sent in armed troops on 11 January 1923 to occupy the Ruhr coalfield, where most of Germany's industry was situated.

On Guard! The Poilu Sentry in the Ruhr. In all but actual warfare France and Germany are at grips. The Germans are maintaining an official attitude of passive resistance helped a little by acts of sabotage on the railways and other public services ... Our picture shows a sentry on guard at a signal box where the instruments were destroyed by the Germans.

The Graphic, Saturday, 3 February 1923

1 *What was a* Poilu *sentry?*
2 *What was the reason for the French and Belgian occupation of the Ruhr?*
3 *How did the Germans oppose them without actually fighting?*

The French and the Belgians hoped to seize coal and steel, and other goods, to make up for the payments promised under the reparations clause of the Treaty. In practice, there was little the German government could do to halt this invasion, since the German armed forces had been drastically scaled down under the terms of the same treaty. Equally there was nothing the French and Belgian armies could do to make German miners actually work down the pits! So the government called for a campaign of passive resistance. This meant that the Germans didn't take up arms against the invaders, neither did they offer them any assistance. Workers were to resist peacefully and to show the foreign troops they were unwelcome.

By the same token, since the German mines and steel works were not producing coal or steel, Germany could not produce the raw materials she needed for her industries. Nor was she earning the wealth which would convince people that her paper money was actually worth the sum of money printed on it. Yet the government continued to print more paper money, as and when it was needed. Soon the printing presses were working flat out to cope with rising prices.

The Worthless Mark

Inflation was already rampant in Germany. Prices increased by four times between 1914 and 1919. But this was as nothing compared with the following years. In 1923 postage stamps were overprinted in *millionen* of marks.

A gold mark, worth two paper marks in January 1919, was worth 11 paper marks in December 1919, 17 in December 1920, 44 in December 1921, and a colossal 1750 in December 1922! Worse was to come. In June 1923 it was worth 37 000 and an incredible 38 000 000 in September 1923! By that time, the paper mark was worthless.

The largest ever denomination of banknote – a one billion mark note issued in 1923. Ten years earlier it would have been worth £50 000 million!

Many tales were told of the effects this rapidly spiralling inflation had on everyday life in Germany. Workers spent their money in the morning, as soon as they were paid, since it had lost some of its value by the afternoon. Photographs show Germans wheeling away their pay in wheelbarrows, using paper money to make kites, or to decorate a room.

The Effects of Inflation

The effects of this catastrophic inflation were felt by Germans of every class, particularly the small businessmen, farmers and middle classes who found their savings were now worthless. A lifetime's frugal living hardly seemed worthwhile when efforts to save money for a rainy day could be wiped out overnight by inflation on such a scale. It wasn't fair. Many of the people who lost their savings looked later to the National Socialist Party for a more effective remedy. This is one reason why there were over 50 000 Nazis in Germany by the end of 1923.

The evils of inflation were not felt by the middle classes alone. Workers, too, found that wages did not keep pace with the rise in the cost of living. Trade unions saw the value of their funds decline. Many workers later looked to the Communists to provide a fairer society. Only the industrialists, landowners and property owners benefited. Their money was invested in factories, land and buildings. These kept their value no matter how rapidly the mark declined in value.

The *Rentenmark*

In August 1923 a new chancellor, Gustav Stresemann, was appointed. He took the common-sense view that the policy of passive resistance in the Ruhr was hurting the Germans as much as the French. The French, for their part, were glad to be let off the hook, since the occupation had given them little material benefit. If anything, it had adversely affected France's relations with her allies. The French and Belgian armies withdrew. The German government replaced the old worthless mark with a new unit of currency,

Gustav Stresemann

the *Rentenmark*. It was backed by land values, so people had more confidence in it than they had in the old mark. One new *Rentenmark* was worth 3 000 000 000 old marks!

In the end the Americans came to the rescue. American bankers supported a proposal to make a large loan to Germany. This would allow the German government to pay the reparations which were overdue. It was called the Dawes Plan because Charles Dawes was the chairman of the committee which proposed the loan in April 1924.

A new German government, led by Wilhelm Marx, accepted the Plan and very soon American loans helped German industry to recover. For the next five years (1924-9) Germany prospered. Industry got back on its feet and as poverty retreated, the attractions of the minority extremist parties (Communist and Nazi) diminished. In 1929 the Young Plan made further reductions in the reparations to be made by Germany to the Allies.

The Treaty of Rapallo

After 1919, German statesmen had to rethink their foreign policy. Friction between Germany and the Allies over the terms of the Treaty of Versailles, especially German anger at the scale of war reparations demanded by France and Belgium, did not promise well for future foreign relations.

In April 1922, Germany signed a treaty of friendship with Bolshevik Russia, the Treaty of Rapallo, which came as a shock to the rest of Europe. Only eight years earlier, Russian–German rivalry had been a main cause of the War. Both countries now agreed to establish diplomatic relations with one another and renounced any financial claims arising out of the War.

The news was greeted with especial anger by right-wing extremists, such as the National Socialists and the former members of the *Freikorps*. Their fury was heightened because the Treaty had been negotiated by Germany's foreign minister, Walter Rathenau, a Jew. He paid a heavy price, however, when he was assassinated ten weeks later, by two young, anti-Semitic German Nationalists.

The Treaty of Locarno

Luckily for Germany, another talented statesman took his place. Gustav Stresemann was foreign minister for six years until his untimely death in 1929. He worked hard, and with considerable success, to re-establish Germany as a powerful force in Europe.

His greatest triumph was the signing of the Treaty of Locarno with France and Belgium on 1 December 1925. This guaranteed that Germany's borders with both countries would not be violated. In other words, Germany renounced any claim to Alsace and Lorraine. In addition, she agreed that the Rhineland would continue to be a demilitarised zone.

> The light of a new dawn is at last breaking upon the world ... Mr Austen Chamberlain [the British representative] did not exaggerate when he called the Locarno Conference the real Peace Congress of Europe. The

profound significance of the Locarno meeting is that the chief belligerents in the war there solemnly bound themselves to make the maintenance of peace in Europe an affair of their mutual honour ... The war is over at last.

The Times, 17 October 1925

The Treaty of Locarno was guaranteed by Britain and Italy. It paved the way for Germany's admission to the League of Nations in 1926. This was generally recognised as a major achievement, considering the harsh treatment which Germany received at Versailles only seven years earlier.

---

1 *Why was Germany able to reach agreement with the Russians in 1922 and with the French in 1925?*

2 *What was unusual about the Treaty of Rapallo in the eyes of the other European powers?*

3 *Why were right-wing extremists, like Hitler, bitterly opposed to the work for peace of Rathenau and Stresemann?*

4 *Why was the Treaty of Locarno signed? How did it improve relations between Germany and the other major European powers?*

5 *What did Austen Chamberlain mean when he called the Locarno Conference 'the real Peace Congress of Europe'?*

THE RISE OF THE NAZI PARTY

Origins

Hitler (centre) watching Nazi Storm Troopers (the Brownshirts) on parade on German Day in Nuremberg in 1923

The National Socialist movement came into being in 1919 when the German Workers' Party was founded by Anton Drexler with about 40 members. One of its first recruits was Adolf Hitler, who soon made his mark as an able and convincing speaker. The fervour with which he attacked Jews and Communists soon helped him to become head of the new party. Its policy was formally announced in 1920 with a list of demands, called the **Twenty-five Points.** These included:

- union between Germany and Austria 'in a greater Germany'
- cancellation of the Treaties of Versailles [with Germany] and St Germain [with Austria]
- 'space and colonies to provide food for our nations and settlement areas for our surplus population'
- only 'fellow Germans' [not Jews] to be citizens
- interests of individuals to give way to those of the State
- confiscation of all wartime profits from the sale of armaments
- nationalisation of all publicly owned companies
- generous improvements in old age pensions
- reform of education and a new curriculum adapted 'to the practical requirements of life ... we must aim to instil national ideas from the earliest age in school'
- improvement in the 'general good health' of citizens 'by making it a legal obligation to participate in sport or gymnastics'
- 'abolition of the paid professional army and its replacement by a people's army' of conscripts
- control and censorship of the press
- freedom of religion 'provided it is not a danger to the German race' [i.e. the Jewish faith]
- 'To achieve all this, we demand the setting up of a strong central government for the Reich'.

At about the same time the German Workers' Party changed its name to the National Socialist German Workers' Party – *Nationalsozialistischen Deutschen Arbeiter Partei* or NSDAP.

---

1 *How and why do you think the new party was soon known throughout the world as the Nazi Party rather than the NSDAP? Where does the word 'Nazi' come from?*

2 *Why did the Nazis call themselves the National Socialists? What was National and what was Socialist about their policies? Whom did they expect to recruit into their Party?*

3 *What was ominous about the Twenty-five Points? What warnings for the future should, a) the Jews, and b) the rest of the world, have taken to heart had they viewed the policies of the NSDAP seriously in 1920?*

Adolf Hitler (1889–1945)

Adolf Hitler in 1923

Adolf Hitler was born in a village in Austria in 1889, the son of a local official called Shickelgruber. In his youth he lived in the slums of Vienna where he developed a hatred of the Jews. He later blamed them for his poverty. In 1913 he left Austria for Munich. When war broke out he joined the German army and won the Iron Cross for bravery.

Adolf Hitler cut rather an unprepossessing figure in the early 1920s. In photographs he is often seen wearing a raincoat and a trilby hat. People who knew him then recalled a rather moody man, who would suddenly launch into an attack on the Jews and Marxists, if sufficiently moved to anger. After the war he was disgusted at the treatment meted out to veterans of the fighting, many of them destitute and unemployed. He contrasted this with the wartime profits made by industrialists from munitions and armaments. This only added fuel to his anti-Semitism. The Spartacist uprising alerted him to the dangers of a Communist revolution. Since Karl Marx and Rosa Luxemburg were Jewish, he blamed the Jews for the spread of left-wing ideas in Germany.

The history of Germany from 1920 to 1945 thereafter became inextricably intertwined with the life of Adolf Hitler. He committed suicide in April 1945, after he finally accepted the fact that Germany had lost the war.

The Munich *Putsch*

The National Socialist Party built up its membership quickly in the early 1920s. Hitler wanted a private army to keep order at his meetings and to put fear into his enemies. So in 1921 the para-military organisation of Storm Troopers, the *Sturmabteilung* or SA, was founded. They wore jackboots, brown uniforms and swastika armbands and were universally known, and feared, as the Brownshirts.

The NSDAP appealed particularly to ex-soldiers and nationalists. It even attracted General Ludendorff, who had been Germany's most able military commander during the war. At first the NSDAP was only a Bavarian political party with little contact with other groups in Berlin and northern Germany. But Hitler began to see his Party as the saviour of Germany as a whole. When French troops occupied the Ruhr without opposition from the German army, many ex-soldiers were appalled. It was one further humiliation for Germany. The patriots and nationalists had more to complain about when the gross inflation of 1923 made their savings and the German mark worthless. They blamed the German government, accusing it of letting the mark decline in value for its own purposes. When the campaign of passive resistance was called off by Gustav Stresemann, Hitler and his aides decided the time was ripe for a *putsch* in Munich, the capital of Bavaria.

The right-wing leaders of Bavaria had themselves rebelled against the authority of the Federal government in Berlin. This is why Hitler planned to use Gustav von Kahr, the State Commissioner, Colonel von Seisser, the Chief of Police and General von Lossow, the commander of the German army in Bavaria to further his plans. He wanted them to head a Nazi revolution against the central government in Berlin.

All three men were due to attend a meeting in the Burgerbräu Keller in Munich on 8 November 1923. In a dramatic intervention halfway through the meeting, they were seized at gunpoint by Hitler and persuaded by Ludendorff to co-operate. But later they escaped from the building and went back on their word. Hitler went ahead anyway and issued this announcement in Munich on 9 November 1923:

> Proclamation to the German People! The Government of the November Criminals in Berlin has today been deposed. A provisional German National Government has been formed, this consists of General Ludendorff, Adolf Hitler, General von Lossow, Oberst [Colonel] von Seisser.

At midday, the Nazis and their Storm Troopers began a march through the centre of Munich led by General Ludendorff and ex-Corporal Hitler. But von Seisser's police and von Lossow's troops were already alerted. The Storm Troopers got no farther than the Odeonsplatz in Munich when police barred their way. Shots rang out and 16 of Hitler's Storm Troopers and 3 policemen were killed. Several others were seriously wounded, including Hermann Göring. Hitler and General Ludendorff were later arrested and charged with treason. The *putsch* was over.

Two of the victims of the Munich putsch. From a German cigarette card album published in 1933. 'These men died on 9 November 1923 for their commanders'

DIESE MÄNNER FIELEN AM 9. NOVEMBER 1923 VOR DER FELDHERRN·

> 1 Why did Hitler's Proclamation refer to the German Government as the 'November Criminals'? Why 'November'?
>
> 2 What made Hitler and General Ludendorff think they would be welcomed by the Bavarian leaders and by the audience at the Burgerbräu beer cellar in Munich?
>
> 3 What was premature about the proclamation?
>
> 4 How did the Nazis regard the 16 men killed in the Munich putsch?

Mein Kampf

Hitler was tried and sentenced to five years imprisonment for his part in the Munich *putsch* but Ludendorff was acquitted. Hitler's nine-month stay in Landsberg Prison was comfortable enough (see photograph on page 73). He had many visitors and his assistant, Rudolf Hess, wrote down his thoughts and philosophy in the book which later became the bible of the National Socialists – Hitler's autobiography, *Mein Kampf* ('My Struggle').

On his release from prison in December 1924, however, Hitler found that Germany had changed. The new German mark was stable. Most of the French troops had gone. There was none of the despair and anger which had fuelled the attempted *putsch* a year earlier. For the next five years the Nazis reorganised the Party and laid the foundations for the years ahead. Men like Josef Goebbels and Heinrich Himmler proved their worth to Hitler.

It was at this time, however, that Hitler first doubted the reliability of the SA. This was why he founded another private army, the *Schutzstaffel* (the notorious and feared SS), as an elite corps of guards owing allegiance only to the Führer. SS members were easily distinguished from the SA because they wore black uniforms and were known as the Blackshirts.

HOW HITLER BECAME FÜHRER

The Depression

By 1929, Germany had become prosperous once again. People were enjoying the same sort of boom in industry and consumer goods as the United States (see page 153). Many industries had been completely modernised. But it was only a false prosperity based on American loans and on the assumption that people would continue to buy everything the factories and the farms could produce.

The Wall Street Crash in October 1929 (see page 163) changed all that. Stocks and shares which had been greatly over-valued in the months before, suddenly plunged sharply on the New York Stock Exchange. Many people and many businesses were ruined. The Wall Street Crash triggered off a slump in industry which had long been overdue.

The outcome for Germany was bleak. American banks and financiers needed the money which they had loaned to Germany as part of the Dawes Plan in 1924. The worldwide depression affected countries as far apart as Japan and Italy. German industries could not sell their goods easily abroad. Many factories closed or severely cut back their workforces. Unemployment figures shot up in Germany: 1.9 million people were out of work in 1929, 3.1 million in 1930, 4.5 million in 1931, and a peak of 5.6 million in 1932. Newsreel film from this period shows poor people sifting through slag heaps in search of coal. Queues of people lined up for help from charities. Banks failed.

---

1 *Draw a graph with columns or bars of different lengths to show the growth of unemployment in Germany between 1929 and 1932.*

2 *If you had been poor and unemployed in Germany in 1932 what sort of election promises would have appealed most to you?*

What was to be done? Successive German governments supported by the centre parties were at a loss. But the extremist parties had a simple answer. The Communists pointed to the example set by Lenin and Stalin in the Soviet Union. Communism could bring similar benefits to Germany. The National Socialists had a different answer. They blamed Germany's problems on the Communists and on the Jews. Vicious street fights broke out between the rival factions.

The Nazis at the Polls

In 1927, a secret German Government report on the Nazi Party concluded

> In spite of their very well prepared and thoroughly organised propaganda ... this is a party that isn't going anywhere.

Five years later, the NSDAP with 37 per cent of the votes had acquired the highest support of any political party in the Weimar Republic. In fact, Hitler despised the electoral system, preferring direct action (the Munich *putsch*) to the ballot box. But after Germany's recovery in the 1920s, he tried to gain power by legal means. At first the results were disappointing. Only 12 Nazis were elected to the Reichstag in 1928 when Germany was prosperous.

Nazi Party Policies

- **Anti-Semitism and racism.** The Nazis blamed the Jewish people for Germany's misfortunes. They believed that Germany's peoples could be divided into two classes. Pure bred Germans, typically tall and blonde, were the Aryans. They were the *Herrenvolk* or the master race. Non-Aryans were racially inferior to the master race. They included peoples, such as the Jews and Slavs. These were the enslaved races who could work for the benefit of the master race.

- **Anti-Communism.** Hitler was an implacable enemy of Communists.
- **Nationalism.** The Nazis wanted to unite all the German-speaking peoples of Germany and those living in Austria and in the new republics created under the terms of the Paris Peace Treaties.
- **Totalitarianism.** The Nazis maintained that the State was more important than the individual and that the interest of the State must come before the interests of the individual.
- **Expansionism.** The Nazis said Germany should expand her territories to gain *lebensraum* or 'living room'.
- **Militarism.** Germany could only get her own way if she was strong. Conscription was essential to build up the army and provide a disciplined training for the youth of Germany. Rearmament was vital to give the armed forces the tanks, planes and ships they needed. Göring summed it up when he demanded 'Guns before butter'.

---

1 *How and why did these policies threaten world peace?*

2 *What were their implications for, a) the Soviet Union, b) Austria, c) Britain and France, d) the Jews, e) German Communists?*

In 1930, nearly a year after the Wall Street Crash, the National Socialists gained 107 seats.

The list of over 100 Nazi members in the next Reichstag seems mainly composed of former officers, small tradesmen, journalists, lawyers, and members of the middle class generally; there are a few working men in it, but not many.

The Times, 18 September 1930

Six and a half million people had voted for the Nazis and now they became the second largest party (Social Democrats 143 seats, Communists 77 seats). No party had an overall majority in the Reichstag, so there was no obvious choice as chancellor.

Heinrich Brüning, who had been nominated as chancellor by President Hindenburg, was a moderate right-wing politician of the Centre Party. The parties which supported him were often defeated in the Reichstag. Since he was unable to carry out many of his policies with the approval of the Reichstag, he had to govern through decrees authorised by President Hindenburg. In other words, he governed as a dictator.

In July 1932, the electoral strength of the National Socialists increased dramatically to 230 (out of 608) seats in the Reichstag. About 14 million Germans voted for Hitler. As you can see from the table on page 88, the Nazi Party could now claim it had the support of far more Germans than any other party. Even so, the Social Democrats secured 133 seats and the Communists 89 seats. Between them the two major left-wing parties had almost as many seats and votes as the Nazis.

No party yet had a majority over all the other parties in the Reichstag. It was still stalemate. President Hindenburg asked Hitler (as leader of the largest party) to serve as vice-chancellor under Franz von Papen, of the German Nationalist Party (who had succeeded Brüning as German chancellor). But Hitler refused. He wanted all or nothing.

Votes cast in German elections 1930–2

	September 1930	July 1932	November 1932
Nazi Party	6.4 million	13.8 million	11.7 million
Social Democratic Party	8.6 million	8.0 million	7.2 million
German Communist Party	4.6 million	5.3 million	6.0 million
Centre Party	5.2 million	5.8 million	5.3 million
German Nationalist Party	2.5 million	2.2 million	3.0 million
Other parties	7.8 million	1.9 million	2.2 million
Total	35.1 million	37.0 million	35.4 million

The deadlock continued when yet another election was held in November 1932. The number of National Socialist seats dropped slightly to 192 but this was still more than enough to convince many right-wing Nationalist German politicians that Hitler's Nazis could be used to keep the Communists and Socialists at bay. By this time, too, the Nazi Party had begun to get substantial support from leading industrialists as well as from many shopkeepers, farmers, and members of the middle classes.

It is common knowledge that on January 27th, 1932 – almost a year before he seized power – Adolf Hitler made a speech lasting about two and a half hours before the Industry Club of Düsseldorf. The speech made a deep impression on the assembled industrialists, and in consequence of this a number of large contributions flowed from the resources of heavy industry into the treasuries of the National Socialist Party.

Fritz Thyssen (former president of a huge German steel works),
I Paid Hitler Hodder and Stoughton, 1941

Hitler was seen as a symbol of hope by millions. His supporters came from a wide cross-section of German society.

It was not the workers or unemployed who gave Hitler their votes but the middle classes, white-collar employees, artisans, shopkeepers and peasants whose economic and social existence seemed threatened.

Zdenek Zofka, translated by Thomas Childers,
The Formation of the Nazi Constituency, Croom Helm, 1986

1 *Where did Hitler get some of the money to pay for the propaganda, parades and Nuremberg rallies?*

2 *Draw a graph to show the growth in support for the Nazi Party compared with the other main parties at the elections in Germany between 1930 and 1932. What did Hitler prove at the election in July 1932?*

3 *Who were the new Nazi members of the Reichstag in 1930? What did The Times find surprising about the list of Nazi members of the Reichstag in 1930? Does this support the view of Zdenek Zofka (page 88)?*

4 *Who voted for Hitler? Compare Zdenek Zofka's statement with the Nazi election posters below and on page 90. What do the posters tell you about the aims and methods of the Nazi Party? At which types of German voter were they aimed? Where did the Nazis expect their support to come from?*

Persuading the Voters

Source A

Nazi election poster. It reads: 'Work, Freedom and Bread! Vote National Socialist!'

Source B

The Nazi Party Election Campaign – July 1932

As I walked through the Berlin streets, the Party flag was everywhere in evidence. Huge posters, pictorial homilies, and Nazi slogans screamed from windows and kiosks, blazoning forth messages about honour and duty, national solidarity and social justice, bread, liberty, and the beauty of sacrifice – all proclaiming the consummate skill with which Hitler had been leavening the masses.

Kurt Ludecke (a Nazi), *I Knew Hitler*, Hutchinson, 1938

Source C

Although the Nazis . . . are forbidden to wear uniforms in Germany, they go about Brunswick as they do in any other city, in their brown uniforms – a brown shirt, brown riding breeches and leggings. The Nazi Storm Troops have lorries on which they race along at great speed. If there is any real or alleged trouble, the lorry dashes to the spot, the storm troops leap down, blows from cudgels, knives, preservers, knuckle dusters are dealt out right and left, heads are cut open, arms raised in self defence are broken or bruised and crouching backs or shoulders are beaten black and blue. Sometimes shots are fired and knives are drawn. In a few moments all is over – the Nazis scramble back into their lorry and are off.

F.A. Voigt in the *Manchester Guardian*, 30 March 1932,
quoted in *The Guardian Omnibus 1821–1971*, edited by David Ayerst, Collins, 1973

Source D

Nazi election posters. Left: 'Workers – Choose the soldier at the front – HITLER!' Right: 'Women! Millions of men without work. Millions of children without food. Vote Adolf Hitler!'

Source E

It must have been during these months [1930–1] that my mother saw an SA parade in the streets of Heidelberg. The sight of discipline in a time of chaos, the impression of energy in an atmosphere of universal hopelessness, seem to have won her over. At any rate, without ever having heard a speech or read a pamphlet, she joined the party.

Albert Speer, *Inside the Third Reich*,
translated by Richard and Clara Winston, Weidenfeld and Nicolson, 1970

> **1** What do you think the author of Source B meant by the phrase 'leavening the masses'?
>
> **2** Make a list of the different methods used by the Nazis to persuade people to support them.
>
> **3** Why did the Nazi Party appeal to Frau Speer? Who had caused much of the 'chaos' in Germany's towns and cities at that time?

Hitler Becomes Chancellor

Since von Papen was still unable to get the support of the Reichstag, he resigned on 17 November 1932. President Hindenburg appointed General Kurt von Schleicher as chancellor but he, too, was unable to secure the support of a majority in the Reichstag. On 26 January 1933, Hindenburg told a German general that he did not intend to appoint 'that Austrian Corporal' as chancellor. Hitler, for his part, bided his time. He explained why to the Nazi leader, Martin Bormann, in a conversation on 21 May 1942:

> If I had seized power illegally, the *Wehrmacht* [German army] would have constituted a dangerous breeding place for a *coup d'état* ... by acting constitutionally, on the other hand, I was in a position to restrict the activities of the *Wehrmacht* to its legal and strictly limited military function.

Hitler's Table-Talk, translated by Norman Cameron and R.H. Stevens,
Weidenfeld and Nicolson, 1953

In the end, Hindenburg had very little choice. He offered the post of German chancellor to Hitler, a few days later, on 30 January 1933.

> **1** When did Hitler first have a legitimate claim to the chancellorship of Germany as leader of the largest party in the Reichstag?
>
> **2** Why do you think Hindenburg resisted this claim for so long?
>
> **3** Why did Hitler want to come to power legally?

For the nationalists who agreed to support Hitler in the Reichstag and for German democracy it was a fatal mistake. Franz von Papen boasted that he would be able to control Hitler, but in the end he was lucky to escape with his life, since Hitler's men later murdered General von Schleicher, von Papen's successor as German chancellor. Many of the more liberal German newspapers, too, drew comfort from the fact that there were only two other Nazis (Göring and Frick) in Hitler's Government. They thought they had little to worry about. Goebbels, on the other hand, was ecstatic,

> It is almost like a dream ... a fairy tale. ... The new Reich has been born. ... The German revolution has begun.

Hitler (right) addressing Hindenburg (left) at a meeting of the Reichstag in Potsdam on 21 March 1933

Hitler could now use his power as chancellor to manipulate public opinion, to control the forces of law and order, and to set the wheels in motion which would establish the Nazi Party as the only political party allowed by law in Germany. The Nazis boasted that the Third Reich (the German Empire) would last for 1000 years. But, as you will see, it lasted for only 12 years.

The March 1933 Election

One of Hitler's first actions was to call a general election, to get public backing for his Nazi policies. Although this sounds as if he was laying himself open to the risk of a defeat at the ballot box, it was nothing of the kind. As chancellor, Hitler controlled the police and the armed services as well as the Nazi private armies of Brownshirts and Blackshirts. During the run-up to this election, Nazi political meetings went unmolested but those of the

Communists and Socialists were broken up. People were encouraged to associate chaos and the collapse of law and order with the left-wing parties but only disciplined and patriotic behaviour from the uniformed supporters of Chancellor Hitler's Nazi Party.

By a stroke of luck (for Hitler) a Dutch Communist, called van der Lubbe, set fire to the Reichstag building on 27 February 1933, a few days before the election. At the time some people suspected that the Nazis started the fire themselves although it now seems clear that van der Lubbe was indeed guilty. Nonetheless it gave Hitler a legitimate legal opportunity, which he seized, to get President Hindenburg to agree to measures leading to the imprisonment of Communists and banning the Communist Party.

At the election, in March 1933, Hitler won a very convincing victory with over 17 million votes and 288 seats. But, despite the bullying and the propaganda, it was not an overall majority of the total of 647 seats in the Reichstag, as you can see from this table:

March 1933 Election

	Total votes cast	Share of poll (percentage)	Seats in the Reichstag
Nazi Party	17.3 million	44	288
Social Democrat Party (Socialists)	7.2 million	18	120
German Communist Party	4.8 million	12	81
Centre Party	4.4 million	11	74
German Nationalist Party (right wing)	3.1 million	8	52
Other parties	2.7 million	7	32

The Enabling Law

Even with the support of von Papen's German Nationalist Party, the Nazis still did not have the necessary two-thirds majority needed under the German constitution to allow Hitler to pass an Enabling Law which would turn Germany from a democracy into a dictatorship. He solved the problem by, a) banning the 81 Communist members from attending the meeting of the Reichstag, b) using a large number of Blackshirts (the SS) to surround the Kroll Opera House, where the Reichstag met after the fire, c) packing the interior of the building with row upon row of Brownshirts (the SA).

On 23 March 1933, the members of the Reichstag had to force their way past the Blackshirts into the building in order to vote on the Enabling Law. A

Socialist member said that youths with swastikas blocked their way and called them 'Marxist pigs'. There was an air of menace in the chamber.

The Enabling Law gave Hitler the power to suspend the constitution and rule as a dictator for four years. Any decrees announced by Hitler were to have the force of law within 24 hours. Hitler promised that his Government would only use these powers 'for carrying out vitally important measures'. To their eternal shame (perhaps understandable in the presence of Hitler's brown- and black-shirted thugs), 153 members of the other political parties in the Reichstag voted with the Nazis to give Hitler unlimited power. Germany ceased to be a democracy. Only 84 Social Democrats had the courage to defy the Nazi bully-boys by voting against the Enabling Law.

---

1 *Why did Hitler want an Enabling Law? How did he get it?*

2 *Why did he not just seize power like many other dictators? Why did he do everything through the German Parliament?*

3 *What percentage of the seats in the Reichstag were held by the Nazi Party after the March 1933 Election? Did the German people genuinely want a Nazi Government in 1933?*

4 *Write a short essay comparing the way in which Hitler took power in Germany with that taken by Mussolini in Italy. What are the similarities and differences?*

TOTALITARIAN GOVERNMENT

A One-party State

Hitler further consolidated his position as Führer when he banned all political parties other than the National Socialists on 14 July 1933. The introduction of a one-party state meant that all democratic opposition was crushed. Many Socialists and Communists were imprisoned and some executed. Hitler also dismantled the loose federation of semi-independent states, such as Bavaria and Prussia, which had come together under the Kaiser in 1871 and which made up Germany before 1933. The Nazis left nothing to chance. Reich governors responsible to Hitler were given the controlling power in each of these states on 7 April 1933. On 30 January 1934, the state assemblies were abolished. *Gauleiters* were appointed as governors of the different provinces which made up Germany (*Gau* meant 'province' and *leiter* meant 'leader').

The Night of the Long Knives

Ernst Röhm with his long-standing friend and colleague Adolf Hitler in 1929

Only one potential source of danger remained, apart from that of foreign invasion. This was the German army, which even in its depleted state after Versailles, was still strong enough to stage a military *coup*. In practice many officers were Nazis who welcomed the role that Hitler had assigned the armed forces, to say nothing of the improvements in morale that the promised introduction of conscription and rearmament would bring.

But there was one serious stumbling block. Ernst Röhm, leader of the SA and one of Hitler's oldest friends, wanted to become a general and form his 2 500 000 Storm Troopers into a people's army under his (Röhm's) command. Himmler and Göring, as well as the aristocratic officers of the German army, affected to despise Röhm and his senior SA commanders as a bunch of loose-living louts, commanding an ill-disciplined, roughneck army of Brownshirts. In reality, they were more alarmed at the size of the power base commanded by Röhm. Unlike many of the other Nazis, the SA leaned towards the left wing in politics. Leading Brownshirts were already disappointed because many of the Socialist policies of the NSDAP had not yet been implemented. In addition they resented the fact that the key role of the Storm Troopers in achieving a Nazi victory at the polls had not yet been sufficiently recognised. They wanted a 'second revolution' in which the Brownshirts would play a glorious part. Röhm was on record as saying 'The SA is the National Socialist Revolution!'

Not surprisingly, Himmler, Göring and the German High Command wanted Röhm and the SA cut down to size. They plotted behind the scenes. An eyewitness reported to Hess that Röhm had even claimed: 'Hitler is a traitor'. They passed on to the prudish Hitler well-founded rumours about the dissolute behaviour of the SA – that they held drunken orgies and that many of the SA leaders (including Röhm) were homosexual.

Hitler's actions in response provided the world with a foretaste of the nightmares to come. The SS, led by Hitler and Himmler, surprised the SA leaders in bed on the Night of the Long Knives (29 June 1934). Ernst Röhm himself, one of Hitler's oldest friends and supporters and a hero of the Munich *putsch*, was executed.

Shortly after dawn Hitler and his party sped out of Munich towards Wiessee in a long column of cars. They found Röhm and his friends still fast asleep in the Hanslbauer Hotel. The awakening was rude. Heines [the SA *Obergruppenführer* of Silesia] and his young male companion were dragged out of bed, taken outside the hotel and summarily shot on the orders of Hitler . . .
[Röhm was arrested and taken to a prison in Munich]
Hitler, in a final act of what he apparently thought was grace, gave orders that a pistol be left on the table of his old comrade. Röhm refused to make use of it. 'If I am to be killed, let Adolf do it himself', he is reported to have said. Thereupon two SS officers, according to the testimony of an eyewitness . . . entered the cell and fired their pistols at Röhm point-blank.

William L. Shirer, *The Rise and Fall of the Third Reich*, Secker and Warburg, 1959

Göring and Himmler executed over 150 SA leaders in Berlin alone. Others who were killed were not even members of the SA. They included the former German chancellor, General von Schleicher (see page 91), Gustav von Kahr (the former dictator of Bavaria who had foiled Hitler at the time of the Munich *putsch*), and Gregor Strasser, another of Hitler's former friends. Afterwards Hitler justified his actions.

I alone during those 24 hours was the supreme court of justice of the German people. I ordered the leaders of the guilty shot.

The news of the massacre appalled many people but it satisfied the German Army, since it guaranteed there would be only one army in Hitler's Germany. Shirer, in Paris at the time, wrote in his diary on 30 June, 'The French are pleased. They think this is the beginning of the end for the Nazis.'

---

1 *What reasons help to explain the 'Night of the Long Knives'?*

2 *Why do you think the officers in the regular army despised the Storm Troopers? Why was it necessary for Hitler to placate the German army, rather than the much larger army of Brownshirts?*

3 *Why do you think many people in Germany and elsewhere accepted the news of the purge with relative calm? What lessons for the future should they have learned from the 'Night of the Long Knives'?*

4 *What powers did Hitler take upon himself on 29 June 1934? Was he justified in taking on these powers?*

Reign of Terror

In April 1933, a month after Hitler became dictator of Germany, Hermann Göring as minister of the interior ordered the formation of a secret police force, the Gestapo (GEheime STAats POlizei), which later became a byword for fear, terror and torture. It was through terror that Hitler and the Nazis dealt with their known or supposed opponents. Concentration camps were established soon after Hitler came to power.

The Munich Police Chief, Himmler, has issued the following announcement: On Wednesday the first concentration camp is to be opened near Dachau with room for 5000 people. All Communists and Socialists who threaten state security are to be concentrated there, since it is not possible to keep them in the state prisons without overcrowding. These people cannot be released because attempts have shown that they persist in their efforts to agitate and organize as soon as they are released. . . . Police Chief Himmler gave an assurance that protective custody is only to be enforced as long as necessary.

Münchner Neueste Nachrichten, 21 March 1933.
From a translation in the *Official Handbook to Dachau Concentration Camp*, 1978

Dachau Concentration Camp. These prisoners had been sentenced by the Gestapo to work as a 'punishment squad'

The prisoners in the first concentration camps were Communists and Socialists, rather than Jews. Other 'undesirable' minorities were sent to the concentration camps as well, such as gypsies and tramps. They lived in tightly packed dormitory blocks under a system of rigid discipline. Their heads were closely shaven. Prisoners were severely beaten if they infringed the Camp's rules. Many were tortured. Many also died from epidemic diseases or ill-treatment, or were shot.

Physical punishment consisted of whipping, frequent kicking (abdomen or groin), slaps in the face, shooting, or wounding with the bayonet. These alternated with attempts to produce extreme exhaustion. For instance, prisoners were forced to stare for hours into glaring lights, to kneel for hours, and so on. . . . A German political prisoner, a communist worker who by then had been at Dachau for four years . . . spoke to me out of his rich experience: 'Listen you, make up your mind: do you want to live or do you want to die?'

Bruno Bettelheim, *The Informed Heart*, Macmillan (New York), 1960

Church leaders who spoke out against the regime, like the Protestant minister Pastor Niemoller, were also sent to concentration camps. Although Hitler signed a Concordat with the Pope in 1933, agreeing to permit religious freedom for German Catholics, he soon broke the terms of the agreement. Many nuns and priests were sent to the camps as well.

---

1 *What reasons did Himmler give for locking up Communists and Socialists in concentration camps instead of in prison? Why? What had they done wrong?*

2 *Was it illegal to be a Socialist on the day that Himmler's announcement was published? How many of the German people had voted for either the Communists or the Socialists in the general election held only a fortnight earlier that month (on 5 March 1933)?*

3 *How did the Nazis 're-educate' the political prisoners in Dachau?*

The Persecution of the Jews

By far the worst aspect of the Nazi reign of terror was the persecution of the Jews. Hitler, Streicher and other Jew-baiters could not forget that although the Jews formed only 1 per cent of Germany's population, they owned a much larger proportion of its shops and businesses. They were also dominant in many intellectual pursuits. About 17 per cent of Germany's bankers, 16 per cent of its lawyers, and 10 per cent of its doctors and dentists were Jewish. But there were also many poor Jews as well. A quarter of Berlin's Jews lived on charity. Despite their great contribution to the quality of life in Germany, the Jews were persecuted by the Nazis for no other reasons than race, religion and envy. Children at school were made to stand in front of a blackboard slogan, 'The Jew is our greatest enemy!' Nazi thugs urged shoppers to boycott premises owned by Jews. Cartoonists drew grotesque pictures of Jewish moneylenders in children's story books. Books were burned and the works of Jewish or subversive writers and composers banned (even the music of Mendelssohn). Great Germans, such as Albert Einstein, the physicist, and Bruno Walter, the conductor, were forced to leave Germany because they were Jewish. Later, the Nuremberg Laws drastically curtailed the rights of Jews in Germany. Inevitably these laws caused great distress.

This was as nothing compared to the horrors to come. On 9 November 1938 the Nazis used the murder of a German diplomat in Paris to launch a government-inspired terrorist campaign, *Kristallnacht*, against the Jews of Germany. But it was the 'Final Solution' (see page 269) – the mass murder of millions of Jews during the Second World War – which provided the most degrading, revolting and appalling evidence of the stark terror and brutal depths to which the Nazi leaders could sink.

Source A

Anti-Jewish posters. Left: 'If you buy from a Jew, you are a traitor to your country'. Right: 'German women remember – Boycott the Jews'. Far right: All Jewish businesses had to carry a sign warning their fellow Germans that theirs was a Juden Geschäft, *a 'Jewish Business'*

Source B

The Jew 'is and remains a parasite, a sponger'. [Hitler]
The Jew 'is the real cause for our loss of the Great War'. [Goebbels]
'The Jews brought international capitalism ... and they also brought Marxism.' [Goebbels]

Source C

We appeal to you, German men and women, to observe this boycott. Don't buy in Jewish shops or warehouses! Don't engage Jewish lawyers, avoid Jewish doctors! Show the Jews that they cannot disgrace and defile Germany's honour without being punished. Those who ignore this appeal prove that they sympathize with Germany's enemies.

Boycott of Jewish shops in 1933,
from a translation in the *Official Handbook to Dachau Concentration Camp*, 1978

Source D

A LAW FOR THE PROTECTION OF GERMAN BLOOD AND GERMAN HONOUR

Recognising that purity of blood is essential to the survival of the German race . . . the Reichstag has unanimously passed the following law:

1. Marriages between Jews and Germans are forbidden. Those marriages which have already been contracted in contravention of this law are declared null and void.

2. Relations between Jews and Germans outside of marriage are forbidden.

Nuremberg, 15 September 1935

Source E

The announcement of the death of the diplomat and party member vom Rath by the cowardly hand of the Jewish murderer has aroused spontaneous anti-Jewish demonstrations throughout the Reich. The German People's deep indignation has given vent to powerful anti-Jewish activities. In Berlin, as in other parts of the Reich, drastic anti-Jewish demonstrations have taken place. In many places Jewish shop windows have been smashed and the show-cases of Jewish shopkeepers wrecked . . . The synagogues from which . . . teachings hostile to the State and People are spread, have been set on fire and the furnishings destroyed . . . The synagogue in Eberwalde went up in flames and Jewish temples in Cottbus and Brandenburg suffered the same fate.

Deutsche Allgemeine Zeitung, 10 November 1938.
Translation from the *Official Handbook to Dachau Concentration Camp*, 1978

---

1 *Why did the Nazis mount a campaign against Jewish shops and businesses and against Jewish doctors and dentists?*

2 *Why did the Nazis look on the Jews as their enemies? What were the Jews alleged to have done? How did the Nazis make life hard for the German Jews before 1939?*

3 *Why was the night of 9 November 1938 called* Kristallnacht *('Crystal Night')? In what ways is the news item in Source E prejudiced?*

HITLER'S GERMANY

Employment

Trade unions were banned in May 1933, since it was inconceivable to the Nazis that workers could be allowed to strike or otherwise put pressure on their employers. Leading trade unionists were rounded up and sent to concentration camps for 're-education'.

In place of unions the Nazis created the German Labour Front which gave workers many benefits, such as subsidised holidays. Welfare benefits were also provided and workers got holidays with pay. Since few were without a job, it was easier for people in employment to remember the good things about National Socialism and to forget the many reminders that Germany was now a police state.

It seems probable that the numbers of people unemployed were actually declining before Hitler took office. But there is no denying the fact that his methods lowered unemployment. By 1934 less than 3 million people were out of work. By 1936 the figure had fallen to less than 2 million. It was under a million in 1937 and negligible by the end of 1939. This dramatic fall contrasted strikingly with what little progress was being achieved in Britain and Italy at the same time – or even in the United States. It is doubtful, however, whether Hitler ever tackled the problem of unemployment deliberately. His success came about largely as a result of policies condemned by the rest of the world.

- The introduction of conscription in 1935 and the expansion of the armed forces obviously employed large numbers of young men.
- Rearmament provided thousands of jobs in arms factories making guns, tanks, planes and ships. This stimulated the growth of the steel and chemical industries which provided the raw materials, and the coal mining industry which provided the fuel.
- The Nazis wanted to be self-sufficient in food, raw materials and manufactured goods. Farmers and manufacturers got government help to stimulate production. This, too, created jobs.

A new motorway between Frankfurt and Darmstadt is opened by Hitler

- Many public works were started, such as public buildings to symbolise the achievements of the Third Reich and fast motorways (autobahns) to speed up the flow of the armed forces across Germany.
- Workers were sent to work wherever there was a shortage of labour. Factory owners were directed to switch production to essentials, or even to close down plants producing non-essential goods. Wages and prices were strictly controlled, so factory owners could keep down their costs.

- It is also true, if sad to relate, that the persecution of the Jewish people, the imprisonment of thousands of Communists and trade unionists in concentration camps, the recruitment of a large secret police force and the establishment of a vast bureaucracy to run the apparatus of the State, also helped to solve the problem of unemployment in pre-war Germany.

Education

Education was strictly controlled. The Nazis taught the young to believe implicitly in National Socialism. Children were trained to obey the State. They were not to think for themselves. The Nazis did not want criticism. One-sided education like this is called indoctrination. It involved telling young children to despise the Jews. German children were taught to think of themselves as the master race. School textbooks were altered to teach Nazi theories about race in biology and history.

Source A

The entire German youth, outside their homes and school, is to be educated in the Hitler Youth physically, spiritually and morally, in the spirit of National Socialism and for the service to nation and national community.

German law dated 1 December 1936, quoted in Henri Lichtenberger, *The Third Reich*, Duckworth, 1938.

Source B

It would be foolish to underestimate the enthusiasm of young Germany for their Führer. . . . Hitler has captured the children heart and soul, and it is one of the oldest adages [sayings] of dictatorship that he who has control of the elementary schools for five years is established in power for ever.

Stephen Roberts, *The House that Hitler Built*, Methuen, 1937

Source C

'Hitler Girls greet the Führer' at Odenwald in 1932

1 *Why was membership of the Hitler Youth made compulsory? Why did the Nazis place such a great emphasis on the various youth organisations? What did they hope to achieve?*

2 *Why did Stephen Roberts say 'it is one of the oldest adages [sayings] of dictatorship that he who has control of the elementary schools for five years is established in power for ever'?*

3 *Write a description of the scene depicted in Source C. What is happening? How would you describe the behaviour of the 'Hitler Girls'? How does Source C support the information in Source B?*

Nazi posters stressed the virtues of physical fitness. This would prove the superiority of the Master Race. Fit Germans were needed to fulfil Germany's destiny. This was why the Nazis took great pride in the fact that Berlin was the venue for the 1936 Olympic Games. Nazi Germany was on show. It was visited by thousands of people from all over the world. Most of these visitors were impressed. The Nazi leaders laid on lavish parties for important foreigners. They took care to ensure that prosperity and ceremony were on show, rather than repression and terror. Less pleasing to Hitler was the fact that the Black American athlete, Jesse Owens, showed up the fallacies of Nazi theories of race by winning four gold medals!

Hitler Worship

Despite the persecution of the Jews, the abolition of the trade unions, the violence of the Brownshirts and Blackshirts, and the activities of the Gestapo, the majority of the German people seemed to idolise Hitler. Newsreel films of processions and rallies show enthusiastic crowds ecstatic in their acclamation of the Führer.

'The Führer speaks' – photographs which children pasted into a cigarette card album called Germany Awakes!*, in 1933*

[4 September 1934]
I was a little shocked at the faces, especially those of the women, when Hitler finally appeared on the balcony for a moment . . . They looked up at him as if he were a Messiah, their faces transformed into something positively inhuman.

William L. Shirer, *Berlin Diary*, Hamish Hamilton, 1941

Hitler had a remarkable gift as an orator, with a fiery and dramatic way with words which undoubtedly attracted and mesmerised the crowds. A British historian called Hitler 'the greatest demagogue in history'. His image as a national leader, sent to save the German people and lead them to greatness once more, was enhanced by the activities of his brilliant but unscrupulous director of propaganda, Dr Josef Goebbels.

Propaganda

Goebbels used all the different types of media – newspapers, pamphlets, books, films, radio – to whip up support for the Nazis and to incite hatred against their enemies. Goebbels was a brilliant and fluent speaker but a liar. He once said, 'If you tell a lie, tell a big lie. If you tell a big lie often enough people will believe it'.

Goebbels made very effective use of the State-controlled radio to inform or misinform the German people. Nazi propaganda urged everyone to tune in to the radio, so that they could listen to the Führer. The German people only heard praise for the regime, never criticism. They were only told the news the Nazis wanted them to hear.

The biggest showpiece of the Nazi year was the annual Nuremberg rally. This always featured splendid uniforms, impressive ceremonies, stirring marches and patriotic songs. Torchlight processions and military parades with goose-stepping standard bearers carrying giant swastikas impressed and thrilled the German crowds. The crowds shouted in unison the slogans of the Nazi Party, such as 'Ein Volk, ein Reich, ein Führer!' (One People, One Country, One Leader!). Rudolf Hess told them, 'The Party is Hitler. But Hitler is Germany and Germany is Hitler!'

[5 September 1934]
The hall was a sea of brightly coloured flags. Even Hitler's arrival was made dramatic. The band stopped playing. There was a hush over the thirty thousand people packed in the hall. Then the band struck up the *Badenweiler March*, a very catchy tune, and used only, I'm told, when Hitler makes his big entries. Hitler appeared in the back of the auditorium, and followed by his aides, Göring, Goebbels, Hess, Himmler, and the others, he strode slowly down the long centre aisle while thirty thousand hands were raised in salute. . . . Great Klieg lights played on the stage, where Hitler sat surrounded by a hundred party officials and officers of the army and navy.

William L. Shirer, *Berlin Diary*, Hamish Hamilton, 1941

Party Day at the Nuremberg Rally in 1933

---

1 *Write a reasoned account explaining how Hitler and Goebbels persuaded the German people to accept the Nazi Party.*

2 *Why was Shirer shocked at the faces of the German women in 1934?*

3 *In what ways do modern politicians use similar techniques to those used by Hitler and Goebbels? Give examples comparing the 1934 Nuremberg Rally with a recent political event seen on television.*

Hitler's Germany Through Foreign Eyes

Despite the fact that many leading Jewish scientists and musicians had already fled from Germany, foreign leaders were impressed by the Nazis. They ignored the reports from British and American journalists which described conditions in the concentration camps and the repression inside Germany. Ex-King Edward VIII visited Hitler in 1937 (much to the disapproval of many people in Britain) only ten months after the abdication. A biographer described the visit as 'something of a nightmare for the poor Windsors' but a photograph shows the Duchess gazing admiringly at the Führer. Sir Henry Channon, a Conservative MP, said of his first glimpse of Hitler, 'I was more excited than when I met Mussolini'. Lord Halifax (later foreign secretary) told Channon after his visit to Berlin, that he

liked all the Nazi leaders, even Goebbels, and he was much impressed, interested and amused by the visit. He thinks the regime absolutely fantastic, perhaps even too fantastic to be taken seriously.

FURTHER QUESTIONS AND EXERCISES

1 *Horst Wessel, killed by a Communist on 23 February 1930, wrote a song which later became the unofficial anthem of the Brownshirts. Explain the words of the* Horst Wessel Song *for the benefit of someone with little knowledge of modern world history.*

> *Hold high the flag! Close up the lines!*
> *The SA marches at a steady pace.*
> *Comrades, slain by the Red Front and the Reaction,*
> *March on in spirit within our ranks.*

> *Keep the streets clear for the Brown Battalions!*
> *Keep the streets clear for the Storm Troopers!*
> *Millions see the Swastika full of hope,*
> *The day of Freedom and Bread is dawning.*

> Translated from the German by Rachel Sauvain

2 *Write brief notes on the following:*

a) *inflation in 1922–3*

b) *the Munich putsch in 1923*

c) *the Dawes Plan of 1924*

d) Mein Kampf

e) *French occupation of the Ruhr, 1923*

f) *the Nuremberg Laws*

g) *Gustav Stresemann*

h) *the Enabling Law of 1933*

i) *President Hindenburg*

j) *unemployment in Germany*

k) *the Olympic Games in 1936*

l) Kristallnacht

3 *You are in a flag-bedecked stadium with thousands of other Germans. Bands are playing. Goose-stepping soldiers march past in smart uniforms. Someone whispers, 'the Führer is coming'. Write a letter to a pen friend describing what happened and the effect it had on you.*

4 *What were the distinctive characteristics of Hitler's system of government? How did he consolidate his position once in power? What methods did Hitler and the Nazi Party use to suppress opposition to their policies? How did they deal with, a) Jews, b) trade unions, c) the Church, d) Communists, e) the SA?*

5 *What do the following extracts all have in common? What do they tell you about Nazi Germany?*

> Göring: *We love Adolf Hitler because we believe deeply and unswervingly that God has sent him to us to save Germany.*

> Goebbels: *You, my Führer, have given us our daily bread this year also.*

> Dr Ley: *Everything comes from Adolf Hitler. His faith is our faith, and therefore our daily Credo [prayer] is: I believe in Adolf Hitler alone!*

Chapter Six

Communist Russia

INTRODUCTION

Soviet painting of Lenin with three peasants

> 1 *Write two or three sentences describing the painting in detail.*
> 2 *What does it tell you about Lenin and about the attitude of the Russian people (and the painter) to Lenin?*

Today, Lenin's tomb in Moscow is a place of pilgrimage for Communists the world over. Yet Lenin died long before Communist Russia could point to any great achievements apart from the Revolution itself and the defence of Russia by the Red Army. Lenin's successor, Josef Stalin, on the other hand, was largely responsible for Russia's transformation into an industrial superpower. Yet he has been reviled ever since his death in 1953. Even the cities which were named after him, such as Stalingrad (now Volgograd), have changed their names.

Both men could be cold and ruthless, Lenin relied on the secret police (the *Cheka*) to instil fear in the early 1920s, just as Stalin used the NKVD in the 1930s. Between them, they governed Russia as dictators for 36 years from 1917 to 1953. In the same period, there were seven US presidents and over 30 French prime ministers!

THE CIVIL WAR

The Opposition

The Civil War which followed the October Revolution (see page 24) was a period of great confusion in Russian history, not least because the Bolsheviks had many different opponents. These could be divided into:

- Political opponents in Russia, such as the discontented members of other political parties like Kerensky's Social Revolutionaries.
- Russians still loyal to the Czar, such as landowners and other members of the upper and middle classes. They had been dispossessed in the Communist takeover. They were the natural enemies of Bolshevism.
- National minority groups in the frontier lands which had been added to the Russian Empire in the past, such as the Poles and the Finns. They saw this as a chance to be free of Russian influence for good.
- Army officers who wanted to continue the war against the Germans and were opposed to the humiliating terms laid down by the Treaty of Brest-Litovsk (see page 31).
- The Western Allies who, in the spring of 1918, desperately wanted Russia to continue the war against Germany. Later in the same year, they supported the anti-Communist White Armies. They feared the effect on their own countries if the Bolsheviks successfully exported Communism to the rest of the world.

State Security

Although Lenin and Trotsky overthrew Kerensky's government with ease they feared a counter-revolution by forces loyal to Kerensky or to the Czar. The Decrees on Land and Workers' Control (see page 29) had made many enemies of the richer classes. They could be expected to join up with the landowners and other patriotic Russians still loyal to the Czar. Lenin and

Trotsky had to eliminate the opposition. They lost little time in creating two organisations to safeguard the security of the State.

- The Red Army – to defend Russia against her external enemies. [It developed out of the Red Guards formed by the Bolsheviks before the October Revolution.]
- The *Cheka*, or secret police – to deal ruthlessly with 'enemies of the State'. [This followed a long Russian tradition – the Czar's secret police system was called the *Okhrana*.]

Many army officers and government workers welcomed the overthrow of the Czar but had no liking for the extremes of Bolshevism. As you have seen (page 28), the elections to the Constituent Assembly showed that Lenin did not have complete popular support.

Some members of Kerensky's Social Revolutionary party began to organise active opposition to the Bolsheviks. Boris Savinkov, a former minister of war, led an unsuccessful uprising in July 1918. An assassination attempt on Lenin's life also failed but the *Cheka* boss in Petrograd was killed. The *Cheka* took a terrible revenge. They eliminated many alleged 'enemies of the State' in an orgy of killings which became known as the Red Terror.

Lenin (1870–1924)

Vladimir Ilyich Ulyanov was born in 1870. He started to use the name Lenin in about 1900. When he was 17 his elder brother Alexander was hanged for taking part in a plot to assassinate Czar Alexander III. Lenin himself was exiled to Siberia in 1897 after organising a revolutionary movement to liberate the working classes.

Thereafter he spent most of his time out of Russia as an exile, living in London and Switzerland. After the March Revolution in 1917 (page 18), he returned to Petrograd and seized power in November. Almost immediately afterwards he negotiated peace terms with the Germans.

Lenin commanded the affection of the peasant as well as the worker. When he died of overwork in 1924, at an age when most world leaders are in their prime, the tearful Russians developed a Lenin personality cult. They worshipped his memory, forgetting the ruthlessness he had used to consolidate the Revolution. His body was embalmed and preserved for all time in a mausoleum in Moscow's Red Square.

Allied Intervention

The Treaty of Brest-Litovsk infuriated Russia's allies, since the war on the Western Front only started in 1914 because France came to the aid of her ally Russia. Now the Russians were pulling out without consulting their allies. The terms agreed with the Germans, if implemented, would give Germany immense gains in Eastern Europe.

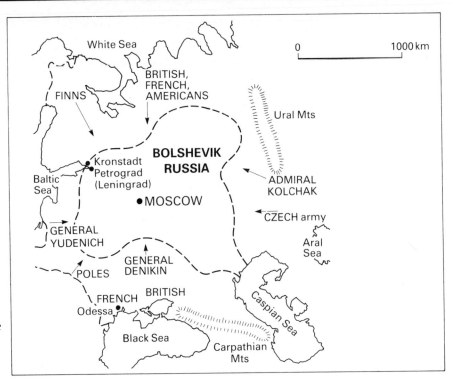

Map of the Russian Civil War showing the greatest advances made by the White Armies

The most worrying aspect of the Treaty, however, was that it released German and Austrian soldiers from the Russian Front to fight against the Allies in the West and on the Italian Front. Some Allied statesmen even suspected the Bolsheviks might fight alongside the Central powers!

They also feared the effect a successful Bolshevik Revolution would have on their own peoples. Russia was not alone in having a society dominated by a small number of landowners and factory owners, whose affluence derived from inherited wealth and the labour of a large working class.

Trotsky and other Bolshevik leaders made no secret of the fact that they wanted to export Communism to other countries. They founded the Third International organisation (the Comintern) in Moscow to do just that. They wanted a world revolution with Russia at its centre. They hoped to inspire workers in other lands to rise up and overthrow their leaders. Rosa Luxemburg, leader of the unsuccessful Spartacist uprising in Berlin in 1919 (see page 48), proved this when she praised Lenin and Trotsky as being

> the first, those who went ahead as an example to the proletariat (working class) of the world; they are still the only ones up to now who can cry: 'I have dared!'

---

1 *Why were the Bolsheviks much admired outside Russia after 1917?*

2 *What incentive did the Allies have to intervene in the Russian Civil War? Had they any legal right to do so?*

The White Armies

Leading Russian generals recruited opponents of the Bolsheviks to fight in the White Armies which began to encircle Russia. The first White Armies were those of General Kornilov and General Denikin in the Ukraine. In the east an army led by Admiral Kolchak took control of a large part of Siberia. Czech nationals, who had been captured as Austrian prisoners of war, had earlier volunteered to form a legion to fight with the Allies against the Central powers. They were being taken by rail across Siberia when they got news of the peace negotiations between Russia and Germany. A rumour spread amongst them that this meant they would be returned to Austria to face trial as traitors. Instead, they rebelled and took control of the towns along the route of the Trans-Siberian railway. Allied forces landed at Vladivostok to support them and Admiral Kolchak took charge of this White Army in the east. It was the advance of these forces which precipitated the execution of the Czar and his family at Ekaterinburg in the Ural Mountains in 1918.

Another White Army was led by General Yudenich in the west. His forces advanced to within striking distance of Petrograd. At different times, French, British, American, Japanese, Polish and Finnish troops gave various levels of assistance to the White Armies. At one stage it looked as if the Whites would crush the Communist Government in Moscow with ease.

Cartoon published in 1919 showing Denikin, Kolchak and Yudenich as dogs led by their different masters

1 *Who controlled the three 'dogs'? What was the point of this cartoon?*

2 *What advantages did the Bolsheviks have in defending Russia against this threat from the White Armies?*

3 *What would have been your reaction to the Allied intervention in the Russian Civil War, had you been a peasant or a worker in Moscow or Petrograd in 1918?*

Lenin and the Bolsheviks reacted to the emergency by putting the country on a war footing. They used propaganda posters to whip up enthusiasm for the war effort. They portrayed the White Armies as terrorist bands, backed by rich businessmen and capitalists. They appealed to the patriotism of the Russian people, convincing them that the White Armies were armed and fully supported by the Western Allies. They drove home the message that foreigners were trying to dictate who should govern Russia; not the Russian people themselves. Russia had to defend herself against the enemies within and the enemies without. This is why two important decisions were made, a) many more soldiers would be recruited into the Red Army, b) War Communism (see page 114) would be introduced to try to increase productivity on the land to support the war effort.

The Red Army

Trotsky was appointed commissar of war to build the Red Army into an efficient fighting force. He toured the country in a train equipped with a radio station, library, office, two motor cars, printing press and bathroom. He used propaganda and his powers as an orator to get the recruits needed. His efficient organisation of the Red Army undoubtedly played a major part in the successful defeat of the White Armies.

Despite the difficulties faced by the Bolsheviks, the combined might of the White Armies was unable to overthrow Lenin's regime. Trotsky's Red Army repelled the White Armies one by one but the cost of the Civil War in human suffering was horrific. Over a million Russians died, many of them brutally and in cold blood – executed as Bolsheviks by the White Armies or as enemies of the State by the Red Army, the *Cheka*, or by special retribution squads.

The Red Army was successful partly because the forces opposing them were spread thinly on the ground. As you can see from the map on page 110, huge distances separated the different White Armies. Communications were bad, so it was difficult for one army to reinforce another or come to its rescue. Nor were the anti-Communist forces agreed on what they would do if they won. Apart from foreign troops they included aristocratic officers from the Russian Imperial Army and also Social Revolutionaries, whose politics were much closer to those of Lenin than they were to those of forces loyal to the Czar. All they had in common was hatred of Communism. The only successful opposition to the Red Army was mounted in Poland, where a Polish army turned back the Russians on the Vistula and then signed a favourable treaty at Riga in 1921, giving Poland the frontier with Russia she wanted.

These are the reasons used by some Communist historians to explain the Red Army victory:

Source A

1 The Soviet Government's policy was supported by the people.
2 The Red Army was loyal and faithful to the people of Russia.
3 The Soviet Government mustered the support of the whole country to serve the needs of the front.
4 The Red Army was heroic because its soldiers understood the aims and purposes of the war.
5 The Bolshevik Party formed the core of the armed forces.
6 The Red Army was able to produce talented commanders like Voroshilov.
7 'The political education of the Red Army was in the hands of men like Lenin, Stalin, Molotov, Kaganovich, Kirov, Mikoyan, Khruschev, and others.'
8 Each army unit had a military commissar from the Communist Party. Lenin said, 'Without the military commissars we would not have had a Red Army'.
9 Bolshevik workers and peasants rebelled against the White Armies behind enemy lines.
10 Workers and Communist sympathisers throughout the world gave the Red Army assistance.

Adapted from *History of the Communist Party of the Soviet Union*, edited by a Commission of the Central Committee, Moscow, 1939

Source B

Trotsky followed the directive he got from Lenin to seek out commanders for the Red Army from among the bourgeois [middle class] officers who had been trained in Czarist military academies.

Khruschev Remembers, translated by Strobe Talbott, Andre Deutsch, 1971
(Nikita Khruschev was Soviet leader from 1953 to 1964)

Source C

The majority of the delegates from the army were distinctly hostile to Trotsky; they resented his veneration for the military experts of the old Czarist army, some of whom were betraying us outright in the Civil War, and his arrogant and hostile attitude towards the old Bolshevik cadres [groups of loyal activists] in the army.

History of the Communist Party of the Soviet Union, edited by a Commission of the Central Committee, Moscow, 1939

Source D

I give this warning: if a unit retreats, the first to be shot will be the commissar, the second will be the commanding officer ... Cowards, profiteers and traitors will not escape bullets. I answer for this pledge before the whole Red Army.

Order issued by Leon Trotsky on 14 August 1918, quoted in Victor Serge, *Year One of the Russian Revolution*, Allan Lane, 1972

The Red Army marches into Odessa in 1919

1 *How did Trotsky try to persuade the Red Army to fight? Was his attitude to army discipline any different from that of the Czar?*

2 *What type of officer did Trotsky recruit into the Red Army? Why?*

3 *What criticisms of Trotsky are made in Source C? Were they justified?*

4 *What types of historical source are represented by Sources B, C and D?*

5 *What was a commissar? What did he do? How do we know he was more important than the commanding officer in an army unit?*

6 *Why did the Red Army triumph in the end?*

7 *What advantages and disadvantages did the different White Armies have in attacking the Bolsheviks on widely separated fronts, instead of attacking them from one direction only?*

8 *Which of the ten reasons given by the Soviet historians in 1939 are obvious examples of bias in favour of Communism? Which reasons seem to you to be acceptable explanations of the Bolshevik victory?*

LENIN'S RUSSIA

War Communism

The growth in size of the Red Army meant that large numbers of soldiers had to be fed by the Government, so too did the large numbers of workers who were producing weapons and other war materials. Insufficient grain and meat were getting through to the troops, or to feed the poor. This is why

Lenin introduced War Communism. As its name suggests, it was intended as a temporary measure during the emergency created by the Civil War.

> The Soviet Government ... took under its control the middle-sized and small industries, in addition to large-scale industry, so as to accumulate goods for the supply of the army and the agricultural population. It introduced a state monopoly of the grain trade, prohibited private trading in grain and established the surplus-appropriation system, under which all surplus produce in the hands of the peasants was to be registered and acquired by the state at fixed prices, so as to accumulate stores of grain for the provisioning of the army and the workers. Lastly, it introduced universal labour service for all classes. By making physical labour compulsory for the bourgeoisie [well-to-do middle classes] and thus releasing workers for other duties of greater importance to the front, the Party was giving practical effect to the principle: 'He who does not work, neither shall he eat'.
>
> *History of the Communist Party of the Soviet Union,*
> edited by a Commission of the Central Committee, Moscow, 1939

---

1 *Why was War Communism introduced? How did the Soviets justify its introduction?*

2 *What happened to Russia's industries? What word would we use to describe this?*

3 *How did the Bolsheviks justify the policy of 'universal labour service for all classes'?*

4 *Do you think War Communism was a sensible policy? Was it fair in view of the sacrifice being made by soldiers at the front? How would you have reacted to War Communism had you been, a) a well-to-do peasant farmer, b) a peasant soldier, c) a factory worker?*

5 *Explain what was meant by the 'surplus-appropriation system'. How and why did it encourage peasants to be dishonest?*

The Peasant Farmers

Under the new policy of War Communism, committees were set up to take the grain surpluses away from the kulaks (the richer peasants) and from other peasants with grain to spare. The committees paid for this surplus grain at prices which were substantially below the fixed prices agreed by the government for normal sales of grain. This did not make sense. The peasants lost any incentive to farm when they had to sell their grain for less than it cost them to plough the land and sow seed. Widespread opposition to these regulations was met by force. Special units of the army were sent to seize the grain. Still the peasants resisted. Many concealed their grain on their farms hoping to sell it later on the black market. A report mentions the case of Irina Ivashkevich, who was fined for hiding grain in a hole in her backyard. Many peasants decided there was little point in working hard and farming efficiently, if at the end of all that effort their surplus grain could be taken at gunpoint. The results for Russia were disastrous. Grain production fell instead of rising as Lenin had planned. What is more, the Russian railway system proved inadequate to cope with both the movement of troops and the movement of food and essential materials to the towns and to the front. Lenin's problems with food production and its distribution were very similar to those which had helped to create the unrest which led to the overthrow of both the Czar and Kerensky in 1917.

The problem of falling food production was aggravated by the Civil War itself and by prolonged drought in some of the grain-growing areas in the Volga valley. In 1920, output from the land (grain, sheep, cattle) was only half that of Russia in 1913 under the Czar.

The Failure of War Communism

Many Russians died of famine in those early years of the Revolution. One estimate put the number at over five million dead.

Source A

Punch, *17 August 1921*

THE CLAIM OF HUMANITY

Source B

Famine in the Volga valley, October 1921

There was no grain because it had been burned in its seed time by a terrible drought, leaving the peasants without food because their reserves had been taken up to feed the Red Army. The villages were as quiet as death. No one stirred from the little wooden houses, though now and again we saw faces at the windows – pallid faces with dark eyes staring at us.

Philip Gibbs, *The Pageant of the Years*, Heinemann, 1946

Source C

Famine in the Volga valley, Autumn 1922

The picture of calamity which opened itself before my eyes was horrible and unbelievable: destroyed husbandry, abandoned fields, covered now with weeds, dead villages with roads covered with grass and huts with closed windows and doors and half-dead people – only a resemblance to human beings. . . . My poor country in great suffering creates her new life, but what sorrow and tears in every moan!

Serge Ivanoff, 'The Terror in Russia', *The Graphic*, 7 April 1923

Although much compassion was shown by people in the West to the plight of the Russian peasants during the great famines of the early 1920s, there was also a lot of gloating at the failure of War Communism. Hatred of the Bolsheviks coloured the news reports which told people in Britain about conditions in the Soviet Union.

Source D

The people live under a perpetual Reign of Terror without parallel in Russian history. Murder stalks abroad in the land. Outrages are committed everywhere. The industrial life of the great nation has been paralysed. Famine has been added to the horrors of the people. Nothing is deemed sacred by the authors of this prolonged orgy of fiendish misrule.

The Graphic, 29 May 1920

1 *What was the point of the drawing 'The Claim of Humanity'? What action had Lenin taken to try to 'save the Soviet Republic'?*

2 *How can we be certain that Sources B and C are eyewitness accounts of the famine? What are the similarities between these two reports?*

3 *What was the cause of the famine? Was it Lenin's fault?*

4 *Is there any evidence that these sources are biased in any way?*

5 *What grains of truth are there in the assertion in Source D? How have they been distorted? Is this propaganda or news?*

6 *What is the value of evidence like Source D to a historian? What does it tell us about Russia and Britain in 1920?*

The Mutiny at Kronstadt

Even when the Civil War came to an end the policy of War Communism continued. But by this time Russia was desperately short of food, raw materials and manufactured goods. The mutiny at Kronstadt in March 1921 helped to prepare the way for new policies. Lenin called it 'the flash which lit up reality better than anything else'.

Kronstadt was a large naval base on the island of Kotlin in the Gulf of Finland. It protected Petrograd. Kronstadt was ice-bound during the winter months and its importance during the Civil War had lessened because of a naval blockade preventing Russian warships from leaving harbour. Many experienced members of the armed forces based there had been sent to fight in other parts of Russia.

By 1921, many of the servicemen manning the defences at Kronstadt came from peasant families. They were discontented. They wanted to get back to their farms. The unrest festered and developed into a full-scale mutiny. The mutineers demanded 'Soviets without Communists'. They wanted local decisions to be made by councils (Soviets) which were not controlled by the Communist Party. They wanted an end to strict Government control of agriculture and industry. In a Resolution dated 1 March 1921, they resolved to liberate all political prisoners and to 'give the peasants complete liberty of action with regard to the land'.

The Bolshevik reaction was callous and predictable. Trotsky sent white-uniformed troops across the frozen ice to Kronstadt, after the mutineers refused to surrender. He said

> I am issuing orders for the suppression of the mutiny and the subjection of the mutineers by armed force.

Trotsky's troops attack Kronstadt in March 1921.

An American noted in his diary for 17 March 1921,

> Kronstadt has fallen today. Thousands of sailors and workers lie dead in its streets. Summary execution of prisoners and hostages continues.

But Lenin took the message of the Kronstadt mutiny to heart. He recognised that there was substance in these grievances and that the appalling shortages in Russia desperately needed new and effective solutions.

---

1 *Why were the loyal Red Army troops clothed in white uniforms?*

2 *What was the main cause of the Kronstadt mutiny?*

3 *How do you think the British or French authorities would have reacted to a similar mutiny on this scale during the First World War?*

The New Economic Policy

Lenin had already decided that a change of policy was needed but the mutiny at Kronstadt gave added point to the change. He made his proposal at the Tenth Congress of the Communist Party, which met less than a week after the start of the mutiny. In November 1922 he told the Moscow Soviet that 'NEP Russia will become Socialist Russia'.

The basic elements of the New Economic Policy were:

- The forcible seizure of surplus grain would be abolished. Instead a new tax would be decided in the spring as a fixed percentage of the peasant's output from the land in the next 12 months. Any surplus, over and above this levy, could be sold by the peasant on the free market. It meant that peasants now had an incentive to produce as much food as possible from the land. In giving the peasants the right to sell their food surplus on the open market, Lenin acknowledged that free enterprise had a part to play in the Soviet Union.

- In addition small businesses were permitted, although all the major undertakings would continue to be run by the State. The 'commanding heights of the economy' – heavy industry, power, transport – remained in State control. In 1923 the State owned about 20 000 enterprises employing some 3 million workers. Private individuals or groups controlled 150 000 enterprises, mainly small workshops with an average of only one or two workers apiece.

Source A

This was a bold, decisive, and dangerous – but absolutely necessary – step for him to take ... In essence the New Economic Policy meant the restoration of private property and the revival of the middle class, including the kulaks. The commercial element in our society was put firmly back on its feet. Naturally this was, to some extent, a retreat on the ideological front, but it helped us to recover from the effects of the Civil War. As soon as the NEP was instituted, the confusion and famine began to subside. The cities came back to life. Produce started to reappear in the market stalls, and prices fell.

Khruschev Remembers, translated by Strobe Talbott, Andre Deutsch, 1971

Source B

The correctness of the New Economic Policy was proved in its very first year. Its adoption served greatly to strengthen the alliance of workers and peasants on a new basis. The dictatorship of the proletariat gained in might and strength. Kulak banditry was almost completely liquidated. The middle peasants, now that the surplus-appropriation system had been abolished, helped the Soviet Government to fight the kulak bands . . . The Party achieved a definite turn for the better on the economic front. Agriculture soon began to forge ahead. Industry and the railways could record their first successes. An economic revival began, still very slow but sure. The workers and the peasants felt . . . the Party was on the right track.

History of the Communist Party of the Soviet Union, edited by a Commission of the Central Committee, Moscow, 1939

---

1 *Compare Source A with Source B. What discrepancy is there between Khruschev's account (written after Stalin's death) and the official Soviet version (written in 1939 at the time of Stalin's Purges)? On what points, if any, do both sources agree?*

2 *Compare the New Economic Policy with War Communism. In what ways was it a backward step for Lenin and the Russian Communist Party to take?*

THE RISE OF STALIN

Tensions in the Party

The New Economic Policy helped Russia to regain her strength. Agricultural output grew, industrial production increased, the new, more liberal measures staved off unrest. Gradually the country recovered from the trauma of the Bolshevik Revolution and the Civil War.

But there was tension among the rulers of the Communist Party. Lenin and Trotsky often took opposing views on issues which were central to the development of a Communist State. In 1921 Lenin and Stalin favoured voluntary trade unions but Trotsky (who lost the dispute) wanted government control of the unions. These tensions figured prominently in the power struggle which developed after the death of Lenin in 1924. There was no obvious successor to Lenin. No one man or woman at that time was able to command the support of all the other Communist leaders.

Trotsky addressing Red Army troops

The brilliant and dynamic Trotsky was easily the most effective of the men at the top. He had helped Lenin to plan the October Revolution and had shaped the Red Army into an efficient fighting machine during the Civil War. Trotsky was an intellectual, an original thinker and a forceful speaker. But he was not liked. He was arrogant, cold, ruthless and callous. He did not suffer fools gladly and was too erratic to get the loyal support of all his comrades.

The other leaders (Kamenev, Zinoviev, Radek, Voroshilov, Bukharin and Stalin) had none of Trotsky's obvious brilliance. For a time it looked as if control of the Soviet Union would be in the hands of the collective leadership at the top – the Politburo – rather than under the control of a single leader or dictator, as had happened from 1917–23 when Lenin was firmly in command.

The Man of Steel

Josef Stalin

Josef Vissarionovitch Dzhugashvili (he later took the name *Stalin* meaning 'man of steel') had other plans and ambitions. In 1917 he had been commissar for the different national groups in the Soviet Union. From this position of power he built up support among many of the representatives of the non-Russian peoples of the USSR. He himself came from Georgia in the south and not from Russia itself. He was also commissar of the Workers' and Peasants' Inspectorate, which meant that he helped to control the work of other Government departments.

In 1922 he took on the newly-created job of general secretary of the Central Committee of the Communist Party. It was this post which gave Stalin control of the Party organisation. It meant that he could manipulate people. He planned the work of committees so that they reached decisions which he had already made.

He outmanoeuvred his rivals, chiefly Kamenev, Zinoviev, Bukharin and Trotsky. They did not identify Stalin as a serious rival for the leadership until it was too late. They despised him. Trotsky called him 'the Party's most eminent mediocrity'. Lenin, however, saw through Stalin shortly before his death.

> 24–25 December 1922
>
> Comrade Stalin, having become Secretary General, has concentrated *unlimited authority* in his hands and I am not certain *whether he will always be capable of using that authority with sufficient caution*.

> 4 January 1923
>
> Stalin is too rude and this defect, although quite tolerable in our midst and in relations among us Communists, becomes intolerable in the post of Secretary General. That is why I suggest that comrades think of a way of removing Stalin from that post and appointing another man to replace him.

> V.I. Lenin quoted in *The Russian Revolution and the Soviet State 1917–1921 Documents*, edited by Martin McCauley, Macmillan, 1975

---

1 *Why was Lenin worried about Stalin? What were Stalin's faults?*

2 *Why did the dying Lenin suggest that Stalin be removed from his post as General Secretary of the Communist Party?*

Kamenev and Zinoviev ignored these warnings, to their eventual peril. Stalin survived. He first allied himself with Kamenev and Zinoviev against Trotsky, the extremist who wanted to abandon the New Economic Policy. Having discredited Trotsky, he allied himself with Bukharin, a right winger, against Kamenev and Zinoviev. Lastly, he allied himself with Voroshilov and Molotov against Bukharin.

Had he tried to take on all his rivals at the same time he might well have sunk into obscurity. Instead, he became the undisputed leader and dictator of the Soviet Union. When he celebrated his fiftieth birthday in 1929 he was acclaimed as 'True Successor of Lenin'. By then three cities had already been named after him: Stalino, Stalingrad and Stalinabad.

Socialism in One Country

In his dispute with Trotsky, Stalin stressed the need to strengthen the Communist Party at home. 'Socialism in one country' was his motto. By this he meant that the first essential for Russia was to complete the Socialist transformation of the Soviet Union. A successful Soviet Union would then be the perfect model of a Communist society. By its outstanding example, it would encourage other Communist Parties to do likewise in their own countries. A strong Soviet Union would also be better able to defend Communism from its enemies.

Trotsky thought differently. He wanted the Party to encourage Communists in other countries at once and to give them all the necessary support they needed to overthrow their leaders. Stalin took the view that this would give other countries the excuse they needed to attack the Soviet Union. He wanted to strengthen the Soviet economy first of all and build up its armed forces to make them capable of withstanding any such onslaught.

Retribution

Zinoviev

Stalin's rivals paid dearly in the end. On 16 January 1925 Trotsky was sacked from his important and very powerful post as commissar for war. From now onwards, Stalin controlled the army and the secret police. The 'Oppositionists' as they were called were spied on by Stalin's agents. On 15 November 1927, Adolf Yoffe, a former Soviet ambassador to Germany and Japan, wrote a last letter to Trotsky shortly before committing suicide. In it, he talked about 'the comrades of the Opposition' and 'how the history of the party and of the revolution is falsified in our country'. At his funeral, on 19 November 1927, Trotsky, Zinoviev, Kamenev and Rakovsky all made speeches.

> The only vehement speech was made by Zinoviev, who spoke of the crimes of Stalin, his accumulation of personal power, his betrayal of the rights of party members, and his deliberate misrepresentation of the party's wishes and purposes ...
>   Stalin received a full report of the speeches made at the grave. In his own time and at his own pace he would punish the speechmakers.
>
> Robert Payne, *The Life and Death of Trotsky*, W.H. Allen, 1978

Kamenev

So, despite their long-standing membership of the Communist Party and the invaluable part they had played in the Bolshevik Revolution, Trotsky, Kamenev and Zinoviev were expelled in 1927 from the Party they helped to found. Trotsky was even exiled from Russia in 1929, despite his major role in defeating the White Armies in the Civil War and making the Bolshevik Revolution possible in 1917.

> *Considered:* The case of citizen Trotsky, Lev Davidovich, under article 58/10 of the Criminal Code, on a charge of counter-revolutionary activity expressing itself in the organization of an illegal anti-Soviet party, whose activity has lately been directed toward provoking anti-Soviet actions and preparations for an armed struggle against the Soviet power.
>
> *Resolved:* Citizen Trotsky, Lev Davidovich, to be deported from the territory of the U.S.S.R.
>
> From Leon Trotsky, *My Life*, Penguin, 1975

During the Purges of 1936–8 (see page 133) Kamenev, Zinoviev and Bukharin were all executed as enemies of the State. In 1940 a Soviet murder squad hunted down the exiled Trotsky in Mexico and assassinated him.

1 *What reasons were given for the deportation of Trotsky? Are there any grounds for thinking that they may have been justified?*

2 *Why were Kamenev, Zinoviev and Bukharin expelled from the Communist Party and later executed?*

3 *How can opponents of a one-party system express their opposition in a totalitarian country? Were these expulsions necessary?*

4 *Was 'socialism in one country' a sensible policy for Russia to adopt in the 1920s?*

Josef Stalin (1879–1953)

Stalin was born in Georgia in 1879, the son of a cobbler. He trained to become a priest but was expelled and later exiled to Siberia as a revolutionary. He escaped but was recaptured and sent back to Siberia. He was released in 1917 after the Revolution in March and later helped Lenin and Trotsky plan the October Revolution. During Lenin's dictatorship he played a relatively minor role, until becoming general secretary of the Russian Communist Party in 1922.

Stalin achieved much during his 25 years as Soviet dictator. He created modern Russia and laid the foundations which enabled the Soviet Union to become a superpower after 1945. During this time a personality cult developed around the figure of Stalin. 'Our great leader' proclaimed the broadcasts. Pictures showed him as a dominant father figure leading his country to greatness. In reality his assistants often loathed and certainly feared him.

He died in 1953, a great hero at the time. Three years later his successor, Nikita Khruschev, shocked Russia and the world, by publicly denouncing Stalin at the Twentieth Party Congress in 1956. In particular he drew attention to the many evils associated with Stalin's dictatorship and the crimes committed during the period of the Purges in 1936–8.

THE FIVE YEAR PLANS

Aims

One of Stalin's first actions as Russian dictator was to begin a programme of reconstruction to modernise and expand Soviet industry. Stalin recognised that the Soviet Union could only become strong economically and militarily if it had a solid foundation of heavy industry to provide the basic raw materials and sources of power needed by other industries, such as factories making tractors, aeroplanes or locomotives.

He wanted to make rapid progress, not wait for slow and gradual improvement. Russia had recovered from the effects of the Civil War but she lagged behind her rivals in Europe and the rest of the world. The New Economic Policy had only produced a half-hearted form of Communism, in which free enterprise played a large part. Now was the time for change.

The Foreign Threat

Stalin recognised that the non-Communist world posed a threat to the Soviet Union. In particular, the existing industrial heartland of the country lay primarily in the basin of the River Don in the Ukraine, a territory which tried to become independent at the end of the First World War. The Ukraine was vulnerable to attack. This is one reason why Stalin decided to build new iron and steelworks in central Russia, well away from the frontier zone. The new steel town of Magnitogorsk (now a city of nearly half a million people) was built in the Ural Mountains in 1929–31, based on local iron ore and nearby coking coal as its main sources of raw materials.

The new steelworks at Magnitogorsk in the Urals in 1930

Stalin's foresight in developing new heavy industry away from the Ukraine was vindicated during the Second World War when the Germans occupied the industrial regions of the Don Basin. This would have crippled the Soviet war effort had this been the only Russian source of steel and coal.

Many other industrial projects were undertaken. Tractor factories were built at Kharkov and Chelyabinsk to mechanise Soviet agriculture. Vast hydroelectricity schemes were constructed on the River Dnieper. The Moscow Underground was built as a showpiece for Communism.

Foreign experts were recruited to provide advice and technical skills but the Russians also developed their own system of technical and university education to train their own experts and technicians. Scientific and engineering research was encouraged. New canals, roads and railways were built to speed up delivery of goods and to aid communications across the the vast land area of the Soviet Union. Electricity pylons criss-crossed the country. Stalin claimed in 1930 at the Sixteenth Party Congress,

> We are on the eve of the transformation of our country from an *agrarian* to an *industrial* country.

---

1 *Why did Stalin concentrate on expanding the power industries (coal, oil, hydroelectricity), raw materials (iron ore) and heavy manufacturing industries (iron and steel, chemicals, vehicles, aircraft, machine tools, agricultural machinery)?*

2 *Why did he place great emphasis on electrification and communications?*

The new industrial policy was marked by the drawing up of the First Five Year Plan, which began in 1928. It set production targets for the different industries to achieve. Coal and steel production was to be doubled, for example, and that of chemicals trebled.

These production targets were used by planners in each industry to set goals for individual mines and factories to meet. Some of these production targets were impossibly high. Factory managers failing to meet these targets were punished. Each manager used the production target to define the norms which had to be achieved by individual workers in the factory. These norms also had to be met or workers, too, were punished.

The Stakhanov Movement

Source A

Bolsheviks must master technique. It is time Bolsheviks themselves became experts. In the period of reconstruction technique decides everything.

Josef Stalin at a Conference of Industrial Managers in February 1931

Source B

On August 31, 1935, Alexei Stakhanov, a coal-hewer in the Central Irmino Colliery (Donets Basin) hewed 102 tons of coal in one shift and thus fulfilled the standard output fourteen times over. This started a mass movement of workers and collective farmers to raise the standards of output, for a new advance in the productivity of labour.

History of the Communist Party of the Soviet Union,
edited by a Commission of the Central Committee, Moscow, 1939

Source C

We have before us people like Comrades Stakhanov [coal], Busygin [automobiles], Smetanin [shoes], Krivonoss [railways], the Vinogradovas [textiles] and many others, new people, working men and women, who have completely mastered the technique of their jobs, have harnessed it and driven ahead. . . . The significance of the Stakhanov movement lies in the fact that it is a movement which is smashing the old technical standards, because they are inadequate . . . and is thus creating the practical possibility . . . of converting our country into the most prosperous of all countries.

Josef Stalin in a speech at the First All-Union Conference of Stakhanovites
held in the Kremlin in Moscow in November 1935

Source D

B. Fedorov, an engineer, drawing on unpublished archives from the mine, has revealed that two assistants – named as Borisenko and Shchigolev – shored up the tunnel and removed the coal while Stakhanov worked at the face with hammer and pick. The event was, moreover, deliberately organised by the local party to meet Stalin's requests for 'heroes', and provide a fitting achievement to mark international youth day, then celebrated on 1 September. Anyone who told the truth, the party warned, would be treated as 'a most dangerous enemy'.

Report by Rupert Cornwell in The *Independent*, 17 October 1988

---

1 *What was the Stakhanov movement? How did it get its name? When, why, how, and where did it begin?*

2 *How do you think workers in the rest of the world would have responded to the Stakhanov movement in 1935? How would you have reacted had you been working then, a) in your home town, b) in the Soviet Union?*

3 *How and why did Stalin encourage the methods of the Stakhanov Movement, a) in 1931, b) in 1935? How did Communist Party officials in the Donets Basin respond to this encouragement?*

4 *How do we know what really happened? What proof is there that Stakhanov did not perform his feat alone?*

Soviet propaganda made much of the achievements of Stakhanov. All workers were encouraged to do likewise. Those who exceeded their norm were rewarded. There were subsidised holidays on the Black Sea, free tickets and special privileges.

The Soviet people were deprived of many consumer goods during this time. Food was short, discipline strict. Many were worse off than they had been under the Czars. But there was little unemployment and, taken as a

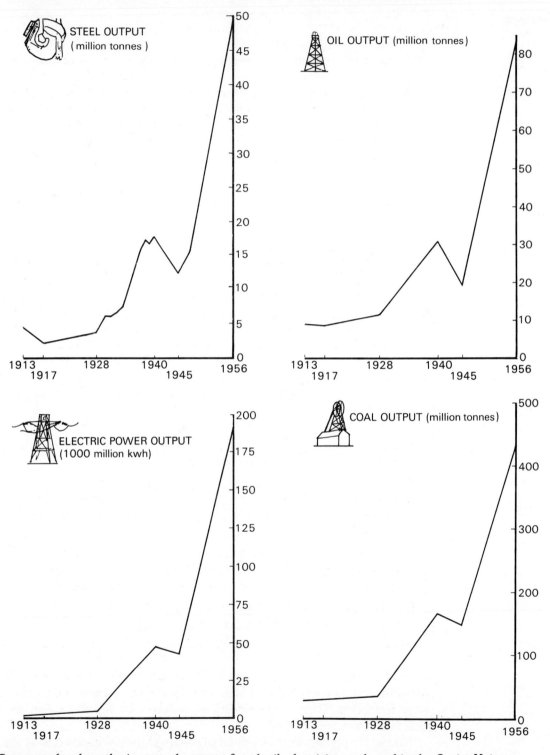

These graphs show the increased output of coal, oil, electricity, and steel in the Soviet Union between 1913 and 1956

whole, Soviet industry showed a remarkable rate of growth. This was at a time when the UK, Germany, USA and Japan were suffering the effects of the great Depression of 1929–34.

---

1 *By how many times did the output of coal, electricity, steel and oil increase between, a) 1917 and 1928, b) 1928 and 1940, c) 1945 and 1956?*

2 *Do the graphs prove that the Five Year Plans were successful in substantially raising the output of Soviet industry?*

The First Five Year Plan (1928–32) was succeeded by the Second Five Year Plan (1933–7) which allowed Russian factories to make more consumer goods than those permitted under the First Five Year Plan. But war loomed ahead. When the Third Five Year Plan (1938–42) was announced, it placed greater emphasis on the manufacture of guns, planes, tanks and munitions.

By 1940 the Soviet Union was producing well over four times as much coal and steel as in 1928 and ten times as much electricity. When Germany attacked in 1941, the Soviet Union had the industrial might to recover from heavy initial losses. Whatever the cost of the Five Year Plans there can be little doubt that they saved the USSR from defeat in the War.

COLLECTIVISATION

Soviet Agriculture

In 1928 Soviet agriculture appeared to have changed little since the days of the Czars. Farming methods were primitive, yields were low and overall output was inadequate to meet the growing needs of the Soviet people. Lenin said, 'There is no escape from poverty for the small farm'. The millions of peasants would only be convinced that Bolshevism was right, 'if we succeed in proving to the peasants in practice the advantages of common, collective, co-operative, cultivation of the soil'.

In December 1928, Stalin told Party workers,

The way out is to turn the small and scattered peasant farms into large united farms based on the common cultivation of the soil, to introduce collective cultivation of the soil on the basis of a new and higher technique. The way out is to unite the small and dwarf peasant farms gradually but surely, not by pressure, but by example and persuasion, into large farms based on common, co-operative, collective cultivation of the soil with the use of agricultural machines and tractors and scientific methods of intensive agriculture. There is no other way out.

Speech to the Fifteenth Party Congress, December 1927

The Fifteenth Congress endorsed Stalin's views and passed a resolution 'calling for the fullest development of collectivization in agriculture' and 'to expand further the offensive against the kulaks'. Stalin needed workers for the new factories and industries to be established under the Five Year Plans. The only source for such extra labour was from the land. Under the New Economic Policy, peasants had produced food for their families and sold the surplus to feed the people in the towns. Taking people away from the land would, therefore, have two main effects:

- It would mean there would be fewer peasants to grow corn and tend livestock. This meant there would almost certainly be a decline, not a growth, in the output of food from the land.
- It would increase the number of people in towns, so even more people would need to be fed from the surplus grain and livestock products produced by the peasants.

Unless there was some radical transformation in Soviet agriculture, it seemed likely that the successful outcome of the Five Year Plans in industry would be jeopardised by a decline in output from the land.

Collective Farming

This is why Stalin abandoned the idea of gradual progress and friendly persuasion. Instead he went ahead with a drastic plan to revolutionise Soviet agriculture. He brought Communism to the countryside, but at an appalling cost in human lives and happiness. The land was already owned by the people but the peasants had the right to work their individual holdings. There were 25 000 000 of these in 1928. Four years later these holdings had been merged to form 250 000 state or collective farms. The state farms were run by the Government and employees received a regular wage for their work. The collective farms, on the other hand, were co-operative ventures. They were run by committees of farmworkers. Each worker had a small plot of land on which to keep a cow, grow a few vegetables, keep hens and a pig or two. In addition he, or she, took a share of the profits from the collective farm in proportion to the amount of work put into the running of the farm. The State took its share of the profits, too, but in return provided facilities and machinery which individual peasants had been unable to afford in the past. Fedor Belov, a leading official on a collective farm in the Ukraine, saw these changes for himself. He said that, in 1928,

> A commune was set up, using two former kulak farms as a base. The commune consisted of thirteen families, with a total of seventy persons, the majority of whom were poor peasants, hired farmhands and orphans. The farm tools taken from the 'dekulakized' farms were turned over to the commune, since its members had almost none of their own. The members ate in a communal dining hall, and income was divided in accordance with the principles of 'co-operative Communism'. The entire proceeds of the members' labour, as well as all the dwellings and facilities belonging to the commune, were shared by the commune members.
>
> Fedor Belov, *The History of a Soviet Collective Farm*, Praeger, 1955

1 *What did Fedor Belov mean when he talked about a 'dekulakized' farm?*

2 *How were the first collective farms in the village set up? Whose land was it? Who were the first collective farmers in the village?*

3 *What was a commune? How do you think the members of the commune divided the farm income by 'the principles of co-operative communism'?*

Smashing the Kulaks

In many parts of the Russian countryside, the Party officials entrusted with the task of implementing the policy of collectivisation met bitter opposition from peasants who had done well under the previous system. Many kulaks were not prepared to see the results of their hard labour over the years turned into common property without putting up a fight. Some even chose to destroy their homes, barns, crops and livestock sooner than hand them over to the State.

Stalin was not prepared to brook any obstacle to his plans. The transformation of agriculture through collectivisation was essential to the success of the First Five Year Plan. Resisting kulaks were sent to labour camps. Many were shot. Stalin urged completion of the collectivisation programme. 'We must smash the kulaks!' he said, and he meant it.

Gains and Losses

In theory, collectivisation meant that farming could be more efficient, since tractors, combine harvesters, heavy ploughs and many other implements were shared and could be used more efficiently on the huge fields of the collectives. The Government could plan farm production in advance, since it could influence which crops were grown and where. It could direct the collectives to produce more meat, milk or grain as the demand in the Soviet Union warranted it.

But there were drawbacks. The workers on the collectives no longer had the profit motive to encourage them to work longer hours than those laid down by the Party. Many devoted more time and energy to their private plots of land than to their official duties on the collectives.

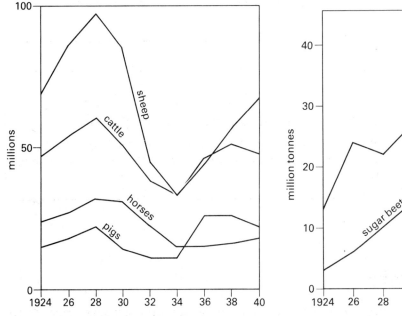
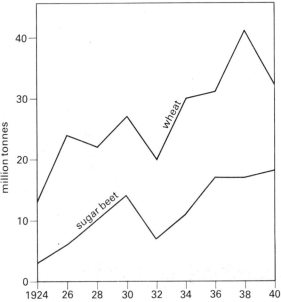

Graphs of Soviet agricultural production 1924–40

Resistance to collectivisation led to a drastic fall in agricultural output. The number of cattle fell by half between 1928 and 1934. The number of pigs fell even further, from 28 million to only 11 million. The number of sheep and goats dropped by a staggering figure, from 146 million to 42 million. Grain production also suffered, falling from 85 million tonnes in 1930 to 69 million tonnes in 1934. As a result millions of Russians starved in the famine which followed.

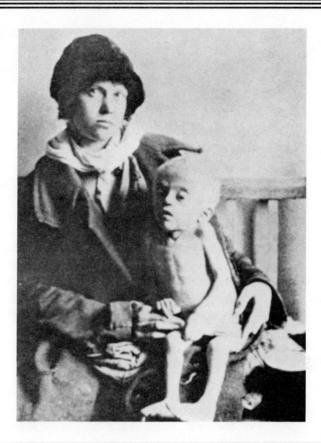

Famine was wide-spread in the Soviet Union in the 1930s. This baby is clearly suffering from malnutrition

1 *Why did Stalin tell the peasants 'we must smash the kulaks'? Was there any alternative to this policy?*

2 *What were the advantages and disadvantages of Stalin's policy on collective farms?*

3 *Look at the graphs opposite. Was the collective farm policy successful in increasing farm output, a) in the short term, b) in the long term? How did collectivisation affect a) arable farming (crops), b) livestock farming?*

THE PURGES

Kirov

In Leningrad on 1 December 1934, Sergey Kirov, the Communist Party boss in Leningrad, was assassinated by a man called Nikolayev. Immediately afterwards, Stalin ordered the trial of all those held responsible for the crime and their prompt execution if found guilty. This was the beginning of the

Purges, a time when hundreds of thousands of Russians were executed between 1936 and 1938. Show trials were staged in Moscow at which the accused almost always confessed to their crimes. Unaccountably, former heroes of the Revolution made little attempt to defend themselves against grave charges of treason. Immediately after sentence was passed, the victims were shot in the neck in a Moscow prison. They were later cremated. The ashes of many of the victims were buried in a mass grave where, today, a simple inscription reads: 'Communal Grave Number 1. Burial place for unredeemed ashes. 1930–1942'.

The reason why the ashes were not reclaimed by the families was simply because they did not know their relatives were in fact dead. Next of kin were told that the prisoners had confessed, been found guilty of crimes against the State, and sentenced to 'exile without the right to receive or send letters'. For many years, they were thought to be still alive in a Siberian labour camp. Only in recent years has the awful truth emerged. In July 1988, the Soviet Politburo made the decision to build a monument to all the hundreds of thousands of Russians who died at the hands of Stalin's executioners 50 years earlier during the Purges of 1936–8.

Enemies of the People

Those brought to trial in this way included party officials, civil servants, scientists, army officers, police officers, veterans of the Revolution and some of the most outstanding figures in Soviet society. They included all the members of Lenin's Politburo, apart from Stalin and Trotsky (who was in exile abroad – soon to be murdered by Stalin's assassins). Kamenev, Zinoviev and Bukharin were all found guilty and shot. Many of Russia's most senior military commanders were executed in an orgy of senseless killing, including the Red Army chief, Marshal Tukhachevsky, and the Navy chief, Admiral Orlov.

Source A

The Soviet Government today published the formal indictment of Zinovieff, Kameneff, Yevdokimoff, and 16 others charging them with complicity in an anti-Stalinist and terrorist plot, including the murder of Kiroff on December 1 . . . A large part of the indictment consists of extracts from the prisoners' alleged confessions of repentance . . . Under the decree of December the participation of defending counsel at these trials is prohibited, and no appeal against sentence is allowed. If a tribunal passes sentence of death the victims must be shot immediately.

The Times, 17 January, 1935

Source B

In the late spring of 1936, a series of arrests of Nazi agents and Trotskyist conspirators revealed the existence of a much wider organization – a central terrorist committee which included, not only Zinoviev and Kamenev, but several leading Trotskyists. Preliminary investigations and evidence given at their trial (in August 1936) revealed that ... the organisation was in close contact with the German Gestapo. Zinoviev, Kamenev and their associates were sentenced to be shot.

Andrew Rothstein, *A History of the U.S.S.R.*, Penguin, 1950

Source C

The Commission has become acquainted with a large quantity of materials in the N.K.V.D. [Secret Police] archives ... It became apparent that many Party, Soviet and economic activists who were branded in 1937–38 as 'enemies' were actually never enemies, spies, wreckers, etc., but were always honest Communists.

Khruschev Remembers, translated by Strobe Talbott, Andre Deutsch, 1971

Source D

The chief instigator and ringleader of this gang of assassins and spies was Judas Trotsky ... These Whiteguard insects forgot that the real masters of the Soviet country were the Soviet people ... These contemptible lackeys of the fascists forgot that the Soviet people had only to move a finger, and not a trace of them would be left.

History of the Communist Party of the Soviet Union, edited by a Commission of the Central Committee, Moscow, 1939

---

1 *What proof did Khruschev have to back his allegations against Stalin?*

2 *What did the writer of Source D mean by the phrases, a) 'Whiteguard insects', b) 'Judas Trotsky', c) 'lackeys of the fascists'? What were the alleged crimes of Trotsky, Zinoviev and Kamenev?*

3 *Why did Stalin hold the show trials in the full blaze of publicity? Why do you think the defendants confessed their crimes? What evidence is there that the show trials were unfair and contrary to most people's ideas of justice and fair play?*

4 *Examine each written source in turn. For each source, identify and explain any signs of bias or prejudice.*

The End of the Purges

When the Purges came to an end in 1938 it is estimated that over 1 million Russians had been put to death and a further 8 million sent to labour camps in Siberia and northern Russia. The Purges seriously reduced the effectiveness of the Soviet armed forces, as Stalin found out to his cost in 1941 when Hitler launched his invasion of the Soviet Union. By then, the Red Army had been deprived of many of its best generals.

Ever since, there has been controversy over the Purges and the extent to which Stalin was justified in his actions. There is even a suspicion that Stalin himself was the instigator of the assassination of Kirov.

Whatever the truth behind the story of the Purges, there can be little doubting the fact that they made Stalin the undoubted strong man of Russia. At a time when the secret police took away suspects in the middle of the night, and when the most eminent people in the Soviet Union could be arrested on trumped up charges and shot, it required considerable courage, or foolhardiness, to stand up to Stalin.

FURTHER QUESTIONS AND EXERCISES

1
> *Uniform British,*
> *Epaulettes from France,*
> *Japanese tobacco,*
> *Kolchak leads the dance.*

> *Uniform in tatters,*
> *Epaulettes all gone,*
> *So is the tobacco,*
> *Kolchak's day is done.*

a) *When, why, and where do you think this song was written?*

b) *What does it tell you about the Russian Civil War?*

2 *Write brief notes on the following:*

a) *the* Cheka

b) *the White Armies*

c) *the mutiny at Kronstadt*

d) *War Communism*

e) *the First Five Year Plan*

f) *the Red Army*

g) *Trotsky*

h) *the* kulaks

i) *the New Economic Policy*

j) *collectivisation*

3 *Study the two photographs opposite carefully. How and why do they differ? Write a long caption explaining the difference you notice between the two photographs. Add sufficient background information to make your explanation clear to someone who only knows a little Russian history.*

4 *Imagine you are 70 years old in 1940. You have either worked in Leningrad factories all your life or you have lived as a poor peasant on a small holding of land which became part of a collective farm in 1932. Describe the changes you have seen in your lifetime. How did they affect you and your family?*

5 *Why did Lenin warn the Russian Communist Party to be suspicious of Stalin? How, then, did Stalin become supreme leader of the Soviet Union on Lenin's death? Were Lenin's suspicions justified?*

6 *How do you account for the fact that Lenin is universally revered in the Soviet Union today but Stalin is reviled?*

Lenin addressing a meeting in Sverdlov Square in May 1920. Trotsky is standing on the right

Lenin addressing a meeting in Sverdlov Square in May 1920. Version published when Stalin was Russian leader

Chapter Seven

Britain and France

INTRODUCTION

In November 1933 French coal miners marched from the Lille coalfield in northern France to Paris

In 1936 shipbuilding workers in Britain marched from Jarrow in the North East to London

1 *What do the pictures opposite have in common? How do they differ?*

2 *Why do you think these workers protested in this way? What was the point of marching? What do these pictures tell you about Britain and France in the 1930s?*

3 *Why was the British march called the 'Jarrow Crusade'?*

4 *The banner carried by the French coal miners is written in two languages. Which languages are these? What does your answer tell you about these workers?*

Only 15 years or so earlier, the men in these pictures shared in the general rejoicing which marked the end of the First World War on 11 November 1918. The people of France and Britain had high hopes then for the future, now that the War was over. 'A new chapter of the world's history is beginning', said the *Daily Mirror*. 'There never again will be such news.' There was, of course, less than 27 years later, in May 1945.

Part of the blame for the Second World War can be laid at the door of the governments of Britain and France. Instead of dealing fairly with the Weimar Republic in 1919, they imposed harsh terms at Versailles. Holding all Germans responsible for the actions of the Kaiser and his Court antagonised good and bad Germans alike.

Successive politicians in Britain and France later acknowledged the injustice done at Versailles and softened their attitude to Germany accordingly. But their subsequent failure to insist strictly on the terms of the Treaty only sent the wrong signals to Hitler. He took it as the green light to dismantle the Paris Peace Settlement, clause by clause.

At the same time, both France and Britain had pressing internal problems of their own to worry about. Both had wasted much of their national treasure fighting the War. In 1914, France was owed 45 billion francs. Four years later the position was reversed. France was now a debtor nation and owed 32 billion francs. The French franc was weak. Demand for goods exceeded supply. Inflation became a problem.

Industrial unrest, unemployment, weak finances, weak government, and the potential menace of Fascism and Communism at home were common to both France and Britain in the 1920s and 1930s. Adolf Hitler identified some of these problems himself when he outlined his future policy at a top secret meeting of his most senior commanders in Berlin on 5 November 1937. Britain, he thought, would continue to have problems with her empire. In particular, he mentioned the struggle of Ireland for independence (see below) and the constitutional struggle in India (see page 390). Preoccupation with empire affairs would make Britain less likely to interfere in Europe. Although France's position (regarding her empire) was more favourable than that of Britain, she 'was going to be confronted with internal political difficulties'.

By this he meant the bitter rivalry between the French Left and the French Right (see page 146). Hitler even thought this could develop into civil war. If so, the French army would be in no position to impede Hitler's plans for Central Europe.

BRITAIN BETWEEN THE WARS

Ireland

Damaged buildings in Sackville Street in the centre of Dublin after the Easter Rising in April 1916. The General Post Office is in the centre of the picture

On Easter Monday, 24 April 1916, Patrick Pearse, James Connolly, and a small group of 1600 Irish Republicans seized Dublin's General Post Office and proclaimed Ireland an independent republic.

British forces soon overwhelmed the Irish Republicans and later executed 15 of the ringleaders. This was a serious mistake. Most Dubliners had been apathetic to the Easter Rising. Indeed, many were hostile when they saw the devastation the rebellion had done to the city centre. But their attitude changed when they learned that Irishmen were being executed for their beliefs. Pearse and Connolly and the men of the Easter Rising became the heroes and martyrs of a free Ireland.

In January 1919, soon after the end of the War, the Irish Nationalist party, Sinn Fein, won most of the Irish seats in the House of Commons. Instead of taking their seats at Westminster, they formed their own parliament in Dublin, the Dail Eireann, and declared Ireland independent. An undeclared Anglo-Irish war followed soon after the British Government banned the Dail Eireann later that year. The Irish Republican Army (IRA) led by Michael Collins waged war on the Royal Irish Constabulary (RIC). They murdered policemen, burned down police barracks and drove the RIC away from the rural areas, leaving much of Ireland under the control of Sinn Fein. In retaliation, the British Government formed a special para-military unit of soldiers who had fought in the First World War. They were known as the 'Black and Tans' from their half-khaki, half-black, police uniforms.

Source A

'Refugee inhabitants of the stricken area [Trim] leaving the town to seek shelter elsewhere'. The Graphic, *2 October 1920*

Source B

Another Irish town, Trim, in the County of Meath, with 1500 inhabitants, has been wrecked by way of reprisal for a Sinn Fein outrage. The revolutionaries on Sunday attacked and greatly damaged the police barracks in the place. In the early hours of Monday, a body, estimated to number about 200, of auxiliary police, the 'Black and Tans', arrived in motor lorries, and as the result of their visit several buildings in the main streets were wrecked by fire, the damage being put at £50 000, while two young men were injured by rifle fire.

The Graphic, Saturday, 2 October 1920

1 *What happened at Trim on Sunday 26th and Monday 27th September 1920?*

2 *Were the actions of the 'Black and Tans' inside or outside the law?*

3 *What reasons may explain why they behaved in this way?*

4 *Why did Herbert Asquith, the previous Liberal prime minister, say 'Things are being done in Ireland which would disgrace the blackest annals of the lowest despotism in Europe'?*

By now it was clear that some form of Irish Home Rule was inevitable. In December 1920, Parliament passed the Government of Ireland Act. It separated the six counties of the north-east from the 26 counties which formed the rest of Ireland and it established two Irish Parliaments, one in Belfast and one in Dublin. Six months later a truce was agreed between the two sides and talks were later held in London. They led to the signing of the Irish Peace Treaty on 6 December 1921.

Michael Collins was one of the Irish delegates who signed that Treaty. 'I signed my death warrant', he said. Collins recognised that, although not perfect, it was the most that the Irish could expect to extract from the British Government at that time. Either they took what they could, or they faced a long, uncertain, and arduous conflict ahead.

Ireland now became the Irish Free State. The six largely-Protestant counties in the North were given the opportunity to join the Free State, or to remain part of the United Kingdom (which they did).

The peace settlement did not satisfy men like Eamon de Valera and other militant IRA leaders. They said they would fight the Treaty all the way. In June 1922, however, the Irish voters endorsed the Treaty, rejecting the more extreme views of the Republican Party led by de Valera.

The IRA split in two, one half supported Michael Collins and the other half formed the 'Irregulars' opposed to the Treaty. In June 1922, the Free State forces, boosted by their election victory, attacked the Irregulars in Dublin and civil war broke out, Irish against Irish. In August, the new Irish prime minister, Michael Collins, was assassinated by the Irregulars in County Cork but early in the new year, the civil war began to peter out and a ceasefire was agreed in April 1923.

De Valera eventually abandoned militancy and got his way in the end through the ballot box when he became Irish prime minister in 1932. He stayed in power for the next 16 years and succeeded in breaking all remaining links with Britain during that period. In 1949, the Republic of Ireland declared its complete independence from Britain and the Commonwealth.

Eamon de Valera

The General Strike

British governments in the 1920s and 1930s also had serious social and economic problems to solve. When British mineowners tried to fight off foreign competition in the coal-mining industry by cutting wages and extending the length of each shift from seven to eight hours, they got a dusty reply from the miners' leader, A.J Cook. He retorted, 'Not a penny off the pay! Not a minute on the day!'

Talks between the miners and the employers eventually broke down and led to a General Strike which began on Monday, 3 May 1926. Workers in many other key industries (transport, heavy industries, printing and power supplies) stopped work.

Stanley Baldwin's Conservative Government, no doubt mindful of the consequences of similar general strikes in other countries (such as Russia in March 1917), drafted in Army units to maintain supplies and put on a show of strength.

Armoured cars escorting food wagons in the centre of London, May 1926

Armoured cars and platoons of soldiers could be seen daily in the streets but there was very little violence. Nonetheless, the General Strike was probably the closest Britain has come to civil war since the seventeenth century, even though the position of the government in Britain was hardly threatened.

During the strike, the newspaper proprietors tried many ingenious ways of getting their newspapers into print. Most were pro-Government in tone. This is why the TUC published its own newspaper, the *British Worker*, to counter the statements put out by the official Government newspaper, the *British Gazette*, which was edited by Winston Churchill.

Source A Thursday, 6 May 1926

WORKERS CALM AND STEADY
Firmer and Firmer Every Day of Strike
BLACKLEGS FAIL

Source B Friday, 7 May 1926

VITAL SERVICES IMPROVING
All Obstacles Being Progressively Surmounted
Defeat Of The Attempt To Silence The Press
RESULT OF THE STRIKE NOW BEYOND DOUBT

Source C Monday, 10 May 1926

Nothing could be more wonderful than the magnificent response of millions of workers to the call of their leaders.

Source D **Wednesday, 12 May 1926**

ORDER AND QUIET THROUGH THE LAND
Growing Dissatisfaction Among The Strikers
INCREASING NUMBERS OF MEN RETURNING TO WORK
850 Omnibuses In The Streets Of London
MORE AND MORE TRAINS – WORK AS USUAL

---

1 *Which headlines come from the* British Worker *and which come from the* British Gazette?

2 *How do the headlines differ in their interpretation of the course of the General Strike? Was this news or propaganda?*

Negotiations behind the scenes continued throughout the strike and on 12 May, the moderate union leaders on the TUC General Council called off the General Strike. When they told Stanley Baldwin, the prime minister, he replied, 'I thank God for your decision'.

The General Strike disillusioned many workers. There was bitter inter-union quarrelling and harsh new trade union legislation. In 1927 the Government brought in The Trade Disputes and Trade Unions Act which banned general strikes, the closed shop and strikes by the police force and other public servants. Trade union membership fell sharply in the next few years. This was partly because a sharp rise in unemployment meant there were fewer workers in industry anyway. The 5.5 million trade union members in 1925 dwindled to only 3.75 million by 1930.

Unemployment

The roots of the unemployment problem lay in the First World War. This had fundamentally changed Britain's position as a trading nation. In order to fight the War effectively, Britain went off the Gold Standard in 1914. This meant that bank notes could no longer be exchanged for gold. The amount of paper money in circulation was increased and this made the value of the pound fall, causing inflation in the war years. Huge sums of money were borrowed from the United States. Income tax rose to an unprecedented 6s in the pound (a rate of 30 per cent). All told, the War cost Britain about 35 billion US dollars. Many of Britain's traditional export markets had been lost for good to non-belligerents, such as Japan and the United States (before 1917). When the Government put Britain back on the Gold Standard again in 1925, this only made the pound more expensive than other currencies. As a result, British exports seemed overpriced to many foreign buyers.

Immediately after the War there was almost full employment. But by 1922 the proportion of people out of work had increased from 3 per cent to 15 per cent. It dropped then to a level of about 10 per cent for the rest of the 1920s, but shot up again to 15 per cent in 1930 and 21 per cent in 1931. It reached a

Labour Party election poster in the 1920s

peak of 22.5 per cent in 1932. This dramatic increase in unemployment was triggered off by the Wall Street Crash in New York in October 1929. This had a serious knock-on effect and caused a severe worldwide depression in trade and industry. In a desperate attempt to counter its effects, many foreign governments put higher tariffs on imported goods to protect their industries. The British industries worst affected by this were those which normally exported much of their output abroad. Coal mining, iron and steel, and textiles suffered severely. Since the depression affected most countries in the world (including the USSR, Germany and Japan) there was a general decline in shipping. Fewer cargo ships were needed. Business slumped in Britain's shipyards, which built most of the world's ships. Some shipbuilding towns, such as Jarrow on the Tyne, were so badly affected, only one worker in three had a job.

Although the unemployment figures fell in the mid-1930s, over 1.5 million people (12 per cent of the workforce) were still out of work in 1939. For almost all of the inter-war years, then, at least one British worker in every ten was out of a job.

France, with a similar population, was far better placed to ride out the problems caused by the Depression. This was partly because a larger percentage of France's workers were farmers (over 9 million in 1921, compared to less than 1.5 million in Great Britain). Even so, unemployment in France soared from 12 000 in 1930 to 312 000 in 1933. It reached a peak of just under half a million in 1935.

Fascists and Communists

A side effect of the Great Depression in Britain was the stimulus it gave to the extremist parties to the left and right of centre. The Communists pointed to Stalin's Five Year Plans and the benefits a planned economy could bring to a nation suffering the effects of a severe slump in trade. Right-wing organisations pointed instead to the achievements and objectives of Hitler's Nazi Party and Mussolini's Fascists. The most successful of these right-wing extremist groups was Sir Oswald Mosley's British Union of Fascists. Despite its name it had more in common with Hitler's Nazis than Mussolini's supporters. Unlike the Italians, Mosley's British Fascists were anti-Semitic and organised provocative marches in London's East End in order to goad the Jews and the Communists.

Sir Oswald Mosley leading a demonstration of the British Union of Fascists in London in 1936

> **1** *Why were the British Fascists able to recruit members in the 1930s?*
>
> **2** *In what ways is this scene similar to those encountered in Fascist Italy and Nazi Germany at this time?*

FRANCE BETWEEN THE WARS

The Right-Wing Leagues

There were similar extremist parties in France. The conflict between them and the moderate parties of the Centre led to serious disturbances and many deaths and injuries.

On the far right stood the Fascist *Croix de Feu* (Cross of Fire). On the far left, the French Communist Party. The *Croix de Feu* organisation was just one of a number of different right-wing leagues. It was founded in 1927 and recruited its members, at first, from the ranks of former soldiers. By 1936, however, it had a substantial following of over 400 000 people. It appealed to the French people with emotional words and phrases, such as 'morality', 'order', 'national flag', 'patriotism', and 'tradition'. Like the Nazi Party in Germany, its policies were anti-Semitic, especially since the leader of the French Socialists, Léon Blum, was a prominent Jew. On 6 June 1936, two days after Blum became prime minister, a Fascist deputy greeted him from the floor of the Chamber of Deputies with the words,

> Your coming to power, Monsieur le Président du Conseil, is undoubtedly an historic occasion. For the first time, this ancient, Roman-Gallic country will be governed by a Jew.

The other leagues varied in their composition, policies and appeal. All were loosely based on the ideas and methods of Mussolini's Fascists and Hitler's Nazis. They included the *Ligue de l'Action Française* (League of French Action), *Jeunesses Patriotes* (Young Patriots), *Ligue des Patriotes* (League of Patriots), *Francistes* (formed by merging '*France*' with '*Fascistes*'), *Solidarité Française* (French Solidarity), and *Front Paysan* (Rural Front). The *Ligue de l'Action Française*, for instance, wanted to restore the French monarchy. Marcel Bucard of the *Francistes* said,

> My revolver is my best friend. It is my best friend because it protected my life in the War and because, today, it permits me to defend the life of my wife, of my children, of my mother, of my family and of my friends.

Procession of the Croix de Feu *on Bastille Day, 1935*

1 *What other photographs in this book resemble the Bastille procession of the* Croix de Feu?

2 *What did the right-wing leagues all have in common? What was significant about the different names they took?*

3 *What was their appeal in the 1930s? Why did they flourish?*

4 *In one of its posters, the* Ligue de l'Action Française, *displayed a crossword pattern linking the words* ORDRE, ROI, PAIX, *and* PATRIE. *What was the policy of the* Ligue de l'Action Française?

The Stavisky Affair

On 6 February 1934, *Solidarité Française* appealed to the French people to demonstrate against the Government at 7.0 p.m. that night. It told them,

> Your Parliament is rotten. Your politicians corrupt. Your country betrayed by the slime of scandal. Your security menaced.

The Stavisky scandal was the reason for this appeal. It came to the surface in January 1934. Serge Stavisky was a Russian-born businessman who had used French government ministers and officials to promote his shady financial deals. Many ordinary people in France, already reeling from the effects of the Depression, had lost a lot of money as a result of Stavisky's fraudulent dealings.

Before the French police could make an arrest, however, Stavisky committed suicide. Police investigations afterwards implicated a number of well-known figures in French political circles. Camille Chautemps, the French prime minister, tried to suppress news of the affair but this only caused widespread anger and suspicion throughout France, especially among the French Fascists and other right-wing groups. Many ordinary people were appalled at the incompetence and corruption revealed in high places.

Chautemps resigned and his place was taken by Édouard Daladier. But by then anger had erupted on to the streets. In Paris, the right-wing police chief, Jean Chiappe, gave the demonstrators so much encouragement that he was dismissed by Daladier in an unexpected show of strength.

It backfired. On 6 February, the right-wing leagues, aided and abetted by the right-wing press, created a massive disturbance in the centre of Paris. But the French police were well prepared. After six hours of fighting with thousands of rioters, 17 demonstrators lay dead, over 1300 were injured, one policeman had been killed and 664 police and soldiers were wounded. Despite the successful suppression of the riot, Daladier immediately resigned and yet another prime minister took his place. The Communists retaliated with their own demonstration three days later when a further 11 demonstrators were killed and 300 wounded. An American journalist described the riot in his diary on 7 February 1934:

Source A

A little dazed still from last night. About five p.m. yesterday . . . we got a tip that there was trouble at the Place de la Concorde. I grabbed a taxi and went down to see. I found nothing untoward. A few royalist *Camelots du Roi, Jeunesses Patriotes* of Deputy Pierre Taittinger, and *Solidarité Française* thugs of Perfumer François Coty – all right-wing youths or gangsters – had attempted to break through to the Chamber [of Deputies], but had been dispersed by the police . . . About eight o'clock a couple of thousand war veterans paraded into the Place . . . we could hear the shooting, coming from the bridge and the far side of the Seine. Automatic rifles they seemed to be using. The mob's reaction was to storm into the square. Soon it was dotted with fires. To the left, smoke started pouring out of the Ministry of Marine . . . Several times the Place de la Concorde changed hands, but towards midnight the police were in control.

[Later:] It's true perhaps that last night's rioting had as its immediate cause the Stavisky scandal. But the Stavisky scandals merely demonstrate the rottenness and the weakness of French democracy . . . [For Daladier] to resign now, after putting down a fascist coup – for that's what it was – is either sheer cowardice or stupidity.

William L. Shirer, *Berlin Diary*, Hamish Hamilton, 1941

A poster published afterwards showed shabbily-dressed, former soldiers, some dead, some on crutches, with a dozen French national flags (the Tricolour) in the background. It carried the slogan:

Source B

These are the unarmed former soldiers who were crying 'DOWN WITH THE SWINDLERS! LONG LIVE FRANCE' when they were killed on 6 February 1934.

Source C

A first salvo of rifle blanks is fired as a warning shot. But the rioters gain ground. The guards fire again into the air, this time with real bullets. It is still not enough to frighten off the extremists determined to overthrow the Republic and the idea of parliamentary democracy. 'Vive Chiappe! Vive Chiappe! Down with the swindlers!' bawl these lunatics. And they throw their bombs under the horses' hooves. This time the Mobile Guards fire in earnest. About ten of the rioters fall; the rest escape. In a matter of seconds, the bridge is captured, *la Place* is empty, as if swept away by a cyclone.

Populaire, 7 February 1934, quoted in *Histoire d'une guerre à l'autre (1914–1939)*,
edited by Régis Benichi and Jean Mathiex, Hachette, 1982

Source D

LE POING FINAL

CHAMBRE DES DÉPUTÉS

Cartoon in the journal, Le Témoin, *4 February 1934*

Source E

The demonstrators, who were they? What did they want? . . . To the Right, they were honest people, ruined by the economic crisis, exasperated by the Stavisky affair, who vented their anger on an incompetent government. To the Left, they were dangerous agitators, recruited by the leagues to overthrow the Republic and set up a Fascist dictatorship in France.

Histoire d'une guerre à l'autre (1914–1939),
edited by Régis Benichi and Jean Mathiex, Hachette, 1982

Source F

It is excessive to see in it any sign of a Fascist threat. The 6 February is not a *putsch*, nor even a riot, only a street demonstration which history would have forgotten had it not had tragic results and if subsequent events had not given it an importance it did not merit.

René Rémond, *La Droite en France*, Aubier-Montaigne, 1963

---

1 *Are any of these sources eyewitness evidence? Which are primary and which are secondary sources? Which primary sources supported, a) the Fascists, b) the anti-Fascists?*

2 *What do you think 'LE POING FINAL' means in English? What was the point of the cartoon? What does the publication of this cartoon just two days before the events of 6 February suggest to you?*

3 *What slogans did the demonstrators shout? What was the cause of the 6 February rioting, judging by these slogans?*

4 *How did the right-wing parties and those of the left wing differ in the way in which they depicted the events of 6 February 1934?*

5 *What evidence is there that it was an attempted 'fascist coup'? What did* Populaire *think it was? What was René Rémond's conclusion? On the evidence given here, what do you think it was?*

The Popular Front

The Stavisky affair had serious repercussions for France, since it brought the entire political system into disrepute and made many people doubt the merits of a democratic system, which seemed incapable of providing strong, honest government. The left-wing parties regrouped in the face of the threat from the leagues. The Communists and Socialists buried their differences and formed the Popular Front. On 14 July, 1935, nearly half a million Radicals (led by Daladier), Socialists (led by Blum) and Communists (led by Thorez) marched through Paris.

Election programme of the Popular Front

1 *Why did the Popular Front march through Paris on 14 July?*

2 *What was the Popular Front against ('contre')? What was it for ('pour')?*

France was rapidly becoming divided between two extremes of right and left. Parliamentary democracy was being discredited. There were serious strikes after the elections of 1936 when many workers occupied their plants. For a time it looked as if the economy of the country would come to a halt. It was only when the Popular Front helped to engineer the Matignon agreement between employers and trade unions, on 7 June 1936, that the threat of further unrest subsided. French workers now enjoyed paid holidays, a 40-hour week, an average 12 per cent pay rise, and trade union bargaining rights, including the legal right to appoint shop stewards. News of the agreement was greeted with ecstasy by the left. 'Victory! Victory! The employers have surrendered!' cried the left-wing journal *Populaire*.

Further political and financial problems afflicted France in the years immediately before the outbreak of war in 1939. Léon Blum, the Socialist premier, had to resign and Radical governments took over. When the political crises of 1938 threatened the peace of Europe, France was ill-equipped to meet them with strength.

FURTHER QUESTIONS AND EXERCISES

1 *What similarities and what differences were there between the problems facing Britain and those facing France in the inter-war years?*

2 *Write brief notes explaining the significance of the following dates in the history of the inter-war years in Britain and France:*

a) *24 April 1916*

b) *6 December 1921*

c) *3 May 1926*

d) *6 February 1934*

e) *14 July 1935*

3 *Explain fully the circumstances in which the following remarks were made. Who made these statements, when, and why?*

a) *'I signed my death warrant.'*

b) *'Vive Chiappe! Down with the swindlers!'*

c) *'Not a penny off the pay!'*

d) *'I thank God for your decision.'*

4 *Draw up a table like this to compile a time chart of the inter-war period:*

Year	Britain/France	Germany/Italy	Soviet Union	Rest of Europe
1918				
1919				
⋮				
1939				

List every year from 1918 to 1939 in the first column. Against each year, note down in the relevant columns the major events which affected Britain, France, Germany, Italy, the Soviet Union and the rest of Europe.

Chapter Eight
Boom and Bust in the USA

INTRODUCTION

Model T Ford motor cars ready to leave the factory in 1925

> 1 What does the phrase 'boom and bust' suggest to you?
>
> 2 Which does the photograph illustrate, boom or bust?

The 1920s was a period of unbelievable prosperity for many Americans – a period called 'the boom years', 'the roaring twenties' and 'the jazz age'. America had fully recovered from the the First World War. After registering 6 million unemployed in 1921, most Americans now had a job, industry was booming, people were enjoying luxuries. Most of the signs of unrest at the end of the War, demonstrations, strikes, and Communist agitation, had gone. President Coolidge told his countrymen 'The business of America is business'. In 1928 his successor, Herbert Hoover, claimed, 'The poor man is vanishing from among us'. The ruling Republican Party boasted 'a chicken in every pot' and 'two cars in every garage'. But by 1930, much of this was just a memory to the average American. Millions were unemployed. In every American city, hungry people lined up at soup kitchens for charity. Many well-to-do families were reduced to poverty. People lived in despair. Americans began to look for a way out. President Roosevelt provided it. He called it the New Deal.

THE ROARING TWENTIES

Normalcy

President Harding

In 1919, many Americans opposed the idea of joining the League of Nations (see page 205), because it might have meant sending American troops to intervene in foreign disputes. They wanted America to follow a policy of isolationism instead. This was the policy of putting America first in everything. America should get on with her everyday business instead of trying to solve the world's problems. Foreign powers were unlikely to attack, let alone invade, the United States. Many Americans had emigrated from Europe to escape oppression and poverty. Why should they fight over Europe's squabbles? When the presidential election was held in 1920, the American people voted by a huge majority for Warren Harding, the Republican candidate who campaigned for 'America First'. President Harding wanted a return to normalcy. He meant an America which would lead a normal life and behave in a normal manner.

Harding was an amiable man but too easily influenced by his advisers, some of whom were corrupt. In 1923, the Teapot Dome enquiry uncovered a financial scandal involving one of Harding's cabinet ministers. Harding died suddenly and Calvin Coolidge took over as president at the start of a period of unprecedented prosperity. His successor, Herbert Hoover, was not so lucky. He came to office only a few months before the Wall Street Crash in October 1929 and the start of the Great Depression of the early 1930s.

Richest Nation

By 1929 the United States had become, beyond any shadow of doubt, the richest nation on earth. There were several reasons for this.

- Although the American army played a big part in the defeat of Germany, she was only involved after April 1917. Since 1914 many American manufacturers prospered by selling arms to the Allies. Britain and France both got huge loans from the US Government to pay for them.
- American manufacturers did very well in the 1920s. They seemed able to sell all the goods they could make. This was partly because foreign manufacturers found it hard to compete. In 1922 the Americans introduced the Fordney-McCumber tariff on foreign imports. It was followed in 1929 by the Hawley-Smoot Tariff Act which raised import duties even higher. Tariffs 'protected' the products of American manufacturers, since they made them cheaper, or no dearer, than competing foreign products (which had to pay the extra tax). Foreign governments retaliated by putting high tariffs on American goods imported into their countries as well.

- The demand for goods was stimulated by advertising. Mail order catalogues, posters, radio and cinema commercials urged customers to buy. If you didn't have the cash you could always borrow the money you needed on hire purchase. Many people began to live on credit.
- People even borrowed money from banks to buy shares on the New York Stock Exchange. Like industry, shares and stocks were booming. This provided extra finance for industry and helped big business to expand and prosper even further. All was well, so long as share prices rose. In 1928 alone, some shares multiplied in value by five times.
- Workers in industry generally got high wages at this time yet the taxes they paid actually fell. Many more people could afford to buy cars, domestic appliances, stocks, shares, and cinema tickets.
- Many new industries boomed in America. Nearly 6 million cars were sold in 1929 compared with only 2 million in 1919. The car manufacturers were good customers for other manufacturers' raw materials. They took four-fifths of America's rubber (for tyres), half the sheet glass which was produced and about one-tenth of the total steel output. Other consumer industries also prospered. The American radio industry sold $60 million worth of radio sets in 1922 and $800 million worth only seven years later in 1929. The same thing happened with washing machines, electric shavers, vacuum cleaners, gramophones, gramophone records and many other luxury and non-essential goods.
- Mass production methods, pioneered by the car-maker Henry Ford, made the manufacture of many of these goods much cheaper than had been the case when they were each individually made by hand. Ford trained each worker to perform a specific task as a vehicle or engine passed by on the assembly line. In this way he greatly increased the output of motor vehicles from his factories.

In 1909 the Model T Ford motor car cost $950. Fifteen years later its price had dropped to only $290 and the Ford motor company was producing them at the rate of 7500 cars a day. Soon everyone seemed to have a car. Some even put it ahead of other purchases for the home. One mother of nine children said, 'We'd rather do without clothes than give up the car'. Another claimed, 'I'll go without food before I'll see us give up the car'. Motoring became a popular leisure-time activity for millions of Americans. The *Saturday Evening Post* urged its readers,

> Get aboard – and be off with smiles down the nearest road – free, loose, and happy – bound for green wonderlands.

Radio, the automobile and the telephone opened up new prospects for many Americans. They made it possible for people to be more mobile and encouraged them to seek their fortunes in the cities or in the Far West on the Pacific coast. Young people found freedom in jazz, ragtime, dancing, smoking, motoring and the cinema. Hollywood film stars influenced the way people dressed, the perfume women used, and the way in which men combed their hair or wore a moustache.

> **1** *Why were the radio and the automobile so important to people living in a country like the United States?*
>
> **2** *Why did they have more importance in the United States than they did in Britain at that time?*
>
> **3** *What events and happenings in Europe between 1918 and 1929 gave normalcy its appeal to Americans?*
>
> **4** *Why do you think 'isolationism' appealed to Americans in the inter-war years? Is America 'isolationist' today?*

The Farmers

There were many Americans, however, who did not share in the prosperity of the boom years. About 1 million people left the land in the 1920s. Some left voluntarily. Others were evicted from their farms and smallholdings because they were unable to pay the rent. Many could not keep up the payments on machinery and buildings which they had bought during the war years when the demand for home-grown food meant high prices for the farmer. Prices soon tumbled after the war but rents, mortgage repayments, machinery costs and fertiliser costs rose by an estimated 30 per cent. Even so, farmers might still have prospered had they been able to sell their surpluses overseas. But the introduction of the Fordney-McCumber tariff penalised foreign manufacturers who wanted to export manufactured goods to the United States. Because these foreign countries earned fewer American dollars from their exports, it meant they had fewer dollars with which to buy American imports such as meat and corn.

The Hawley-Smoot Tariff Act introduced in 1929 only made matters worse. It imposed even higher tariffs. As a consequence, American trade fell by 50 per cent in the next two years. Wheat prices fell from 233 cents a bushel in 1920 to 32 cents a bushel in 1932. Foreign tariffs made it harder for American farmers to sell their surplus produce abroad. The small and less efficient farmers went bankrupt. Many farm incomes in 1932 were only a third of what they had been some twelve years earlier.

By the end of the 1920s tempers were rising and there were ugly demonstrations in the Mid-West. Farmers demanded protection against falling prices. They wanted the Government to buy their surplus grain and livestock in order to keep farm prices high. They added weight to their protests by stopping the sale of bankrupt farms. A farmer explained,

> If they was gonna call a farm sale, we would send a group there to stop the sale.

The greatest tragedy in farming occurred after the Wall Street Crash in 1929. Farm prices collapsed even further. In 1932, Oscar Ameringer told a Congressional sub-committee on unemployment,

Migrant farmworker's family in 1936 on their way to California to face an uncertain future

While Oregon sheep raisers fed mutton to the buzzards [because freight costs were too high], I saw men picking for meat scraps in the garbage cans of the cities of New York and Chicago.

The position of many Mid-Western farmers worsened in the 1930s when drought and poor farming methods caused crop failure and widespread soil erosion. Winds blew the soil across fields and on to roads. Cars and homes were buried as ploughland was stripped of its valuable topsoil. Thousands of poor tenant farmers had to abandon their homes and holdings. Many emigrated to California. Oscar Ameringer told Congress,

The roads of the West and Southwest teem with hungry hitchhikers. The campfires of the homeless are seen along every railroad track. I saw men, women, and children walking over the hard roads.

---

1 *Why was American farming in such a poor way by 1932?*

2 *How does the photograph sum up the problems of the poor farmer in the 1920s and 1930s?*

The Blacks

The poorest families in America in the 1920s and 1930s lived in the American South in states such as Alabama, Louisiana, and Mississippi. Many were Blacks, the descendants of former slaves who had only been freed 60 years or so earlier. Many former slaves were still alive. Most of the Blacks lived in rural slums and worked long hours on cotton and tobacco plantations for low pay. They suffered the added humiliation of living in a society where they were not regarded as the equals of the Whites.

The laws of the South did not protect them against racial discrimination. They were expected to 'know their place'. Racial bullies implemented the unwritten law. Lynchings, brandings, tarrings and beatings were common, many of them carried out at night by the nightriders of the Ku Klux Klan.

The Klan was a secret society of Whites, usually drawn from the poorest sectors of the community. Many were sharecroppers. These were poor farmers who had been hit hard by the slump in farm prices after the war. The Ku Klux Klan also had the support, in many southern states, of members of the police force, and even of judges, state senators and congressmen. Victims of the Klan also included Jews, Catholics, foreign immigrants and other minority groups as well as Blacks.

The Klan had originally been founded in the South in the 1860s at the end of the Civil War. It was revived again in 1915 by a travelling preacher called William Joseph Simmons ('the Imperial Wizard'), whose

> converts, largely of startlingly feeble intelligence, were enveloped and overawed by a weird and meaningless code of ceremonies, signs, signals and words. The Klansmen sang 'klodes', held 'klonversations', swore blood oaths, ignited crosses and whispered passwords.
>
> Stephen Webbe in *History of the Twentieth Century*, Purnell, 1968

By 1926, their numbers had grown to several million. But a scandal involving a national Ku Klux Klan leader and the increasing prosperity of the later 1930s helped eventually to lessen the Klan's appeal.

The position of the Blacks in the South showed few signs of improvement to match the increasing prosperity of the nation as a whole. Their lot in life, like that of most of the White labourers and small tenant farmers of the South, was at the bottom of the pile. Even in 1938 these problems were still acute. A US Government report claimed that,

> Southeastern farms are the smallest in the Nation . . . the South has cut away a large part of its forest, leaving acres of gullied, useless soil . . . Overgrazing, too, has resulted in serious erosion throughout the Southwest . . . The low-income belt of the South is a belt of sickness, misery, and unnecessary death.
>
> National Emergency Council Report, 25 July 1938, in *Documents of American History*, edited by Henry Steele Commager, F.S. Crofts, 1941

> **1** *Who were the members of the 'low-income belt of the South'?*
>
> **2** *What problems affected farming in the American South in the 1930s?*
>
> **3** *Why do you think the members of the Ku Klux Klan engaged in such 'weird and meaningless' ceremonies? What was their aim?*
>
> **4** *Why did the Ku Klux Klan pick on Jews, Catholics, foreign immigrants and other minorities? What was their motive?*

The Immigrants

Source A

Jewish immigrants from Russia entering New York Harbour in 1892. This view of New York was very familiar to millions of Americans. A poster in 1917 with a similar picture and the slogan 'Remember Your First Thrill of AMERICAN LIBERTY' urged them to buy US Government Bonds to help the American Army fight the war against Germany

Source B

The annual quota of any nationality shall be two per cent of the number of foreign-born individuals of each nationality resident in continental United States as determined by the United States census of 1890, but the minimum quota of any nationality shall be 100.

The Immigration Act of 1924

Source C

Give me your tired, your poor,
Your huddled masses yearning to breathe free,
The wretched refuse of your teeming shore.
Send these, the homeless, tempest-tost to me,
I lift my lamp beside the golden door!

From *The New Colossus*, by Emma Lazarus.
A poem inscribed in bronze at the base of the Statue of Liberty in New York Harbour

Source D

Quota of immigrants

Country	1921	1924
	3 per cent of 1910 population	2 per cent of 1890 population
Germany	68 059	51 227
British Isles incl. Ireland	77 342	62 574
Sweden and Norway	32 244	16 014
Poland	25 827	5 982
Italy	42 957	3 845
Czechoslovakia	14 382	3 073
Russia	34 284	2 248
All Countries	356 995	164 667

Bureau of the Census, US Department of Commerce,
The American Almanac, Grosset and Dunlap, 1973

Source E

Immigrants into the USA (000s)

	1881–90	**1891–1900**	**1901–10**	**1911–20**	**1921–30**	**1931–40**
British Isles	1462	660	865	487	551	42
Scandinavia	656	372	505	203	198	11
Germany	1453	505	341	144	412	114
Russia	213	505	1597	921	62	1
Italy	307	652	2046	1110	455	68
Asia	70	75	324	247	112	16
Others	1086	919	3117	2624	2317	276
Total	5247	3688	8795	5736	4107	528

Collier's Encyclopedia, 1979

Source F

The war [First World War] had also revealed some alarming facts in regard to our foreign population. (1) Many immigrants neglected to become naturalized American citizens. They retained their real allegiance to the lands from which they had come. (2) Radical labor agitators were suspected of 'taking their orders from Moscow'. (3) Over one thousand newspapers in the United States were printed in foreign languages. (4) Over 10 per cent of the people here could not speak English. (5) American labor leaders [trade unionists] were disturbed over the hordes of incoming foreigners who were accustomed to work for low wages. (6) Patriotic citizens generally were alarmed at the number of newcomers who had no knowledge of American institutions or ideals.

David Saville Muzzey, *Our Country's History* (the USA), Ginn, 1961

1 What was the average reduction in the number of immigrants allowed into the United States in 1924 compared with 1921?

2 Which countries fared better in 1924, compared with other countries, than they did in 1921? From which countries were the numbers of potential immigrants drastically cut in 1924? Why do you think the quota system was altered in this way? Suggest reasons why the American Government tried to encourage emigration from some countries at the expense of others.

3 What was the quota system? Why was it introduced? What did the American Government hope to achieve by this policy? What do you think Emma Lazarus would have thought of this system had she lived to see it introduced in the 1920s?

4 *Germany was the birthplace of over 2 500 000 Americans in 1890. How do you think this affected their attitude to the poster referred to in Source A? What do you notice about the immigration statistics for Germany in the 1930s? Suggest a reason for this.*

5 *What changes took place in the pattern of emigration to the United States between 1881 and 1940? Draw a graph, or a series of graphs, to illustrate your answer.*

The Gangsters

A United States marshal pours bootlegged liquor down the sewers during the days of prohibition

The Volstead Act of 28 October 1919 amended the American Constitution, prohibiting the manufacture or sale of intoxicating liquor. When it was first passed by Congress, it was vetoed by President Wilson. But the Minnesota congressman, Andrew Volstead, persisted and Congress overruled the President. Prohibition had been the target of temperance movements for many years. They hoped that by banning alcohol completely they could abolish organised crime!

Far from making the United States free from drink, prohibition had the opposite effect. Millions of Americans drank in illegal bars, or 'speakeasies', run by criminals. Much of the alcohol they sold was of poor quality, having been brewed or distilled illegally. The suppliers were called bootleggers. They had many ingenious ways of hiding alcohol. 'The man that used to distil the booze and beer used to hide it in the basement of the church', recalled one American.

Bootlegging expanded at a rapid rate when gangsters like Al Capone of Chicago moved in and took control. They had the money and the power to bribe the police. City mayors were even put on the pay roll. Al Capone earned well over $100 000 000 from crime in 1928 alone. When other gangsters tried to muscle in on the racket they were eliminated. Gangland killings multiplied and cities like Chicago seemed to be lawless. Yet the gangsters were so skilful in concealing their operations, that Capone was eventually sent to prison for tax evasion instead of for theft, extortion, or murder! Prohibition was eventually repealed in 1933.

THE WALL STREET CRASH

Warning signs

In the summer of 1929 people in the know began to worry whether the boom years could last much longer. Prices on the stock market were still rising. After the election of President Hoover, a Republican, people put even more of their savings and their borrowings into the stock market. Some even mortgaged their houses or their businesses to invest on New York's Wall Street. They borrowed large sums of money from banks to buy shares. On trains and buses, people read the stock market quotations instead of the headlines or the sports pages. Nurses, window cleaners, film stars, widows, cowboys and grocers all played the market. Some made huge fortunes, buying shares when they were low in price and selling them a few months later when they had rocketed in value.

> The Crash – it didn't happen in one day. There were a great many warnings. The country was crazy. Everybody was in the stock market, whether he could afford it or not. Shoeshine boys and waiters and capitalists . . . It wasn't only brokers involved in margin accounts. It was banks. They had a lot of stinking loans. The banks worked in as casual a way as the brokers did.
>
> John Hersch (a former stockbroker's clerk) in
> *Hard Times: An Oral History of the Depression*, by Studs Terkel, Pantheon Books, 1986

As a result many companies were over-valued by the stock market. Their factories, resources and profits were not worth as much as the investors seemed to think they were. What was worse, American industry was producing more manufactured goods than people could buy. Some experts said as much and forecast that share prices would go down. So long as investors were confident their money was safe and likely to make a profit, there seemed little cause for alarm. It was only when some people began to sell their shares, and others started to follow, that the calamity happened.

1 *Why was the New York stock market booming in 1929? Why did John Hersch say 'the country was crazy'? What did he mean when he said that many banks 'had a lot of stinking loans'? What were the 'great many warnings'? What should a sensible investor have done with his or her shares at that time?*

2 *What is oral history? How is it of value to a historian? What are its possible advantages and disadvantages?*

The Crash

Shareholders wait anxiously for news, Wall Street, 1929

Source A **Thursday**

MARKET IN PANIC AS STOCKS ARE DUMPED
IN 12,894,600 SHARE DAY BANKERS HALT IT

The stock markets of the country tottered on the brink of panic yesterday as a prosperous people, gone suddenly hysterical with fear, attempted simultaneously to sell a record-breaking volume of securities for whatever they would bring.

The *World*, Friday, 25 October 1929

Source B

STOCK VALUES CRASH IN RECORD STAMPEDE
BANKERS HALT ROUT
CURIOUS JAM WALL STREET TO SEE THE 'SHOW'
Huge Crowd Throngs 'Money Lane' Seeking Thrill
in Battle of Bulls and Bears

The *Philadelphia Inquirer*, 25 October 1929

Source C **Monday**

Monday was a rout . . . Leading stocks broke through the support levels as soon as trading started and kept sinking all day. Periodically the news would circulate that the banks were about to turn the tide as they had done on Thursday, but it didn't happen . . . When the market finally closed, 9,212,800 shares had been sold.

Jonathan Norton Leonard, *Three Years Down*, J.B. Lippincott, 1944

Source D **Tuesday**

STOCKS COLLAPSE IN 16,410,030 – SHARE DAY,
BUT RALLY AT CLOSE CHEERS BROKERS;
BANKERS OPTIMISTIC,TO CONTINUE AID
240 Issues Lose $15,894,818,894 in Month;
Slump in Full Exchange List Vastly Larger

The *New York Times*, Wednesday 30 October 1929

Source E

This was real panic. It was what the banks had prevented on Thursday, had slowed on Monday. Now they were helpless . . . When the closing bell rang, the great bull market was dead and buried. 16,410,000 shares had changed hands. Leading stocks had lost as much as 77 per cent of their peak value.

Jonathan Norton Leonard, *Three Years Down*, J.B. Lippincott, 1944

Source F

October 29, 1929, yeah. A frenzy . . . Suicides, left and right, made a terrific impression on me, of course. People I knew. It was heartbreaking. One day you saw the prices at a hundred, the next day at $20, at $15. On Wall Street, the people walked around like zombies. . . . You saw people who yesterday rode around in Cadillacs lucky now to have carfare [bus fare].

Arthur A. Robertson (a businessman) in *Hard Times: An Oral History of the Depression*, by Studs Terkel, Pantheon Books, 1986

---

1 What did the writers of these sources mean when they talked about, a) 'Bulls and Bears', b) 'securities', c) 'selling orders', d) 'the great bull market', e) a '16,410,030–share day'?

2 Why did share prices continue to fall after the 'panic' on Thursday, 24 October 1929? Why didn't they rise again? How and why did the banks and large financial institutions try to stop the 'Crash'? When and why did they give up trying?

3 What effects did the 'Crash' have on some shareholders? Why did it make such an impact? Why were millions of Americans suddenly plunged into debt after seeing the value of their shares fall? What effect was this likely to have on the banks?

Results of the Wall Street Crash

The Wall Street Crash not only proved disastrous for the American economy it started a crisis in almost every country in the world. It didn't actually cause the Great Depression because this would almost certainly have happened anyway. But it set it off – like Sarajevo and the First World War. Some speculators committed suicide. Thousands of businesses collapsed and many banks closed their doors. So even the people who put their savings into banks rather than into the stock market lost their money. Factories shut their gates. A coal miner recalled,

> All mines shut down – stores, everything. One day they was workin', the next day the mines shut down.

People tightened their belts and bought fewer luxuries – so many more factories closed their gates as a result. The social consequences were appalling. One writer described her horror in Chicago, early in 1932, at seeing a crowd of about 50 men fighting over a tub of leftovers outside a restaurant – American citizens fighting for scraps of food like animals!

In every large American city there were long queues as men stood in line to get a piece of bread and a bowl of hot soup. There were beggars on every street. Down-and-outs hitched lifts and rode illegally on freight trains.

Unemployment

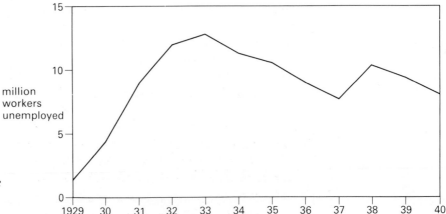

Unemployment in the United States: 1929–40

The numbers of unemployed rose to record levels. In 1932, 14 million Americans were out of a job, but there were no welfare benefits and no unemployment pay. Unemployed workers carried billboards asking for a job. Some towns even put up large signs telling the jobless to move on, since there was no work for them there. Inevitably there were evictions. Families were thrown out of their homes.

Around the large cities the new homeless poor slept in the parks, under bridges, in the doorways of shops and public buildings, or in empty railway waggons. Shanty towns sprang up on the outskirts of the major cities, with crude huts built out of waste materials, such as scrap iron, packing cases, and dumped cars. The unemployed workers who built them called their settlements *'Hoovervilles'*. This was a sarcastic reminder that the Republican President, Herbert Hoover had done nothing, and was doing nothing, to remedy matters or to alleviate distress. Hoover believed in 'rugged individualism' – in the capacity of any American worker to get out of a rut and get rich. This was the 'American dream'. Self-help was all the working man needed. To many Americans this wasn't enough. The boom of the 1920s had been promoted under Republican presidents.

They got us into this mess, they should get us out again.

Me? I blame Hoover. He's done nothing. He just doesn't care.

Hooverville, on the outskirts of Los Angeles in 1932

---

1 *How would we describe 'rugged individualism' today?*

2 *What did Hoover see as the alternative to rugged individualism? Why was he opposed to it?*

3 *Was the 'mess' the fault of the Republicans?*

Hoover did in fact spend Government money on projects designed to put the unemployed to work. In December 1930 he got Congress to agree to spend $116 million on the construction of various public works such as new roads and public buildings. But unemployment continued to rise whilst more and more businesses failed. By 1932 the average income was less than two-thirds of the 1929 figure and American industry was operating at half capacity. A songwriter summed up the effects of the Depression:

> Once I built a railroad, I made it run.
> Made it race against time.
> Once I built a railroad, now it's done.
> Brother can you spare a dime?

In June 1932 President Hoover belatedly introduced a much bigger relief scheme. A Reconstruction Finance Corporation was founded with the vast sum of $2 billion to be used to provide loans to railways, insurance companies, banks and other organisations in danger of going to the wall for want of capital. But it was too late. By then the American people had had their fill of the Republicans and false promises, such as Hoover's 'Prosperity is just around the corner' (March 1931).

THE NEW DEAL

President Roosevelt

America turned to the Democrats for salvation. In 1932 Franklin Delano Roosevelt struck a chord when he called for a 'new deal' for the people of America. This was what many people had wanted to hear, a government prepared to take direct action. At the Democratic Party Convention, in 1932, Roosevelt said that they (the Democrats) were the 'Prophets of a New Order of confidence and courage'. He issued a 'call to arms' which would enable the Democrats 'to win in this crusade to restore America to its own people'. His bounding confidence, despite a severe disability, and cheerful optimism hit home and the American people elected him president by a convincing majority. Roosevelt had many pressing problems to solve when he took office in January 1933. If he had any doubts he didn't show them. He told the crowd who listened to his inauguration,

> So first of all let me assert my firm belief that the only thing we have to fear is fear itself. Nameless, unreasoning, unjustified terror which paralyzes needed efforts to convert retreat into advance . . . Our greatest primary task is to put people to work. This is no unsolvable problem if we face it wisely and courageously.

Roosevelt told them he was going to demand from Congress powers as great as those needed in wartime to wage 'war against the emergency'. And he did. One of his first actions was to close all the banks for a few days whilst his advisers decided how to deal with the financial problems facing America. Roosevelt followed this by putting forward 15 major new laws in the next 100 days. At last, Americans thought, the country is on the move again. One of the junior members of his government said,

> They were exciting, exhilarating days. It was one of the most joyous periods of my life. We came alive, we were eager. We were infected with a

gay spirit of adventure, for something concrete and constructive finally was being done about the chaos which confronted the nation.

Thomas L Stokes, *Chip Off My Shoulder*, Princeton University, 1940

Roosevelt had three main aims. First he would alleviate distress. Second he would create new jobs. Third he would try to ensure that nothing like this ever happened again. He reformed the stock market. In future shares could not be bought on credit without payment of a substantial deposit.

Policies

Apart from the Social Security Act of 1935 (see below) which provided welfare benefits, the most lasting and most memorable achievements of the New Deal were the imaginative and far-reaching projects instigated by the Federal Government under the so-called Alphabet Laws. These Government agencies and organisations were specifically designed to create new jobs. In this they succeeded. Millions of Americans got jobs under the schemes and millions more regained confidence in America and the American dream. Roosevelt faced opposition from many quarters, particularly from American big business. Some said he was a Fascist! Others thought he was a Communist! Roosevelt faced both criticisms with equanimity. This is what he said in one of his regular broadcasts to the American people:

> It is true that the toes of some people are being stepped on and are going to be stepped on. But these toes belong to the comparative few. A few timid people who fear progress will try to give new and strange names for what we are doing. Sometimes they will call it Fascism and sometimes Communism and sometimes Regimentation and sometimes Socialism. But in so doing they are trying to make very complex and theoretical something that is really very simple and very practical. I believe in practical explanations and in practical policies.

1 *Why do you think many Americans felt, like Thomas L. Stokes, that the first few months of Roosevelt's new administration were 'exciting, exhilarating days'?*

2 *What was happening in Europe at this time, in France, the UK, Germany, Italy and the USSR? With whom was Roosevelt likely to be compared?*

3 *How would the policies of Roosevelt and the New Deal be viewed today in Britain and America?*

The Alphabet Agencies

AAA – Agricultural Adjustment Act 1933   The aim of this Act was to lower farm production and so cause prices to rise, since over-production kept prices below their pre-war level. Farmers agreed to plough up growing crops and to kill off young livestock in return for cash. Six million piglets were killed in 1933 alone. As a result farm incomes rose two to three times between 1932 and 1935. Critics who hated Government interference in industry or agriculture denounced the Act. In 1936 the Supreme Court ruled that it was unconstitutional. So Roosevelt replaced it and paid farmers to grow different crops instead.

Members of the Civilian Conservation Corps filing past President Roosevelt when he visited their camp in 1933

CCC – Civilian Conservation Corps 1933   The CCC was one of the most popular schemes and Roosevelt's favourite. Unemployed youths volunteered to join the Conservation Corps, where they were sent to temporary camps to care for the American countryside. There they were paid a wage and given accommodation and meals. In return they laid forest trails, built forest roads, sprayed pests, and planted 200 million trees. Over 2 million boys and young men took part in the scheme, wearing the green CCC uniform. Most enjoyed the experience and were fitter and healthier as a result. Many trade union leaders disapproved. Some claimed it was Fascism. They said it was similar to the activities of the Hitler Youth. But President Roosevelt was undeterred and on Saturday, 12 August 1933, went to see for himself how the system worked. Harold Ickes, one of his colleagues, recalled,

> The first camp we visited was in course of construction. The second was up in the Blue Ridge Mountains along the new Skyline Drive. This was a well established camp. In all the camps the men seemed fit, and we were told by the commander of this corps area that the average gain in weight had been fifteen pounds [7 kg] per man. The average age is about nineteen years. . . . The camps are well set up, sanitary and comfortable, and clean. Army officers are in charge.

The Secret Diary of Harold L. Ickes, Simon and Schuster, 1953

---

1 *Why was the Civilian Conservation Corps founded?*

2 *How do you account for the fact that, despite all the heavy physical exercise they got, the average young person put on over a stone (7 kg) in weight when working for the Civilian Conservation Corps? What does this tell you about the state of America in 1933?*

3 *Compare the Civilian Conservation Corps with the Italian Fascist youth organisations (page 65) and the Hitler Youth (page 102). What did they have in common? How were they different?*

4 *How would you react today to the establishment of a Civilian Conservation Corps in Britain? What are the nearest modern equivalents to the CCC?*

CWA – Civil Works Administration 1933   Like the WPA (see below), which later took over much of its work, the CWA put the unemployed to work on projects such as the construction of new dams, roads, schools and other public buildings.

FERA – Federal Emergency Relief Administration 1933   This was a temporary measure providing unemployment benefit or dole money. It wasn't much but it helped to bring some comfort to people suffering deprivation and poverty.

FHA – Federal Housing Administration 1934   This organisation provided Government loans to help householders buy, repair or improve their homes.

FSA – Farm Security Administration 1937   This was the system through which the Government made loans to help farmworkers and tenant farmers.

NLRB – National Labor Relations Board 1935   This Board was established to deal with strikes and disputes between the workers (labor) and the employers. In its first two years it successfully resolved 75 per cent of the disputes it reviewed.

WE DO OUR PART

The Blue Eagle of the NRA

NRA – National Recovery Administration 1933 This was another popular scheme, since it aimed to improve working conditions in factories, encouraging employers to set minimum wages, to eliminate cheap labour and to recognise the trade unions. Firms were encouraged to agree to codes of behaviour. In return they could display the NRA Blue Eagle badge with its slogan 'We Do Our Part'. But some of the major companies refused to take part in the scheme or to comply with its codes. So in the end, the NRA had only a limited success.

Many US employers were violently opposed to the growing strength of the American Labor Movement and refused to recognise the unions. During the 1930s, the unions organised many factory sit-ins and strikes. These demonstrations were sometimes broken up by private armies of strike-breakers organised by the employers.

PWA – Public Works Administration 1933 This scheme undertook various public works, such as slum clearance, until most of its work was taken over by the WPA.

REA – Rural Electrification Administration 1935 As its name suggests, this organisation was set up to help build power lines to cover the many parts of rural America which were not already served by the private electricity companies.

TVA – Tennessee Valley Authority 1933

> An ACT to improve the navigability and to provide for the flood control of the Tennessee River; to provide for reforestation and the proper use of marginal lands in the Tennessee Valley; to provide for the agricultural and industrial development of said valley . . .
>
> The Corporation . . . Shall have power to construct dams, reservoirs, power houses, power structures, transmission lines, navigation projects, and incidental works in the Tennessee River and its tributaries, and to unite the various power installations into one or more systems by transmission lines.
>
> The Tennessee Valley Act, 18 May 1933. Quoted in *Documents of American History*, edited by Henry Steele Commager, F.S. Crofts, 1941

This was probably the best known of all the New Deal schemes. In this area of the American South (see Report on page 158) the rivers frequently flooded. Soil had been eroded from the valleys because trees no longer protected the river banks. There was little industry and the people were very poor. Few homes had electricity.

TVA achieved all its aims. Large areas were saved from soil erosion. Over 30 dams were eventually built. Many huge areas of forest were planted. Lakes were created. Hydroelectric power stations were constructed. New roads and factories were built. The living standards of the people of the area rose sharply and tourists were attracted to the lakes and forests, giving yet another boost to the area. The Tennessee River and its tributaries were

One of the new dams on the Tennessee River

brought under control. Flooding ceased to be a problem. It was possible to send goods by barge all the way along the valley. An interesting side effect of TVA was the fact that its plentiful supply of cheap electricity made it possible for the United States to manufacture the world's first atom bomb in 1945.

WPA – Works Progress Administration 1935   The WPA took over much of the work of the CWA and PWA (see above). It was responsible for the construction of hydroelectric dams (such as Boulder Dam, which the Republicans later renamed Hoover Dam), bridges, airports, power stations, sewers, waterworks and many public buildings (including 70 per cent of all new schools built in this period). These public works improved America, at the same time employing eight million workers, who would otherwise have been unemployed. But again many critics denounced these schemes. They were particularly unpopular with employers who now found that unemployed workers who had worked on WPA projects were reluctant to accept the low rates of pay which they offered instead.

> 1 *Why were they called the Alphabet Acts? How do you account for their popularity in America in the 1930s? Would methods like this work in Britain or America today?*
>
> 2 *How did they attempt to solve the problems of unemployment?*
>
> 3 *Write a short essay saying in what respects the methods employed by Roosevelt's New Deal policies were similar to those used by Hitler, Mussolini and Stalin in Europe. How were they different?*

Achievements and Failures

Roosevelt persuaded Congress to pass many other laws designed to improve living conditions, to eliminate injustices and to come to the aid of those Americans who were unable to help themselves. For instance, the Social Security Act of 1935 set up an unemployment insurance scheme for workers. It provided social welfare benefits for the handicapped. It also introduced a compulsory retirement pension scheme. All of these were long overdue in the United States.

However, Roosevelt did not get everything his own way. In 1936, the Supreme Court ruled that the Agricultural Adjustment Act was unconstitutional. Although he got round this later, Roosevelt was disturbed that the Supreme Court could overrule laws, which the elected President and Congress had passed. He attributed this to the fact that they were old men who still lived in 'the horse and buggy days'.

Cartoon in the
Washington Post

DON'T SEND MY BOYS TO PRISON

1 *What was the point of this cartoon?*

2 *What does it tell you about the relationship between Roosevelt and the Supreme Court?*

After his re-election in 1936, Roosevelt proposed a new law to make Supreme Court judges retire at the age of 70. He also proposed to increase their number by appointing judges sympathetic to the New Deal. Congress turned the bill down. For all its faults, they preferred a Supreme Court which could curb the power of the President if he tried to go above the law. Roosevelt argued differently in one of his famous 'fireside chats' on the radio.

Source A

By bringing into the judicial system a steady and continuing stream of new and younger blood, I hope, first, to make the administration of all Federal justice speedier and therefore less costly; secondly, to bring to the decision of social and economic problems younger men who have had personal experience and contact with modern facts and circumstances under which average men have to live and work.

Radio broadcast by President Roosevelt, 9 March 1937. Quoted in
Documents of American History, edited by Henry Steele Commager, F.S. Crofts, 1941

Source B

Rejection of the Proposal by the Senate Judiciary Committee

It would not banish age from the bench nor abolish divided decisions . . . It would not reduce the expense of litigation nor speed the decision of cases . . . It would subjugate the courts to the will of Congress and the President and thereby destroy the independence of the judiciary, the only certain shield of individual rights.

Documents of American History, edited by Henry Steele Commager, F.S. Crofts, 1941

Source C

Punch, *21 April 1937*

1 *How did Roosevelt use the radio during his presidency?*

2 *What was the point of the* Punch *cartoon on page 175? Did the cartoonist approve or disapprove of Roosevelt's proposals?*

3 *What arguments did Roosevelt use to plead his case? What was the response of the Senate Judiciary Committee to each of these arguments?*

4 *Do you think it is right that the courts of law should be able to overturn the decisions of a government elected by the people? Are the courts able to do this in Britain?*

Franklin Delano Roosevelt (1883–1945)

Franklin Delano Roosevelt was born in 1883, the son of wealthy and prominent parents. He trained as a lawyer and became a member of President Wilson's administration during the First World War.

In 1921 he was struck down with poliomyelitis and was disabled for the rest of his life. But this did not deter him from standing and winning the election for the Presidency in 1932. Subsequently the American people elected Roosevelt to the Presidency for a record four terms of office; so he was President from 1933 to 1945.

Although he was disabled he did not let that stand in his way. In particular he was determined to act with vigour and decisiveness and do something positive about the problems caused by the Great Depression.

His first 100 days in office (1933) produced a rich array of measures designed to put American industry and agriculture back on its feet and to help cure the problem of unemployment.

In foreign policy he was less successful, since Americans were fearful they might be drawn unwillingly into the war which now seemed inevitable in Europe. After the Japanese attack on the American naval base at Pearl Harbor in 1941, however, Hitler declared war on the United States and America entered the Second World War at last.

Roosevelt threw himself into his new role as a war leader and prosecuted the American war effort with determination and confidence. He spared no effort to reach an agreement with the other allies and attended the wartime conferences with Churchill and Stalin. But his health deteriorated. He died in April 1945 only days before the victory in Europe.

FOREIGN POLICY
Japan

The United States and Japan were at loggerheads for most of the time President Roosevelt was in office. The US Government protested in 1931 when Japan invaded Manchuria (see Chapter 9) but did nothing concrete to back up its protest. In 1937 the Japanese invaded China again and relations between Japan and the USA deteriorated once more, particularly when an American naval vessel was sunk by Japanese planes. In 1939 action was at last taken to stop the sale of arms to Japan (see page 178) when America herself felt threatened by Japanese ambitions in the Far East.

Isolationism

Although the United States refused to join the League of Nations and, for much of the next 20 years, tried to stand aside from Europe's squabbles, she could not ignore world problems entirely. As you have seen, US bankers played a major part in resolving Germany's financial problems with the Dawes Plan (see page 80). The USA antagonised the Japanese military with the plans which limited the navies of Britain, America and Japan at the Washington Conference (see page 181). The USA also helped to arrange the signing of the Kellogg Pact (see page 215).

But isolationism delayed America's entry into the Second World War until December 1941. This did not mean that Americans necessarily approved of aggression by Mussolini or Hitler but it did mean they were not prepared to fight unless they had to. Roosevelt felt differently. He did not always stand idly by. He intervened during the Czech crises of 1938 and 1939 by sending telegrams to Hitler and Mussolini. Since they were not backed by anything stronger than disapproval, they were ignored.

Punch, 13 October 1937

WILL HE COME RIGHT OUT?

On 1 May 1937 Roosevelt signed the Neutrality Act which prevented the sale of American arms and munitions to countries which were deemed to be at war. In addition, the Act had a 'cash and carry' clause which stated that any warring nations buying goods which were permitted must, a) pay *cash* for them immediately, b) *carry* them in their own merchant ships.

After Hitler's aggressive acts of 1938 and March 1939, however, Roosevelt tried to get Congress to amend the Neutrality Law but was rebuffed. It was only when Hitler invaded Poland in September 1939 that Congress finally agreed to repeal the ban on arms sales to countries at war, much to the relief of the British and French governments.

The war divided American opinion between those who wanted the United States to intervene and those who still favoured isolationism (like Colonel Lindbergh, the famous aviator). Although the time was not yet ripe for American participation in the war, Roosevelt gave Britain invaluable material support by supplying arms on credit and by stepping up the production of armaments.

---

1 *What was the point of the cartoon on page 177? Why did people in Europe look with disfavour on American policy at this time?*

2 *What did the US Government do to help solve world problems in the 1920s and 1930s?*

3 *Why was the Neutrality Act introduced?*

4 *Imagine you are an opponent of isolationism in the 1930s. What points would you have wanted to make to Congress to try to make the Senators and Representatives change their minds?*

The Good Neighbour policy

The United States has always been conscious of its role as the most powerful nation in the New World. In 1823 President Monroe told Congress that European powers were no longer free to interfere in North or South America. These issues were the exclusive concern of Americans. The Monroe Doctrine has been upheld by the United States ever since. In his inaugural address as President, in 1933, Roosevelt had this to say,

> In the field of world policy I would dedicate this nation to the policy of the good neighbour – the neighbour who resolutely respects himself and because he does so, respects the rights of others.

President Roosevelt recognised that all the countries of North and South America were equal and that they should therefore respect each other's rights without attempting to interfere. This policy was also called Pan-

Americanism (*'pan'* meaning 'all the members of'). At a Conference in Lima (in Peru) in 1938 the 21 countries meeting there agreed that common action would be taken if any member state was threatened.

FURTHER QUESTIONS AND EXERCISES

Source A

It took this guy with the long cigarette holder to do some planning about basic things – like the ... WPA and even the lousy Blue Eagle. It put a new spirit in the country.

Source B

Oh, I'm for you, Mr President
I'm for you all the way
You can take away the alphabet
But don't take away this WPA.

1 Who was the 'guy with the long cigarette holder'? What was the WPA? What was the Blue Eagle? Who was most likely to call it 'lousy'?

2 Write notes explaining what was meant by each of the following:

a) Isolationism

b) the boom years

c) normalcy

d) mass production

e) rugged individualism

f) Hoovervilles

g) prohibition

h) the Ku Klux Klan

i) the Tennessee Valley Authority

j) the 'Good Neighbour' policy

3 Explain carefully what was meant by the New Deal. What were the Alphabet Agencies? How successful were they in creating new jobs and bringing new prosperity to the United States?

4 What were the Acts from which the following extracts are taken? When and why did they become law? Were they successful in achieving those aims?

Extract A

Whenever ... there exists a state of war between, or among, two or more foreign states ... it shall thereafter be unlawful to export ... arms, ammunition, or implements of war from ... the United States to any belligerent state.

Extract B

No person shall manufacture, sell, barter, transport, import, export, deliver, furnish or possess any intoxicating liquor.

Chapter Nine

Conflict in the Far East

INTRODUCTION

Mao Tse-tung in northern China during the civil war

On 16 October 1934, Mao Tse–tung and a large army of Red Chinese soldiers, began a gruelling Long March across the mountains of western China. They were evading the Kuomintang armies (the Government forces of Chiang Kai-shek). A year later, with much depleted forces, the Red Army reached safety at Yenan in northern China. This legendary journey took place at a time when the very existence of China as an independent nation was threatened by Japan. But instead of joining forces against the foreign aggressor, the Kuomintang and the Communists fought a vicious civil war.

> **1** *Why do you think Mao Tse-tung's force was called the Red Army?*
> **2** *What other legendary 'marches' took place in the 1920s and 1930s?*

Only eight years earlier, in 1926, Mao Tse-tung and Chiang Kai-shek had been allies together on the Northern Expedition to unify China. Two years after the Long March, they buried their differences for the time being and fought a long war against the Japanese. The conflict between the

Kuomintang and the Communists was finally settled in 1949, when the Red Army drove Chiang Kai-shek into exile on Taiwan.

During this epic struggle which lasted 22 years (from 1927 to 1949) Japan was at war with China, off and on, for about two-thirds of that time. Only in the early 1920s had there been any real prospect of peace in the Far East.

JAPAN

The First World War

When the First World War broke out in August 1914, Japan soon joined her ally, Britain, in declaring war on Germany. China remained neutral. A month later, on 7 September 1914, Japan took over Germany's interests in Shantung Province in China, including the important seaport of Tsingtao. When China asked Japan to leave, the Japanese presented the Chinese leader, Yuan Shih-kai, with an impossible list of Twenty-one Demands on 18 January 1915. Apart from claiming Germany's rights and concessions in Shantung Province, the list demanded that the privileges Japan already enjoyed in Southern Manchuria and Inner Mongolia be enlarged. The Japanese even demanded the right to send financial, military and political experts as advisers to the Chinese Government.

The implication was clear. Japan intended to make China part of the Japanese Empire. China had no allies she could turn to for help. The great powers were at war in Europe. The Allies protested to Japan but did not press the argument too hard since Japan was a valuable ally.

In May 1915 the Japanese modified their demands but threatened military action if they weren't accepted. Yuan Shih-kai had to agree but leaked the 'secret' demands to the press. The Chinese people were furious. They held protest meetings throughout China and boycotted Japanese goods. At the end of the War, Germany's interests in Shantung were officially granted to Japan under the terms of the Treaty of Versailles. But as you will see on page 189, news of the concession provoked a massive protest in China.

The Washington Conference

By 1919, it was clear that the Royal Navy was no longer the undisputed mistress of the seas. The US Navy was nearly as big. That of Japan ranked third in the world. The United States wanted to ensure that an Open Door policy, giving equal trading rights to all countries in China and the Far East, would now prevail – instead of the pre-war system of granting exclusive trading rights and privileges to the different powers.

This is why the United States called a conference of interested nations in Washington in November 1921. Delegates from nine countries attended: the United States, Japan, Britain, Italy, France, Portugal, the Netherlands, Belgium and China. The Conference limited the size of the navies of Britain, the United States and Japan. It did so according to the ratio 5:5:3. This meant that for every five warships in the Royal Navy, the Americans could also build five and the Japanese could build three. In addition the Conference agreed that no new naval bases were to be built in the Far East.

These agreements especially favoured the Japanese because:

- Her navy was deployed exclusively in the Pacific, whilst those of the United States and Britain operated throughout the world.
- The fact that naval bases had already been built in Japan meant that she would continue to dominate the Far East.

In return, Japan agreed under pressure to renounce her claims to Shantung Province in China. All nine powers agreed to guarantee China's independence and territory in future (the Nine Power Treaty of 1922). Under the terms of an associated agreement, the Four Power Treaty, the United States, Japan, Britain and France also agreed to consult with one another in the event of any act of aggression in the area, or if their interests came under threat from any other power.

---

1 *How can you tell from the Washington Conference that Britain still regarded Japan as an ally?*

2 *How did the Nine Power Treaty affect, a) Japan, b) China?*

Western Influence

After 1918 Japan seemed to be strengthening her democratic system. In 1925 every male adult was given the right to vote and political parties flourished, including those on the left. But there were limits to political freedom and the enactment of the Peace Preservation Law effectively suppressed the budding Japanese Communist Party.

The most encouraging sign in postwar Japan was the sight of politicians who seemed committed to peace rather than war. This was one reason why the Washington Conference was able to reach agreement on limiting naval power and why Japan gave up her claims to Shantung Province.

Western ideas were making a big impact on the Japanese people. Classical music was popular. Many more people wore Western clothes. Golf courses were built. Jazz came to Japan. When an appalling earthquake destroyed much of Tokyo in 1923, the old wooden buildings were replaced with fine new buildings of steel and concrete.

The old customs of Japan seemed to be fading, too, but to the regret of many Japanese. Japan had always been ruled by the military in the past. Only 60 years earlier, the *Shogun* (a military dictator) had been more important than the Emperor. Many officers longed for a revival of the days when military glory was all-important in Japan. But in the 1920s, the armed forces were contracting in size, not expanding.

> **1** *How do you think the military greeted the Nine Power Treaty in 1922?*

MILITARISM

The Showa Emperor

Crown Prince Hirohito of Japan in London in 1921

In 1926 the old *Meiji* (Enlightened Government) Emperor died and was succeeded by the *Showa* Emperor Hirohito. The Japanese gave him the title *Showa* because it meant 'Enlightened Peace'. This later proved to be an appropriate description of the last two-thirds of the Emperor's long reign, but only after Japan was defeated in 1945. In the first 19 years of his reign militarism dominated Japanese foreign policy. The nation prepared for, and waged, war.

Militarism, as its name implies, gloried in parades, flags, oaths of loyalty, and the idea of heroic sacrifice. Militarism was seen as an excellent training ground for the young. It emphasised war as a way of solving problems. It gained in strength in Japan in the late 1920s and 1930s for a number of reasons.

- The politicians brought little credit to the Diet, the Japanese parliament. There were fights between rival groups, and bribery and corruption among officials and politicians were commonplace. Ordinary Japanese had little reason to respect their elected assembly. In any case many of the older Japanese disliked the idea of democracy. They preferred direct action rather than protracted debate.
- Japan was badly hit by the Great Depression after 1929, since her industrial strength depended on exports. These were cut by 50 per cent between 1929 and 1931. Declining trade hit most workers in Japan, such as the peasant farmers who cultivated silk and the mill workers who turned it into yarn or cloth. Silk was a luxury. It was obvious that the demand for luxury goods would fall sharply in a depression. Many peasants had to take a two-thirds cut in income. Without exports Japan could not buy the imports she needed, such as coal, oil, iron ore, and other raw materials. Desperate times called for desperate measures. Workers tried strikes, riots and demonstrations.
- Militant army officers had other plans to resolve the crisis. Many came from peasant homes and resented the circumstances which made their families poor. Japan was too small and had too few raw materials (such as coal, oil, iron ore) to support its rapidly growing population. Only 15 per cent of the land area of Japan was habitable. The Japanese needed more 'living space'. But they were not allowed to emigrate to the United States or Australia, while the Washington agreements stopped them expanding

in Far Eastern Asia, an area they regarded as being part of Japan's sphere of influence.

These pressures resulted, first, in political assassination and, second, in war when the Japanese militarists invaded Manchuria in 1931.

Assassination

Prime Minister Hamaguchi – a moderate

In 1930 the Japanese prime minister, Osachi Hamaguchi, signed the London Naval Treaty. This extended the terms agreed at the Washington Conference and limited the tonnage of other warships. Extremists in the Japanese army and navy saw this as treason. They regarded Hamaguchi as unfit to advise the Emperor. An assassin gunned him down at Tokyo's railway station. Two years later, yet another Japanese prime minister, Tsuyoshi Inukai, was also assassinated.

> 1 *Which single cause best helps to explain why the ideas of the Japanese militarists became increasingly popular in the 1930s?*
>
> 2 *What reason did the Japanese have for resenting European and American influence in the Far East?*
>
> 3 *What is meant by the phrase 'Japan's sphere of influence'? Where today would you find the 'sphere of influence' of, a) the United States, b) the Soviet Union?*

MANCHURIA

Japanese Business Interests

Ever since the 1900s, Japanese business interests had worked hard to develop the resources of Manchuria after special rights and concessions had been granted to Japan under the terms of various treaties. Port Arthur and Dairen were developed as modern ports. The South Manchurian Railway was built and controlled by a Japanese army stationed near Mukden.

The Japanese hoped eventually to make Manchuria part of their empire. But these plans were endangered when it became clear in the late 1920s that the local ruler of Manchuria, Chang Hsueh-liang (known in China as 'the Young Marshal'), seemed close to reaching an agreement with the Kuomintang (Chinese Nationalist) leader, Chiang Kai-shek, who wanted to unite China. What would happen to Japan's business interests if the Chinese Government controlled Manchuria?

Chiang Kai-shek had already persuaded the European powers to give up many of the trading concessions they held in China. The Japanese felt they had too much to lose if the Kuomintang suddenly terminated Japanese business interests in Manchuria or if China used its raw materials for her own industries.

The Plot

This is why a number of Japanese Army officers in Manchuria decided to strike first. They plotted to take over the country. However, Japan's civilian Government heard of the plan and sent an officer to Manchuria to order the army not to attack. If the order had been delivered in time, the officers concerned would have had to obey. The officer, however, delayed handing over his orders until after a bomb explosion blew up part of the railway line on 18 September 1931. The incident was then used by the Japanese Army as an excuse to seize control of the whole of Manchuria.

Source A

Foreign Observers at Mukden Hold Japanese
Military Deliberately Caused Incident

NANKING Sept 20 – 'Appropriate steps are being taken to apprise [tell] the League of Nations and the powers signatory to the Kellogg pact [see page 215] of the unwarranted actions of Japanese troops'. C.T. Wang, Foreign Minister of the Nanking Government, declared in a statement this morning concerning the lodging of vigorous protests by the Nanking Government with the Japanese Government . . .

Foreign opinion here is that the Japanese were angry . . . so, according to all foreign observers here, the outbreak on Friday night was premeditated. A Japanese statement says:

'We were always prepared for an emergency, but we were surprised on the night of Sept. 18, when Chinese tried to blow up the South Manchuria Railway tracks and to attack a Japanese garrison. The occupation in various cities and towns was necessary to protect everybody. The incident is unfortunate.'

Hallett Abend in the *New York Times*, Monday, 21 September 1931

Source B

At 10 o'clock last night, [Japanese] railway guards picked a quarrel by blowing up a section of the S.M.R. at Huankutun, and subsequently accused the Chinese military of having done this. The Japanese immediately staged a surprise attack upon Peitaying, bombarding the place at random. Many houses were burnt and many people shot dead. At 5.30 a.m. large groups of Japanese soldiers began entering the city of Shenyang [Mukden] and immediately occupied all Government buildings.

Official Report by Mr Tsang Shih-yi, Chairman of the Provincial Government, 19 September 1931, quoted in *Source Materials in Chinese History*, edited by Charles Meyer and Ian Allen, Frederick Warne, 1970

Source C

Amidst the atmosphere of perturbation and anxiety thus created, a detachment of Chinese troops destroyed the track of the South Manchuria Railway in the vicinity of Mukden and attacked our railway guards at midnight on September 18. A clash between Japanese and Chinese troops then took place . . . In order to forestall an imminent disaster, the Japanese army had to act swiftly. The Chinese soldiers garrisoned in the neighbouring localities were disarmed, and the duty of maintaining peace and order was left in the hands of the local Chinese organisations under supervision of the Japanese troops . . . It may be superfluous to repeat that the Japanese Government harbours no territorial designs in Manchuria.

Japanese Government statement, dated 24 September 1931,
from *The China Yearbook 1931-32* quoted in *Source Materials in Chinese History*,
edited by Charles Meyer and Ian Allen, Frederick Warne, 1970

---

1 *How did the incident begin according to, a) China, b) Japan, c) Western sources?*

2 *What action did the Chinese propose to take against the Japanese aggressors?*

Japanese soldiers inspecting arms taken from the Chinese garrison at Mukden

The Japanese army immediately used the bomb explosion incident as an excuse to march on Mukden the capital. They followed this by occupying the whole of Manchuria. The speed and efficiency of the invasion left little doubt that it had been planned in advance and that the bomb attack had been deliberately staged to give them a valid excuse. They later installed the former Chinese Emperor, Pu Yi, as the puppet (figurehead) ruler of the newly created 'independent' state of Manchukuo which they based on the old Manchuria. This attempt to make it look as if the Manchurians were seeking independence from China fooled no one.

Chiang Kai-shek's Government in Nanking did very little to help the Manchurians, apart from making a complaint to the League of Nations. The Kuomintang army could have been used to confront the Japanese in Manchuria but this would have risked an all-out war between China and Japan. Chiang Kai-shek preferred to concentrate his forces against the Communists instead (see page 197). The Japanese went unpunished, apart from a Chinese boycott of Japanese goods.

The League of Nations

The League of Nations sent a team led by Lord Lytton to investigate the Chinese complaint of Japanese aggression. Japan was condemned and ordered to leave Manchuria forthwith, but none of the member nations were prepared to back words with force. In any case, the Japanese Government might well have complied with the order, had they been able to control the army. Their failure to do so paved the way for the later full-scale Japanese invasion of China in 1937 and the development of a military regime in Tokyo. Not surprisingly, Japan left the League of Nations in 1933, but not before the League's failure to act decisively had shown clearly to Hitler and Mussolini that aggression could be made to pay.

Preparation for War

In the 1930s the influence of the army and navy began to penetrate into every corner of Japanese life. Children and young people were brainwashed into accepting war as normal and military strength as right. Army officers taught in schools. Children were given training in the martial arts, such as judo and karate, and taught the supposed virtues of war. Even young children were shown how to march and to salute. To die for the Emperor and for Japan was portrayed as noble and heroic.

Military parades, martial music, flags and propaganda put the country in a militaristic mood. The armed forces controlled the press, the cinema and the radio. The successful invasions of Manchuria (1931) and central China (1937), and the unwillingness of the Western powers to intervene, stirred national pride and added further fuel to the arguments of those who planned a Japanese empire in Asia. Japan's military strength grew. The country spent over two-thirds of its budget on rearmament and defence.

In 1936 a group of young officers attempted to stage a coup in Japan. Several cabinet ministers were assassinated and the Tokyo Revolt, as it was called, was crushed by senior army officers. The ringleaders were executed. Nonetheless, the incident demonstrated only too clearly where the power lay in Japan. The military controlled Japan even though civilians headed the government. This was because the armed forces derived their authority from the Emperor and could bypass the politicians. The civilians were powerless to go against their wishes.

---

1 *In what ways was militarism in Japan similar to Fascism in Europe?*

2 *How did the Japanese Army ensure that militarism would be supported by the next generation of the Japanese people?*

CHINA BEFORE 1923

The 1911 Revolution

China had also seen considerable changes since the early years of the twentieth century. A rebellion in 1900, the Boxer Rising, had been directed mainly against the foreigners in China (British, American, Russian, Japanese, French, German) who had forced the Chinese to grant them special trading privileges. Many of their nationals treated China as a colony rather than as an independent nation.

On 10 October 1911 ('the Double Tenth'), a revolution began which ended the rule of the hated Manchu Dynasty of the Chinese emperors. Sun Yat-sen, an outstanding revolutionary leader, helped to kindle resentment against the Manchu domination of China and against the foreign influence in China. Sun Yat-sen put his nation first. He was a Nationalist.

The 1911 revolution spread like wildfire. Within five weeks most of the provinces of China had declared their independence. There was very little fighting. A powerful general, called Yuan Shih-kai, became president when Sun Yat-sen accepted that the Chinese Army posed a threat to his government. The leaders of the revolution had wanted a democratic system of government but Yuan Shih-kai became a dictator instead. He planned to make himself Emperor. Sun Yat-sen, who had only just founded the Kuomintang (Chinese Nationalist) Party in 1912, fled from China. But Yuan Shih-kai's attempt to become Emperor failed. He died in 1916.

The Warlords

His death left China without effective government. There was no hereditary emperor. Nor was there an effective electoral system in place to elect a new president. Yuan Shih-kai's successor was weak and incompetent. China lapsed into chaos. It broke up into hundreds of separate regions each ruled by a different military leader or warlord. All were nominally under the control of the Government in Peking, except the Canton area which was controlled by Sun Yat-sen after his return to China in 1917. The warlords press-ganged young men to serve in their private armies. The soldiers often lived off the land, looting food and valuables to pay for their upkeep.

The May the Fourth Movement

Despite its inability to govern China properly, the Peking Government declared war on Germany and Austria in 1917, hoping this would give it a say in the peace negotiations at the end of the war. But the Allies had already made certain promises to Japan. In April 1919, the Allies at the Versailles Peace Conference confirmed that Germany's rights and privileges in Shantung Province had been granted to Japan.

This came as a tremendous shock to most people in China. They were unaware of the secret agreements. They assumed the defeat of Germany would mean that Shantung Province would be free at last from foreign interference. It was no business of the peace negotiators in Paris to say what should or should not be done with China. When the news reached Peking there was an immediate outcry. On 4 May 1919, outraged Peking university students led an angry demonstration against the Government.

Source A

Modern painting of the student revolt in Peking, 4 May 1919

Source B

We marched off in force to the Legation Quarter, intending to demonstrate before the Japanese Legation first of all. We shouted a wide variety of slogans and carried many different banners. Chief among them were 'Return our Tsingtao', 'Abolish the Twenty-one Demands', 'Punish the Traitors', 'Refuse to Sign the Peace Treaty', and 'China for the Chinese'. . . . A leading pro-Japan official – Chang Tsung-hsiang, who was then Minister to Japan – happened to be in the Legation. He had not managed to escape in time, so the students gave him a harsh beating. Meanwhile they turned their wrath against the house's furnishings and recklessly destroyed things. Some students set fire to a pile of this wreckage in one of the courtyards.

Chang Kuo-tao (a student in Peking at that time), Rise of the Chinese Communists,
Kansas University Press, 1971–2

Source C

Banners Carried by the Peking Students

We may be beheaded, but Tsingtao must not be lost
China has been sentenced to death
Boycott Japanese goods
Protect our Country's soil
China belongs to the Chinese
The people should determine the destiny of the traitors
Don't just be patriotic for five minutes

Quoted in Chow Tse-tsung, The May the Fourth Movement,
Harvard University Press, 1960

---

1 *What is a legation? Why did the students march to the Legation Quarter in Peking to make their protest?*

2 *Why did the news from Versailles shock the Peking students? What did they think it meant for China? Quote evidence from Source C to support your answer.*

3 *Whom did the Peking students blame for the humiliation of China at Versailles? Quote evidence from Sources B and C to support your answer. Who were the 'traitors'?*

4 *What action did the protesting Peking students want the government to take? What did they want the Chinese people to do?*

5 *What type of evidence is Source A? In what ways is it different from Sources B and C?*

The demonstrations spread to other parts of China, encouraged by political opponents of the regime. There were strikes, boycotts of Japanese goods and many meetings. Over a thousand students were arrested but they got their way at last. The strength of the protests forced the Government to give way and China became the only country to refuse to sign and ratify the Versailles Treaty (see page 38).

The New Culture Movement

The May the Fourth Movement sparked off a renewed interest in China in Western ideas. Chinese students and intellectuals discussed Western attitudes to religion, science, Socialism, Marxism and education, and to society in general. This was the New Culture Movement. The old values of China were examined in the light of Western notions of freedom and justice, fair play and authority, democracy and constitutional change. Study groups and societies were founded by students and intellectuals. They wanted to change the face of Chinese society. Newspapers, books, pamphlets and periodicals widened public interest in the new ideas.

Many of the students, thinkers and intellectuals of the New Culture Movement came from Peking University, the centre of the demonstrations on 4 May 1919. The May the Fourth Movement had reawakened the revolutionary spirit in the Chinese. It made them receptive to many of the ideas of Lenin's Bolsheviks, such as state ownership of farms and factories and opposition to European imperialism. Indeed, the Russians helped two Peking University professors to found the Chinese Communist Party in 1921. Two of its founder members, Mao Tse-tung (an assistant in Peking University Library) and Chou En-lai (a radical student), later became the outstanding leaders of Communist China in 1949.

The great Chinese leaders of the twentieth century were in no doubt about the significance of the May the Fourth Movement. Chiang Kai-shek said it was proof of the desire for revolution in China. Mao Tse-tung claimed it started a 'new democratic revolution'.

---

1 *What was the appeal of, a) Communism and b) Nationalism, to the Chinese people after the events of 4 May 1919?*

2 *What did the Nationalists and Communists both have in common? How did they differ?*

3 *From which class or type of people did the demand for revolution spring? Were they typical of the Chinese people as a whole?*

THE KUOMINTANG

Russian assistance

After Sun Yat-sen returned to Canton in southern China, in 1917, he formed a Kuomintang government there to rival the one in Peking. The May the Fourth Movement gave it the impetus it needed to grow. Sun Yat-sen was a fervent Nationalist. He wanted to develop the Kuomintang as a truly national party capable of controlling the whole of China, not just Canton. But he needed military help to create an army capable of defeating the warlords in the north. Only then would China be strong enough to rid itself of foreign influence and eject the Japanese. The Bolsheviks offered help, so handpicked members of the Kuomintang were sent to Russia to be trained by Red Army experts. Chiang Kai-shek was one of them and on his return he took charge of a military academy for Kuomintang officers near Canton.

A Russian expert, called Michael Borodin, also helped Sun Yat-sen reorganise the Kuomintang into an effective political party by creating small groups of activists, called cells. In 1924 the members of China's growing Communist Party were allowed to join the Kuomintang as well. Preparations were made for a push against the northern warlords, but the Northern Expedition, as it was called, received a setback when Sun Yat-sen died prematurely in 1925.

The Northern Expedition

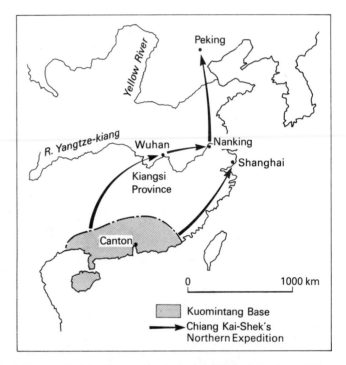

Map showing the route taken by Chiang Kai-shek on the Northern Expedition

The gifted Chiang Kai-shek was the obvious choice as leader of the expedition against the warlords. But he had one major disadvantage. He was a right-wing member of the Kuomintang and distrusted the Communists. Yet, without their support, the expedition could not succeed. A compromise was reached and Mao Tse-tung and other Communist leaders joined the expedition. Their role was to organise peasant and worker revolts in advance of the main Kuomintang armies as they drove northwards through China. By September 1926 Chiang Kai-shek's troops had occupied Hankow and Wuhan. In the spring of 1927 they took Shanghai and Nanking.

> **1** What advantages did the Kuomintang have when fighting the different armies of the warlords? Why do you think they were successful?
>
> **2** How did Russia assist the leaders of the Northern Expedition?

The Shanghai Massacre

It was at this juncture that Chiang Kai-shek decided to deal a mortal blow to his rivals, the Communists, in the Kuomintang. After his military victories, he felt strong enough to assert his authority. In any case he believed there might be a Russian-backed plot to overthrow him once he completed the conquest of China. His right-wing views, and the support he got from wealthy landowners and businessmen, made him suspect the motives of Mao Tse-tung and the other Communists who had helped to stir up peasant and worker revolts. The actions he took were little different from those taken by Hitler on the 'Night of the Long Knives'.

On 12 April 1927, Kuomintang soldiers, aided by members of Shanghai's secret societies (old friends of Chiang Kai-shek), rounded up Communists, trade union leaders and Communist sympathisers. Hundreds, possibly thousands, were executed. Only a few escaped.

The Shanghai Massacre in 1927. The soldiers are shooting at gunmen in the windows opposite

The Communists who remained free were in a dilemma. Lenin's Bolshevik Revolution began in Petrograd. Like Marx and Lenin, most Chinese Communists believed that a successful revolution, when it came, would start in the industrial cities, such as Shanghai, Nanking and Peking.

Mao Tse-tung, however, argued that China was primarily a land of peasants rather than a nation of industrial workers – the proletariat that Karl Marx had had in mind. Mao urged his comrades in the Chinese Communist Party to concentrate their strength in one place and to build up support among the hundreds of millions of Chinese peasants. In 1928 he joined Chu Teh and other Communist leaders in seeking refuge on a plateau in the mountains of southern China. They established a Chinese Soviet Republic there, in Kiangsi Province, in 1929, and in 1931 Mao was elected Chairman of the Kiangsi Soviet while Chu Teh became the Red Army Commander.

> **1** *Why did the Shanghai Massacre take place?*
> **2** *Was a clash between the Communists and the Nationalists likely anyway?*
> **3** *Why did Mao Tse-tung set up a Chinese Soviet Republic in Kiangsi Province in 1929? What did he hope to achieve by this?*
> **4** *How did Mao Tse-tung's ideas differ from those of Marx and Lenin?*

Chiang Kai-shek's government

Chiang Kai-shek turned his attention to the conquest of the remaining parts of China. He entered Peking in 1928. He defeated other warlords and made contact with the leaders of more distant provinces, such as 'the Young Marshal' in Manchuria. Chiang Kai-shek made Nanking the new capital city of China. His Kuomintang Government was recognised by the major world powers as the legitimate government of China. It looked as if Chiang Kai-shek could well achieve Sun Yat-sen's ambition to complete the unification of China under Kuomintang leadership.

Chiang introduced a number of important reforms, constructed roads and railways, and modernised the densely populated region between the Yangtze and the Yellow rivers. But he did not stick to Sun Yat-sen's Three Principles on which the Kuomintang had been based – Democracy (free elections), Nationalism (China for the Chinese) and Socialism (peasant ownership of the land). Nor did he unify China. Instead, he established a one-party system under a military dictator. He did not improve the lot of the industrial workers. Nor did he liberate the hundreds of millions of peasants who remained landless and oppressed by their landlords.

Chiang Kai-shek (1887–1975)

Chiang Kai-shek was born in 1887, the son of a wealthy farmer. He trained at first to become an officer in the Japanese army but later played an active part in the 1911 revolution. He joined the Kuomintang Party soon after it was formed and became one of Sun Yat-sen's most trusted officers. In 1922 he saved Sun Yat-sen's life and was given the post of commander of the Kuomintang military academy. When Sun Yat-sen died in 1925, Chiang Kai-shek took command of the Kuomintang forces and led the successful Northern Expedition to subdue the warlords of northern China.

During the Second World War he was treated as one of the big five Allied leaders, even though his control of China was far from complete. At the end of the war America helped him dominate China after the defeat of Japan. But the long-standing feud with the Communists erupted into civil war once more in 1946. Mao Tse-tung controlled the countryside and Chiang Kai-shek was eventually forced to flee with his supporters to the island of Taiwan off the Chinese mainland, where he died in 1975.

MAO TSE-TUNG'S CHINA

A Prairie Fire

Mao Tse-tung aimed to establish soviets (local governments of workers and peasants) throughout China which would later be the pillars of the Communist Revolution. In the Kiangsi Soviet he built up the strength of the Red Army and developed friendly relations with the peasants. Mao believed that great things could have small beginnings. In 1930 he wrote an article entitled 'A Single Spark Can Start A Prairie Fire'. He listed the things that were wrong with China: high rents paid by peasants to the hated landlords, high taxes to pay for the army, famine, bandits everywhere and a very low standard of living.

Source A

All China is littered with dry faggots which will soon be aflame. The saying, 'A single spark can start a prairie fire', is an apt description of how the current situation will develop. We need only look at the strikes by the workers, the uprisings by the peasants, the mutinies of soldiers and the strikes of students which are developing in many places to see that it cannot be long before a 'spark' kindles 'a prairie fire'.

Selected Works of Mao Tse-tung, Foreign Languages Press, Peking, 1967

Mao Tse-tung talking to a peasant in the 1930s

Mao's methods paid off. In 1929 the Communists only had the support of about 20 000 people (half of them being soldiers). By 1934 there were 200 000 soldiers in the Red Army and the Communists had the support of about 10 million peasants. This was still only a tiny proportion of China's total population of about 500 million people. By the early 1930s, the

Communists had formed about 15 soviets throughout China, besides the Kiangsi Soviet.

Mao was confident that Communism would triumph in China because the Red Army was expert in guerrilla warfare. This is how he described their tactics in 1930:

Source B

Divide our forces to arouse the masses, concentrate our forces to deal with the enemy. The enemy advances, we retreat; the enemy camps, we harass; the enemy tires, we attack; the enemy retreats, we pursue.

Selected Works of Mao Tse-tung, Foreign Languages Press, Peking, 1967

He issued strict instructions to the soldiers serving in the Red Army.

Source C

Be courteous and polite to the people and help them when you can. Return all borrowed articles. Replace all damaged articles. Be honest in all transactions with the peasants. Pay for all articles purchased.

Edgar Snow, *Red Star Over China*, Gollancz, 1937

In this way Mao's Red Army earned the respect, and often the affection of the peasants – unlike the Kuomintang armies, who followed the traditional way of life of a Chinese soldier, living off the countryside and treating brutally anyone suspected of sympathising with the enemy. Red Army soldiers told Edgar Snow how the peasants helped them.

Source D

When the White Army comes to a village in Kansu, nobody helps it, nobody gives it any food, and nobody wants to join. When the Red Army comes, the peasants organize, and form committees to help us, and young men volunteer to join.

Edgar Snow, *Red Star Over China*, Gollancz, 1937

1 *What did Mao identify as the causes of unrest in China in 1930?*

2 *What events did Mao think might provide 'the single spark' which could 'start a prairie fire'?*

3 *Why were Mao's guerrilla tactics successful, even when the Red Army was smaller than the Kuomintang Army?*

4 *Mao wanted the Red Army to muster the support of the peasants. Why? How did he do this? Quote evidence from these sources.*

The Extermination Campaigns

Chiang Kai-shek could not ignore the soviets. The Northern Expedition had destroyed the power of the warlords. It would have been illogical to stand by and see Mao's Communists take their place. He set out to eliminate them in a series of extermination campaigns. But although his forces outnumbered the Red Army, they had little initial success.

Peasants helped the Red Army to set up ambushes and booby traps. Many revenged themselves on the Kuomintang soldiers who stole their food and destroyed their homes. Many Kuomintang prisoners were taken. Some joined the Red Army instead. Thousands of rifles were seized.

When the Japanese invaded Manchuria in 1931 there was a lull in the fighting but in 1932 Chiang Kai-shek launched a new campaign, this time with a large well-equipped army of 500 000 men. His German advisers recommended a change of tactics. The Kuomintang soldiers were grouped into much larger units. The Red Army found it difficult to use guerrilla tactics against them. When the Communists did try conventional warfare (against Mao's advice) they were defeated. The area controlled by Mao's Kiangsi Soviet got smaller as the Kuomintang troops surrounded the area. Chiang Kai-shek intended to starve them out or beat them in the field.

The Long March

At an historic meeting in October 1934 the ruling Communist Party leadership decided to evacuate the Kiangsi Soviet. On 16 October they left, after first loading weapons and valuables on to mules, ponies and donkeys. Over 100 000 people departed on one of the greatest journeys of survival in world history. The Communists called it the Long March.

Source A

If you mean, did we have any exact plans, the answer is that we had none. We intended to break out of the encirclement and join up with the other soviets. Beyond that there was only a ... desire to ... fight the Japanese.

Mao Tse-tung in Robert Payne, *Mao Tse-tung*, Weybright and Talley, 1969

Source B

Around five o'clock in the evening [16 October 1934], Mao and about twenty others left Yutu by the North Gate, and then turned to the left towards the river, which was all yellow, roaring and foaming, as though calling on the armies to advance. Soon the sun set and the gusts of bitter wind chilled us. The Chairman wore a grey cloth uniform and an eight-cornered military cap, with no overcoat. He walked along the river banks.

Mao's batman quoted in Dick Wilson, *The Long March*, Hamish Hamilton, 1971

Source C

Ahead of them is the Tatu River, behind is the Golden Sand River [the Yangtze-kiang]. They're caught like fish in a bottle. Now is the time to annihilate the Red bandits.

Kuomintang General Liu Wen-hui, quoted in Dick Wilson The Long March,
Hamish Hamilton, 1971

At first, the Red Army used ferries to cross the fast-flowing Tatu, one of the tributaries of the Yangtze. They soon realised it would take weeks to get everyone across. Chiang Kai-shek's bombers were already raiding the crossing point and his armies were converging on their position. Mao changed tactics. The Red Army would capture the Luting bridge – a narrow, partly dismantled chain bridge perched precariously above the turbulent River Tatu.

Source D

We began our attack at four in the afternoon. The regimental CO and I directed it from the west end of the bridge . . . Carrying tommy-guns, big knives strapped across their backs, twelve grenades apiece tucked into their belts, twenty-two heroes, led by Commander Liao, climbed across the swaying bridge chains in the teeth of intense enemy fire. Behind them came the officers and men of 3rd Company, each carrying a plank in addition to full battle gear; they fought and laid planks at the same time. Just as the assault squad reached the opposite side, huge flames sprang into the sky outside Luting City's West Gate. The enemy was trying to block us by fire, to consume us in its flames . . . Emboldened by our cries, the twenty-two men, at the sound of a clarion bugle call, plunged boldly into the flames.

Yang Cheng-wu quoted in Dick Wilson, The Long March, Hamish Hamilton, 1971

Source E

Poem by Mao Tse-tung

The Red Army does not fear the difficulties of the Long March,
the thousand rivers and hundred mountains are but routine . . .
We greatly delighted in the thousand *li* of snow which covered Min Mountain,
and as the three armies left it behind,
we all broke into smiles.

Translation in Andres D.Onate, Chairman Mao and the Chinese Communist Party,
Nelson Hall, 1979

The Red Army, never fearing the challenging Long March,
Looked lightly on the many peaks and rivers . . .
A thousand joyous *li* of freshening snow on Min Shan,
And then, the last pass vanquished, Three Armies smiled!

Translation in Edgar Snow, Red Star Over China, Gollancz, 1937

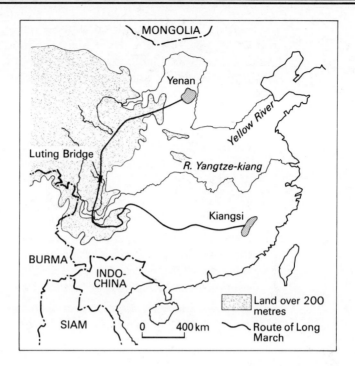

Map showing the route taken by the Chinese Communist forces during the Long March 1934–5

Source F

This mass migration was the biggest armed propaganda tour in history. The Reds passed through provinces populated by more than 200 000 000 people. Between battles and skirmishes, in every town occupied, they called great mass meetings, gave theatrical performances, heavily 'taxed' the rich, freed many slaves (some of whom joined the Red Army), preached 'liberty, equality, democracy', confiscated the property of the 'traitors' (officials, big landlords, and tax-collectors) and distributed their goods among the poor. Millions of peasants have now seen the Red Army and heard it speak, and are no longer afraid of it.

Edgar Snow in Red Star Over China, Gollancz, 1937

Only 30 000 members of Mao's original army of 100 000 Chinese Communist soldiers, who left Kiangsi in October 1934, reached journey's end at Yenan in northern China a year later. The marchers took 368 days to cover the 10 000 kilometre journey. For most of that time they fought running battles with Chiang Kai-shek's Kuomintang armies. They rested on only 44 days, covering a distance which averaged well over 30 kilometres each day, not counting delays caused by major battles en route.

Edgar Snow estimated that they fought 'an average of almost a skirmish a day' and devoted 15 days to 'major pitched battles'. They climbed and crossed five snow-capped mountain ranges, to say nothing of 13 other ranges of hills or mountains. They crossed 24 major rivers, including the turbulent Yangtze – one of the world's greatest rivers. They also passed through a dozen provinces and captured over 60 cities.

At last the Red Army reached safety in Yenan, a Communist stronghold in the north-west of China. Here Mao Tse-tung trained agents (called the cadres) to spread Communism to the people. He wrote training manuals which they could use and bided his time, waiting for Chiang Kai-shek's next move.

---

1 *Why do you think the local Chinese were reluctant to blow up the Luting Bridge? How did they defend the bridge instead? Why was the capture of the Luting Bridge vital to the success of the Long March?*

2 *Why did Edgar Snow say the Long March was 'the biggest armed propaganda tour in history'? What did he mean by this?*

3 *Study Source E. How do these translations of Mao's poem about the Long March differ from each other? Do the differences alter the meaning of the poem in any way? Why is it always necessary to be cautious when reading a translation from another language?*

4 *Why was the Long March undertaken in the first place? What was its aim? Was it a victory for Mao Tse-tung or for Chiang Kai-shek?*

Mao Tse-tung (1893–1976)

Mao Tse-tung in 1959

Mao Tse-tung was born in 1893 and started his career as a teacher. He was influenced at an early stage by the thinking of Karl Marx and became one of the first members of the Chinese Communist Party when it was founded in 1921. Mao was extremely astute and recognised early on that the secret to the eventual control of China lay in the hands of the peasants, since they were by far the largest group in the country. After the war against Japan, he used his power over the peasants to overthrow Chiang Kai-shek and became the leader of Communist China in 1949.

Mao Tse-tung was a remarkable leader. He aroused adulation among the Chinese people, not merely because he was their leader, but also because he inspired them with his poetry. In the 1960s millions of young people carried with them a little red book containing the thoughts of Chairman Mao. He died in 1976, having helped to create modern China and to establish beyond doubt the right to be regarded as one of the most influential leaders the world has ever known.

---

1 *Why do many people, irrespective of their political beliefs, look on Mao Tse-tung as the greatest leader of the twentieth century? What did he do to justify this claim?*

2 *What part did the Long March play in establishing Mao Tse-tung's claim to that title?*

AT WAR WITH JAPAN

Sian

Even before the Long March had been successfully concluded, the Red Army renewed its call to Chiang Kai-shek and the Kuomintang to face squarely the threat presented by Japan. On 1 August 1935, the Chinese Communist Party issued the following statement,

> The Communist Party solemnly declares: if the Kuomintang troops cease their attacks on the Red Army and if any units carry out resistance to Japan, then the Red Army, regardless of any old feuds or present conflicts or differences on domestic issues, will not only immediately cease its hostile actions against these units, but willingly work closely with them to save the nation . . . An anti-Japanese united army should be formed of all troops willing to fight Japan.

> *Selected Works of Mao Tse-tung*, Foreign Languages Press, Peking, 1967

Chiang Kai-shek patched up his differences with Mao Tse-tung and the Communists early in 1937. At a meeting in Sian with Chou En-lai, he agreed that Mao's Communists would be allowed to stay at Yenan. In return, the Red Army would fight under his orders. This was the Second United Front. Leaders from both sides immediately drew up plans to combat Japanese aggression.

The Invasion

After making Manchuria part of their empire in 1931, the Japanese annexed other Chinese territory between Manchuria and Peking in 1933. However, the new alliance, early in 1937, between the Kuomintang and the Chinese Communists, seriously threatened the stability of these Japanese acquisitions in China. Hitherto, Chiang Kai-shek and the Kuomintang had been too preoccupied with the internal conflict with Mao Tse-tung to worry unduly about Japan. Now it looked as if a combined Kuomintang/Red Army might even be formed, which in numbers alone would be capable of launching a successful campaign against Manchuria.

The Japanese High Command decided to strike first. They made plans and mobilised their troops. On 7 July 1937, fighting broke out again between the two sides after an incident on the Marco Polo bridge near Peking. The Japanese used it as an excuse to invade China.

Source A

On the evening of July 7, Japanese troops held illegal manoeuvres at Lukouchiao . . . in the vicinity of Peking . . . Alleging that a Japanese soldier was missing, Japanese troops demanded, after midnight, to enter the adjacent city of Wanping to conduct a search. When permission was refused by the Chinese authorities, the Japanese suddenly opened an attack on Wanping with infantry and artillery forces, and the Chinese garrison was compelled to offer resistance.

The China Yearbook 1938, quoted in *Source Materials in Chinese History*,
edited by Charles Meyer and Ian Allen, Frederick Warne, 1970

Source B

Lukouchiao is about a Chinese mile west of Fengtai and the Japanese forces are always engaging in manoeuvres on the plain north of it. On the night of July 7, part of the Japanese detachment was carrying out night exercises ... Unexpectedly, the Japanese unit exercising north of Lukouchiao was fired on about 11.40 p.m. by Chinese troops. While preparing to reciprocate the Chinese challenge, the men reported the incident to their superior officer, who rushed to the scene with assistants to work out expedient measures.

Speech by General H. Sugiyama, minister of war,
in the Japanese Diet (Parliament) on 27 July 1937

Source C

U.S. CONDEMNS JAPAN AS INVADER OF CHINA
DROPS NEUTRALITY POLICY TO BACK LEAGUE

State Department Says Tokyo Breaks 9-Power and Kellogg Treaties
Senator Asserts an 'Economic Quarantine' Would End Conflict
in 30 Days

Headlines in The *New York Times*, 7 October 1937

This time Chiang Kai-shek took action. He said

> If we allow any more of our land to be taken, we shall be guilty of an unforgivable crime against China.

But words didn't stop the Japanese advance. They captured Peking, Nanking and Shanghai and invaded Canton from the sea. By the end of 1938 they had captured a large part of north-eastern China which, with Manchuria, was several times larger than Japan itself. When the victorious Japanese troops seized Nanking their troops were allowed to go on the rampage and, in an orgy of looting and killing (the Rape of Nanking), the Chinese capital suffered one of the worst atrocities ever committed by an army on a civilian population.

Japanese troops marching into China in 1937

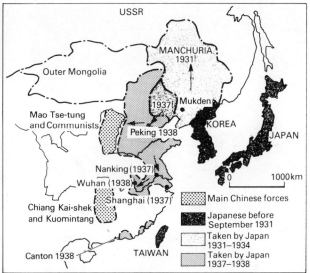

Map showing the extent of Japan's conquests in China

1 What happened on 7 July 1937 according to, a) Japan and b) China? What discrepancies are there between the two accounts?

2 What was unusual about the American reaction to the Japanese invasion? Why do you think the Americans were prepared to change their foreign policy in the Far East but remained indifferent to events in Europe?

3 In what ways was the incident on 7 July 1937 similar to the incident on 18 September 1931 (see page 185)?

As the Japanese advanced into China, Chiang Kai-shek retreated into the mountains of western China. He established his headquarters there at Chungking on the River Yangtze. The Japanese made no serious attempt to destroy his army, since they had obtained most of what they wanted in the area of China now under Japanese occupation. The Red Army played a more active role, however, harassing the Japanese with the same guerrilla tactics they had used successfully against Chiang Kai-shek before the Long March.

FURTHER QUESTIONS AND EXERCISES

1 You were a student at Peking University in 1919. You are writing your memoirs in 1969. Write a brief extract from your chapter describing what happened on 4 May 1919, the events leading up to it, and the effect it had on China afterwards.

German strip cartoon drawn in the early 1930s

2 *To which event does this strip cartoon refer? Where, when, and why did that event take place? Explain the sequence of cartoon pictures. Whom do the characters represent? How have they been portrayed by the artist?*

3 *Write brief notes explaining carefully the significance of the following in the history of modern China:*

a) *Sun Yat-sen*   d) *the Treaty of Versailles*

b) *the warlords*   e) *the Twenty-one Demands*

c) *Yuan Shih-kai*   f) *the Kiangsi Chinese Soviet Republic*

4 *Describe carefully the events leading up to and including the Long March in 1934–5. How did Mao Tse-tung lead his soldiers to safety? Draw a map to illustrate your answer. Was it a victory for the Kuomintang or for the Communists?*

5 *Put these events in their correct chronological order. Write brief notes explaining their significance.*

a) *The meeting at Sian*   e) *The Shanghai Massacre*

b) *The invasion of Manchuria*   f) *The Rape of Nanking*

c) *The Northern Expedition*   g) *The Double Tenth*

d) *The capture of the Luting Bridge*   h) *Death of Yuan Shih-kai*

Chapter Ten

The League of Nations

INTRODUCTION

Source A

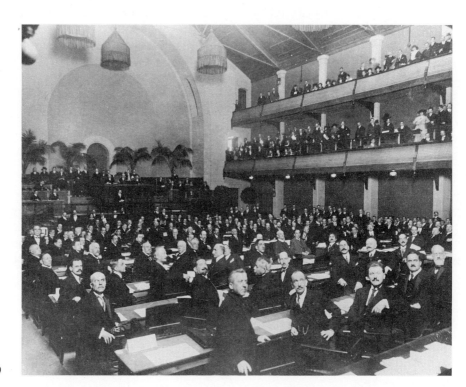

The League of Nations in session, The Graphic, 27 November 1920

Source B

The first session of the Assembly of the League of Nations at Geneva the Swiss Capital, which has been selected as the headquarters of the new organisation, constitutes a great landmark in the history of the world. As yet it is incomplete in its composition. The United States, the originator of the idea, is, paradoxically enough, unrepresented, though it summoned the delegates to the present gathering. And Germany, Austria, Bulgaria and Turkey, of course, are as yet outside the pale, while Russia in the shackles of Bolshevism, also has no voice in the deliberations.

The Graphic, 27 November 1920

> **1** Why did the writer of the caption use the words 'of course' when mentioning the fact that Germany, Austria, Bulgaria and Turkey were not represented at the first session of the League?
>
> **2** Why was Russia excluded from the League of Nations in 1920?
>
> **3** Which country should have been there but wasn't? Why?

Before 1920 there was no international forum which could be used by national delegates to argue problems and resolve disputes. But the appalling waste of life, and the scale of the conflict during the First World War, persuaded many belligerent countries and neutrals, that an international peace-keeping organisation was needed in the future.

SETTING UP THE LEAGUE

The Covenant

The reception of the Covenant was all that could be desired . . . Henceforth there will be no neutrals in any wars or punitive measures of economic blockade in which the League takes part. The assumption is that if the League is taking part the struggle will be one for the maintenance of common civilization, and that in such a struggle no one has any right to be neutral.

The Times, 29 April 1919

The Covenant, which set up the League of Nations, had 26 articles. These described the aims and objectives of the League and provided the machinery for its government and smooth running from day to day. Since it formed part of each peace treaty, each nation signing the Covenant agreed,

to promote international co-operation and to achieve international peace and security by the acceptance of obligations not to resort to war, by the prescription of open, just and honourable relations between nations, by the firm establishment of the understandings of international law as the actual rule of conduct among Governments, and by the maintenance of justice and a scrupulous respect for all treaty obligations in the dealings of organized peoples with one another.

Speeches and Documents on International Affairs,
edited by Arthur Berriedale Keith, Oxford, 1938

1 *What is the modern equivalent of the League of Nations?*

2 *What did the writer in* The Times *mean when he used the phrases 'punitive measures' and 'economic blockade'? What is a Covenant?*

3 *Why would there be no neutral countries in any wars in which the League took part?*

4 *What did the nations who signed the Covenant promise to do? What did they hope to achieve?*

Article	Covenant
1	Explained how to join the League.
2, 3, 4 5, 6	Set up the rules governing the organisation of the Assembly, Council, and the Permanent Secretariat.
7	Fixed the headquarters of the League in Geneva in Switzerland. 'All positions under or in connexion with the League, including the Secretariat, shall be open equally to men and women.'
8, 9	Laid down that member nations would seek to reduce armaments.
10	'The Members of the League undertake to respect and preserve as against external aggression the territorial integrity and existing political independence of all Members of the League. In case of any such aggression or in case of any threat or danger of such aggression the Council shall advise upon the means by which this obligation shall be fulfilled.'
11	'Any war or threat of war, whether immediately affecting any of the Members of the League or not, is hereby declared a matter of concern to the whole League, and the League shall take any action that may be deemed wise and effectual to safeguard the peace of nations.'
12	'The Members of the League agree that if there should arise between them any dispute likely to lead to a rupture, they will submit the matter either to arbitration or to inquiry by the Council ...'
13, 15	Established the procedure for dealing with such disputes.
14	Set up the Permanent Court of International Justice.
16	'Should any Member of the League resort to war in disregard of its covenants under Articles 12, 13, or 15 [i.e. if it disregarded the League's procedures for dealing with such disputes], it shall be deemed to have committed an act of war against all other Members of the League, which hereby undertake immediately to subject it to the severance of all trade or financial relations, the prohibition of all dealings between their nationals and the nationals of the covenant-breaking State, and the prevention of all financial, commercial, or personal dealings between the nationals of the covenant-breaking State and the nationals of any other State, whether a Member of the League or not.

It shall be the duty of the Council in such case to recommend to the several Governments concerned what effective military, naval, or air force the Members of the League shall contribute to the armed forces to be used to protect the covenants of the League.'

17   Established the procedure for dealing with disputes between a Member of the League and a non-Member.

18, 19, 20, 21   Dealt with separate treaties made between Members of the League.

22   Dealt with the way in which the Mandates of the League (i.e. the former colonies administered by countries, such as France and the United Kingdom) should be administered by the League.

23   By this covenant, the Members of the League agreed to a number of important civil rights, including the following:

     a) 'Fair and humane conditions of labour'

     b) The 'just treatment of the native inhabitants of territories under their control'

     c) League intervention in cases involving the traffic in women and children, opium and other dangerous drugs

     d) League supervision of the arms trade

     e) Freedom of communications

     f) Prevention and control of disease.

24, 25   Dealt with relations between the League and some other international organisations, such as the Red Cross.

26   Dealt with the procedure for making amendments to this Covenant.

Adapted from *Speeches and Documents on International Affairs*, edited by Arthur Berriedale Keith, Oxford, 1938

---

1 *Who ran the League of Nations?*

2 *What actions did members of the League promise to take to reduce the likelihood of war?*

3 *What actions did members of the League promise to take if they had a dispute with another country?*

4 *What did all the members of the League promise to do if another member of the League went to war and ignored the League's solution to the problem?*

5 *How do we know the League of Nations was in favour of women's rights? What other social problems concerned the members of the League?*

6 *In what circumstances could members of the US Armed Services have been involved in war had Congress ratified the Treaty of Versailles?*

Organisation

The headquarters of the League of Nations in Geneva

The League consisted of an Assembly or parliament for debates; a Council or committee of important states, which made most of the League's decisions; a Secretariat which ran the League; and a Court of International Justice.

The **Assembly** met once a year, where the delegates of all the member nations could speak. Every member country had one vote, whatever its size. The Assembly decided the policy of the League and controlled its finances, but most of its decisions had to be unanimous. Although, in theory, this gave any nation the right of veto, it did not prove an obstacle to the work of the Assembly.

The **Council** met more frequently than the Assembly. This committee, of four (later five) great powers and four elected nations from the Assembly, decided many of the problems put before the League. Each member had one vote. Initially the Council had four permanent representatives (the British Empire, Japan, Italy and France) and four representatives elected by the Assembly (Belgium, Spain, Greece and Brazil in 1920). When Germany joined the League in 1926 she immediately became a permanent member of the Council; and when Hitler left, Germany's place was taken by the Soviet Union (1934).

The **Secretariat** ran the day to day business of the League. It was manned by officials who carried out the decisions made in the Assembly and in the Council. The first Secretary General was a British official called Sir Eric Drummond. The League had its headquarters in Geneva in Switzerland.

The **Court of International Justice** was presided over by 15 judges, chosen from 15 different countries. It met in The Hague (in the Netherlands) and heard cases brought before it, by countries complaining of infringements of international law.

UP-HILL WORK

Punch, *10 July 1935*

JOHN BULL "EVEN THOUGH IT'S ONLY HALF A LEAGUE,
IT MUST GO ONWARD."

Unfortunately, it was the behaviour of the major powers, when they were Council members, which reduced the credibility of the League of Nations as peace-maker and guarantor of frontiers *not* the behaviour of the minor powers in the Assembly. Japan left in 1933 after seizing Manchuria. Germany left in 1933 after Hitler came to power. Italy left in 1937 after seizing Abyssinia. The Soviet Union left in 1939 after invading Finland.

> **1** *Why does John Bull say 'Even though it's only half a league it must go onward'? What had happened to the League? What was the point of the cartoon?*
>
> **2** *To which other historical event and to which poem is this a reference?*

THE LEAGUE IN ACTION

The failure of the League of Nations to deter Hitler, Mussolini or the Japanese military leaders from acts of aggression in the years before 1939 is often held up as evidence that the League of Nations was a total failure. Yet, even though the League had relatively few major successes, it did provide an international forum to debate the actions of member states, or non-member states, who broke the rules of international behaviour. In time the League of Nations Assembly became the parent of the United Nations General Assembly in 1945. The Council of the League became the parent of the United Nations Security Council.

Successes

The League did much valuable work behind the scenes.

- It helped solve the refugee problem after the First World War.
- It administered those German and Turkish colonies which had been allocated to the colonial powers as mandates of the League of Nations. It was the League's responsibility to see that those mandates were carried out in accordance with the Treaty of Versailles. It did this through the work of the Mandates Commission.
- The League also administered the plebiscites in the various frontier territories to decide whether or not they wanted to stay in Germany. A League Commissioner ran the free city of Danzig. The League also administered the Saar until the 1935 plebiscite.
- The ILO (International Labour Organisation) was founded in 1919 and was linked to the work of the League of Nations. However, non-League countries, like the United States, could also join. It helped to encourage the formation of trade unions and to improve working conditions, pensions and minimum wage schemes throughout the world. The ILO was one of the few organisations set up by the League which continued in the same form after the end of the Second World War.
- The Health Organisation helped to combat the spread of epidemic diseases. The League was also concerned with many other matters affecting the everyday lives of the peoples of the world, such as women's rights, providing loans to developing nations, the eradication of slavery and the control of drugs.

League Decisions Before 1931

The League attempted to resolve the various disputes which were brought before it. Before 1931 its decisions could be, and were, criticised, but they were usually accepted. This encouraged many statesmen to think that the League could resolve major disputes as well.

1920 Aaland Islands: Dispute between Finland and Sweden over possession of these islands. The inhabitants were of Swedish origin but the islands had been part of the Russian Empire. The League awarded the islands to Finland but granted the islanders a certain amount of independence.

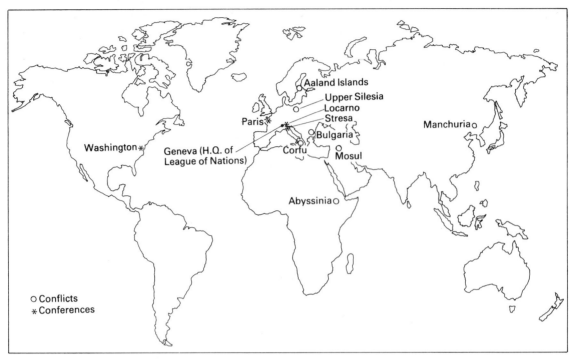

The League of Nations was involved in disputes all over the world. The headquarters of the League at Geneva and the locations of the main peace conferences in the inter-war years are also shown here

1921 Upper Silesia: The League decided the problem of how to divide this industrial area between Germany and the newly-created state of Poland. Neither side was satisfied with the result, since both coveted Silesia's mineral resources and both were eventually left with substantial numbers of their nationals in the other's country.

1923 Corfu: Italy's General Tellini and his companions were assassinated in Greece when attempting to resolve a frontier dispute between Greece and Albania (then under Italian protection). Mussolini over-reacted to the news and demanded compensation from the Greek government. When this was not immediately forthcoming, he shelled and then captured the Greek island of Corfu. Greece protested to the League of Nations. Italy was one of the four permanent members of the Council, so the League trod carefully. Mussolini refused to accept the League's ruling, so the matter was decided by the Council of Ambassadors, which was linked to the League. Greece paid up and Mussolini was persuaded to withdraw. But the action of Italy was not condemned by the League – unlike that of Greece in 1925 (see below).

1922–6 Mosul: The League decided this frontier dispute in favour of Iraq rather than Turkey. Both claimed Mosul with its rich oilfield. The area had been part of the Ottoman Empire and its population was mainly Kurdish (one of the Turkish peoples). But it fell into British hands towards the end of the war and they wanted to see it become part of Iraq (a British mandate).

1925 Greece v Bulgaria: A Greek army invaded Bulgaria after a border incident. The League ordered the Greeks to withdraw and condemned their action.

League Decisions After 1931

The League of Nations proved powerless, however, when the major powers infringed its Covenant. There were a number of such incidents but the two most important were in 1931 in the Far East and in Abyssinia in 1935.

1931 Manchuria: The members of the League failed to take decisive action when Japan invaded Manchuria in 1931 (see Chapter 9). Not surprisingly the Japanese delegate vetoed a motion calling on Japanese forces to withdraw. Lord Lytton (page 187) led an investigation on behalf of the League but his report was unacceptable to the Japanese. Sanctions were not applied. Force was not used or contemplated. The only result was Japan's resignation from the League in 1933.

> 1 *Which Articles of the League applied to this case? What actions should the members of the League have taken?*
> 2 *Why was it hard to prove that Japan was the aggressor in Manchuria?*
> 3 *Why did the League fail to act decisively in this dispute?*
> 4 *What effect do you think the League's handling of this dispute had on Mussolini and Hitler?*

1935 Abyssinia: With even less cause than the Japanese, Mussolini invaded Abyssinia and overthrew the Emperor Haile Selassie (see page 221). Italy was clearly condemned as the aggressor. The League applied economic sanctions. It told its members to stop trading with Italy. But the members of the League were reluctant to enforce the ban with regard to the sale of oil, which would really have hurt the Italians. In the end the sanctions were removed and the League suffered a blow from which it never recovered. When Hitler threatened Czechoslovakia in 1938 the crisis was resolved outside the League of Nations.

> 1 *What actions should the members of the League have taken against the Italians according to its Covenant?*
> 2 *Why was the failure of the League to act decisively over Abyssinia so crucial to its later success or failure?*

Why the League Failed

The League of Nations failed to resolve the major political disputes for a number of reasons:

- Trade sanctions could not be made to bite. For one thing the League could not control the trade of non-League nations, such as the United States. Member nations were unwilling to contribute troops to a League of Nations force. So the League had no effective way of compelling other countries to accept its decisions. Small or weak nations could be forced to accept League decisions but powerful states could choose to obey League decisions, or ignore them. This destroyed the faith which smaller countries had in the League.

- The founder members of the League of Nations did not include Russia (because of the Bolshevik Revolution), the United States (because the US Senate refused to ratify the Treaty of Versailles) and Germany (because she was labelled the aggressor in the First World War). Yet these were major world powers. Germany became a member in 1926 and the Soviet Union in 1934 but the United States, the most powerful nation on earth, remained outside the League of Nations. As a consequence the League could never speak for the world as a whole.

- It was set up as a result of a Peace Conference which imposed harsh terms on five countries (one of them a permanent member of the Council in 1926) and which disappointed several others (e.g. China and Italy).

- A major part of its work consisted of administering the plebiscites and mandates laid down by the Paris Peace Treaties. This was not the concern of nations which had been neutral during the War.

- The member nations of the League were rarely united on the great issues which came before them, such as disarmament.

It was only in the late 1920s that the League worked really well – at a time when the permanent members of the Council were supported by three talented foreign ministers: Gustav Stresemann of Germany, Aristide Briand of France and Austen Chamberlain of Britain.

INTER-WAR DIPLOMACY

The absence of American, German and Russian delegates from the League of Nations led diplomats to seek international agreements outside the League. These conferences were concerned primarily with a) guaranteeing international frontiers, b) renouncing war as a means of settling international disputes, c) seeking a reduction in armaments.

The Treaty of Locarno

This Treaty was signed in Locarno, Switzerland, in December 1925. The principal signatories were Germany, France and Belgium. It was a notable diplomatic breakthrough at a time of international tension, since French and Belgian troops had earlier occupied the German Ruhr (in January 1923). Gustav Stresemann (Germany) and Aristide Briand (France) later won the Nobel Peace Prize (1926) for their work in seeking and ratifying this agreement. All three countries agreed to confirm existing frontiers and to abide by arbitration, not war, if any disputes arose between them. Other agreements were signed at Locarno between Germany, Poland and Czechoslovakia. All were guaranteed by Britain and Italy (see page 80).

Punch, *21 October 1925*

A LEAGUE TRIUMPH

The Kellogg–Briand Pact

Aristide Briand, foreign minister of France

In 1927 the French foreign minister, Aristide Briand, wishing to involve isolationist America in peaceful diplomacy, suggested to the US secretary of state, Frank Kellogg, that France and the United States should jointly renounce war as a means of settling international disputes.

Kellogg felt that this might be construed as an alliance between France and America. He proposed, instead, that other nations should be invited to sign the declaration as well. So, on 27 August 1928, the Kellogg–Briand Pact was signed in Paris. Fifteen nations, including Germany, the United States, Belgium, France, Britain, Italy, Japan, Poland and Czechoslovakia, took part. Over 60 nations eventually signed the Pact, including the Soviet Union. Its provisions were very simple:

• The 'High Contracting Parties' (i.e. the respective governments) declared that they condemned war as the way to solve international disputes and renounced it 'in their relations with one another'.

● They agreed to settle all disputes between them by peaceful means.

But the Kellogg–Briand Pact had two fatal flaws. These were:

● There was no means of enforcing the Pact.

● The great powers signed the Pact on the understanding that it did not stop them using force in self defence. Kellogg himself said, 'any nation has the right to defend its interests anywhere in the world'.

The Pact was meaningless, since many wars begin with an incident which both belligerents use as an excuse to say they were attacked first (for example, the Manchurian bomb incident). All the Pact did was to give other nations the right, which they already had under the Covenant, to condemn acts of aggression. But many people at the time thought differently.

> Short and simple as were the proceedings, the ceremony was most impressive, and those who were present will not easily forget the occasion when the plenipotentiaries of the greatest Powers of the modern world 'solemnly declared', in the names of their respective peoples, that they condemned recourse to war for the solution of international controversies, and renounced it as an instrument of national policy in their relations with one another.

The Times, 28 August 1928

THE AUTOGRAPH HUNTER

LITTLE MISS PEACE "Isn't it splendid? I've got fifteen — and I hope to get the rest."

> **1** *Why was* The Times *impressed by the signing of the Kellogg Pact?*
>
> **2** *Is it ever possible to prove beyond dispute that one nation was the only aggressor or the sole cause of a war?*
>
> **3** *What was the point of 'THE AUTOGRAPH HUNTER' cartoon in Punch?*
>
> **4** *Who took the 'Right Turning' in 'A LEAGUE TRIUMPH' (page 215)? What was the 'Right Turning'? Why was it important at that time?*

Disarmament

One of the fundamental causes of the First World War had been rearmament, the heavy build-up of weapons, warships and conscripted armies in the years up to 1914. After the War the great powers made a number of efforts to reduce and limit stocks of weapons and the recruitment of armed forces.

- Germany and the other Central powers were forced to reduce their armed forces under the terms of the Paris Peace agreements (see Chapter 3).
- The Washington Conference in 1921, and subsequent treaties, limited the size of the British, US and Japanese navies (see Chapter 9).
- The League of Nations had been charged with the duty of securing disarmament under the terms of the Covenant. But it was not until 1932 that a Disarmament Conference actually met in Geneva. The delegates spent many months in debate from 1932 to 1934 but could not agree. The French were stubborn and, even before Hitler came to power, the German Government demanded equality with the other European powers. All hope of such agreement vanished when Germany left the Conference in October 1933 and announced, in March 1935, that it was rearming the German armed forces (see also page 233).

Britain, France and Italy reacted to the news of German rearmament by calling the Stresa Conference (April 1935) at which their leaders, Ramsay MacDonald (Britain), Mussolini (Italy) and Flandin and Laval (France), condemned the German repudiation of the Treaty of Versailles. They formed the Stresa Front to co-ordinate their opposition to German rearmament. But the alliance broke down when Mussolini invaded Abyssinia six months later.

FURTHER QUESTIONS AND EXERCISES

1 *Argue the case in 1919 for or against the League of Nations from the point of view of a) a US senator, b) Czechoslovakia, c) Germany.*

2 *Write brief notes on each of the following, a) the Locarno Pact, b) the Kellogg–Briand Pact, c) the Disarmament Conferences of the 1930s.*

THE WAR SALAD

Punch, *11 December 1935*

MUSSOLINI "LET ME SEE — THEY SAY 'A MISER FOR THE VINEGAR: A SPENDTHRIFT FOR THE OIL, AND A MADMAN TO STIR IT.' BUT — IS THE OIL GOING TO HOLD OUT?"

3 *To which crisis does this refer? What was the point of the cartoon?*

4 *Describe the structure and organisation of the League of Nations. What did the following do: a) the Secretariat, b) the Assembly, c) the Council, d) the Court of International Justice?*

Chapter Eleven
Origins of the Second World War

INTRODUCTION

NINETEEN YEARS AFTER

Punch, *1 March 1933*

Will the Maniac break loose again?

> **1** *Why was the cartoon called 'Nineteen Years After'?*
>
> **2** *Who was 'the Maniac'?*
>
> **3** *Why was this cartoon drawn in March 1933?*

On 3 September 1939, Neville Chamberlain, the British prime minister, declared war on Germany. He said what a blow it had been, to him personally, to know that his 'long struggle to win peace' had failed. This chapter is about that 'long struggle to win peace'. His policy, and that of French leaders in the 1930s, is usually called *appeasement*. This is a policy of trying to buy off dictators by negotiating agreements which give in to some of their demands under threat of war. At best, this type of policy can only delay the ambitions of a ruthless dictator like Hitler. Appeasement became an issue after 1933 when Hitler, step by step, dismantled the Treaty of Versailles. Fifteen years earlier, Britain and France imposed harsh terms at Versailles which had been specifically designed to stop Germany going to war again. Why, then, did France and Britain allow Germany to become the dominant power in Europe once more?

Part of the answer lies in the fact that many people were ashamed of the Paris Peace Treaties and could see that the German-speaking peoples had many genuine grievances. Germany had been forced to disarm but other countries had not done the same. German-speakers living in the borderlands of countries like Czechoslovakia had been unfairly treated. East Germans had been artificially separated from the rest of Germany by a strip of Poland called the Polish Corridor.

In the 1930s, many people in Britain and France were worried more by the spread of Communism than they were by Fascism. Russia's Communists had world revolution in mind. Communism had great appeal to desperate working people hit hard by the effects of the depression. Mussolini's Fascists were strongly anti-Communist; so too were Hitler's Nazis. Were they not suitable allies in the struggle against international Communism? Many people envied the way in which Mussolini's trains ran on time. There were no strikes under Fascist regimes. Hitler had even reduced unemployment with his public works and grandiose plans for the Third Reich.

Above all, statesmen in Britain and France could not forget the appalling slaughter of the First World War when their friends had been lost on the battlefields of Flanders. War had to be avoided at all costs. Anthony Eden told the League of Nations:

> There is in our judgement, no dispute between nations that cannot be settled by peaceful means.

Cartoon by Low in 1937. Anthony Eden is the man in front trying to stop Hitler and Mussolini from marching forward

> **1** *How has the artist drawn the soldiers compared with the two dictators? What was the point of the cartoon?*
>
> **2** *What was wrong with Eden's view that there is no dispute 'that cannot be settled by peaceful means'?*

ABYSSINIA

Wal Wal

Hitler and Mussolini had entirely different perceptions of the First World War from those of Anthony Eden, Harold Macmillan, Edouard Daladier, and other politicians in Britain and France. Fascism relished war. It saw military conquest as the road to national glory. This was one reason why Mussolini sent a modern army of 100 000 men into Abyssinia in 1935. It would be excellent war experience. Pride in a military victory would curb criticism of the regime and give renewed vigour to Fascist Italy.

Mussolini's opportunity came in December 1934 when an incident occurred at the small Abyssinian desert oasis of Wal Wal, close to the border with Italian Somaliland. Italian troops had camped at Wal Wal for years but Abyssinia wanted it back. A peaceful confrontation between the two sides suddenly escalated into battle and over a hundred soldiers were killed. The Italians demanded compensation and acknowledgement that Wal Wal was Italian. The dispute was put to the League of Nations for settlement.

Abyssinia was then one of only two independent states in Africa. It had been ruled by Haile Selassie as Emperor since 1930, and as the Regent, Ras Tafari, since 1916. Abyssinia became a member of the League of Nations in 1923 and later signed the Kellogg–Briand Pact (see page 215). She was fully entitled to the protection – 'collective security' – which membership of the League conferred on all its members.

The Italians argued that Abyssinia should never have been admitted to the League. The Italian delegate, Baron Aloisi, claimed on 10 October 1935 that Abyssinia had flouted the terms of the Covenant which dealt with human rights. He said that slavery still flourished there. Prisoners of war were mutilated. Minority tribes had been eliminated. Abyssinia should have been expelled from the League.

Italy's Reasons

The Italians, however, had other reasons for wanting Abyssinia.

- In 1919, Italy had not been given any of the League of Nations mandates to administer a former German colony in Africa. Mussolini was determined to grab 'a place in the sun' for Italy (see page 52).

- They wanted revenge. Italian national pride had been badly hurt in 1896 when an Abyssinian army heavily defeated 12 000 Italian soldiers at the battle of Adowa. After their victory in 1936, the Italians erected a war memorial, 'To the Dead of Adowa – Avenged at last'.
- Italy needed to expand. She wanted a colony with resources and raw materials which she could develop and which could be used to settle emigrants from an overcrowded Italy.

War

Despite the fact that Italy had signed a Treaty of Friendship with Abyssinia in August 1928, promising 'durable peace and perpetual friendship' between the two nations, Mussolini went ahead with plans for an invasion. These were hardly kept secret. It was obvious to everyone in 1935 that Italy would invade Abyssinia. Italian troops were mobilised in the spring of 1935 and sent by troopship through the Suez Canal to the Italian Somaliland (south of Abyssinia) and Eritrea (to the north). The League investigated the Wal Wal incident but the solution it proposed was unacceptable to Italy. The newspapers in the summer and autumn of 1935 were filled with gloomy predictions. War correspondents were sent to Africa. Time was running out. What would Mussolini do?

AT THE HOTEL DE LA PAIX

"DEARY ME! DOES THIS MEAN THAT
THE NICE ITALIAN GENTLEMAN IS GOING
TO LEAVE US?"

A Punch *cartoon, 3 July 1935*

THE AWFUL WARNING

FRANCE AND ENGLAND (together?)

"WE DON'T WANT YOU TO FIGHT,
BUT, BY JINGO, IF YOU DO,
WE SHALL PROBABLY ISSUE A JOINT MEMORANDUM
SUGGESTING A MILD DISAPPROVAL OF YOU."

B Punch *cartoon, 14 August 1935*

"BY THAT SIN FELL THE ANGELS"

THE EXILED KAISER "THINK TWICE BEFORE
YOU DEFY WORLD OPINION.

I TRIED ONCE, AND FOUND IT DIDN'T PAY."

C Punch *cartoon, 28 August 1935*

THE BLACK MAN'S BURDEN

ABYSSINIA "I SOMETIMES WONDER WHETHER
IT WAS WORTH MY WHILE JOINING THIS
EUROPEAN LEAGUE."

D Punch *cartoon, 11 September 1935*

---

1 *What was the 'Hotel de la Paix' in cartoon A? What picture clue tells us that this cartoon deals with Mussolini's plans to invade Abyssinia? What was the point of the cartoon?*

2 *Look closely at cartoon D. What was 'The Black Man's Burden'? How were the European nations trying to exploit Abyssinia in 1935?*

3 *What do you think were the main talking points in Europe in 1935, a) in early July, b) in early August, c) in late August?*

4 *This Music Hall song was extremely popular in 1878 (at a time when war with Russia was being advocated by some hotheads):*

> *'We don't want to fight,*
> *But, by jingo if we do,*
> *We've got the ships, we've got the men,*
> *We've got the money too.'*

a) *What is meant by 'jingoism'? How did it get this name?*
b) *What attitude do you think France and England were taking to Mussolini's proposed invasion of Abyssinia in early August 1935?*
c) *Was it jingoism to demand something tougher than trade sanctions against Italy in 1935?*
d) *What was the point of cartoon B?*

5 *How does cartoon C appear to contradict cartoon B?*

Invasion

At five o'clock on the morning of October 2, the thunderous roar of a column of motor trucks awakened me. I rose and went down to Asmara's main street, Viale Benito Mussolini. The procession of motor trucks continued hour after hour, manned by drivers sunburned to the colour of old leather, dusty, begoggled, with their mouths and noses swathed in handkerchiefs to keep them from breathing the clouds of talcum-like dust. On some of the trucks was chalked the inscription, 'Rome to Addis Ababa' ... At one a.m. .... I started to General De Bono's observation post on the brow on Coatit Mountain ...

Four-fifty-five a.m. I write first a series of bulletins for release at exactly 5 a.m.; only six words, 'Italians commenced invasion Ethiopia 5 a.m.' These six words will set thousands of presses spinning in forty-nine countries, spewing out extras. At 8.03 a.m. I heard a series of heavy explosions from the direction of Adowa ... Within a few minutes nine huge, tri-motored Caproni bombers glistening in the early morning light droned back towards Asmara.

Webb Miller (an American journalist), *I Found No Peace*, Gollancz, 1937

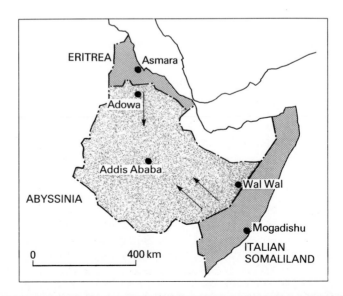

Abyssinia in 1935

1 *In which direction were the trucks moving through Asmara? Why did they start moving 24 hours before the invasion started? What clue tells us the Italians had been preparing the invasion for many weeks?*

2 *What precautions did the Italian transport drivers take? Why? What does that tell you about the nature of the campaign facing the Italian forces in Abyssinia?*

Despite the bravery of the Abyssinian soldiers, the result was never in doubt, since they were ill equipped to face a modern army armed with the very latest weapons. Four days after the invasion, the League of Nations branded Italy the aggressor and agreed to impose economic sanctions prohibiting trade with the Italians. In this way it hoped to make Mussolini withdraw his troops. But the sanctions were ineffective, since the League failed to include a ban on oil supplies. Mussolini later admitted to Hitler that if oil had been banned he would have had to call off the invasion.

In December the British foreign minister, Sir Samuel Hoare, and the French prime minister, Pierre Laval, proposed a secret plan which would have given Italy much of the territory she had already conquered but would have guaranteed Abyssinia's frontiers against further attack. The news was leaked before it became official and the Hoare–Laval Plan was scrapped in the face of scandalised public opinion, which saw it as appeasement in the face of naked aggression. Even so, no effective alternative plan was ever put forward to deter Mussolini.

The Italians completed their conquest in May 1936 with the capture of Addis Ababa, the Abyssinian capital. Italy could now develop it as an Italian colony. Mussolini combined all three colonies (Abyssinia, Eritrea and Somaliland) into one and called it Italian East Africa.

1 *Quote evidence from the extract on page 224 to support Mussolini's claim that an oil ban would have forced him to call off the invasion.*

2 *What action should the League of Nations have taken under the terms of the Covenant signed by all the member nations (see pages 207–8)? Argue the case for or against taking such action.*

End of Sanctions

Sources A and B, which follow, are extracts from two important speeches made during the debate at the Assembly of the League of Nations (30 June–4 July 1936). The League voted to end trade sanctions against Italy.

Source A

The Emperor Haile Selassie

The issue before the Assembly today is not merely a question of a settlement in the matter of Italian aggression. It is a question of collective security; of the very existence of the League; of the trust placed by States in international treaties; of the value of promises made to small States that their integrity and their independence shall be respected and assured. I ask the fifty-two nations. What are they willing to do for Ethiopia? What measures do they intend to take? What answer am I to take back to my people?

The Emperor Haile Selassie, in *Speeches and Documents on International Affairs*, edited by Arthur Berriedale Keith, Oxford, 1938

Source B

Anthony Eden, who later gained a reputation as an opponent of appeasement, answered that, while the Emperor's appeal had evoked sympathy,

the facts should be squarely faced . . . The course of military events and the local situation in Ethiopia have brought us to a point at which the sanctions at present in force are incapable of reversing the order of events in that country . . . In our view [i.e. that of the British Government] it is only military action that could now produce this result. I cannot believe that, in present world conditions, such military action could be considered a possibility. . . . So far as His Majesty's Government is concerned, our policy has been based on the principles for which the League stands.

Anthony Eden, British foreign secretary, in *Speeches and Documents on International Affairs*, edited by Arthur Berriedale Keith, Oxford, 1938

Source C

An American foreign correspondent spoke up for Mussolini in 1937,

I felt that the Italian invasion was in fact no less and no more reprehensible than the series of unprovoked aggressions and land grabs by which England, France, Belgium, Spain, Portugal and Germany had gobbled up the entire continent of Africa, excepting Ethiopia and Liberia, previous to the World War . . .

I had seen how the other Allies after the World War cheated Italy out of her share of the territorial war loot. And I knew, as other European nations admitted, that Italy needed territorial expansion to care for her rapidly increasing population, whose previous outlets by emigration had been cut off by immigration restrictions of the United States and the South

American republics. I also realised that Italy needed raw materials more urgently than any other European nation . . . Of all the populous areas in the world, I found Ethiopia the most savage, uncivilised, and unknown. Its social fabric rested upon the institution of slavery . . . Not one person in ten thousand could read or write; intertribal wars and criminal punishments involved cruel mutilations; unchecked disease was rapidly killing off the population, and the vast majority lived in filth, poverty, and degradation.

Webb Miller, *I Found No Peace*, Gollancz, 1937

---

1 *Make a list of Miller's reasons for backing Mussolini's invasion of Abyssinia. Write a reply to each argument on your list.*

2 *Which of Miller's arguments accuses Britain and France of hypocrisy? Was he justified in saying this? Were Abyssinia's alleged backwardness and Italy's need for raw materials and room for expansion sufficient reasons to justify Mussolini's invasion?*

3 *Was Anthony Eden right or wrong in his speech to the League of Nations? Would you have been prepared to fight for a League of Nations' force against Italy in 1936? If not, why not?*

4 *How did Haile Selassie effectively put an end to the League of Nations as an influential world body?*

5 *Was Eden justified in claiming, 'So far as His Majesty's Government is concerned, our policy has been based on the principles for which the League stands'? Was it?*

The Axis Pact

Hitler and Mussolini in 1938

Italy resented British and French interference in the Abyssinian Crisis and the actions of the League. This is why Italy left the League of Nations in 1937. By then, Mussolini was already drawing closer to Hitler. On 21 October 1936, he signed the Axis Pact (see page 69) with Germany. On 6 November 1937, he joined Germany and Japan in agreeing the Anti-Comintern Pact against the spread of international Communism. A triumphant Ribbentrop claimed that Germany and Italy would keep Communism at bay in Europe, while Japan would do the same in the Far East. Both Britain and the United States saw the new alliance as a threat to their own special interests in Europe, the Mediterranean and the Pacific.

One reason why Germany and Italy had come closer together was their joint interest in the future of Spain. Both were heavily involved in the Spanish Civil War, aiding their fellow Fascist, General Franco, in his rebellion against the democratically-elected, left-wing, Republican government of Spain.

THE SPANISH CIVIL WAR

The Republic

Communists, Basque and Catalan Separatists (seeking independence for Catalonia and the Basque country in the border region close to France), Socialists, Anarchists (who wanted to abolish the government), Syndicalists (a trade union movement), Nationalists, and Falangists (a would-be Fascist working-class movement) were just some of the different groupings of left- and right-wing activists in Spain before 1936.

The right-wing parties wanted to preserve the privileges of the landed classes, including the dominant roles of the Catholic Church and the army in Spain. Yet the liberal and left-wing parties had greater reason on their side. Over half of Spain was owned by only 1 per cent of the population and the Church had huge estates as well. The army took a quarter of Spain's national budget and was top heavy with officers.

Revolution

Spanish Government forces (Republicans) in action against Franco's Nationalists in Toledo in 1936

On 18 July 1936 General Franco led an army revolt against the Republican Government, which the Spanish people had elected to power only a few months earlier by a majority of nearly 5 million votes to 4 million. Franco's supporters (the Falangists, Nationalists, Church, landowners, industrialists and middle classes) were afraid that the Government, which was supported by Liberals as well as by Socialists and Communists, might create the conditions which would enable the Communists to stage a 'Bolshevik' Revolution in Spain. They struck first. The rebellion began in Spanish Morocco and soon spread to the mainland of Spain.

The resulting civil war lasted just under three years. It was marked by the most appalling atrocities on both sides and ended in the deaths (many of them cold-blooded executions) of between half a million to 1 million Spaniards plus 20 000 of the 60 000 volunteers from Europe and America who joined the International Brigade fighting on the Republican side. Many Communists and Socialists in Britain and France felt it their duty to fight against the 'forces of Fascism'. Equally, some volunteers (see Source C on page 230) felt a similar call to fight on the side of the Nationalists against Bolshevism.

Foreign Intervention

Not surprisingly, Europe's Fascists offered their support to the Spanish Nationalists. Mussolini sent 50 000 Italian soldiers ('Fascist volunteers') to fight for Franco. Together with Hitler, he supplied Franco with weapons, munitions and aircraft. This interference in Spain's internal affairs caused a world outcry but there was little the other powers could, or wanted, to do about it. Stalin reacted by supplying some arms, weapons and troops to the Republican forces.

France had an agreement to supply the Spanish Government with arms but, not wishing to get involved, helped Britain to form a Non-Intervention Committee to try to prevent arms and munitions reaching either side. This only served to weaken the Republican forces, while doing little to curb the activities of Hitler and Mussolini.

---

1 *Was there any justification for the German, Italian and Soviet intervention in the Spanish Civil War?*

2 *Why did the League of Nations play little part in bringing the war to an end?*

General Franco (1892–1975)

Francisco Franco was born in 1892 and served in the army, reaching the rank of general by the time of the Spanish Civil War in 1936. His rebellion against the elected Republican Government was supported by both Hitler and Mussolini. This, together with his right-wing, Nationalist policies, the one-party state, and his status in Spain as 'the leader' (*El Caudillo*), led observers to assume he was Fascist too.

In fact, there was little persecution of Jews in Spain. Franco kept his distance from the other Fascist leaders. Spain stayed neutral during the War, for instance, despite Nazi pressure to join the conflict. This is why Franco's Falangist government survived after 1945, at a time when democracies were being restored in Germany and Italy. He died in 1975.

Guernica

When bombers destroyed the town of Guernica in northern Spain on 26 April 1937, the world was horrified, not least because it showed the terrors which air raids would bring in wars to come. But, as you can see from these sources, the Nationalists and their Fascist allies would not admit responsibility for the raid. They blamed the Republicans instead.

Source A

We were about eighteen miles east of Guernica . . . my heart shot into my mouth when I looked. Over the tops of some hills appeared a flock of planes. A dozen or so bombers were flying high. But down much lower, seeming just to skim the treetops were six Heinkel 52 fighters. The bombers flew on towards Guernica . . .

[Later] I saw a priest in one group. I stopped the car and went up to him. 'What happened Father?' I asked. His face was blackened, his clothes in tatters. He couldn't talk. He just pointed to the flames, still about four miles away, then whispered, 'Aviones . . . bombas . . . mucho, mucho' . . .

One middle-aged man spoke English. He told me, 'At four, before the market closed, many aeroplanes came. They dropped bombs. Some came low and shot bullets into the streets . . .' I moved among survivors. They had the same story to tell, aeroplanes, bullets, bombs, fire. Within twenty-four hours, when the grim story was told to the world, Franco was going to brand these shocked, homeless people as liars. So-called British experts were going to come to Guernica, weeks afterwards . . . and deliver pompous judgments: 'Guernica was set on fire wilfully by the Reds'.

Noel Monks, *Eyewitness*, Muller, 1955

Source B

On 28 April Guernica fell. Foreign journalists with the Nationalists were next told that, while 'a few bomb fragments' had been found in Guernica, most of the damage had been caused by Basque incendiarists . . . later, the word 'Garnika' was found in the diary for 26 April of a German pilot shot down by the Basques. The pilot explained that this referred to a girl he knew in Hamburg . . .

But the truth of the story has long since been known. In October 1937, a Nationalist staff officer told a *Sunday Times* correspondent: 'We bombed it, and bombed it and bombed it, and *bueno* why not?' The German air ace, Adolf Galland, who shortly afterwards joined the Condor Legion admitted that the Germans were responsible . . . Göring himself admitted in 1946 that Germany had regarded Guernica as a testing ground.

Hugh Thomas, *The Spanish Civil War*, Pelican, 1965

Source C

To compensate for their loss of Bilbao the Republicans achieved in this campaign their greatest propaganda victory of the war: the myth of Guernica, according to which that ancient centre of Basque liberties was set alight and totally destroyed by German Stukas. The truth was quite different, as I learned at the time from two journalist friends, an Englishman and a Frenchman, who entered the town with the first Nationalist troops on 29th April and closely questioned the inhabitants . . . The Nationalist – not the German – air force did bomb Guernica, an important communications centre crowded at the time with troops, and hit the railway station and an arms factory. The burning and destruction of the town, however, were the work of Republican militiamen . . . they had done the same to Irun and other Basque towns I myself visited.

Peter Kemp (a volunteer who fought for the Nationalists) in *History of the 20th Century*, Purnell, 1969

Source D

Picasso's painting of Guernica, painted in May 1937

Source E

In Berlin, the Nazi Minister of War, Field Marshal von Blomberg, sent the [Condor] Legion High Command repeated cables demanding to know who had bombed Guernica. According to Sergeant-Telegraphist Kurt Albrecht, he was ordered to reply: 'Not Germans'.

Years later, Squadron Leader Freiherr von Beust said that it was about this time that 'we were suddenly told to "hush up" about the raid.' . . . Most members of the [Condor] Legion who were involved in the planning and execution of the raid on Guernica died in World War II. We talked to many of those who survived; they, too, were anxious that at last the truth, however painful, should emerge.

Gordon Thomas and Max Morgan-Witts, *The Day Guernica Died*, Hodder and Stoughton, 1975

1 *Which of these sources are, a) primary, b) secondary sources? Which are based on eyewitness evidence?*

2 *Did Picasso support the Republicans or Franco's Nationalists? Describe the details in his painting which tell you how he reacted to, and what he felt about, the air raid on Guernica.*

3 *Which source tells a different story from that of the others? How does the writer justify his case?*

4 *All four written sources use the words 'the truth' or 'liars' in describing what did, or did not happen, at Guernica. What do you think was 'the truth'? Which evidence do you find most convincing? Why? Who bombed Guernica? Write a short essay, backed by evidence, explaining what you think happened on 26 April 1937.*

Results

THE QUESTION

Punch, *30 March 1938*   **"Was this done for *my* sake? If not, for whom?"**

The war came to an end in March 1939 with the surrender of Madrid. Many Republicans were later executed in the reprisals which took place as Franco took the powers of a dictator. He owed his victory partly to the superiority of his professional soldiers, partly to the fact that his right-wing parties were more united than those of the left-wing, and partly to the foreign aid he received from Germany and Italy.

As for Hitler and Mussolini, their armed forces (especially the bomber and fighter pilots) had gained invaluable experience fighting a modern war.

HITLER'S MARCH TOWARDS WAR

Intentions

Whether Hitler set out deliberately in 1933 to achieve world domination is a matter of debate. If every promise he ever made is taken as representing his foreign policy, then there seems little doubt that he intended to enlarge the boundaries of Germany well beyond those of 1914. But some experts believe he had no master plan and had no real idea of what he intended to do. They think he just exploited opportunities as and when they arose. Initially, at least, he seemed to know just how far he could go without provoking Britain and France. He dismantled the Treaty of Versailles, stealthily, clause by clause. He didn't do it all at once. His success in putting Germany back on her feet, albeit at the expense of many thousands of imprisoned intellectuals, Jews, trade unionists and other potential opponents, gave him the support and backing of the vast majority of the German people. When he was successful, as he was before 1942, they cheered and applauded. Newsreel film of his reception after the Fall of France in 1940 leaves no doubt that, in Germany, Hitler was regarded as a hero.

Rearmament

One of Hitler's first actions was to rearm Germany's armed forces. As you saw in Chapter 3, the Treaty of Versailles severely restricted the size and nature of the German army and navy. It stopped Germany from creating an air force. In 1933 the German army, officially limited to 100 000 men, was smaller than that of Czechoslovakia (140 000) or Poland (270 000). This was intolerable to Hitler.

In October 1933, Germany withdrew from the Disarmament Conference. In other words, Germany proposed to rearm. Göring had already started to form a German air force (the Luftwaffe). Pilots were trained privately and factories were producing warplanes. The Allies knew about this in 1934 but made no effective protest. On 16 March 1935, Hitler shocked the world by announcing plans to create a conscript army of over half a million men organised *'in 12 Korpskommandos und 36 Divisionen'.*

Nine days later, on 25 March 1935, Hitler met two British cabinet ministers, Sir John Simon and Anthony Eden, in Berlin where he told them that his actions were directed at the Soviet Union, not the West.

> We are only safe against the Bolshevists if we have armaments which they respect.

When Sir John Simon argued that the rearmament clauses of the Treaty of Versailles could not be broken by Germany on her own,

> Hitler replied with his well known thesis that it was not Germany but the other Powers that had first broken the disarmament provisions of the

Treaty of Versailles, in that they had failed to carry out the clearly expressed undertaking to disarm themselves.

[Hitler told them],

We shall not let conscription be touched but we are prepared to negotiate regarding the strength of armed forces. Our only condition is parity [equality] on land and in the air with our most strongly armed neighbour.

Dr Paul Schmidt, *Hitler's Interpreter*, edited by R.H.C. Steed, Heinemann, 1951

Hitler also said he wanted to enlarge the German navy until it was one-third the size of the Royal Navy.

His actions were condemned by the Council of the League of Nations on 17 April 1935. Six days earlier, on 11 April 1935, the British and French prime ministers and their foreign ministers had seen Mussolini at Stresa on Lake Maggiore and agreed,

to oppose with all suitable means any unilateral [one-sided] denunciation of treaties.

But the effectiveness of this protest was soon set at nought by the action of Italy in Abyssinia and by the signing of the Anglo-German Naval Agreement in June 1935. This limited the size of Germany's navy to 35 per cent of the size of the Royal Navy, as Hitler had earlier demanded. When the British foreign minister asked how long the agreement should last, Ribbentrop replied, '*Ewig*', which means 'for ever'!

Since Germany had already been banned at Versailles from building submarines, to France and other states it looked as though Britain was accepting Hitler's right to rearm. Laval protested that

A question which affects all the signatories of the Treaty of Versailles has been treated more or less as a private matter between Germany and Great Britain.

Meanwhile France had already taken steps to safeguard her own position. Pierre Laval negotiated a treaty of alliance, on 2 May 1935, with the Soviet Union, Hitler's avowed enemy. When Göring saw Laval later that same month, he greeted him with the words,

I trust you got on well at Moscow with the Bolsheviks, Monsieur Laval.

---

1 *What do you think Göring meant by that remark?*

2 *Why do you think Germany was allowed to rearm, despite the restrictions placed on German rearmament in the Treaty of Versailles only 16 years earlier? Had Hitler any genuine reason to fear the Soviet Union?*

3 Write an explanatory caption for the cartoon by Low on page 220.

4 What merit was there in Hitler's argument, that since the Western powers had not observed all the clauses of the Treaty of Versailles, why should Germany do so on her own?

5 If you had been a politician in Nazi Germany in 1935, how would you have interpreted the actions of Britain, France and Italy in the three months or so following the announcement of Germany's rearmament plans on 16 March?

The Rhineland

CLASSIFIED RESULTS   FINAL NIGHT

Don't be Vague — ASK FOR **Haig**

Evening Standard

To-morrow's Weather— Bright periods ; showers.

Lighting-up Time To-day 6.19 p.m.

No. 34,799   LONDON, SATURDAY, MARCH 7, 1936   ONE PENNY

—BUT WAIT UNTIL YOU'VE TASTED **Dunville's** OLD IRISH WHISKY THERE'S NOTHING BETTER

GERMAN TROOPS ENTER RHINELAND

Hitler Denounces Locarno And Offers New Pacts

FOOTBALL RESULTS And League Tables BACK PAGE

25 YEARS' PEACE WITH FRANCE | RE-ENTRY INTO THE LEAGUE

Hurried Talks in Paris Follow Breaking of Treaties

HITLER TO-DAY SMASHED THE LOCARNO AND VERSAILLES TREATIES BY SEND-ING TROOPS INTO THE DEMILITARISED RHINE ZONE.

FRANTICALLY CHEERING CROWDS THREW FLOWERS AT THE SOLDIERS AS THEY MARCHED, WITH DRUMS BEATING AND COLOURS FLYING, INTO COLOGNE, MAINZ, COBLENCE AND FRANKFURT.

In Berlin Hitler handed to the Ambassadors of Britain, France, Italy and Belgium, the guarantor Powers, a Note which said : "The Government declare themselves liberated from the obligations imposed on them by the Treaties of Versailles and Locarno. They have effected during the night of Friday and Saturday the re-occupation of the Rhineland zone. The operation is now being completed."

Front page of the Evening Standard, 7 March 1936

I was in a tram passing near [Cologne] cathedral shortly before noon, when we noticed several groups of police and police wagons. A passenger asked the conductor what was happening.

He replied that the soldiers were marching in. 'What, French soldiers?' asked the passenger. 'No, the German army', was the reply. 'The Rhineland is to be re-militarised.'

The Daily Telegraph, 9 March 1936

Hitler deliberately sent a small contingent of soldiers into the demilitarised Rhineland to test Allied reaction. This, too, was a blatant breach of the Treaty of Versailles (and of the Locarno Pact). But as Hitler hoped and expected, the Allies did nothing, even though many German generals had warned him that the reoccupation of the militarised zone would mean certain war. Hitler himself admitted to his personal interpreter, Dr Paul Schmidt,

The forty-eight hours after the march into the Rhineland were the most nerve-racking in my life. If the French had then marched into the Rhineland, we would have had to withdraw with our tails between our legs, for the military resources at our disposal would have been wholly inadequate for even a moderate resistance.

Dr Paul Schmidt, *Hitler's Interpreter*, edited by R.H.C. Steed, Heinemann, 1951

But the French did not make a move. Nor did the British. Once again the League of Nations did nothing positive to uphold the Treaty of Versailles. In any case many people could see no good reason why Germany should not be allowed to deploy her own troops wherever she pleased – in her own country.

---

1 *Refer back to Chapter 7 and the section on France in the 1930s. Why do you think Germany was allowed to re-militarise the Rhineland in 1936 without intervention by France?*

2 *What was its effect on the border between Germany and France?*

Anschluss

VIENNA, February 16 [1938]
A terrible thing has happened. We learned the day before yesterday about Berchtesgaden. Hitler took Schuschnigg [the Chancellor of Austria] for a ride, demanded he appoint several Nazis led by Seyss-Inquart to the Cabinet, amnesty [free] all Nazi prisoners, and restore the political rights of the Nazi Party – or invasion by the *Reichswehr*.

William L. Shirer, *Berlin Diary*, Hamish Hamilton, 1941

Hitler's ultimatum forced von Schuschnigg to admit Nazis into his government. Three weeks later, on 9 March, Schuschnigg suddenly announced a plebiscite or referendum for the following Sunday. Austrians would be able to vote whether or not they wanted to be free and independent. Hitler saw this as a threat to his plans for a union of all the German-speaking peoples. Again he threatened to invade Austria, this time if Schuschnigg went ahead with the plebiscite. Again Schuschnigg capitulated in the face of a threat. But Hitler had further demands to make. In a broadcast, Schuschnigg told his fellow Austrians that Hitler had demanded that the Austrian President, 'nominate as Chancellor a person designated by the German government ... otherwise German troops would invade Austria'.

Schuschnigg resigned and was replaced by the Austrian Nazi leader Arthur Seyss-Inquart who immediately invited in German armed forces 'to help preserve the peace'. At dawn, the next day, 12 March 1938, the German army crossed into Austria.

> Cheers greeted German troops as they arrived over the frontier and came into Austrian towns. Swastikas hung from windows, crowds gave the Nazi salute; buttonholes, not bullets, greeted the marching men as they penetrated further into the land where Hitler was born.
>
> *These Tremendous Years*, Daily Express Publications, 1938

Front page of the News Chronicle, 12 March 1938

On 13 March 1938, Seyss-Inquart announced that Austria was now a province of Germany's Third Reich. Three days later Hitler drove through

---

NEWS CHRONICLE, Saturday, March 12, 1938.

News Chronicle

No. 28,662   ONE PENNY   SATURDAY, MARCH 12, 1938

POSTAGE in U.K., Canada, and Newfoundland ... 1d. Other Places Abroad 1½d.

Hitler Marches Troops Into Austria: Fuehrer's Deputy Flies To Vienna

BERLIN ORDERS SCHUSCHNIGG OUT OF OFFICE

Nation Told Not To Resist Invaders

HITLER INVADED AUSTRIA LAST NIGHT. HE THUS DROVE FROM OFFICE CHANCELLOR KURT VON SCHUSCHNIGG, WHO HAD PLANNED TO HOLD ON SUNDAY A PLEBISCITE TO DECIDE WHETHER THE NATION STOOD FOR A "FREE, GERMAN AND INDEPENDENT STATE."

At 7 p.m. Schuschnigg went to the microphone in Vienna and broadcast:

"The German Government sent President Miklas an ultimatum that unless my Government fell in with the proposals of the German Government, German troops would march into Austria.

"I declare before all the world that reports of workers' unrest in Austria, and of blood flowing in the streets, are fabrications from A to Z.

HERR ENDER

Suggested As New Chancellor

MUNICH IN FERMENT AS NAZIS MOVE

Reservists Called Up, Cars Seized

From Our Own Correspondent

MUNICH, Friday.

MUNICH woke this morning to find itself in a state of mobilisation and to read the first news of Dr. von Schuschnigg's proposal to hold a plebiscite on Austrian independence.

Early in the day large detachments of regular troops and units of Brown Shirts and Black Guards were seen driving through the streets, curiously enough in a northerly direction.

Dispatch riders were racing along, breaking all the rules of the road.

Reservists, especially those with fast cars, were called up and their cars were commandeered.

The municipal buses were also seized and the "Motor Caravan Journalists"—a fleet of lorries with most elaborate wireless, ambulance and complete equipment—left their garages before daybreak.

Drone of Planes

LATE NEWS

MINISTERS READY IF NEEDED

The Political Correspondent writes: Cabinet Ministers had not received any instruction from Downing Street last night to "stand by" in case the

BRITAIN'S PROTEST

On the Government's instructions, the British Ambassador in Berlin (Sir Nevile Henderson) last night called upon the German Government and, in reference to the contents of the second German ultimatum to Austria, registered a protest in the strongest possible terms against "such a use of coercion, backed by force, against an independent State, in

Vienna in his native Austria. Crowds tried to break through the police cordons shouting, 'We want to see our Führer! Hitler! Hitler!' A British reporter said that the older men and women had 'tears of joy in their eyes'.

A month later Austrians (and Germans) got a chance to vote on whether they wanted the union (Anschluss) to take place or not. They did so by a massive 99 per cent of those qualified to vote! By then the persecution of Austria's Jews had already begun.

---

1 *What evidence is there that the Austrian people genuinely wanted the Anschluss? What discrepancy is there between the actual vote in the plebiscite in April 1938 and Hitler's reaction to von Schuschnigg's referendum proposal only a month earlier?*

2 *What arguments do you think were used by some people in Britain and France to justify the merging of Austria with Germany? What merit is there in such arguments?*

3 *What action do you think the League of Nations could have taken over the Anschluss? In what circumstances would they have been justified in using military force?*

THE MUNICH CRISIS

The Sudetenland

Konrad Henlein

In 1937 Konrad Henlein, leader of the local Nazi Party, asked Hitler for assistance in solving the problems of the large German minority living in the Sudetenland region of Czechoslovakia. This was one of the states which had been created out of the old Austro-Hungarian empire. There were about 3 million Germans living there in a country of 15 million people. Although Czechoslovakia was a democracy, the German minority claimed, with some justice, that the Czechs (about 7 million of them) discriminated against them in the civil service and when making promotions in the army. The minority group of Slovaks (just over 2 million) also had cause to resent Czech domination.

Neither Germans nor Slovaks could count on receiving justice, in their own tongue, in the law courts. Unemployment was chronic in the German region, about twice the rate of the country at large, but unemployment benefit for Germans was wholly inadequate, and much lower than for Czechs.

K. Feiling, *The Life of Neville Chamberlain*, Macmillan, 1946

Reforms had been promised but the German minority could see a much better future for the Sudetenland if it formed part of Hitler's Germany, where unemployment was rapidly declining. Konrad Henlein's Sudeten German Homeland Party was formed and gained the eventual support of most of the German-speakers living in Czechoslovakia. During the spring and summer of 1938, they began to agitate for self-government, encouraged by Hitler and the German Nazis. At a conference in Berlin, on 29 March 1938, Ribbentrop reassured the Sudeten German Homeland Party,

> The Sudeten Germans must realise that they are backed up by a nation of 75 million which will not tolerate a continued suppression of the Sudeten Germans by the Czechoslovak Government.

Czechoslovakia reacted by calling up some of her reserve troops in May and stationing them in the Sudetenland.

---

1 What justification did Hitler have for the attitude he took to the Sudetenland problem?

2 If you thought Hitler was basically a reasonable man (which many British people did), what sympathy would you have had for Germany's attitude to rearmament in 1935, to the remilitarisation of the Rhineland in 1936, to Anschluss in the spring of 1938, and to Hitler's stand with regard to the Sudetenland in the summer of 1938? At what point would you have called a halt to the step by step breakdown of the Treaty of Versailles?

War Clouds

Neville Chamberlain

The war clouds gathered during the course of the summer. France confirmed she would come to Czechoslovakia's aid in the event of an invasion. Britain warned Germany that she too might be forced to take action if France went to war. In private, Chamberlain had already made his position clear. He told his sisters in a letter dated 20 March 1938,

> You have only to look at the map to see that nothing France or we could do could possibly save Czechoslovakia from being overrun by the Germans, if they wanted to do it. The Austrian frontier is practically open; the great Skoda munitions works are within easy bombing distance of the German aerodromes, the railways all pass through German territory, Russia is 100 miles [160 km] away. Therefore we could not help Czechoslovakia – she would simply be a pretext for going to war with Germany. That we could not think of unless we had a reasonable prospect of being able to beat her to her knees in a reasonable time, and of that I see no sign. I have therefore abandoned any idea of giving guarantees to Czechoslovakia, or the French in connection with her obligations to that country.

K. Feiling, *The Life of Neville Chamberlain*, Macmillan, 1946

1 *Neville Chamberlain had been, and still is, much reviled as a weak man committed to appeasement at all costs. What reasons did he give in March 1938 for not coming to the aid of Czechoslovakia? In your opinion, are these convincing reasons or are they the excuses of an appeaser?*

2 *In what circumstances did Chamberlain envisage resistance to Hitler's demands?*

3 *Would you have fought to preserve Czechoslovakia's frontiers in 1938?*

The Soviet Union proposed collective action to support the Czechs but neither Britain nor France trusted Stalin. The Soviet Union was not a democracy. The main news from Moscow in 1938 was of Purges not freedom.

In August, Germany started large scale military exercises near the Czech border. People began to think that there might really be a war. But voices were already being heard in France and Britain advising caution and recommending the partition of Czechoslovakia (i.e. separating the Sudetenland from the rest of the country). In early September the Czech Government announced far-reaching concessions to the Sudeten Germans. But these were now too late to mollify Hitler and the Nazis. Accordingly, the Czech proposals were rejected. On 12 September Hitler whipped up German support for the Sudeten Germans in a vitriolic speech at Nuremberg.

Peace Talks

Two days later Chamberlain made his first journey to see Hitler at Hitler's Alpine home at Berchtesgaden in Bavaria. Hitler would not budge. So on his return Chamberlain consulted the French and together they drew up a plan conceding the Sudetenland to Germany. The Czech government reluctantly agreed and Chamberlain made another trip to Germany, this time to the Rhine Valley, where he met Hitler at Godesberg on 22 September 1938. Once again he was bitterly disappointed at the outcome of the meeting. Hitler had new demands to make on Czech territory.

Pressure built up during the next few days. Poland (attacked by Hitler less than a year later), and Hungary, both demanded a share of Czech territory. Poland sent troops to the Czech border to support her claim. Russia prepared to intervene. Czechoslovakia rejected Hitler's latest demands. The Czech Government directly appealed to Britain and France for their support,

We rely upon the two great Western Democracies, whose wishes we have followed much against our own judgment, to stand by us in our hour of trial.

On 26 September Hitler made yet another vicious attack on Czechoslovakia in the Berlin Sports Palace before a vast crowd of 30 000. He threatened an invasion by the following Monday if his demands were not met:

> Our patience is at an end. Benes [the Czech President] will have to surrender this territory to us on October 1.

He also made a promise:

> It is the last territorial claim which I have to make in Europe, but it is the claim from which I do not recede and which I shall fulfil, God willing.

Meanwhile, Henlein's supporters armed themselves with rifles and formed *Freikorps* (Free Corps) to fight a guerrilla campaign against the Czech army – if it came to war. By now the Czech Government had declared martial law in the Sudetenland. Troops massed on the borders. The atmosphere in Europe was electric.

War Preparations

Most people feared the worst and expected war. Trenches were dug in London's parks. Air raid shelters were constructed. Gas masks were issued. Children were evacuated from London. On 27 September Neville Chamberlain broadcast to the people of Britain and told them,

> How horrible, fantastic, incredible it is that we should be digging trenches and trying on gas masks here because of a quarrel in a far away country between people of whom we know nothing.

That same day, Chamberlain also told the Czechs the stark truth, that if Germany crossed the Czech frontier,

> That must result in Bohemia being overrun and nothing that any other Power can do will prevent this fate for your own country and people, and this remains true whatever may be the ultimate issue of a possible world war.

---

1 *Did the Allies have any reason to believe Hitler when he said this 'is the last territorial claim which I have to make in Europe'?*

2 *If you had been a Czech citizen would you have been reassured by Neville Chamberlain's broadcast on 27 September?*

3 *Compare Neville Chamberlain's statement on the Sudetenland to the Czechs on 27 September 1938 with Anthony Eden's attitude to Abyssinia in July 1936 (see page 226).*

Although Chamberlain is generally regarded as an appeaser, he did mobilise the Royal Navy on 27 September. In other words, he prepared for immediate war. This may well have convinced Hitler that he really did mean business. Hitler is reported to have told Göring afterwards,

> Do you know why I finally yielded at Munich? I thought the Home Fleet might open fire.

However, thanks to the intervention of his fellow Fascist, Mussolini, Hitler was persuaded to call a final conference at Munich. Chamberlain was making a long speech in the House of Commons, on the grave prospects facing the nation, when a minister plucked at his coat and handed him a note. Chamberlain paused. Tension in the House rose. Then he turned to the waiting MPs and announced,

> Herr Hitler has just agreed to postpone his mobilisation for twenty-four hours and to meet me in conference with Signor Mussolini and Monsieur Daladier at Munich.

'Chips' Channon (Conservative) described how Parliament received the news,

> We stood on our benches, waved our order papers, shouted – until we were hoarse – a scene of indescribable enthusiasm – Peace must now be saved, and with it the world.

Harold Nicolson, a National Labour MP, remained seated and a Conservative behind hissed at him, 'Stand up, you brute!'

The Munich Agreement

Chamberlain flew to Germany once again. In Munich, on 29 and 30 September, 1938, he met the leaders of the other three powers (Germany, Italy, France) who had taken it upon themselves to decide the fate of Czechoslovakia. Russia, a guarantor of Czech frontiers, was not invited, much to Stalin's fury. As for Czechoslovakia, she, too, was not officially invited to Munich. A Czech delegation did fly there but, according to Dr Hubert Masarik of the Czech foreign ministry, 'The reception we met with at the aerodrome was roughly that accorded to police suspects'. A British official told them that, if they did not accept the decision of the Conference, 'you will have to settle your affairs all alone with the Germans'.

In fact, Czechoslovakia had already agreed to the main proposals for the future of the Sudetenland. The differences between the Munich Agreement and the earlier proposals at Godesberg were relatively slight. Some German historians think that Hitler even yielded at Munich, contrary to the view of Russian, Czech and many British and French historians, who think that Daladier and Chamberlain bowed to force once more.

The Munich Peace Agreement is forever associated with the idea of appeasement and the piece of paper which Chamberlain brandished to the crowd at the airport on his return.

This morning I had another talk with the German Chancellor, Herr Hitler. And here is the paper which bears his name upon it as well as mine. We regard the agreement signed last night, and the Anglo-German Naval Agreement, as symbolic of the desire of our two peoples never to go to war with one another again.

Chamberlain said Hitler jumped at the idea of signing the declaration, in which both leaders agreed to continue efforts 'to remove possible sources of difference and thus to contribute to assure the peace of Europe'. He told his sisters,

As the interpreter translated the words into German, Hitler frequently ejaculated '*Ja, Ja*', and at the end he said 'yes, I will certainly sign it'.

The interpreter, Dr Paul Schmidt, was left with a different impression,

My own feeling was that he [Hitler] agreed to the wording with a certain reluctance, and I believe he appended his signature only to please Chamberlain, without promising himself any too much from the effects of the declaration.

DAILY HERALD, October 1, 1938

Daily Herald

No. 7061   SATURDAY, OCTOBER 1, 1938   ONE PENNY

COME TO WOMEN'S FAIR OLYMPIA Nov 2nd–26th 1938

Easy on the t.. FRANKLY MILD TOBACCO 8d

MR. CHAMBERLAIN DECLARES
"IT IS PEACE FOR OUR TIME"

5,000 British Troops Will Be Sent To Sudetenland

PRAGUE'S DAY OF SORROW

To a frenzied welcome from tens of thousands of Londoners, Mr. Neville Chamberlain came home last night and announced to all the world : "I believe it is peace for our time."

GERMANS WILL MARCH AT NOON

The Premier had two agreements in his pocket:

1.—The Munich Four-Power Pact for the transfer of Sudetenland from Czechoslovakia to Germany; and

2.—An Anglo-German declaration of the "desire of

From a Window at No. 10

BUT—
Poles Rush Ultimatum

BY OUR OWN CORRESPONDENT
WARSAW, Friday night.

WITHIN 24 hours of one threat of an immediate war on the Czechs being averted, Poland to-night handed a new ultimatum to Prague.

Imposing a 24-hour time limit, the ultimatum insisted on an immediate answer to the demand that all Czech territory inhabited by Poles shall be evacuated at once.

A Warsaw Foreign Office spokesman announced that the Note would reach Prague by ten o'clock to-night.

An official communiqué explained that Czechoslovakia's answer to the Polish Note, sent last Tuesday, containing a detailed plan of frontier adjustments in Teschen Silesia, reached Warsaw at 1 p.m. to-day, but had been found unsatisfactory.

The Polish Government had therefore sent another Note requesting a "clear and precise" answer and the cession of the territory.

The answer to the Note is expected by noon to-morrow.

Simultaneously with the sending of the ultimatum the threat was

"will resort to measures which may have the gravest consequences."

Suggestions were made that Polish troops would enter the Teschen district of Czechoslovakia to-morrow at the same time that the Germans occupied the areas ceded to them.

The official wireless broadcast a message from Teschen which declared: "The hour is approaching when Polish troops will free the Poles in Czechoslovakia with their fixed bayonets."

Reports were circulated in Wa'd saw to-day of alleged "incidents" on the Czech border.

An urgent meeting was called, attended by General Smigly-Rydz, virtual Dictator of Poland, President Moscicki, the Premier, vice-Premier and Foreign Minister.

Colonel Beck, the Foreign Minister, then received in' turn the Ambassadors of Germany, France, Italy,

Headlines in the Daily Herald, *1 October 1938*

> **1** *What differences were there between Neville Chamberlain's account of his meeting with Hitler and the account written by Dr Paul Schmidt, Hitler's interpreter? How do you account for these differences?*
>
> **2** *How do you account for the 'frenzied welcome' which the* Daily Herald *said Londoners gave Chamberlain on his return to Downing Street?*

The Results of Munich

The fact remains that Hitler got almost everything he demanded through a peace treaty instead of having to use force to get the same concessions directly from Czechoslovakia. The four powers signed away a substantial part of Czechoslovakia, including most of that country's heavy industry, coal mines and fortifications, together with 3 million Sudeten Germans and 700 000 luckless Czechs.

- It encouraged Hitler to believe that when the crunch came neither Britain nor France would fight. Both had promised support to Czechoslovakia, and made warlike preparations, but in the end both failed to back Czechoslovakia with force.
- It convinced the Russians that neither Britain nor France could be relied upon to form a military alliance to guarantee existing frontiers. This is why the Soviet Union signed the notorious Nazi-Soviet Pact ten months later (see page 248).
- It provided Britain and France with a brief respite in which to begin rearmament in earnest. However it has been said that had Germany's enemies combined to take collective action (as Russia wanted), their combined forces would have heavily outnumbered those of the Germans. Czechoslovakia and France combined had over twice as many troops, Russia had four times as many, and the Royal Navy was far more powerful than the German navy.

Reactions to the Munich Agreement were almost always either definitely for or definitely against. Few people lacked a point of view on the subject. Some argued that Czechoslovakia had not been an issue 'that Britons should be asked to die for'. Some welcomed the fact 'that precious time had been won in which to rearm'. Others, no doubt recalling the First World War and recent events in Nanking and Guernica, were only too glad to be spared the abominations and horrors of modern warfare.

But there were many critics as well. Winston Churchill called it 'a disaster of the first magnitude'. Hitler said, 'that fellow Chamberlain has spoiled my entry into Prague'. A few days later he warned,

> We cannot tolerate any longer the tutelage of governesses . . . they should busy themselves with their own affairs and leave us in peace.

Clement Attlee (Leader of the British Labour Party) said,

We have seen a gallant and civilised democratic people betrayed and handed over to ruthless despotism.

Neville Chamberlain, himself, was in little doubt. As his car struggled through the cheering, jubilant crowds on his return (on 30 September 1938), he told Lord Halifax that 'all this will be over in three months'. And he warned the Cabinet that same day,

It would be madness for the country to stop rearming until we were convinced that other countries would act in the same way. For the time being, therefore, we should relax no particle of effort until our deficiencies have been made good.

Quoted by D.B. Adams in *History of the 20th Century*, Purnell, 1969

On 3 October 1938, he told the House of Commons,

Let no one think that because we have signed this agreement at Munich we can afford to relax our efforts in regard to the rearmament programme.

The following March, he told an audience,

I did not go there [i.e. to Munich] to get popularity . . . I have never denied that the terms which I was able to secure at Munich were not those that I myself would have desired.

K. Feiling, *The Life of Neville Chamberlain*, Macmillan, 1946

THE HAPPY ELEPHANTS, Picture Post, *15 October 1938.*
'The elephants are happy. They are flying about in the sky. The elephants are happy because they have got peace. For how long have the elephants got peace? Ah, that alas! no one can say'.

1 *What evidence is there that Neville Chamberlain was not quite as inept as he is often depicted? What alternative explanation is there of his actions at Munich?*

2 *Was Chamberlain right to warn Czechoslovakia, on 27 September, that if no agreement was reached, Hitler's troops would march into Czechoslovakia and, 'That must result in Bohemia being overrun and nothing that any other Power can do will prevent this fate for your own country and people'?*

3 *Who were the 'happy elephants'? Why were they happy? Why did* Picture Post *print this photograph?*

LAST YEAR OF PEACE

Bohemia, Moravia, the Memel

The following March, Hitler bullied the Prague Government once more and got the Czechs to agree to make Bohemia and Moravia into German Protectorates. Czechoslovakia now ceased to exist as an independent state. Chamberlain argued that this was not aggression, calling for a British military response. But within a week Hitler struck again and took the Memel, which was predominantly German, away from Lithuania. People who had cheered Chamberlain the previous September now set their teeth against appeasement.

The Polish Corridor

Hitler's next move was to take steps to link Germany to East Prussia, which as you can see from the map on page 249, was divided from the rest of the country by a strip of territory known as the Polish Corridor. This gave Poland an outlet to the sea and a port she could use – Danzig. But this 'free city' was predominantly German and had a government and a population which wanted to return to Germany. Poland stood firm against Hitler's demands and rumours of German troop movements prompted France and Britain to warn Germany that they guaranteed Poland's independence.

On 26 March 1939, Chamberlain wrote that he profoundly distrusted Russia and had no faith in her ability to act as an effective ally. In any case, Poland (part of the Russian Empire in 1917) hated the Russians as much as she hated the Germans. On 31 March Chamberlain gave the Poles a pledge:

any action which clearly threatened Polish independence, and which the Polish government accordingly considered it vital to resist with their national forces, His Majesty's Government would feel themselves bound at once to lend the Polish government all support in their power.

K. Feiling, *The Life of Neville Chamberlain*, Macmillan, 1946

AN OLD STORY RETOLD

Hitler and Mussolini in a cartoon from Punch, *5 April 1939*

HERR HITLER. 'IT'S ALL RIGHT; YOU KNOW THE PROVERB — "BARKING DOGS DON'T BITE"'?'
SIGNOR MUSSOLINI. 'OH, YES, *I* KNOW IT, AND *YOU* KNOW IT; BUT DOES THE DOG KNOW IT?'

This infuriated Hitler and he ordered his army to prepare to invade Poland. At the same time he renounced the agreements he had made with Poland (the 1934 Non-Aggression Treaty) and Britain (the 1935 Naval Agreement). The Soviet Union, alarmed by these moves, talked about collective action with Britain and France, but both countries were still reluctant to ally themselves closely with a Communist power and delayed making a decision about an alliance until it was too late. Meanwhile the pro-Western Russian foreign minister, Litvinov, was replaced by Molotov.

1 *What was the point of the cartoon? What private path was Hitler proposing to cross? Who was the barking dog? Why was there some doubt as to whether the dog would bite?*

2 *Which country could most easily have come to the aid of Poland? Was it Great Britain, France, or the Soviet Union?*

3 *Why do you think Britain and France were reluctant to ally themselves with the Soviet Union?*

War preparations were already being made in Britain. Plans to double the size of the Territorial Army were announced on March 29, civil defence plans (evacuation of children and provision of air raid shelters), and conscription were approved by Parliament in April. On 22 May 1939 Mussolini and Hitler signed a treaty of alliance, the Pact of Steel, which guaranteed immediate aid from the other partner in the event of war.

Then in August the bombshell fell. On the 23rd the world was told startling and blood-chilling news. The Soviet Union and Nazi Germany – hitherto the deadliest of enemies – had signed a Non-Aggression Pact in Moscow.

> In case one of the contracting parties [i.e. Germany] becomes the object of aggression by a third power [i.e. Poland], the other partner [i.e. Russia] shall not support the aforesaid third power [Poland] in any matter whatever.

Report in the *Daily Telegraph*, 26 August 1939

Russia's Stalin (centre) and foreign minister Molotov (right) with German foreign minister Ribbentrop (left), Moscow, 23 August, 1939

It was obvious now that Hitler intended to invade Poland. There was nothing to stop him. There would be no retaliation from the Red Army, the only armed force in Eastern Europe capable of pushing back the German forces. What the world didn't know was that, secretly, Germany and Russia had also agreed to partition Poland between them.

FURTHER QUESTIONS AND EXERCISES

1 *Read the extracts which follow and say what each of these statements tells you about the Munich Peace agreement. Identify the speaker in a) and referred to in b).*

　　a) *'I believe it is peace for our time. Now I recommend you to go home, sleep quietly in your beds.'*

　　b) *'Twice he asserted that if the Sudeten territories were ceded this would be the last territorial demand Germany would make.'*

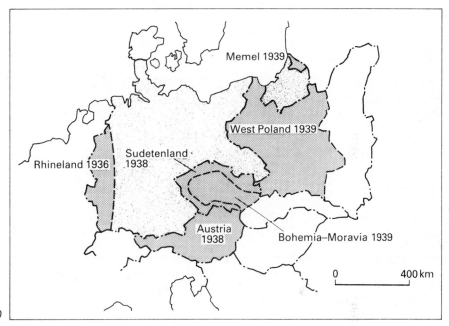

Map showing the expansion of Nazi Germany before 1940

2 *With the aid of the map, write brief notes explaining how each of the following contributed to the outbreak of the Second World War:*

　　a) *German rearmament in 1935*　d) *the Anschluss, 1938*

　　b) *the Rhineland in 1936*　　　　e) *Czechoslovakia, 1938-9*

　　c) *the Spanish Civil War 1936-9*　f) *Poland, 1939*

3 *You were born in 1894. You survived the First World War after volunteering in 1914 as a soldier or as a nurse. Many of your friends and relatives were killed or wounded. It is now Saturday, 1 October 1938. You are 44 years of age and have a son (20) and a daughter (18). Write a long letter to an American relative explaining in detail what happened at Munich, what you feel about Hitler, appeasement and Chamberlain's promise of 'Peace for our time'.*

THE SWEETS OF AGGRESSION

Punch *cartoon,*
18 December 1935

HAILE SELASSIE "HAVE I GOT THIS RIGHT? — HE'S TAKEN NEARLY HALF OF WHAT I HAD AND NOW YOU GENTLEMEN WANT TO DISCUSS WHETHER HE SHOULD TAKE ANY MORE!"

4 a) *Identify Pierre Laval (France), Sir Samuel Hoare (UK), Mussolini (Italy), and Haile Selassie (Abyssinia).*

b) *What was the point of the cartoon?*

c) *To which event does it refer?*

d) *What happened in the following months? How did Mussolini and Haile Selassie react to the intervention of Britain and France?*

Cartoon by Low,
1939

RENDEZVOUS

5 *Explain carefully why and when this cartoon was drawn. What was the point of the cartoon? To which event and which city does the cartoon refer? How important was that event to world history?*

Chapter Twelve
The Second World War

INTRODUCTION

Friday, 1 September 1939: German armed forces invade Poland and advance rapidly using tanks, mechanised infantry, dive bombers and fighters to shock the enemy. They call it *Blitzkrieg*, 'lightning war'.

Two days later, on Sunday, 3 September 1939, Hitler's interpreter, Dr Paul Schmidt, stands in for Ribbentrop at the German Foreign Office in Berlin. The British ambassador, Sir Nevile Henderson, is expected at 9.0 a.m. He brings an ultimatum. It gives Germany just two hours to agree to withdraw German troops from Poland. Dr Schmidt takes it to Hitler's office and translates it slowly. Afterwards there is complete silence.

Source A

Hitler sat immobile, gazing before him. He was not at a loss, as was afterwards stated, nor did he rage as others allege. He sat completely silent and unmoving.

After an interval which seemed an age, he turned to Ribbentrop, who had remained standing by the window. 'What now?' asked Hitler with a savage look, as though implying that his Foreign Minister had misled him about England's probable reaction.

Dr Paul Schmidt, *Hitler's Interpreter*, edited by R.H.C. Steed, Heinemann, 1951

Source B

I remember it well. We sat in a semi-circle round the wireless set instead of going out. We were supposed to be on holiday. I remember a man talking but what he said meant little to me. The silence and the grim looks made the day stick out for fifty years.

Man recalling (in 1989) the outbreak of war in 1939 (when he was six years old)

Source C

11.15 a.m.

I am speaking to you from the Cabinet Room at 10 Downing Street. This morning the British Ambassador in Berlin handed the German Government a final note stating that, unless we heard from them by eleven o'clock that they were prepared at once to withdraw their troops from Poland, a state of war would exist between us. I have to tell you that no such undertaking has been received, and that consequently this country is at war with Germany.

Prime minister, Neville Chamberlain, on BBC Radio, 3 September 1939

Source D

Crowd outside Downing Street, Sunday 3 September 1939

Source E

Crowd in Munich, Germany, listening to Hitler's speech, Friday 1 September 1939

Source F Sunday, 3 September 1939

I was standing in the Wilhelmplatz [Berlin] about noon when the loud-speakers suddenly announced that England had declared herself at war with Germany. Some 250 people were standing there in the sun. They listened attentively to the announcement. When it was finished, there was not a murmur. They just stood there as they were before. Stunned. The people cannot realize yet that Hitler has led them into a world war . . . In 1914, I believe, the excitement in Berlin on the first day of the World War was tremendous. Today, no excitement, no hurrahs, no cheering, no throwing of flowers, no war fever, no war hysteria. There is not even any hate for the French and British.

William L. Shirer, *Berlin Diary*, Hamish Hamilton, 1941

---

1 *What evidence is there that neither Hitler, nor the German people, expected Britain to declare war? Write a paragraph explaining their reaction to the news, using evidence from these sources.*

2 *Compare these sources with those on page 1 describing the outbreak of war in 1914. What are the similarities and differences?*

3 *Can any of your relatives remember Sunday, 3 September 1939? Write down or record their memories of that day. Compare the oral history you collect with that recorded by your friends.*

Bonnet, the French prime minister, also declared war on Germany at 5.0 p.m. the same day. But no other country entered the war at once, apart from the countries of the Commonwealth. Russia attacked Poland herself a fortnight later and didn't fight against Germany for nearly two years. The United States waited even longer and only declared war after the surprise Japanese attack on Pearl Harbor extended the war to every continent and every ocean.

THE BATTLE OF FRANCE

The Phoney War

Even though Britain and France were at war with Germany, their land forces saw little action for seven months. This was the *phoney war*. Hitler made little attempt to attack the Allies and they made little attempt to attack Germany. Instead the German Army completed its invasion of Poland. On 17 September, Soviet troops invaded Poland in accordance with a plan secretly agreed with Germany, in Moscow, in August. On 5 October they partitioned Poland between them.

Hitler hoped Britain and France would agree peace terms, since the war with Poland was over. His speech in the Reichstag was reported by the *Volkischer Beobachter* under the headline,

> 'GERMANY'S WILL FOR PEACE – NO WAR AIMS AGAINST FRANCE AND ENGLAND'.

But Hitler was rebuffed. Chamberlain no longer felt that Hitler could be trusted. By then, anyway, the aims of the war had changed. Winston Churchill told Parliament on 3 September 1939,

> This is not a question of fighting for Poland. We are fighting to save the whole world from the pestilence of Nazi tyranny.

Norway

The land war in Europe erupted again in 1940, when German forces attacked Denmark and Norway on 9 April to prevent the Allies mining the waters off the coast of Norway. This would have stopped the shipment of Swedish iron ore from the ice-free port of Narvik to the Ruhr for use in the German iron and steel industry. Allied troops did land in Norway but were soon forced to withdraw. The failure of the expedition helped bring about the downfall of Neville Chamberlain as prime minister, the man of peace. His successor was Winston Churchill, the man of war. A leading Conservative, Leo Amery, quoted Oliver Cromwell's words to tell Chamberlain, 'Depart, I say, and let us have done with you. In the name of God, go!'

Winston Churchill (1874–1965)

Winston Churchill was born in 1874. In 1900 he entered Parliament as a Conservative but six years later became a minister in the Liberal government at the early age of 32. As First Lord of the Admiralty he took charge of the navy in 1914. In the 1920s and 1930s he was a controversial figure, arguing forcefully for rearmament and against appeasement.

On 3 September 1939 he became First Lord of the Admiralty again. The news was sent to the fleet with the signal 'Winston's back!' He became Prime Minister on 10 May 1940, the day that Hitler launched his blitzkrieg on the Low Countries.

Churchill was in his element as a war leader. He took an active but sometimes ill-informed part in military decisions, but his greatest value to Britain was as an orator. When things looked bleak, he raised morale. When he died in 1965, people of all parties acclaimed him as one of the greatest British leaders of all time.

Dunkirk

On 10 May 1940 Hitler launched an attack on the Low Countries, even though they were neutral. French and British troops rushed to the assistance of the Belgian army. But it was a trap.

The main German attack came, instead, through the Ardennes. This is the hilly area of southern Belgium which the French had assumed to be unsuitable for modern tank warfare. It was not. German tanks sliced through the weakened French armies and raced for the Channel coast.

In ten days von Kleist's Panzers (tanks) had reached the sea. In doing so, they trapped the Allied armies to the north, including the British Expeditionary Force (BEF) of about a quarter of a million men. Instead of annihilating the cream of the British professional army, the main German forces drove onwards towards Paris to knock France out of the war. It gave the BEF just enough time to escape. A fleet of 222 Royal Navy ships and 665 other vessels successfully took 225 000 British servicemen and over 110 000 French and Belgian troops back to Britain.

Soldiers waiting to be evacuated from Dunkirk in 1940

Three long thin black lines protruded into the water, conveying the effect of low wooden breakwaters. These were lines of men, standing in pairs behind one another far out into the water, waiting in queues till boats arrived to transport them, a score or so at a time, to the steamers and warships that were filling up with the last survivors ... On either side, scattered over the sand in all sorts of positions, were the dark shapes of dead and dying men, sometimes alone, sometimes in twos and threes ... Splinters from bursting shells were continually whizzing through the air, and occasionally a man in one of the plodding groups would fall with a groan.

John Charles Austin, *Return Via Dunkirk*, Hodder and Stoughton, 1940

The owner of a large private yacht described the conditions on board his vessel as it swerved sharply to avoid the Luftwaffe,

> The effect on the troops below, in a stinking atmosphere with all ports and skylights closed, can well be imagined. They were literally packed like the proverbial sardines, even one in the bath and another on the W.C., so that all the poor devils could do was sit and be sick.
>
> Commander Lightoller, in A.D. Divine, *Dunkirk*, Faber and Faber, 1945

Dunkirk was a massive, demoralising defeat for the British Army since it left most of its vehicles and equipment behind. But there were relatively few casualties and the soldiers lived to fight another day. Churchill had said only three weeks earlier, 'I have nothing to offer but blood, toil, tears and sweat'.

Now he rose to the occasion with yet another stirring speech, which at the time made Dunkirk seem almost like a victory.

> We shall not flag or fail. We shall go on to the end; we shall fight in France; we shall fight on the seas and oceans; we shall fight with growing confidence and growing strength in the air; we shall defend our island whatever the cost may be. We shall fight on the beaches; we shall fight on the landing grounds; we shall fight in the fields and in the streets; we shall fight in the hills. We shall never surrender.

---

1 *What sort of an ordeal did the survivors at Dunkirk have to go through before they returned safely to Britain?*

2 *What did Churchill mean when he said he had nothing to offer the British people but 'blood, toil, tears and sweat'?*

3 *Why were so many survivors successfully evacuated from Dunkirk?*

Fall of France

After Dunkirk there was very little the French army could do to resist the German advance. On 10 June Mussolini declared war on Britain and France. The *New York Times* said it was, 'With the courage of a jackal at the heels of a bolder beast of prey'. On 14 June German troops goose-stepped into Paris and on 21 June the French Government surrendered at Compiègne – in the very same railway carriage where the Armistice had been signed less than 22 years earlier. The German people greeted the victory with ecstatic enthusiasm. Even Hitler danced a little jig.

Germany now occupied most of northern France, including the Channel ports and much of the Atlantic coast. Unoccupied France became a neutral country, led by First World War hero, Marshal Pétain, and prewar prime minister, Pierre Laval, from the small town of Vichy in central France. An army general, Charles de Gaulle, however, escaped to London where he formed a Free French Government in exile. Relations between France and Britain deteriorated. In July, the Vichy Government nearly declared war on her former ally after British forces destroyed or captured French warships in North Africa rather than let them fall into German hands.

The Battle of Britain

On 18 June 1940 Churchill urged his fellow countrymen,

> Let us therefore brace ourselves to our duty and so bear ourselves that if the British Commonwealth and Empire last for a thousand years men will still say, 'This was their finest hour'.

Churchill followed his own advice. He dismissed a German peace offer. In retaliation, Hitler and his staff prepared to invade Britain. Hitler said,

> A great Empire will be destroyed which it was never my intention to destroy or even harm.

The Nazi High Command codenamed the plan, 'Operation Sealion'. First they needed to secure command of the air. Without it the Royal Air Force could destroy the German landing craft before they reached the beaches of southern England. Göring promised this would be done. He ordered the

The London Blitz in 1940

Luftwaffe to bomb airfields and destroy other essential targets, such as the newly-created radar installations which gave warning of German air attacks. The Royal Air Force resisted bravely and, though hard pressed, managed to stave off defeat. Churchill said,

> Never in the field of human conflict was so much owed by so many to so few.

The Battle of Britain might have been lost, however, if Göring had not changed Luftwaffe tactics by bombing London in September instead of the airfields where the RAF fighters were based. The London Blitz did a vast amount of damage and killed many civilians, but it failed to break the spirit of Londoners and it gave the RAF the chance to recover. On 15 September a massive Luftwaffe raid on London ended with the shooting down of 56 German planes. Soon afterwards Hitler called off 'Operation Sealion' and the danger of an invasion of Britain had passed – for good.

---

1 *Why did France surrender? What might have happened to Britain in June 1940 had it been connected to Europe by land?*

2 *Why did Hitler call off 'Operation Sealion'? What sort of British Army would have faced the German Panzer units and mechanised infantry, had Hitler landed his troops on the south coast of England?*

3 *Why was the bombing of London called the 'Blitz'? Which group of people were later called 'the Few' and why?*

RUSSIA ENTERS THE WAR

Operation Barbarossa

Hitler turned his attention instead, to his old arch-enemy, the Soviet Union, despite the Non-Aggression Pact of 1939. In July 1940 he told his generals, 'The sooner we smash Russia the better'. Stalin didn't trust Hitler either and had already taken military action against Finland, and annexed Lithuania, Latvia, Estonia and Bessarabia to give Russia a buffer zone between east and west.

Hitler first aimed to invade Russia on 15 May 1941 but postponed 'Operation Barbarossa' so that German forces could attack Greece and Yugoslavia in April. This was a mistake. The delay of five weeks stopped the German forces knocking the Soviet Union out of the War before the onset of the Russian winter.

Source A

22 June 1941: The attack will begin at 3.30 a.m. 160 Full Divisions along a 3000 kilometre-long battlefront. Everything is well prepared. The biggest concentration of forces in the history of the world. The Führer seems to lose his fear as the decision comes nearer . . . 3.30. Now the guns will be thundering . . . I pace up and down restlessly in my room. One can hear the breath of history.

The Goebbels Diaries 1939–1941, translated and edited by Fred Taylor, Hamish Hamilton, 1982

Source B

The camp was asleep. Suddenly the roar of motors was heard. The battle alarm was sounded and our unit was up instantly. The first enemy aircraft were over our native soil. The Fascists tried to bomb our camp and perhaps to break through into the depth of the country. They succeeded in neither – the powerful fire of the anti-aircraft batteries forced them back. Faster than ever we completed the eight-kilometer march to the border to meet the Nazi usurpers, to check without delay their advance.

Senior Sergeant N. Shabota quoted in *The Voice of Fighting Russia*, edited by Lucien Zacharoff, Alliance Book Corporation (New York), 1942

Source C

The infantry had a hard time keeping up. Marches of twenty-five miles [40 km] in the course of a day were by no means exceptional, and that over the most atrocious roads . . . Even when encircled, the Russians stood their ground and fought . . . It was appallingly difficult country for tank movement – great virgin forests, widespread swamps, terrible roads, and bridges not strong enough to bear the weight of tanks. The resistance also became stiffer, and the Russians began to cover their front with minefields; it was easier for them to block the way because there were so few roads.

German General Guenther Blumentritt, quoted in *The War 1939-1945*, edited by Desmond Flower and James Reeves, Cassell, 1960

Source D

Despite the reports indicating that Germany was preparing for aggression against the Soviet Union, Stalin believed right till the last moment that it would be possible to ward off the impending war through diplomatic means . . . A directive to the frontier areas warning of a possible surprise attack by the Germans was only issued on the evening of the 21 June and did not have time to reach many formations and units. The first blow struck by the aggressor took the Soviet troops by surprise.

History of the USSR, translated from the Russian by Ken Russell, Progress Publishers (Moscow), 1977

1 *Why did 'Operation Barbarossa' start at 3.30? What was unique about the attack on Russia?*

2 *What errors did Stalin and Hitler both make in 1941? What evidence can be used to correct the view that Hitler was a fearless leader? Is it a reliable source?*

3 *How does Source B help to confirm Source D? Does it help to confirm any of the information in Source C?*

4 *What problems did the German forces encounter as they advanced into Russia? How were these problems likely to change with the onset of winter and as they advanced deeper into the Soviet Union?*

By the autumn of 1941, German forces had captured Kiev, capital of the Ukraine, were laying siege to Leningrad, and even threatening Moscow itself. But that fatal delay of five weeks in the summer prevented the German army from completing the conquest of Russia before the end of 1941. The onset of the Russian winter caught the German army unprepared. Their soldiers had inadequate winter clothing and their tanks and vehicles ran into difficulties, first in the autumn muds and later in the intense cold of the Russian winter.

No such problems hindered the Russians fighting on their native soil. In December white-uniformed Russian soldiers, some on skis, drove the Germans back in front of Moscow. Their leader, Marshal Zhukov, was probably the most successful of all the Soviet commanders. By this time Britain and the United States were helping to supply the Russians with arms and munitions.

Stalingrad

The following spring the German army renewed the offensive but with a change of plan. Hitler ordered them to take the oilfields of the Caucasus in the south-east. A large German army laid siege to Stalingrad but once again the Russian winter intervened. What was worse, Zhukov led them into a trap, encircling the German Sixth Army under von Paulus and forcing them to surrender on 31 January 1943 (against Hitler's orders to 'fight to the last man'). That same month another Russian army relieved Leningrad, after a devastating siege in which hundreds of thousands of Russians died. In July Russian and German armies fought a vast tank battle at Kursk in central Russia. From this time onward the Russians were on the offensive. The war had turned in favour of the Allies in the east.

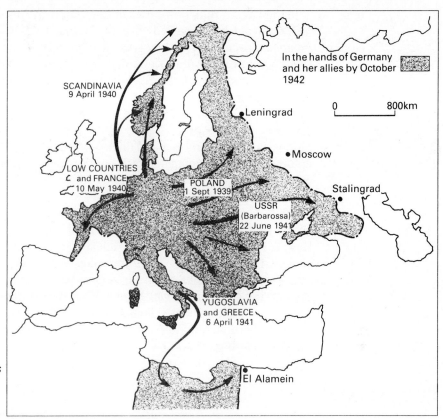

Map of Axis conquests and campaigns in Europe and North Africa 1939–42

1 *Write two or three sentences describing the maximum extent of the conquests made by the Axis powers by 1942.*

2 *What reasons help to explain why the Soviet Union fought back so successfully against the Germans in 1942–3?*

THE WAR IN THE PACIFIC
US–Japanese Relations Before 1941

The United States maintained its neutrality throughout the first two years of the war in Europe. Both the French and the British asked the Americans to intervene before the Fall of France in 1940 but to no effect. Many influential Americans, including the American ambassador in London, thought Britain was doomed. The United States was not neutral, however, when it came to supplying friends and hampering enemies. The Lend-Lease Act of Congress in March 1941 enabled the President to lend or lease military equipment to Britain (and later the Soviet Union).

In the Pacific, relations between the USA and Japan deteriorated in 1941. American aid to China led to a crisis which came to a head when the Japanese forced Vichy France to let them use airfields and naval bases in French Indo-China (now Vietnam). Japan was anxious that her supplies of vital raw materials should not dry up and told France these bases were needed to protect her trade.

The US Government saw it differently, suspecting rightly that the Japanese had designs on the oilfields of the Dutch East Indies (now Indonesia) and the rubber and tin producing areas of Malaya (then a British colony). Roosevelt retaliated by banning oil and petrol sales to Japan. On 15 October 1941, Roosevelt wrote to Churchill, 'The Jap situation is definitely worse!'

While US and Japanese delegations talked, the Japanese navy made secret preparations for an attack on the US Naval Base at Pearl Harbor in Hawaii. On 17 October, General Hideki Tojo, the Japanese minister of war, replaced Prince Konoye as prime minister of Japan. Tojo was a military hardliner. Two weeks later he approved Admiral Yamamoto's plan to destroy the American Pacific Fleet in Pearl Harbor. Talks still continued with the US Government but the final decision to attack was made on 1 December 1941. By this time Admiral Nagumo's task force was already at sea, on course for Pearl Harbor.

Pearl Harbor

7 December 1941. American war planes on fire at Pearl Harbor after Japan's unexpected and devastating bombing raid

Six Japanese aircraft carriers, supported by battleships, cruisers and destroyers, had steamed to within striking distance of Pearl Harbor. Yet there was no special alert in Hawaii. The Americans thought the Japanese would attack first in Malaya or in the Philippines. At 6.0 a.m., the Japanese planes started to take off. When they swept over Hawaii nearly two hours later, they were picked up on American radar but the report of a massive formation of planes was dismissed out of hand as 'nothing to worry about'. It was Sunday morning. Nobody had declared war.

> War struck suddenly and without warning from the sky and sea today at the Hawaiian islands, and Japanese bombs took a heavy toll in American lives. Wave after wave of planes streamed over Oahu which the army said started at 8.10 a.m. Honolulu time and which ended at around 9.25, an hour and 15 minutes later.
>
> Associated Press

The shock raid completely surprised the American forces. The Japanese blitzkrieg destroyed nearly 200 American warplanes on the ground, sank four battleships at anchor and badly damaged four others, as well as ten other ships. Luckily, the US aircraft carriers *Lexington*, *Saratoga* and *Enterprise* were at sea. Had they been in port, the war might even have ended differently. More than 2300 Americans died, war was declared, and Roosevelt called 7 December 1941, 'a date that shall live in infamy'.

Four days later, the other Axis powers, Germany and Italy, also declared war on the United States. This was a fatal mistake for both Hitler and Mussolini. Meanwhile, Japanese forces attacked Hong Kong, the Philippines, Malaya, Thailand, Singapore and Guam. The world was at war.

---

1 *Why did Japan make a surprise attack on Pearl Harbor without first declaring war on the United States?*

2 *Why were the US Forces at Pearl Harbor caught by surprise? Was a Japanese attack completely out of the question?*

3 *What arguments would a Japanese officer have used to justify the attack on Pearl Harbor, the Philippines, and on British and Dutch possessions in the Far East?*

On Christmas Day 1941 Japanese forces captured Hong Kong and in January invaded the Dutch East Indies. A stunning series of victories followed. Singapore fell on 15 February 1942 because the large British garrison assumed an attack would come from the sea. Instead the Japanese army advanced through the jungles of Malaya. Thousands of British and Commonwealth troops were taken prisoner. The fall of this great Far Eastern port was called the greatest disaster in British military history. It was followed in March–May 1942 by the defeat of General MacArthur's forces in the Philippines. Before he left, MacArthur promised the people of the Philippines he would return.

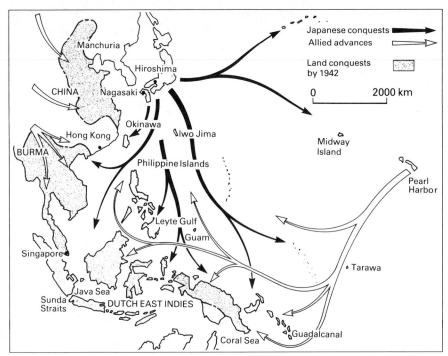

Japanese conquests
Allied advances
Land conquests by 1942
0 2000 km

Map of the war in the Far East

By the beginning of June 1942, the Japanese controlled a vast Far Eastern empire. They called it the Greater East Asia Co-Prosperity Sphere. It included all or part of Hong Kong, Malaya, Burma, Thailand, Indo-China, Java, New Guinea, the Philippines, Borneo and the Dutch East Indies. A Japanese Foreign Office official told John Morris in Tokyo that, 'it could be roughly interpreted, where the Far East was concerned, as a continuation of the British Empire, but with a change of rulers!'

The Battle of Midway

So far the tide of battle had been in favour of Japan. But now it turned against them. The Japanese had expected the Allies to sue for peace in the face of these lightning conquests and the disabling of the American Pacific Fleet. But although they sank battleships at Pearl Harbor they had not sunk the American aircraft carrier fleet. Their own attack on Pearl Harbor had shown only too clearly the effectiveness of the aircraft carrier compared to the battleship. Now it was the turn of the Americans. At midday on 18 April 1942, John Morris said,

I happened to be in the Ginza, the main thoroughfare of Tokyo, at the time ... American bombers appeared over the city, flying so low that their distinguishing marks were clearly visible ... There was not the slightest sign of panic. The police halted the traffic, but nobody made any attempt to take shelter ... as a realisation of what was happening gradually dawned upon them, one heard people starting to criticise the army for having misled them.

John Morris, *Traveller from Tokyo*, Penguin, 1946

---

1 *Why do you think people in Tokyo criticised the army for having misled them? What had they been led to believe? Why was this air raid worrying to the Japanese? What did it demonstrate?*

2 *Study the map. Which other countries would have been worried by Japan's recent conquests and expanding empire?*

In May 1942 American and Japanese aircraft carriers fought the first battle in the history of naval warfare in which the opposing warships did not see each other. This was the battle of the Coral Sea, near Australia and the Solomon Islands. Although the Americans lost one of their biggest carriers, the *Lexington*, they severely damaged a Japanese carrier, sank another, and prevented the Japanese from taking Port Moresby in Papua, which would have been an effective base from which to invade Australia.

One month later, on 4 June 1942, the American navy avenged Pearl Harbor in a battle off Midway Island in the middle of the Pacific. American planes managed to sink four of the Japanese aircraft carriers which had taken part in the raid on Pearl Harbor, together with 332 Japanese planes. American losses were relatively light by comparison (147 planes and one aircraft carrier). Thereafter American forces were on the offensive against Japan. In August 1942 American forces landed on the island of Guadalcanal, the first of a number of Pacific islands which were taken by American marines in the teeth of bitter Japanese opposition. In the next three years the Americans captured many other islands. They called it 'island-hopping'. They took the Philippines in 1944 and Okinawa and Iwo Jima (on the fringe of Japan itself) early in 1945.

THE END OF THE WAR

North Africa

After Stalingrad and Midway, a third major turning point in the war came in Egypt, when Montgomery's Eighth Army decisively defeated Rommel's crack Afrika Korps at the battle of El Alamein on 4 November 1942. The war in North Africa had originally been fought between Italian and British troops but a crushing defeat for Italy persuaded Hitler to send German troops to aid Mussolini. Now Hitler's Afrika Korps was on the run.

At 21.40 hours our guns commenced the barrage. The ground shook. It was fantastic . . . like hundreds of pneumatic-drills breaking up Piccadilly Circus while you lay, with Eros above you, in the middle! It went on for hours; one lost count. Then it ceased and we moved forward beneath 'Monty's Moon' which by then had risen.

Jack Partridge, in *From Oasis Into Italy*, Shepheard-Walwyn, 1983

---

1 *How and when did the battle of El Alamein begin?*

2 *What was 'Monty's Moon'?*

Four days after El Alamein, American and British forces landed in North Africa ('Operation Torch'). Churchill and Roosevelt held the first of the major wartime conferences at Casablanca (see page 275) soon afterwards. In January 1943, they decided that Italy would be the next target for the Allied armies. The North African invasion forces joined up with Montgomery's Eighth Army and invaded Sicily in July 1943. Mussolini was deposed by the Italians on 25 July and imprisoned, but was later freed by German paratroopers after a daring raid.

When the Allies invaded the Italian mainland in September, Italy surrendered, to the disgust of the Germans who called it treachery and cowardice. Hitler immediately sent troops into Italy to halt a possible Allied advance into Austria. The Allies pressed forward but had to fight for every inch of ground in the face of stubborn and tenacious German resistance, led by Field Marshal Kesselring.

Invasion of Europe

Since it was now clear that the Red Army alone was capable of defeating fascist Germany, the Western Allies decided, at long last, to open the second front in Europe. The circumstances were highly favourable for such a move, since the bulk of Germany's forces continued to be deployed along the Soviet–German front . . . By the beginning of 1945 . . . 204 enemy divisions were concentrated [there], whereas the British and American troops had to face less than 70 divisions.

History of the USSR, translated from the Russian by Ken Russell, Progress Publishers (Moscow), 1977

---

1 *What was 'the second front'? Was it accurate to call it the 'second'? How do we know the Russians expected an Allied invasion before 1944?*

2 *What reason did the Soviet historian give for the success of D-Day?*

3 *Is there any evidence that 'the Red Army alone was capable of defeating fascist Germany'?*

Stalin had urged Churchill and Roosevelt to open a second front in Europe in order to take the pressure off the Soviet Union. But the Allies knew the risk involved if such an invasion failed. This is why they made detailed and comprehensive plans in advance. The decision to go ahead was agreed at the Teheran Conference (see page 275) at the end of 1943.

General Dwight Eisenhower was appointed Supreme Allied Commander of 'Operation Overlord', as it was called. He assembled a team of high-ranking officers from Britain and the United States to train the forces, make preparations and ensure that supplies could be quickly sent to the armies once they had secured a bridgehead in France. Floating harbours (codenamed Mulberry) and an underwater oil pipeline (PLUTO) were constructed to speed up supplies to the invasion force in France.

Troops landing in Normandy on D-Day 1944

Bad weather nearly postponed the invasion of France but a favourable forecast persuaded Eisenhower that Operation Overlord could go ahead as planned. 'O.K. Let's go', he said. On Tuesday 6 June the great armada sailed, the greatest naval invasion in history. As the Allied troops neared the Normandy beaches, an American naval officer said,

> Then we all spied it. A red glow lighted the western horizon. Silhouetted by this light was the unmistakable outline of low-lying land.

The German defenders were caught by surprise. A private said,

> When the sun rose the next morning, I saw the invasion fleet lying off the shore. Ship beside ship. And without a break, troops, weapons, tanks, munitions and vehicles were being unloaded in a steady stream.

An American soldier described the actual landing,

> We were late in getting to the beaches. Our rope ladders got wet on the way over. We were dumped out and had to wade several hundred feet in to the beach, and all the time the Germans were firing at us from the top of the big bluff we had to storm. Some of us were shot crossing the sand to the foot of the cliff. When we climbed, the Germans shot down at us. Finally, we threw grenades at the cliff, making furrows up the side and giving us some protection.

Ranger Alban Meccia, in the *Saturday Evening Post*, quoted in *D-Day*, by Warren Tute, Sidgwick and Jackson, 1974

---

1 *Why was D-Day successful?*

2 *What was especially difficult about Ranger Meccia's task on D-Day?*

3 *Imagine you are one of the troops in the photograph landing in Normandy on D-Day. Write an entry for your diary dated 6 June 1944.*

In August the Allies broke through the opposing German forces and launched a rapid advance across northern France and the Low Countries. Paris was liberated on 25 August and Brussels on 3 September. Temporary setbacks included the failure of the Arnhem landings in September 1944 and

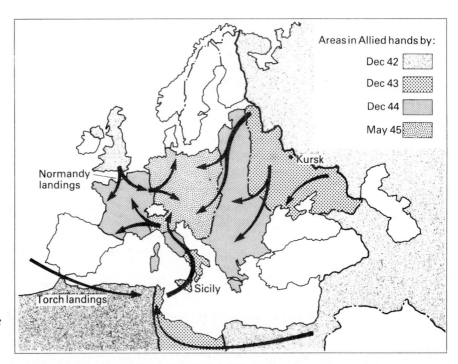

Map showing Allied conquests and campaigns in Europe and North Africa 1942–5

the battle of the Bulge in December – a major German counter-attack in Belgium. In February 1945, Stalin, Churchill and Roosevelt met at Yalta (see page 276) to draw up plans to deal with Poland, the occupation of Germany, and the setting up of the United Nations. The War was rapidly drawing to a close.

In March 1945 Eisenhower's armies crossed the Rhine. At the same time the Red Army drove towards Berlin from the east. On 25 April American and Russian soldiers shook hands when they met at Torgau on the River Elbe. Four days later Mussolini was killed by partisans in Italy and the next day Hitler committed suicide. Berlin fell to the Russians on 2 May and on 8 May it was all over. Germany had surrendered. The Allies called another conference at Potsdam (see page 277) to draw up a treaty to end the war.

The Holocaust

Holocaust means 'great loss of life'. As the advancing Allied forces entered Germany, Austria and Poland, they were horrified to discover the true scale of the war crimes perpetrated by the Nazis on millions of innocent victims throughout Europe, such as the cold-blooded execution of Russian prisoners of war. They discovered concentration camps with gas chambers which had been used to put to death millions of German, Polish and Russian Jews. Photographs of hundreds of corpses in a pit at Bergen-Belsen, a huge pile of shoes of the murdered at Auschwitz, and pictures of survivors looking like walking skeletons, chilled the blood.

Six million Jews are thought to have been killed in this way, one-third of them in the gas chambers at Auschwitz in Poland. The Nazis called this the 'final solution' to disguise what they were doing. The term dates from July 1941 when Göring instructed Heydrich (Himmler's right-hand man) to submit his proposals for carrying out, 'the desired final solution of the Jewish question'. On 4 October 1943, Himmler said,

> This is a glorious page of our history which never has and never will be written.

He was wrong. It was. The camp commandants, prison guards, doctors and assistants brought to trial by the war crimes tribunals looked little different from other people. They were just doing their job, they said. Providing the machinery to exterminate thousands of human beings had even been treated as a normal business deal. A Berlin engineering company wrote to the Reichsführer SS and Chief of the German Police [Heinrich Himmler] on 18 May 1943 offering a reduced price if two of their 'coal burning 'Reform' incinerators' were purchased for use at Dachau. Camp doctors conducted experiments on human guinea pigs instead of saving lives. Dr Sigmund Rascher, one of the leading doctors at Dachau, wrote to his 'Esteemed Reichsführer', Heinrich Himmler, on 9 August 1942, asking if it would be possible to test the effects of our different combat gases in these chambers using the persons who are destined for those chambers anyway . . . Because of this paragraph I am marking this letter 'Secret'.

In December 1945, the Dachau camp commandant, Obersturmbannführer Martin Gottfried Weiss, in evidence at the war crimes trial at Dachau, claimed he

was absolutely powerless in the face of the experiments of Dr. Rascher . . . Himmler said: Rascher and Schilling are responsible to me personally for their experiments and you must obey their orders.

Concentration Camp Dachau 1933–1945, the official handbook to the Dachau Museum, published by the International Dachau Committee, 1978

The Munich newspaper _Süddeutsche Zeitung_ headed its report of the trial with the sarcastic headline,

EACH ONE BLAMES THE OTHER, ALL WERE INNOCENT.

Some Germans committed suicide on learning what had been done in their name. Ever since, the fact of the holocaust has remained uppermost in the minds of all those who have tried to understand the actions of Nazi Germany, both before and during the War.

When Allied troops entered Hitler's concentration camp at Dachau in April 1945, they were cheered by the inmates

1 *How do we know from this evidence that the Nazis intended the 'final solution' to be kept secret?*

2 *What was the Dachau commandant's defence against the accusation that he had been guilty of war crimes? What do you think of this line of defence? Would Dr Sigmund Rascher have been convincing had he offered the same defence? If not, why not?*

3 *Visitors to Dachau cannot miss the huge slogan, 'THOSE WHO CANNOT REMEMBER THE PAST ARE CONDEMNED TO REPEAT IT'. Why? Is the Holocaust sufficient reason in itself to justify the compulsory teaching of history in schools?*

Victory Over Japan

After Victory in Europe Day, the Allies could concentrate on defeating Japan in the Far East. American commanders made plans for the invasion of Japan in 1946. But they knew that these invasions would be costly in both men and materials. The Japanese defenders of Iwo Jima and Okinawa, which had been captured as a result of bitter fighting in March and June 1945, fought tenaciously to the last man. Over 100 000 Japanese died on Okinawa alone (American dead numbered 12 000). Forecasts of a million casualties were mentioned.

The Japanese Government sent peace feelers to Moscow, hoping to negotiate a settlement (through Stalin) with the United States. But the Soviet Union was itself preparing to fulfil an earlier promise to attack the Japanese in Manchuria. Whether a peace settlement could have been negotiated is a matter of some controversy. It wasn't in the Japanese nature then to surrender – as you can see from their Okinawa casualties. But the threat of an attack from the Soviet Union might well have alarmed them, as it did the Americans, who had no desire to partition Japan into separate occupation zones as had happened in Germany.

However, President Truman of the United States (Roosevelt died in April 1945) had a secret weapon – the atom bomb. It came as a dramatic shock to the world when, at 9.15 a.m. on Monday, 6 August 1945, a superfortress bomber, the *Enola Gay*, dropped an atom bomb on Hiroshima, a large Japanese industrial city on the coast. It killed 80 000 people. While the Japanese Government considered what to do, a second bomb was dropped on Nagasaki, on 9 August 1945, killing another 40 000 people. On 14 August the Japanese surrendered. The Second World War was over.

Source A

After the missile had been released I sighed and stood back for the shock. When it came the men aboard with me gasped 'My God', and what had been Hiroshima was a mountain of smoke like a giant mushroom. A thousand feet above the ground was a great mass of dust, boiling, swirling and extending over most of the city.

US Naval Captain, William Parsons, an observer in the *Enola Gay*, quoted in the *Daily Mail*, 8 August 1945

Source B

6 August 1945: Towards Hiroshima [said Mr Katsutani] I saw a big black cloud go billowing up, like a puffy summer cloud ... I saw no badly wounded people around Itsukaichi, but when I reached Kusatsu, nearly everybody was badly hurt. The nearer I got to Hiroshima the more I saw until by the time I had reached Koi, they were all so badly injured, I could not bear to look into their faces.

Between the Red Cross Hospital and the centre of the city [said Dr Hanaoka] I saw nothing that wasn't burned to a crisp. Tramcars were standing at Kawaya-cho and Kamiya-cho and inside were dozens of bodies, blackened beyond recognition.

It was a horrible sight. Hundreds of injured people who were trying to escape to the hills passed our house [said Dr Tabuchi]. The sight of them was almost unbearable. Their faces and hands were burnt and swollen; and great sheets of skin had peeled away from their tissues to hang like rags on a scarecrow.

Eyewitnesses quoted in *Hiroshima Diary*, by Michihiko Hachiya, translated and edited by Warner Wells, Gollancz, 1955

Source C

By God's mercy British and American scientists outpaced all German efforts. The possession of these powers by the Germans at any time might have altered the result of the war and profound anxiety was felt by those who were informed.

Winston Churchill quoted in the *New York Times*, 7 August 1945

Source D

Protests against the use of the atomic bomb have been sent to Mr. Attlee and President Truman by the Rev. A.D. Belden, chairman of the 'Christianity Calling' Council. The message to Mr. Attlee said: 'Unparalleled terrorism disgraces the United Nations. Beg you secure veto of its use.'

News report in the *Daily Mail*, Wednesday, 8 August 1945

Source E

The atom bomb was no 'great decision'.... It was merely another powerful weapon in the arsenal of righteousness. The dropping of the bombs stopped the war, saved millions of lives.

President Truman

Source F

On the 6 August, without any military necessity, an American plane dropped an atomic bomb on the Japanese city of Hiroshima, causing the deaths of many thousands of civilians, including women, children and old men . . . It was a senseless, cruel and barbarous crime against not only the Japanese people, but also mankind as a whole.

> *History of the USSR*, translated from the Russian by Ken Russell, Progress Publishers (Moscow), 1977

Source G

The devastation after the atom bomb was dropped on Hiroshima

---

1 *What happened at Hiroshima on 6 August 1945? Use the facts in these sources to write a detailed account of the dropping of the atom bomb on Hiroshima and its effects.*

2 *Compare the accounts given by eyewitnesses in Hiroshima with the facts and opinions in the other sources. Make a list of the different points of view which people had about the dropping of the atom bomb.*

3 *Was it 'a senseless, cruel and barbarous crime'? Write a reasoned essay arguing the case either for or against the dropping of the atom bombs on Hiroshima and Nagasaki in August 1945.*

WARTIME DIPLOMACY

The Second World War began in Europe with the German advance into Poland on 1 September 1939 and Hitler's subsequent refusal to withdraw his forces in response to the British and French ultimatums. In other words, the War began because Britain and France guaranteed Polish independence and with it Poland's existing frontiers. When the War was over, a substantial slice of Polish territory was ceded to the Soviet Union and Britain found she was no nearer securing Polish independence than she had been in 1939.

What had happened, as in all great wars, was simply that circumstances changed during the course of the fighting. The belligerents had new war aims, new enemies, new allies. The United States and the Soviet Union, which stood by while Hitler occupied most of Europe, later bore the brunt of the fighting, though not without complaint. This gave them the right, which they took, to determine how the war should end.

The Allies tried to reach agreement on what would be done with the lands they regained or conquered. For the Western Allies, at least, it was not to be a war of gain. It was unthinkable, therefore, to allow Italy to retain Abyssinia (1935) or let Japan keep Manchuria (1931).

The Atlantic Charter

In August 1941 Winston Churchill and President Roosevelt held an historic meeting on board a warship anchored in Placentia Bay, Newfoundland. Here they drew up a list of eight war aims. These were war aims to show the sort of world they hoped to see after the war. A British newspaper called it 'The Atlantic Charter'. It was later used to help formulate the aims and objectives of the United Nations Organisation in 1945.

Roosevelt and Churchill wanted to ensure that all countries would have free access to the raw materials they needed. People should be free to cross the seas without hindrance. They wanted international co-operation in improving labour standards, welfare measures and economic growth. After the defeat of the Nazi tyranny they wanted a lasting peace. All nations should abandon the use of force. Disarmament was essential. Both leaders agreed that territorial changes should only be made with the consent of the people living there. They respected the right of all peoples to choose their own type of government, although Churchill did not extend this right to the people of India at the time.

Five months later, these war aims were endorsed by representatives of the 26 nations then at war with the Axis powers. In a Joint Declaration, on 1 January 1942, the United Nations (as they called themselves) looked forward to a world which would involve 'the establishment of a wider and more permanent system of general security'.

> **1** *Why did they call themselves the United Nations in 1942?*
>
> **2** *What do you think they meant by 'a wider and more permanent system of general security'?*

The Casablanca Conference

The Casablanca Conference was held in French Morocco on 14–24 January 1943. Stalin was 'too busy' to attend (not surprisingly, since this was the month when Leningrad and Stalingrad were both relieved).

Stalin had urged Britain and America to invade the mainland of Europe and start a Second Front, to relieve the pressure on the Red Army. Some American admirals and generals, on the other hand, wanted the United States to concentrate first on defeating the Japanese – if an invasion of France was no longer possible in 1943. For his part, Churchill felt the Allied forces were not yet ready for such a major operation. He pressed instead for a joint invasion of Mediterranean Europe – the underbelly of Germany and the Axis Powers. This is what the Allied leaders decided to do. Sicily, and then Italy, would be invaded as soon as the Axis powers had been defeated in North Africa.

> **1** *What different courses of action did the Allies consider at Casablanca? What were the advantages and disadvantages of each of these proposals?*
>
> **2** *Why do you think the Allies eventually decided to invade Italy?*

The Teheran Conference

This conference, held between 28 November and 1 December 1943 was the first to be attended by all three leaders. Churchill said that he only realised how small Britain was after sitting between Stalin on one side and Roosevelt on the other. In fact Roosevelt took Stalin's side when the leaders discussed strategy in Europe. Churchill proposed an Anglo-American invasion of the Balkans but Roosevelt supported Stalin in opposing it. Stalin was afraid the Allies might liberate Hungary and Austria before the Red Army. The main decisions were:

- that the D-Day landings should take place the following May or June.
- that the Soviet Union should declare war on Japan as soon as the war against Germany was over.
- that there should be a world organisation after the war to take the place

of the League of Nations. Britain, China, the Soviet Union and the United States would be the 'four policemen' of the security council.

• that the Polish frontier with the Soviet Union should be redrawn to give Russia a buffer zone. In return Poland would be given part of eastern Germany as compensation.

The Yalta Conference

Churchill, Roosevelt and Stalin at the Yalta Conference in February 1945. Standing behind them, from left to right, are Lord Leathers, Anthony Eden, Stettinius, Sir Alexander Cadogan, Molotov and Averill Harriman

This was the second meeting between Stalin, Churchill and Roosevelt. It was held in the Russian Black Sea holiday resort of Yalta between 4–11 February 1945. By this time the War was nearly over in Europe and the Allies had to make important decisions about the shape of Europe after the War. Stalin wanted to clear up the question of what to do with Poland. Sir Alexander Cadogan, a leading British official at Yalta, thought him

> much the most impressive of the three men. He is very quiet and restrained ... he never used a superfluous word, and spoke very much to the point. He's obviously got a very good sense of humour – and a rather quick temper! ... I have never known the Russians so easy and accommodating. In particular Joe has been extremely good. He is a great man, and shows up very impressively against the background of the other two ageing statesmen.
>
> *The Cadogan Diaries*, edited by David Dilkes, Cassell, 1971

The Conference decided:

• The eastern boundary of Poland should follow the approximate line of the partition which Russia had agreed with Hitler in 1939.

- To compensate, Poland should have part of eastern Germany, probably on a line approximately following the Rivers Oder and Neisse. No firm decision was reached on this.
- Representatives of the London-based Polish and Yugoslav Governments in exile were to be involved in their respective governments after the War.
- Free elections were to be held after the War in countries liberated by the Allies. This was embodied in the *Declaration on Liberated Europe*.
- The Soviet Union would declare war on Japan within three months of the end of the war in Europe. In return she would regain territories lost to Japan in the War of 1904–5.
- The United Nations Organisation should go ahead on the lines already drawn up at the Dumbarton Oaks Conference (see Chapter 13). The three leaders cleared up issues still unresolved, such as the power of veto and difficult questions about entitlement to membership.
- There should be four occupation zones in Germany when the War ended (American, British, French, Soviet). Stalin only agreed to the inclusion of France after pressure from the other two leaders.
- Germany should pay reparations. Roosevelt agreed that the sum of $10 000 million should go to the Soviet Union and another $10 000 million to other victims of Nazi aggression. These would be the approximate sums the Allies would have in mind at the end of the War.

---

1 *Did the division of Germany into four occupation zones adequately reflect the contribution which each power made to the Allied victory? Why do you think Stalin opposed the idea of a French occupation zone?*

2 *Why was the Soviet Union still neutral in the war against Japan?*

3 *What happened to the original cause of the war in 1939?*

4 *Why were the Western Allies worried about the way in which new governments were being formed in eastern Europe?*

The Potsdam Conference

This was the last of the wartime conferences between the three great powers. It was held in occupied Germany at Potsdam near Berlin. One of the 'ageing statesmen' at Yalta, Roosevelt, had died. His place was taken by President Truman. Churchill was the British prime minister at the start of the Conference on 16 July 1945. At the close, on 2 August 1945, his place had been taken by Clement Attlee, leader of the newly-elected Labour Party.

At Potsdam the Russians held most of the cards. Eastern Europe was in their hands. The most the Allied leaders could do was to bring as much pressure to bear as possible. But the atmosphere had changed. Sir

Attlee, Truman and Stalin at the Potsdam Conference in 1945

Alexander Cadogan said Stalin was being 'very tiresome' about Poland's frontiers. He noted that, 'Russia tries to seize all that she can and she uses these meetings to grab as much as she can get'.

The Conference decided:

- to endorse many of the decisions made at Yalta, such as the boundaries of Poland. But the Oder–Neisse line was still regarded as temporary, depending upon the formal agreement of the Germans as part of a peace treaty. In fact a peace treaty was never signed. It was only in 1970 that the Federal Government (West Germany) finally accepted the Oder–Neisse line.
- to form a Council of Foreign Ministers to draw up the peace treaties with the different Axis powers.
- to prosecute Nazi war criminals.
- to approve payment of reparations by Germany to Russia and the other countries she had invaded. These reparations were to be paid in kind – whole factories were to be dismantled and the equipment and machinery sent to Russia. Since Germany's leading industrial region, the Ruhr, lay in the occupation zones of the Western Allies it was agreed that, in return for machinery and equipment from the West, the Russians would exchange corn and coal from their zone.

---

1 *Why do you think Sir Alexander Cadogan changed his mind about Stalin between the meeting in Yalta (in February) and the meeting in Potsdam (July–August) only six months later?*

2 *Which Conference decided the fate of Poland after the war?*

PEACE

Peace In Europe

The Second World War did not end with an impressive conference attended by the world's leaders – as had happened after the First World War, when the Paris Peace Treaties were signed. Perhaps it was as well, in view of the tension and aggravation caused by the provisions of the Treaty of Versailles in 1919.

Germany was never reunited. The separation of the country into four occupation zones led eventually to the division into East and West Germany. Long before Germany had recovered sufficiently to contemplate reunification, the Cold War (see Chapter 14) intervened. The failure to reunite Germany led ultimately to the formation of the North Atlantic Treaty Organisation (NATO) and the Warsaw Pact. When West Germany joined NATO it was no longer possible to think of a united Germany. Since there was no one Germany there was no peace treaty.

Map of the territorial changes at the end of the Second World War

Russian gains

1, 2, 3 from Finland	7 from Germany
4 Estonia	8 from Poland
5 Latvia	9, 10 from Czechoslovakia
6 Lithuania	11 from Romania

The other Axis powers came out of the war with a more certain future. **Italy** lost Fiume, Trieste, and her African colonies (under UN supervision), paid reparations and cut back her armed forces. These terms formed part of the Treaty of Paris (1947) which inflicted similar conditions on the other Axis powers of **Bulgaria**, **Finland**, **Hungary** and **Romania**. Their territorial losses can be seen on the map.

Austria, which had been united with Germany under Hitler, was also divided into occupation zones. In exchange for a guarantee of strict neutrality, however, the Russians eventually agreed to withdraw their troops and allowed Austria to become independent once more. But it wasn't until 1955 that the Austrian State Treaty was signed.

---

1 *Why was no peace treaty signed to end the war with Germany? Why was Italy let off lightly after the War? What happened to Austria?*

2 *How did the end of the Second World War differ from the end of the First World War?*

Peace in the Far East

It has sometimes been argued that one of the reasons why Truman decided to drop an atom bomb on Hiroshima was his desire to end the war against Japan as quickly as possible without calling for help from the Soviet Union. Russian stubbornness at the conference table, the practical difficulties of co-ordinating the work of the different occupation zones in Germany, and Russian unwillingness to co-operate, strengthened American determination to exclude the other Allies, including Britain, from the pacification of Japan after the War. The Americans argued that their forces had borne the brunt of the fighting in the last three years of the war. This is why the army of occupation in Japan was almost exclusively American. There were no quarrels, no arguments, no vetoes in Japan, only General Douglas MacArthur, Supreme Commander for the Allied Powers (SCAP) with dictatorial powers. MacArthur had a number of objectives. Some of these had been determined for him at the Cairo Conference during the War, when China, Britain and the United States met in November 1943 and agreed to insist on unconditional surrender and the splitting up of Japan's overseas empire.

General MacArthur

- Parts of the empire went to the Soviet Union in the north;
- Pacific islands which Japan had acquired as League of Nations mandates after the First World War were to be administered by the United States;
- Taiwan and other lands, once Japanese, were to be returned to China;
- Korea, scheduled to be independent, was divided between two occupying armies – Soviet in the north and US in the south.

These territorial changes were later ratified by the Treaty of San Francisco in 1951.

General MacArthur's policy as SCAP in Japan was laid down in a document dated 29 August 1945:

The ultimate objectives of the United States in regard to Japan are:
a) to insure that Japan will not again become a menace to the United States or to the peace and security of the world.
b) to bring about the eventual establishment of a peaceful and responsible government which will respect the rights of other states.
   i) Japan's sovereignty will be limited to the islands of Honshu, Hokkaido, Kyushu, Shikoku and . . . minor outlying islands . . .
   ii) Japan will be completely disarmed and demilitarized. The authority of the militarists and the influence of militarism will be totally eliminated from her political, economic, and social life. Institutions expressive of the spirit of militarism and aggression will be vigorously suppressed.
   iii) The Japanese people shall be encouraged to develop a desire for individual liberties and respect for fundamental human rights, particularly the freedom of religion, assembly, speech, and the press. They shall also be encouraged to form democratic and representative organizations.
   iv) The Japanese people shall be afforded opportunity to develop for themselves an economy which will permit the peacetime requirements of the population to be met.

Quoted in *The Japan Reader 2*,
edited by Livingston, Moore and Oldfather, Penguin, 1976

---

1 *What is meant by 'sovereignty'?*

2 *Why was it necessary to demilitarise Japan?*

3 *What are the 'fundamental human rights' of people living in Britain?*

4 *What did the document mean when it said that the Japanese people would be given the opportunity 'to develop for themselves an economy which will permit the peacetime requirements of the population to be met'?*

Despite a clause which said 'It is not the responsibility of the Allied Powers to impose upon Japan any form of government not supported by the freely expressed will of the people', the Americans forced Japan's politicians to accept a new Japanese Constitution. On 6 March 1946, Wataru Narahasi, secretary of the Japanese Cabinet said,

the Emperor himself proclaims the people sovereign . . . Through the adoption of this constitution, the Emperor will become a symbol above the people.

In other words, the emperor ceased to be a divine ruler and became a symbol of power instead as head of state. He no longer took an active part in the decisions of the Government. The power rested with the people through their elected representatives.

All adult Japanese citizens, male or female, over 21, were given the vote – to elect representatives to the Diet (the Japanese Parliament). The Government was to be chosen from the majority party in the Diet. Trade unions were permitted and political parties allowed to flourish freely. The Japanese were given new liberties, such as freedom of speech (provided they didn't criticise the occupation forces).

The law courts were given powers which made them independent and beyond the control of the Government. The educational system was overhauled. The large organisations (called *zaibatsu*) which used to control Japanese industries, banks and businesses were broken up. Until then half of Japan's farmers were tenants, who paid their rent in crops and farm produce. They were now given the opportunity to buy their land cheaply with government loans.

---

1 *What was the role of SCAP in the years immediately after the end of the War?*

2 *What was the position of the emperor after 1945? How had it changed since before the War?*

Militarism was eliminated as a force in Japan. The major war criminals were tried and punished, including General Tojo (ex-prime minister) and General Yamashita (conqueror of Singapore) who were both executed. Government departments and the big business enterprises of Japan were purged of their top officials. The armed forces were disarmed and all traces of authoritarian rule wiped clean (e.g. political prisoners were freed).

American aid

Tokyo in ruins in 1945. Over 200 000 people were killed in the American raids on the city

The road to recovery in Japan looked insuperable. Japan's industrial might had been shattered by Allied bombing. Cities lay in ruins. The transport system was in chaos. The people were poor and desperate. Japan's overseas empire had been broken up. Even Taiwan (Japanese since 1895) and Korea (Japanese since 1910) had gone. Japan no longer controlled the production of raw materials on the mainland of Asia, such as Manchurian coal and iron ore. Many of Japan's traditional markets had been lost and the goodwill of nations, such as Australia, dispelled by the actions of her forces during the war years.

The Americans increasingly began to realise that a friendly Japan could become a bulwark of freedom, to counter what the Americans viewed as a world-wide Communist conspiracy, which they later held responsible for the Communist Revolution in China in 1949 and the Korean War in 1950.

In 1951, 48 nations, including the United States, signed the Japanese peace treaty in San Francisco. The Americans signed a security treaty as well, which gave them valuable military bases in the Far East, at the same time providing an effective defence system for Japan.

At first Japan made only a slow recovery from the effects of the War. In 1947 the Americans provided $400 million worth of aid to prevent the people from starving. By 1951, the value of this aid had escalated to $2000 million a year. In the next few years, however, Japan received a huge boost when United Nations' forces intervened in the Korean War. Japanese businesses worked flat out to supply the American armed forces who formed the vast bulk of the non-Korean forces fighting in Korea.

Trade increased rapidly, particularly with the United States, and Japan's industries thrived as managements and workforces adapted skilfully to the changes of the postwar world. Living standards inside Japan rose dramatically and this too stimulated the boom in industry, since Japanese customers also wanted the new consumer goods and electronic products which have been developed by Japan's space age factories.

---

1 *Why did Japan become one of the world's most powerful economies despite losing the War?*

2 *How important was American aid in enabling Japan to recover?*

3 *What did the United States get in return for all the American aid given to Japan?*

FURTHER QUESTIONS AND EXERCISES

1 *Draw a large scale map of Europe. Colour in the changes that were made to the frontiers of the Soviet Union and neighbouring states at the end of the War. What other international boundaries were altered in 1945?*

2 *Interview older relatives and friends who can remember the period between 1939 and 1945. What can they recall? What effects did the war have on their lives and on their families?*

3 *To which important events, battles and happenings of the Second World War do the following statements refer? Write brief notes to explain the circumstances in which each extract was said or written,*
   a) 'Winston's back!'
   b) 'O.K. Let's go.'
   c) 'I could see a mushroom of boiling dust.'
   d) 'I shall return.'
   e) 'a date that shall live in infamy'
   f) 'the final solution'.

4 *For each of the conferences listed below, say briefly, i) who attended, ii) what issues were discussed, and iii) with what results.*
   a) Casablanca 1943   *c) Yalta 1945*
   b) Teheran 1943   *d) Potsdam 1945*

5 *Göring, Ribbentrop, Hess, and other leading Nazis, were tried at Nuremberg in 1946. Many of those found guilty were hanged. Why? What crimes had they committed? How would you distinguish between war crimes and legitimate acts of war? Who is responsible for a war crime – the soldiers or officials who carry it out, the people who give the orders, or both?*

Chapter Thirteen

The United Nations

INTRODUCTION

The United Nations Building in New York

The Second World War was unquestionably the worst war the world has ever known. About 50 million people died. The Holocaust and the dropping of the atom bombs on Hiroshima and Nagasaki made many people fear for the future of civilisation. The Second World War significantly changed international relationships. It saw the emergence of the two great superpowers: the United States and the Soviet Union. Their disagreement about the future of the world led to the Cold War.

But there was a positive side as well. The Second World War brought democracy to Japan, Germany, Austria and Italy. It stimulated hopes of independence among the millions of subject peoples in the colonies of the great European powers. By destroying much of Europe it made necessary a new mood of economic, social and political co-operation. This later led to the creation of the European Community as a union of like-minded nations bound by a common purpose.

Above all it gave birth to the United Nations which, for all its faults, has proved to be a far more comprehensive, longer-lasting, and more effective peace-keeping world organisation than its predecessor the League of Nations. It has also proved an effective tool in the struggle to achieve equality for all peoples, to establish basic human rights, and to eliminate human suffering.

> **1** *Who were the superpowers before the War? What happened between 1939 and 1945 to allow the United States and the Soviet Union to dominate the postwar world?*
>
> **2** *Why do you think the Allies decided to start the United Nations from scratch, instead of just improving the old League of Nations?*

FOUNDING THE UNITED NATIONS

The Old League

When Churchill and Roosevelt spoke of the need for 'a wider and more permanent system of general security' at the Atlantic Charter summit conference in 1941, they had in mind the failure of the League of Nations to provide any such security in the years before the war. To all intents and purposes, the League of Nations was already dead. It was finally disbanded in April 1946 when all its assets and property were transferred to the United Nations.

By 1941 the United Kingdom was the only great power still technically a member of the League. The United States never joined the League. The Soviet Union was expelled in 1939. Italy, Germany and Japan all resigned in the 1930s. Vichy France was no longer a great power. Any future world organisation could only work if it included both the United States and the Soviet Union.

This didn't mean that the League had little influence on the shaping of the United Nations. Far from it. The structure of the UN – with its Secretariat, Security Council, General Assembly, International Court of Justice and Specialised UN Agencies – bears a very strong resemblance to that of the old League of Nations – with its Secretariat, Council, Assembly, Court of International Justice and Specialised Organisations. The Covenant setting up the League of Nations also influenced the officials who drew up the UN Charter. But the United Nations is much more than a League of Nations, as you will see.

Dumbarton Oaks

In January 1942, Britain and America were joined by 24 other nations in confirming the principles enshrined in the Atlantic Charter (see page 274). They included the Soviet Union, China and the Commonwealth Dominions. Roosevelt called this grouping *The United Nations*.

The Allied foreign ministers, Molotov (USSR), Eden (UK) and Hull (USA) took the first steps forward when they met in Moscow in October 1943, a month before the Teheran Conference. At these discussions, they agreed on the desirability of setting up a United Nations Organisation.

Accordingly a special conference, to draw up the Charter and decide the structure of the UN, was called for the autumn of 1944. It met at Dumbarton Oaks near Washington DC. Only the United States, the United Kingdom and the Soviet Union met initially to draw up this Charter.

They decided that the UN would have a General Assembly and a Security Council consisting of permanent representatives (the three great powers) and other representatives appointed for a fixed term from the other member-countries of the UN. Later, China took part in discussions with the UK and the USA but not with the Soviet Union, which was neutral at that time in the war between the Allies and Japan.

Although much of the Dumbarton Oaks Conference went well, there was one crucial sticking point. This was the proposed right of any of the great powers to veto proposals which affected their own interests. The Soviet Union was adamant that decisions of the great powers should always be unanimous. The British delegates, on the other hand, were equally determined that a country involved in a dispute should not be able to vote on any course of action proposed by the UN. They argued that no other country in the world would agree to the great powers having privileges which they were not allowed to share. Without such an agreement, there could be no United Nations, they warned.

> Thursday, 7 September 1944 Washington
> Ed. [Stettinius of the USA], Gromyko [Russia] and I [Sir Alexander Cadogan, head of the British Foreign Office] lunched together and Ed. and I tried to hammer him on the main point – the Great Power Veto. But he was quite wooden on that. Best he could say was that we should 'leave the point open'. I explained to him again and again that this was an illusion and that, if one 'left it open' one simply wouldn't get a World Organisation . . .
> [Wednesday, 13 September]
> Gromyko informed us his Government's final answer on voting question was definitely 'No'.
>
> *Diaries of Sir Alexander Cadogan*, edited by David Dilks, Cassell, 1971

The Soviet position was understandable, however. Stalin had every reason to believe that the Soviet Union would be outvoted by the Western nations in combination with the US-influenced countries of Latin America. He told Roosevelt they had 'certain absurd prejudices' against the Soviet Union.

San Francisco

The same issue dominated the San Francisco Conference from April to June 1945, attended now by 40 other nations besides the big four (Britain, the United States, Soviet Union and China). Later on in the Conference it became the big five with the addition of France.

The San Francisco Conference April–June 1945

Source A

9 April 1945: I had lunch today with . . . John Foster Dulles [the hardline US Secretary of State 1952–9]. Dulles indicated great misgivings as to whether the hopes of the nation for an international peace organization flowing out of Dumbarton Oaks and San Francisco might not be raised to too great heights. He said that these questions of a viable machinery for world peace are questions that have been perplexing the minds of statesmen for centuries and that it was unwise, he thought, to assume they would be settled now over night . . . Mr Dulles expressed doubt that it was wise to permit all of the small nations to express their opinions on all matters of international relationships.

James Forrestal (US Secretary of the Navy in April 1945), *The Forrestal Diaries*, edited by Walter Millis, The Viking Press, 1951

Source B

Wednesday, 23 May 1945: Old Smuts [prime minister of South Africa] sent for me yesterday morning for a chat about things – mainly about voting powers of the Council, about which he's rather worried. I think he's all right himself on the subject but has been got at by Evatt the Australian [foreign minister], who's the most frightful man in the world; he makes long and tiresome speeches on every conceivable subject, always advocating the wrong thing and generally with a view to being inconvenient and offensive to us, and boosting himself.

Diaries of Sir Alexander Cadogan, edited by David Dilks, Cassell, 1971

Source C

May 23, 1945: By hammering it out, we have found an answer which satisfies practically everybody. In my view, that is the great hope for the new League itself. If we do nothing more than create a constant forum where nations must *face* each other and *debate* their differences and strive for common ground, we shall have done infinitely much.

The Private Papers of Senator Vandenberg, Houghton Miflin, 1952

Source D

Saturday, 26 May 1945   San Francisco

Later, at 9, we've got a Big Four meeting on voting powers of the Council. I think we shall agree about that, so that it can come before a Committee on Monday and we can get a final decision on it in the course of a day or two. But we shall have all the little fellows yapping at our heels, and it won't be too easy. Of course one could crack the whip at them and say that if they don't like our proposals there just damned well won't be any World Organization. But I don't know that that would pay and would have to be put tactfully.

Diaries of Sir Alexander Cadogan, edited by David Dilks, Cassell, 1971

Source E

June 23, 1945: We have finished our job. I am proud of it. It has been the crowning privilege of my life to have been an author of the San Francisco Charter. It has an excellent chance to save the peace of the world *if* America and Russia can learn to live together and *if* Russia learns to keep her word.

The Private Papers of Senator Vandenberg, Houghton Miflin, 1952

---

1 *What was meant by 'a viable machinery for world peace', 'a constant forum', the 'Big Four', the 'Council'?*

2 *Why was the question of the great power veto of such importance in the discussions of the Conference? Look at the voting procedures on page 294. How did the negotiators finally settle how votes were to be counted in the United Nations?*

3 *To whom was Cadogan referring when he talked of the 'little fellows'? Name one of the 'little fellows' he had in mind. Why were they 'little'? Why were they 'yapping'?*

4 *How did Cadogan and Vandenburg differ, on 23 May 1945, in the way in which they reacted to the progress of the Conference so far?*

5 *What evidence is there here, and at Dumbarton Oaks, a) that the Cold War had already begun, b) that members of the Commonwealth didn't always agree, c) that American politicians differed sharply in the way in which they viewed future prospects for the United Nations?*

6 *In what respects were Cadogan and Dulles in agreement but at odds with the views of Senator Vandenburg? Was it a 'united' nations?*

There were also discussions over rights to membership. At one stage the Soviet Union insisted that all 16 Socialist Soviet Republics should each have a representative and a vote in the General Assembly. This was because the countries of the British Commonwealth would all be represented separately. In the end the Soviet Union agreed to compromise with three delegations – from the Soviet Union, the Ukraine and Byelorussia.

The debate about the role of the veto showed clearly, long before the first meeting of the United Nations, that great power rivalry would dominate its proceedings, and that without great power support and agreement the UN would be just as helpless as the League.

The Charter

The UN Charter was signed by representatives of 50 Allied nations on 26 June 1945 at San Francisco. It came into being officially on 24 October 1945, later to be known as 'United Nations Day'. General Smuts said,

> It provides for a peace with teeth; for the unity of peace-loving peoples against future aggressors; for a united front amongst the greatest powers, backed by the forces of the smaller powers as well.

The Charter began like this:

San Francisco   26 June 1945

We, the peoples of the United Nations, determined –
to save succeeding generations from the scourge of war, which twice in our lifetime has brought untold sorrow to mankind, and
to re-affirm faith in fundamental human rights, in the dignity and worth of the human person, in the equal rights of men and women and of nations large and small, and
to establish conditions under which justice and respect for the obligations arising from treaties and other sources of international law can be maintained, and
to promote social progress and better standards of life in larger freedom, and for these ends:
to practise tolerance and live together in peace with one another as good neighbours, and
to unite our strength to maintain international peace and security, and
to ensure, by the acceptance of principles and the institution of methods, that armed force shall not be used, save in the common interest, and
to employ international machinery for the promotion of the economic and social advancement of all peoples,
have resolved to combine our efforts to accomplish these aims.
Accordingly, our respective Governments, through representatives assembled in the city of San Francisco, who have exhibited their full powers found to be in good and due form, have agreed to the present charter of the United Nations and do hereby establish an international organisation to be known as the United Nations.

The Charter stated clearly the purposes of the United Nations as being:

- To maintain international peace and security by acting collectively to deter aggressors and to settle disputes peacefully.
- To develop friendly relations among nations based on respect for the principle of equal rights and self-determination of peoples.
- To achieve international co-operation in solving economic, social, cultural and humanitarian problems.
- To be a centre for harmonising the actions of nations in the attainment of these common ends.

---

1 *Compare the preamble to the United Nations Charter with the opening words of the League of Nations Covenant (on page 206). What are the similarities and differences? Did the UN Charter add anything new? Did it leave anything out?*

2 *Give examples from your own knowledge of recent events which show that the great powers do not always abide by these principles.*

President Truman addressing the United Nations General Assembly in October 1945

In July 1945, the US Senate voted on whether to ratify US membership of the United Nations. Would they repeat the débâcle, 26 years earlier, when the Senate refused to allow the USA to join the League of Nations? The US Senate Foreign Relations Committee was in no doubt that the new United Nations could not guarantee world peace:

Source A

Neither this Charter, nor any other document or formula that might be devised can prevent war. And the committee would be performing a disservice to the public in its action with respect to the Charter should it declare any such opinion for its part. The establishment of the UN will at best be a beginning towards the creation of those conditions of stability throughout the world which will foster peace and security.

The US Senate Foreign Relations Committee, July 1945

Source B

SENATE RATIFIES CHARTER OF UNITED NATIONS 89 TO 2
TRUMAN HAILS AID TO PEACE

WASHINGTON, July 28 – The United States Senate paid a first installment on an old debt today. It ratified, 89 to 2, the United Nations Security Charter, successor to the League of Nations Covenant which it rejected twenty-six years ago, and thereby fulfilled Woodrow Wilson's prophecy that one day the upper chamber would reverse its decision.

James B. Reston, The *New York Times*, 29 July, 1945

Source C

Results of a poll taken by the Roper organization in 1945

Which one of these comes closest to expressing what you would like to have the United States do after the war?

a	Enter into no alliances and have as little as possible to do with other countries	9.7%
b	Depend only on separate alliances with certain countries	4.8%
c	Take an active part in an international organization	71.8%
d	Don't know	13.7%

Quoted by John Gunther in *Inside U.S.A.*, Hamish Hamilton, 1947

---

1 *What was the 'old debt'? What policy was overturned by the US Senate? Is there any evidence that this was a popular decision?*

2 *Which of the alternative policies in Source C (a, b or c) had been followed by the United States before the War?*

3 *Why did members of the Senate Foreign Relations Committee ratify the Charter? What were their hopes and fears for the United Nations?*

San Francisco, 26 June 1945. The Earl of Halifax signs the United Nations Charter on behalf of the United Kingdom

ORGANISATION

Membership

Membership of the United Nations is continually changing as new countries gain their independence and when countries merge to form a union or federation (such as Tanzania in 1964). By 1988 there were 158 member states, from Afghanistan and Albania to Zambia and Zimbabwe. Of the major countries of the world only Switzerland, North and South Korea were not in membership at that time. South Africa's membership was suspended in 1974. Indonesia resigned in 1965 but returned in 1966.

The Nationalist Chinese Government on Taiwan was expelled in 1971 and the Communist Chinese Government in Peking took its place. This had long been a matter of bitter dispute in the UN. Indeed, the reason why the Soviet Union was unable to prevent UN involvement in the Korean War (see page 314) was simply because its delegate was boycotting the Security Council at the time – in protest at the American refusal to agree to the admission of Red China to the UN. For 22 years, the United States had effectively vetoed proposals to admit the world's largest country! China only gained her rightful place in the General Assembly and became one of the five permanent representatives on the Security Council in 1971. The *New York Times* called this a 'crushing American defeat' and White House officials described it as being, 'the most important defeat ever suffered by the United States in the world organization'.

How the United Nations is organised

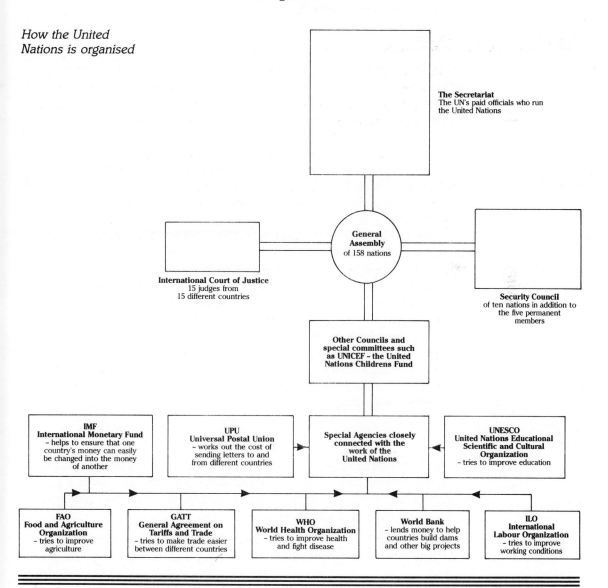

The Secretariat
The UN's paid officials who run the United Nations

General Assembly of 158 nations

International Court of Justice
15 judges from 15 different countries

Security Council
of ten nations in addition to the five permanent members

Other Councils and special committees such as UNICEF – the United Nations Childrens Fund

IMF International Monetary Fund
– helps to ensure that one country's money can easily be changed into the money of another

UPU Universal Postal Union
– works out the cost of sending letters to and from different countries

Special Agencies closely connected with the work of the United Nations

UNESCO United Nations Educational Scientific and Cultural Organization
– tries to improve education

FAO Food and Agriculture Organization
– tries to improve agriculture

GATT General Agreement on Tariffs and Trade
– tries to make trade easier between different countries

WHO World Health Organization
– tries to improve health and fight disease

World Bank
– lends money to help countries build dams and other big projects

ILO International Labour Organization
– tries to improve working conditions

The General Assembly

Each member country can be represented in the General Assembly by up to five delegates. The General Assembly is the parliament of the United Nations, and meets to discuss and debate issues brought before it and to send proposals to the Security Council for approval.

Each country has one vote in the General Assembly, so China with 1 000 000 000 people has the same vote as Grenada with 100 000. A simple majority is sufficient to decide most issues, except where a matter of crucial importance is discussed. Then a two-thirds majority is needed.

The General Assembly meets once a year in the third week of September, but special meetings can also be held in an emergency. Much of its work is carried on in seven special committees, on which every member country is entitled to be represented.

The Security Council

The Security Council is authorised to take immediate action on behalf of the General Assembly. It has 15 members, each with the right to send one delegate with one vote. The five permanent members are the United States, United Kingdom, Soviet Union, China and France. The ten other members are elected from the General Assembly for a period of two years. Unlike decisions taken in the General Assembly by a simple majority, the rules of the Security Council require that a motion can only be carried if nine of the 15 members vote *for* the motion and *if* none of the five permanent members on the Council votes *against*. A single *no* vote (called the veto) from any one of the big five is sufficient to stop a proposal going through.

This great power veto was used by the Soviet Union, in particular, to block many proposals made by the General Assembly. So in 1950, the General Assembly approved the 'Uniting for Peace' Resolution, which enables the General Assembly to take emergency action to override a Security Council veto provided an emergency meeting is called within 24 hours and approves the vetoed motion by a two-thirds majority.

On 19 September 1960, for instance, the Soviet Union vetoed a resolution approving Dag Hammarskjold's policy on the Congo. Within 24 hours a meeting of the General Assembly was called. An emergency resolution was passed overriding the Soviet veto by 70 votes to nil. The Iron Curtain countries abstained.

The Secretariat

The Secretary General has ultimate responsibility for the smooth functioning of the United Nations Organization, aided by officials drawn from the different member countries. Since its foundation in 1945 this important post has been held by only five men:

- **Trygve Lie (Norway), 1946–53** – he helped to organise the UN forces sent to South Korea in 1950.

Dag Hammarskjold

- **Dag Hammarskjold (Sweden), 1953–61** – he was probably the most influential of all the UN Secretary Generals. He sent a UN peace-keeping force to help dampen down the Suez Crisis in 1956. He was killed on UN business, trying to bring peace to the Congo (now Zaire) in 1961.

- **U Thant (Burma), 1961–71** – he sent a UN peace-keeping force to Cyprus in 1964. His withdrawal of the UN peace-keeping force in the Sinai Peninsula in Egypt helped start the Six Day War between Egypt and Israel in 1967. He arranged a ceasefire between India and Pakistan in Kashmir in 1965.

- **Kurt Waldheim (Austria), 1972–81** – he played little part in resolving the crises of the 1970s. Progressively the major powers settled disputes outside the UN (e.g. the Camp David agreement between Israel and Egypt).

- **Perez de Cuellar (Peru), 1981 onwards** – he tried to prevent the United Kingdom and Argentina going to war in 1982, but without success. His reported aim as Secretary-General was 'Negotiate, negotiate, negotiate'.

Perez de Cuellar, UN Secretary General since 1981

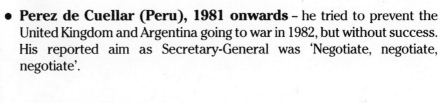

1 *From which parts of the world have the UN Secretary Generals been drawn? Why have they not come from the great powers?*

2 *What was unfair about the voting system in the United Nations in 1945? Has the 1950 amendment made it fair?*

The International Court of Justice

The International Court of Justice is a direct descendant of the pre-war League of Nations Court of International Justice which was also based at The Hague in the Netherlands. The Court consists of 15 judges. Each is elected to serve for a nine-year term. Not more than one judge may come from any one country.

The Court is unusual in that it can only hear cases brought by member states, not by individuals. Decisions of the Court are by a simple majority of the judges hearing a case. In its first decision in 1949 the Court awarded damages to Britain after two British destroyers were badly damaged by Albanian mines in the Corfu Channel.

The Councils

Trusteeship Council: This committee of the big five was set up to administer territories, not yet independent, which were placed under the control of the United Nations at the end of the Second World War. By 1980 only the Trust Territory of the Pacific Islands, administered by the United States was left. South West Africa (Namibia), a former German colony, was handed over to South Africa as a League of Nations mandate, but South Africa refused to accept the authority of the Trusteeship Council as the successor to the League.

Economic and Social Council: This is a committee of 54 members elected by the General Assembly who serve for three years and have responsibility for supervising the work of the United Nations specialised agencies in health, education, welfare, economic, social and other areas of concern.

The Organisations

WHO officials in Ethiopia in 1980, travelling by horse, search for cases of smallpox and vaccinate the people they meet en route

World Health Organization [WHO]: was formed to raise health standards throughout the world by trying to control epidemics, evaluating new drugs and medicines, promoting positive health measures such as better diets, child care, health education, etc.

Food and Agriculture Organization [FAO]:   was founded to help farmers (particularly those in the Third World) to grow more food through the proper use of fertilisers, crop sprays and other forms of pest control, agricultural education, etc. It is also concerned to promote healthier diets, combat famine, and raise living standards.

United Nations Educational Scientific and Cultural Organization [UNESCO]: was founded to implement the UN Charter's call to 'to re-affirm faith in fundamental human rights, in the dignity and worth of the human person, in the equal rights of men and women'. It does this through its work in promoting higher educational standards, scientific research and cultural exchanges. UNESCO has been particularly concerned to eradicate illiteracy by helping to train teachers and to facilitate the exchange of ideas between member countries.

International Labour Organization [ILO]: was founded by the League of Nations in 1919. Its aim is to improve working conditions throughout the world by encouraging member states to insist on minimum safety standards, good labour relations, sound management methods, vocational training, etc.

UN Agencies

There are a number of different international organisations which operate under the auspices of the United Nations. They include:

Universal Postal Union [UPU]: founded to co-ordinate and improve the world's postal services.

The General Agreement on Tariffs and Trade [GATT]: founded to promote and develop world trade and settle disputes between trading nations.

International Bank for Reconstruction and Development [IBRD or World Bank]: founded to provide loans to help develop resources in many of the countries of the Third World.

International Monetary Fund [IMF]: founded to help promote international trade by keeping a steady exchange rate between different currencies – if necessary, by providing loans.

World Meteorological Organization [WMO]: founded to enable member states to share weather information.

International Telecommunication Union [ITU]: founded to help develop world telecommunications and make them easier and cheaper to use.

International Civil Aviation Organization [ICAO]: founded to make air travel safer and more efficient throughout the world.

International Atomic Energy Agency [IAEE]: founded to help develop the peaceful uses of atomic energy.

KEEPING THE PEACE

The Veto

SOVIET VETO BARS ACTION IN COUNCIL
Censure Move in U.N. Over New Attack
on Hungary Carried to Assembly

The Soviet Union early today vetoed a United States resolution proposing Security Council censure of the Russian military attack on Hungary. Nine nations favored the United States proposal and one abstained, Yugoslavia . . . Angrily, Mr Lodge [the US representative] told the Council that the will of the world organization had been 'thwarted' by the Soviet veto and that the eleven-nation body had been prevented from fulfilling its responsibilities.

Lindesay Parrott in the *New York Times*, 4 November 1956

---

1 *Why did the headline read 'Censure Move in U.N. Over New Attack on Hungary Carried to Assembly'?*

2 *Why was it premature to say 'that the will of the world organization had been "thwarted" by the Soviet veto'?*

This was recorded as being the seventy-ninth use of the veto by the Soviet Union in just over ten years! The great power squabbling over the right of veto when the UN was founded in 1945, showed clearly that neither the Soviet Union nor the United States was prepared to allow the UN to intervene where its own vital interests were at stake. Although the United Kingdom argued against the veto at Dumbarton Oaks, she later used it when the occasion suited, such as joining with France in vetoing the Security Council motion condemning the use of force during the Suez Crisis in 1956. This was later carried by a huge majority in the General Assembly.

The massive influx of newly-independent countries, who joined the UN in the 1950s and 1960s, changed the pattern of voting in favour of the non-aligned nations (countries which are not allies of the East or West). This seriously weakened the position of the great powers in the General Assembly, if not in the Security Council.

Inevitably it is the peace-keeping role of the United Nations which has come in for the greatest criticism. As you have already seen, the League of Nations failed, not for the excellent work it did in improving public health and working conditions throughout the world, but because it failed to stop Japan invading Manchuria and Italy seizing Abyssinia.

Most of the failures of the UN can be attributed to the unhelpful attitude often adopted by the great powers and to the inability of member countries to see beyond their own regional or power groupings, such as the

Communist bloc, the Western Alliance, and the Third World. Nonetheless supporters of the United Nations can point to some solid achievements during the first 40 years in the history of the organisation, and to some valiant, if unsuccessful, efforts to preserve the peace in trying circumstances.

Palestine 1947–8: The UN sent a commission to Palestine, which reported back, recommending the partition of Palestine into two states – one Arab, one Jewish. This was passed by the General Assembly in 1947 but the proposals were rejected by the Arabs. The UN tried to mediate in the Arab–Israeli war which followed, but the chief UN mediator, Count Bernadotte, was assassinated in 1948 by Jewish terrorists. The UN later played a part in supervising a ceasefire.

Indonesia 1947–9: The UN intervened in the war between Dutch troops and Indonesian Nationalists, calling for a peaceful settlement. Much later U Thant successfully intervened over Dutch and Indonesian claims to West Irian (New Guinea) in 1962.

Kashmir 1949: The United Nations arranged an armistice which ended fighting in a dispute between Pakistan and India over Kashmir.

Korea 1950–3: The Security Council voted by seven to one (at a time when the Soviet delegate was boycotting Security Council meetings) to intervene in South Korea to halt North Korean aggression (see page 314). Although 16 countries sent soldiers to Korea, the armed forces were almost entirely American and South Korean.

Suez 1956: British, French and Israeli forces seized the Suez Canal in a campaign which was overwhelmingly condemned by the United Nations. In November a large peace-keeping force of 6000 soldiers from ten different nations was sent to separate the two sides.

The Congo 1960–4: A large peace-keeping force (mainly African) was sent to keep law and order in the Congo, which had only just been given its independence by Belgium.

Cyprus 1964: War between the Greek and Turkish people on the island of Cyprus led to UN intervention. The UN Secretary General, U Thant, sent a peace-keeping force to separate the two sides.

Other successful ventures included the imposition of sanctions against Rhodesia in 1966 and intervention in the Lebanon in 1968. But for every successful intervention there were failures. The United Nations was powerless to intervene (apart from passing votes of censure):

- when the Soviet Union invaded Hungary in 1956
- during the Cuban missiles crisis in 1962
- in the war in Vietnam 1964–75
- when the Warsaw Pact nations invaded Czechoslovakia in 1968

- in the India–Pakistan war 1971–2
- when American hostages were seized in Iran in 1979
- when the Russians invaded Afghanistan in 1979.

Canadian troops manning an observation post in Cyprus in 1974 as members of the United Nations peace-keeping force

---

1 *What are the limitations of the United Nations? What can't it do?*

2 *What positive advantages does membership of the United Nations bring?*

THE UNITED NATIONS AND THE LEAGUE

The United Nations closely resembles the old League of Nations but there are a number of important differences:

a) The United Nations has been able to send peace-keeping forces, drawn from the forces of member nations, to separate the belligerents in a conflict, such as in the Middle East in 1956 and 1967.

b) Almost all countries are members of the United Nations, including the United States and the Soviet Union.

c) There are more specialised agencies of the United Nations than there were under the auspices of the League.

d) The United Nations secretary-general has more power, and more scope for initiative, than had the secretary-general of the League.

e) The ability of the General Assembly to over-ride the veto of the Security Council has given its discussions greater significance.

Nonetheless, it is still disturbing that few nations seem able to accept United Nations' criticism. Many have ignored or rejected its proposals.

FURTHER QUESTIONS AND EXERCISES

> *Thursday, 28 September 1944*   *Washington*
> *Then we talked a bit about Dumbarton Oaks results. I said altho' we'd agreed 90% there was a nasty snag in the remaining 10%. I think he understands this. He talked of the necessity of a top-level meeting to iron it out. Said Joe had agreed that a meeting was necessary. He (F.D.R.) proposes the Hague, or Stockholm or Scotland – in November.*
>
> *Diaries of Sir Alexander Cadogan*, edited by David Dilks, Cassell, 1971

1 *Who was 'F.D.R.'? Who was 'Joe'? What were the 'Dumbarton Oaks results'? When was the next 'top-level meeting' held and where? What was the 'nasty snag in the remaining 10%'? How was it finally agreed, when, and where?*

2 *Write brief notes on each of the following:*

  a) Dag Hammarskjöld   *d) the UN in Suez 1956*

  b) U Thant   *e) the UN in the Congo 1960*

  c) the UN in Palestine 1948   *f) WHO*

3 *Read the aims and objectives of the United Nations (page 290). Make a list of what you think are the ten most important aims and objectives. Against each item on your list write down whether you think the United Nations has successfully achieved its intended objective or not.*

4 *Explain carefully the circumstances which led to the formation of the United Nations Organization. How, why, when and where was it founded?*

Chapter Fourteen

The Cold War

INTRODUCTION

Military police on duty at a crossing point in Berlin

1 *Which sector of Berlin are you, a) entering and b) leaving, at this point? Why was Berlin divided into sectors like this?*

2 *Is Berlin still a divided city?*

From Stettin in the Baltic to Trieste in the Adriatic, an Iron Curtain has descended across the Continent. Behind that line lie all the capitals of the ancient states of central and eastern Europe . . . all are subject, in one form or another, not only to Soviet influence but to a very high and, in many cases, increasing measure of control from Moscow.

This was the first public occasion when a Western leader used the term 'Iron Curtain' to describe the frontier between eastern and western Europe after the War. Winston Churchill was speaking at Westminster College in the small American town of Fulton, Missouri. He made his speech on 5 March 1946 but had already used the same phrase in a telegram to President Truman on 12 May 1945:

An Iron Curtain is drawn down upon their front. We do not know what is going on behind . . . Surely it is vital now to come to an understanding with Russia, or see where we are with her, before we weaken our armies.

One year after Churchill's Fulton speech, an American friend of his, Bernard M. Baruch, told politicians in South Carolina:

Let us not be deceived – we are today in the midst of a cold war.

By this he meant a war of words between the Soviet Union and the West. It was not a 'hot' war, nor a 'shooting' war. But it was a war, nonetheless, in which there were enemies and friends, losers and winners, defeats and conquests. Coupled with Churchill's idea of an Iron Curtain, separating and isolating the Communist world, these two ideas helped to shape postwar relations between East and West.

---

1 *What was the attitude of the West to Russia, a) before the War, in 1936–9 and b) after the First World War, in 1918–20? What was the attitude of Russia to the West then?*

2 *Why was the use of the terms 'Iron Curtain' and 'cold war' unhelpful to the peace process after the War?*

3 *What was Churchill implying when he sent his telegram to Truman on 12 May 1945? Why was he worried?*

THE IRON CURTAIN

The Cold War

The Cold War should have come as no surprise to the world in view of the pre-war policies of both sides. It was only hope which led people to imagine that the War had changed fundamental attitudes and long-held government policies. Churchill still hated Communism. Communism still hated Capitalism.

The Allies had been united in their desire to defeat the Axis powers but this didn't mean they saw eye to eye. It was simply that all Hitler's friends were their enemies. All Hitler's enemies were their friends. Churchill said, 'If Hitler invaded Hell I would make at least a favourable reference to the Devil'. Immediately after the start of the German invasion of Russia in June 1941 he told radio listeners,

No one has been a more consistent opponent of Communism than I have . . . I will unsay no word that I have spoken about it. But any man or state who fights on against Nazidom will have our aid.

In 1945, that fight had been won. Now earlier fears and prejudices were revived on both sides.

● Western statesmen could not forget that only six years earlier, in 1939, Stalin and Hitler had agreed a Non-Aggression Pact. It was this which had precipitated the start of the Second World War, since it cleared the way for Hitler to invade Poland and for the later partition of Poland between Nazi Germany and Stalin's Russia. In 1939–40 Stalin annexed Bessarabia (part of Romania), the Baltic states (Lithuania, Latvia, Estonia) and invaded Finland. What reason had the West to suppose the leopard had changed his spots?

● Communism and Capitalism are opposites. Churchill had pressed the West to intervene in the Russian Civil War only 25 years earlier. Churchill and Truman were known opponents of Communism. What reason had Stalin to suppose the Western leopards had changed their spots?

● Germany was in chaos after the war, with her economy in ruins, and millions close to starvation. Massive aid was needed. But the Soviet Union, too, had suffered terribly in the War. Millions of Russians had died.

Map of Eastern Europe showing the Iron Curtain countries

Stalin's priority was Russia, not Germany. Western concern and compassion for Germany – to ensure the return of democracy and stable government – was not shared by Stalin.

- Both sides had substantial grounds for distrust in 1945:
  - The United States had the atom bomb – a closely guarded secret. Truman only told Stalin about it a short time before Hiroshima.
  - Stalin promised that the people living in the liberated territories would be free to choose their own governments after the War. But it was already clear that the Russians were only prepared to see the formation of pro-Communist governments in the territories they had overrun. There was nothing the Allies could do about this, short of going to war.

The charitable view was that Russia still feared a Western crusade against Soviet Communism. According to this theory, Stalin wanted a buffer zone of satellites between Russia and the West. This would act as 'a strong defensive perimeter'. The hostile view, taken by many Americans, was that the Communist takeover of eastern Europe was simply a subtle form of Soviet aggression, enlarging the frontiers of world Communism by peaceful means instead of by force.

---

1 *Where was the Iron Curtain?*

2 *Which were the Iron Curtain countries?*

Eastern Europe

At first Stalin moved slowly in eastern Europe. There was no sudden imposition of Soviet Communism. Opposition parties were allowed. At the first elections the voters were given a relatively free choice, provided the governments they chose were at least sympathetic to Communist aims and ideals. But gradually the east European Communists took over the running of their countries.

- Georgi Dimitrov became Communist leader of Bulgaria in 1946.
- A Coalition Government dominated by Communists controlled Poland until all opposition parties were banned in 1947.
- A left-wing Coalition Government in Hungary, dominated by the non-Communist Smallholders' Party after free elections, made sweeping reforms until it was replaced by a hardline Communist Government led by Matyas Rakosi.
- A Communist-dominated Coalition Government controlled Romania, which had a king until December 1947 when King Michael was made to abdicate.

- In Czechoslovakia the 1946 elections gave the Communist Party about 40 per cent of the vote. A Coalition Government led by Klement Gottwald, a Communist, came to power. But in a coup in February 1948, Gottwald managed to get rid of the non-Communists in his government and left President Benes with no option but to resign.

The Cominform

The Cominform was the abbreviated name for the Communist Information Bureau, an organisation which Stalin set up in October 1947 after a conference of Communist Party leaders from Eastern Europe and also from the West (France and Italy). Apart from providing information, it co-ordinated the work of the Communist Party in Europe and made sure that European Communist leaders toed the Party line from Moscow. In 1948, for instance, the Cominform condemned and ordered the expulsion of Yugoslavia, when President Tito refused to follow Party directives.

Tito, a guerrilla leader during the War, remained a thorn in Stalin's side. He was a Communist who took an independent, not a Stalinist, line. He was able to keep Yugoslavia independent of the other Iron Curtain countries because it had not been 'liberated' by the Red Army at the end of the War.

Yugoslavia's Communist dictator, President Tito

---

1 *Why was the Communist Information Bureau called the Cominform?*

2 *Why did the countries of Eastern Europe turn Communist after the War?*

3 *Which of the countries of Eastern Europe was a democracy in the 1930s? Which had a Communist government after the First World War?*

The Truman Doctrine

Only one of the Balkan countries remained outside the Iron Curtain. This was Greece. Greece had been involved in a civil war during the closing months of the War. Communist guerrillas, calling themselves the National People's Liberation Army (ELAS), fought the Germans with considerable success. When Hitler's occupation forces withdrew, ELAS tried to take over the legitimate government of Greece. At this stage they controlled over two-thirds of the country. But when the Germans left, their place was immediately taken by British forces, committed to the restoration of the Greek monarchy. ELAS changed from fighting the Germans to fighting the Greek Government and the British until a truce was agreed in January 1945. The establishment of pro-Communist regimes in other parts of Eastern Europe encouraged ELAS to lead another uprising in northern Greece in

1946. By this time the British forces were unable to provide the Greek Royalist government with the support and material aid it needed to counter the new rebellion. By then, however, US President Truman had decided to withstand all signs of Communist aggression whatever the cost. On 12 March 1947 he enunciated the Truman Doctrine:

> I believe that it must be the policy of the United States to support free peoples who are resisting attempted subjugation by armed minorities or by outside pressures.

Truman put his Doctrine into practice by supplying the Greeks with advisers and arms. As a result the attempted Communist takeover of Greece was successfully resisted, partly because President Tito withdrew his support from the guerrillas when he broke away from the Cominform.

---

1 *What was the Truman Doctrine? How was it different from the duty of UN member states to resist aggression by one state against another?*

2 *What possible dangers were there in carrying out the Truman Doctrine?*

3 *How do you prove that an 'armed minority' actually does represent the minority and not the majority of the people? How do you prove that there are 'outside pressures'?*

4 *How would the Truman Doctrine have worked out had the Americans applied it to Spain, ten years earlier, in 1937?*

The Marshall Plan

General George Marshall

The Truman Doctrine signalled a change in American foreign policy, from one of co-operation with Soviet Communism to one of confrontation. Truman was not going to stand idly by and watch while Stalin took by stealth other territories in Europe.

But what if freely elected Communist governments came to power? What could America do then? This was a distinct possibility, since Europe was still suffering the after-effects and ravages of the War. There were severe food shortages. Lack of money prevented European governments rebuilding their shattered cities. The Americans recalled the end of the First World War. Communism thrived wherever there was poverty and despair.

This is why the Americans devised a plan to provide massive financial aid to help the governments of Europe. It was to help them recover from the damage which the War had done to their economies. It was first outlined, in June 1947, by a former American wartime commander – General Marshall – now US secretary of state (foreign minister).

The Marshall Plan was yet another way in which the Americans could carry out the Truman Doctrine, of helping democratic governments counter the spread of Communism. In Greece, the Americans used the 'stick'. Now Marshall Aid was to be the 'carrot'.

Marshall Aid to European countries which fought in the War

	$ (million)		$ (million)
United Kingdom	3 176	Austria	677
France	2 706	Belgium/Luxembourg	556
Italy	1 474	Denmark	271
West Germany	1 389	Norway	254
Netherlands	1 079	Yugoslavia	109
Greece	694		

Any country accepting aid was assumed to be friendly to the United States. This was why the Americans offered help to Iron Curtain countries as well as the West. Czechoslovakia, governed by a pro-Communist Coalition Government, originally accepted an offer of Marshall Aid but eventually turned it down on instructions from Moscow. Yugoslavia accepted – demonstrating, once again, Tito's independence from Stalin.

The Russians later provided their own substitute for Marshall Aid when they founded COMECON in January 1949 (COuncil for Mutual ECONomic Assistance). Marshall Aid was administered by the Organization for European Economic Co-operation (OEEC). It eventually distributed grants totalling $13 000 million as the European Recovery Programme. Countries receiving Marshall Aid included Britain, France, Belgium and Norway of the countries which had been at war with Germany, and Austria, Italy and West Germany of the former Axis powers.

ICE-COLD WAR

Cartoon by Vicky in the News Chronicle, *5 February 1948, published shortly after news that Russia had tested an atom bomb. Bevin (British foreign secretary) is in goal (left) while Molotov (Russian foreign secretary) keeps goal (right). The other two players are General Marshall and Stalin. They are playing with an atomic puck.*

1 *Draw a graph from the statistics to show the extent of American aid to Europe under the Marshall Plan. Which countries benefited most?*

2 *What was the point of the cartoon opposite? What part did Marshall Aid play in the Cold War?*

3 *Why were the Americans able to offer massive financial assistance to the Europeans after the War? Why did they offer it to their former enemies: Germany, Austria and Italy?*

CRISIS

The Berlin Blockade

When the War ended Germany was divided into four occupation zones: British, American, French and Russian. Because of the importance of Berlin as capital of Germany, this too was divided into four occupation zones, even though it was over 150 km inside the Russian occupation zone (see photograph on page 302). This meant that access to and from Berlin and West Germany had to be across Soviet-controlled territory.

It had originally been intended that both the Berlin and the German occupation zones would eventually be governed jointly by the four occupying powers. But by 1948, three years after the War, deteriorating relations between East and West held out little hope that Germany would ever be reunited. Since the Soviet authorities did not allow free access to their zone, the other three occupying powers took steps to merge their zones into one. In retaliation, the Soviet authorities put obstacles in their way. They demanded the right to board Allied military trains en route to Berlin. On 1 April 1948, two American passenger trains were refused entry into the Soviet zone because the train commandant in each case was not prepared to accept inspection by Soviet border guards. On 20 April and 20 May the Russians demanded that the movement of canal barges should be brought into line with the new procedures.

The crisis came to a head on 18 June 1948, when the Allies announced that a revised Deutschemark would be used in future in the Allied zones of West Germany. The Soviet authorities responded immediately by closing all road routes into Berlin, all passenger train services, and restricting rail freight train services and canal traffic. On 22 June, the Allies told the Soviet authorities that they proposed to introduce the new Deutschemark into West Berlin as well, to make it easier for goods to be traded between Berlin and the Allied zones. To the Russians, it looked as if the Allies intended to incorporate West Berlin permanently in West Germany, making both independent of the Russian-dominated Eastern zone. This would give the West a base well inside the Iron Curtain.

Source A

On June 23, the Soviet authorities suspended all railroad passengers and freight traffic into Berlin, because of alleged 'technical difficulties' on the Berlin-Helmstedt rail line. They also stopped barge traffic on similar grounds.

Shortly before midnight of June 23, the Soviet authorities issued orders to the Berlin central electric switch-control station (located in their sector) to disrupt delivery of electric power from Soviet zone and Soviet sector plants to the Western sectors. Shortage of coal was given as a reason for this measure.

The Berlin Crisis: A Report, US Department of State, 1948

Source B

28 June 1948
Meeting at White House – Berlin Situation
When the specific question was discussed as to what our future policy in Germany was to be – namely, were we to stay in Berlin or not? – the President [Truman] interrupted to say that there was no discussion on that point, we were going to stay period . . . we were in Berlin by terms of an agreement and the Russians had no right to get us out by either direct or indirect pressure.

James Forrestal (US secretary of the Navy in April 1945), *The Forrestal Diaries*, edited by Walter Millis, The Viking Press, 1951

Source C

This reform [the new currency] . . . sparked off a dangerous crisis. The devalued old marks poured into the Soviet occupation zone. The Soviet military administration was obliged to take urgent steps to protect the East German economy and monetary system. In order to foil currency speculators, checks were carried out on passengers arriving from West Germany and certain restrictions were imposed on transport links between Berlin and the Western zones. Nevertheless, the Soviet side was ready to maintain the supply of food and fuel to the whole of Berlin . . .

Every day 380 American transport planes made several flights each into Berlin. All this was simply a propaganda move and was also intended to intensify the cold war. The restraint shown by Soviet diplomacy and its readiness to accept a reasonable compromise helped to preserve the peace during those tense months. Nevertheless, the 'Berlin crisis' accelerated the complete division of Germany and the formation of a separate West German state.

History of the USSR, translated from the Russian by Ken Russell, Progress Publishers (Moscow), 1977

Source D

The Berlin Blockade. Food is unloaded straight on to lorries from American cargo planes, June 1948. Allied cargo planes, flying night and day, supplied Berliners with everything, including coal.

Source E

Just as the morning sun rose over the jagged skyline of this broken but defiant city a Soviet zone locomotive chugged wearily into the Charlottenburg Station in the British sector hauling the first train to reach Berlin from the West in 328 days. Arrival of the train completed the relief of the city from the iron vice of the Soviet blockade. At one minute after midnight . . , two jeeps and a convoy of cars, buses and trucks roared out of the city for the western zones.

Drew Middleton in the *New York Times*, Thursday, 12 May 1949

---

1 *How long did the Berlin Blockade last? How did the Allies beat it?*

2 *How and when was the Blockade begun by the Russians?*

3 *What reason did Truman think explained the Soviet Blockade? How does Source C refute this explanation?*

4 *Why do you think the Russians allowed aircraft to fly into Berlin but not rail, road, or canal traffic? Why do you think the Allies chose not to force their way into Berlin with tanks?*

5 *Quote evidence which contradicts the explanation in Source C of the events which led up to the imposition of the Berlin Blockade.*

6 *How did the Russians explain the reasons for the disruption of communications to Berlin, a) to their Western counterparts in 1948 and b) in the Soviet history published 30 years later?*

NATO and the Warsaw Pact

When the Berlin Blockade ended on 12 May 1949, the future course of Europe had changed irrevocably:

- the Western Allies had formed a defensive alliance – NATO.

- plans for the creation of the German Federal Republic had been finalised and came into being 11 days after the lifting of the Blockade.

Both these results had an important 'knock-on' effect, since the Russians and their allies regarded the formation of NATO (Source A below) as a hostile act, as an endorsement of the Cold War and a threat to their own security. This led, inevitably, to the formation of their own Warsaw Pact alliance (Source B opposite) in 1955.

The founding of the Federal Republic made it possible for Germans in the three Western occupation zones to start rebuilding their country. But it also ensured that Germany would now be split permanently in two.

The German Democratic Republic (East Germany) came into being on 7 October 1949, little more than four months after the foundation of its rival, the Federal Republic, on 23 May 1949. When the Federal Republic joined NATO on 9 May 1955, it was followed five days later by the signing of the Warsaw Pact. The North Atlantic Treaty Organization came into being on 4 April 1949. You can see the principal terms of the Treaty in the panel below and the names of the countries who signed it. The most significant feature of the Treaty was not so much the fact that it was an alliance of 12 powers – ten in Europe and two in North America – but the fact that it committed the United States, bigger than all the other countries put together, to the defence of Europe. This was a convincing answer, at last, to Churchill's worries, in May 1945 at the end of the war, about the future defence of Europe.

Source A

The North Atlantic Treaty

Article 1
The Parties undertake, as set forth in the Charter of the United Nations, to settle any international disputes in which they may be involved by peaceful means in such a manner that international peace and security, and justice, are not endangered, and to refrain in their international relations from the threat or use of force in any manner inconsistent with the purposes of the United Nations . . .

Article 5
The Parties agree that an armed attack against one or more of them in Europe or North America shall be considered an attack against them all; and consequently they agree that, if such an armed attack occurs, each of them, in the exercise of the right of individual or collective self-defence recognised by Article 51 of the Charter of the United Nations, will assist the Party or Parties so attacked by taking forthwith, individually and in concert with the other Parties, such action as it deems necessary, including the use of armed force, to restore and maintain the security of the North Atlantic area.

Any such armed attack and all measures taken as a result thereof shall immediately be reported to the Security Council. Such measures shall be terminated when the Security Council has taken the measures necessary to restore and maintain international peace and security.

Signed Belgium, Canada, Denmark, France, Iceland, Italy, Luxembourg, Netherlands, Norway, Portugal, United Kingdom, United States.
Washington. 4 April 1949

Since 1949, NATO has remained strong, despite one or two upsets. In 1952 Greece and Turkey joined the organisation, followed three years later by West Germany. France later withdrew her forces from NATO command (1966). This is why the NATO headquarters moved from Paris to Brussels.

Source B

The Warsaw Treaty of Friendship, Co-operation, and Mutual Assistance

Article 1
The Contracting Parties undertake, in accordance with the Charter of the United Nations Organization, to refrain in their international relations from the threat or use of force, and to settle their international disputes peacefully and in such manner as will not jeopardize international peace and security.

Article 4
In the event of armed attack in Europe on one or more of the parties to the Treaty by any state or group of states, each of the parties to the Treaty, in the exercise of its right to individual or collective self defence in accordance with Article 51 of the Charter of the United Nations Organization, shall immediately, either individually or in agreement with other Parties to the Treaty, come to the assistance of the state or states attacked with all such means as it deems necessary, including armed force. The Parties to the Treaty shall immediately consult concerning the necessary measures to be taken by them jointly in order to restore and maintain international peace and security.

Measures taken on the basis of this Article shall be reported to the Security Council in conformity with the provisions of the Charter of the United Nations Organization. These measures shall be discontinued immediately the Security Council adopts the necessary measures to restore and maintain international peace and security.

Signed Albania, Bulgaria, Hungary, East Germany, Poland, Romania, Soviet Union, Czechoslovakia. 14 May 1955.
[Albania withdrew from the Pact on 13 September 1968]

1 *What similarities and differences are there between the Warsaw Pact and the North Atlantic Treaty?*
2 *Why do Soviet historians question Greek and Turkish membership of NATO? What reasons help to explain why they joined the alliance?*

3 Look at the cartoon below. Work out why it was drawn. What is the chain made of? Who is speaking and to whom? Who is the 'he' on the end of the chain? What was the point of the cartoon?

4 How has the existence of NATO and the Warsaw Pact helped or hindered the cause of world peace since 1949–55?

'DO NOT FEAR, HE IS ON A CHAIN.' Russian cartoon drawn in 1955 after the Western powers allowed West Germany to rearm and join NATO. The Russian word on each link means 'guarantee'.

The Korean War

When Japan was defeated in 1945 the Allies were faced with the problem of deciding the future of the old Japanese empire. The Korean peninsula had been Japanese since 1910. The Allies (but not Stalin) promised it would become independent after the War. But in 1945 it was partitioned along the 38th parallel (38° North) with the Japanese forces surrendering to the Red Army in the north and to the Americans in the south.

Plans to unite the two halves failed, so in 1948 both occupation zones were granted their independence. The Republic of Korea (formerly the American zone in the **South**), led by Syngman Rhee, came into being on 15 August 1948. The Korean People's Democratic Republic (formerly the Soviet zone in the **North**), led by Kim Il Sung, was founded on 9 September. The Soviet forces left North Korea by the end of 1948. US forces left South Korea by June the following year.

Neither of the two Korean governments was happy with the partition of their country. Both claimed to be the rightful government. The United

Nations tried in vain to unify the two Koreas as both sides built up their armed forces. Not surprisingly, there were frequent skirmishes on the frontier between the two Koreas. In 1949, the UN Commission in Korea warned of the danger of civil war.

An uncomfortable peace kept the two sides apart until 4.0 a.m., Sunday, 25 June 1950. A large North Korean army led by Marshal Choe Yong Gun, supported by tanks, crossed the border and rapidly moved south. Its seven divisions easily outnumbered the four poorly equipped South Korean divisions which faced them.

Source A

On Saturday, June 24, 1950, I was in Independence, Missouri, to spend the weekend with my family. It was a little after ten in the evening when the telephone rang. It was the Secretary of State calling from his home in Maryland. 'Mr.President', said Dean Acheson, 'I have very serious news. The North Koreans have invaded South Korea.'

Memoirs of Harry S. Truman, Doubleday, 1956

President Truman flew back to Washington.

Source B

I had time to think aboard the plane. In my generation, this was not the first occasion when the strong had attacked the weak. I recalled some earlier instances: Manchuria, Ethiopia, Austria. I remembered how each time that the democracies failed to act it had encouraged the aggressors to keep going ahead. Communism was acting in Korea just as Hitler, Mussolini, and the Japanese had acted ten, fifteen, and twenty years earlier. I felt certain that if South Korea was allowed to fall Communist leaders would be emboldened to override nations closer to our own shores.

Memoirs of Harry S. Truman, Doubleday, 1956

Source C

TRUMAN ORDERS U.S. AIR, NAVY UNITS TO FIGHT IN AID OF KOREA; U.N. COUNCIL SUPPORTS HIM; OUR FLIERS IN ACTION; FLEET GUARDS FORMOSA

SANCTIONS VOTED
Council Adopts Plan of U.S. for Armed Force in Korea, 7 to 1
THE SOVIET IS ABSENT
Yugoslavia Casts Lone Dissent – Egypt and India Abstain

Headlines in the *New York Times*, Wednesday, 28 June 1950

Source D

HONG KONG. June 27 – The North Korean Government issued a statement today saying that it regarded the cease fire order of the United

States Security Council illegal for two reasons. It said these were, one, because the Democratic People's Republic of North Korea was not represented when its affairs were discussed and, two, because the Soviet Union and (Communist) China did not participate. On the latter point, it cited the United Nations Charter, which requires unanimity of five permanent members of the Security Council on questions of substance.

News report in the *New York Times*, Wednesday, 28 June 1950

Source E

5th July: The Prime Minister (Mr Attlee): I am asking the House to support the [Labour] Government in the action which they have taken in resisting aggression. That action is fulfilling our obligations under the Charter of the United Nations . . .

On 25th June there started the invasion of South Korea by the armed forces of North Korea. Here, again, we have one of these extraordinary inversions of the facts, it being alleged that South Korea attacked North Korea. Anything less likely, in view of the fact that North Korea was heavily armed and South Korea was not, could not possibly be imagined.

Report of the Parliamentary Debate in the House of Commons, 1950

1 How do you account for the discrepancy in dates in Sources A and E? What was the cause of the Korean War according to, a) the West, b) North Korea, c) the United Nations? Which do you believe? Why?

2 Does the UN Charter (page 294) require the 'unanimity of five permanent members of the Security Council on questions of substance'?

3 What were President Truman's reasons for intervening in South Korea? What assumption did he make about the aggressors? Did he see the war as only being between North Korea and the United Nations?

4 Would it have made any difference to the outcome of the war had Communist China been a member of the United Nations in 1950?

On 28 June, the North Korean forces captured Seoul and rapidly drove the South Korean forces southwards into a small corner of the Korean peninsula near the port of Pusan. However, the American troops fighting in Korea managed to delay the North Korean advance long enough to let US General MacArthur plan a daring counter-attack.

MacArthur was an outstanding and original commander. Instead of reinforcing the troops caught inside the Pusan perimeter zone (see map), he made a landing at Inchon, near Seoul, 300 km inside enemy-occupied territory on 15 September 1950. Caught off guard, the North Koreans were routed and fell back as the soldiers inside the Pusan perimeter linked up with the Inchon landing forces. Together they drove the North Koreans behind the 38th parallel and back into their own republic.

Instead of staying in South Korea, having forced the North Koreans to obey the UN demand (that they withdraw their troops), MacArthur's armies (backed by another UN resolution on the reunification of Korea) advanced

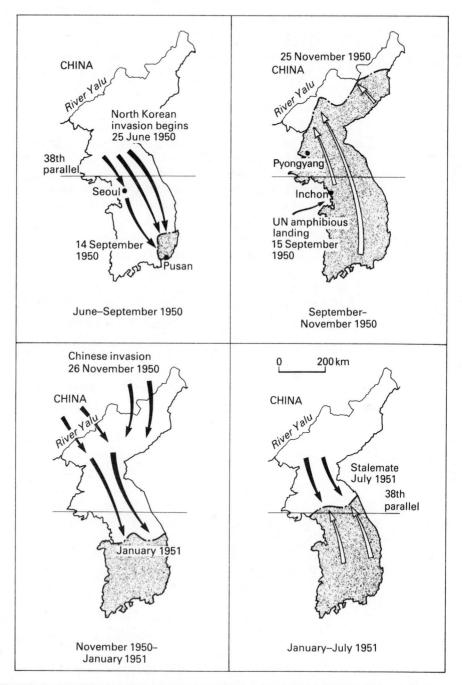

CHINA

River Yalu

North Korean invasion begins 25 June 1950

38th parallel

Seoul •

14 September 1950

Pusan

June–September 1950

25 November 1950
CHINA

River Yalu

Pyongyang

Inchon

UN amphibious landing 15 September 1950

September– November 1950

Chinese invasion 26 November 1950

CHINA

River Yalu

January 1951

November 1950– January 1951

0   200 km

CHINA

River Yalu

Stalemate July 1951

38th parallel

January–July 1951

Maps showing the course of the Korean War

into North Korea. In doing so, MacArthur ignored a clear warning from Chou En-lai, that China would intervene in the war if he did so.

This time the UN forces (mostly South Korean and American) could be branded as aggressors. They seized Pyongyang, the North Korean capital, and advanced rapidly towards the Chinese border. By mid-November they had nearly completed the reunification of the two Koreas.

But on 25 November 1950, the war changed course for yet another time. Massive Chinese armies crossed the Yalu River between China and North Korea and drove a huge wedge between the two main UN armies. MacArthur's forces had no alternative but to retreat. The Chinese advance southwards was just as rapid as that of the UN forces northwards, only days earlier. On 31 December 1950, the Chinese and North Korean armies crossed the 38th parallel again and Seoul fell once more, this time to the Communists. After much hard fighting, the UN forces managed to drive the Red armies back again. They recaptured Seoul on 14 March 1951 and then held on to a front line on or about the 38th parallel.

MacArthur was not the man to be satisfied with stalemate. He disagreed in public with the President on the future conduct of the war. MacArthur wanted to extend the war into China itself, using American air superiority to attack Chinese bases in Manchuria and American sea power to blockade the Chinese mainland. This was dangerous talk. It could have led to Soviet intervention, in Korea or in Europe.

Truman was his commander-in-chief and Truman sacked him. General Omar Bradley, the chairman of the joint chiefs of staff, later justified MacArthur's dismissal with the comment that these policies would have involved the US armed forces in 'the wrong war, at the wrong place, at the wrong time, and with the wrong enemy'.

The stalemate convinced Truman and other Allied leaders that hopes of unifying Korea were completely out of the question. Restoration of the line of partition along the 38th parallel was the best they could hope for. After holding virtually the same front line for two years, both sides eventually signed an Armistice agreement in July 1953.

The significance of the Korean War lay not so much in the fact that the UN forces regained South Korea for the South Koreans, but in the decisive and convincing way in which the Americans rushed troops to defend the victim of an act of aggression. This, in itself, should have told the Russians and the Chinese that the Americans would be no pushover in any future conflict. But victory was bought at a terrible cost. Over 50 000 Americans were killed and an estimated 3 000 000 Korean civilians died. Yet technically the United States had not been at war – as President Truman explained to an interviewer:

Interviewer: Mr President, everyone is asking in this country, are we or are we not at war?

Truman: We are not at war.

Interviewer: Would it be correct to call it a police action under the United Nations?

Truman: Yes, that is exactly what it amounts to.

1 *Why did Truman stress that the United States was not at war?*

2 *Why was it foolhardy of the UN forces under MacArthur to advance north of the 38th parallel? Could this be justified as being a necessary part of the 'police action under the United Nations'?*

3 *What did the Korean War achieve?*

RUSSIA AFTER STALIN

Stalin's Successor?

Nikita Khruschev

When Stalin died in 1953 the Russian leaders were thrown into confusion. Stalin, 'the man of steel', had ruled the Soviet Union with an iron fist ever since the late 1920s. When he first came to power the Bolshevik Revolution was not yet ten years old, the country was still weak, its agriculture backward and its communication systems poor. Most of its industrial resources had yet to be developed.

When Stalin died, the Soviet Union had become a gigantic superpower, second only to the United States. Who would succeed Stalin as ruler of this powerful empire? Would it be another dictator like Lenin or Stalin? Or would Russia be governed by the Politburo (the Russian equivalent of a British Cabinet)? At first, Georgi Malenkov was named as prime minister. But Nikita Khruschev, his rival on the Politburo, took the post of first secretary of the Communist Party, the position which Stalin used to gain power when Lenin died.

Khruschev Denounces Stalin

By 1956, Khruschev had replaced Malenkov as Russian leader. At the Twentieth Party Congress in Moscow, in 1956, he astounded the world when he denounced Stalin and the many injustices committed during the Purges in the 1930s (see page 133). Khruschev told the delegates that Stalin had deliberately encouraged the 'cult of personality' – getting too much power for himself and persuading the public that he alone was the saviour of Russia – a superman to be worshipped rather than criticised.

In the end these criticisms could be, and were, made about Khruschev himself! In particular the Chinese Communist Party accused him of revisionism – unwarranted modifications to the principles of Marx and Lenin. Khruschev's denunciation of Stalin and his belief in a policy of peaceful co-existence were attacked because they undermined the general belief in the infallibility of Communism.

1 *What was meant by the 'cult of personality'? Of which other figures in twentieth-century history could this accusation be made?*

2 *What was 'revisionism'? Why was this a crime in the eyes of Mao Tse-tung? Why was 'peaceful co-existence' thought to be at odds with the aims of Communism?*

3 *Why did Khruschev's denunciation of Stalin in 1956 startle the world?*

Peaceful Co-existence

People in the West didn't quite know what to make of Khruschev. He had a cheerful face and a fiery temper. One minute he seemed to want to be friends, the next moment he was an enemy.

There seems little doubt that Khruschev genuinely believed in peaceful co-existence between East and West. In doing so, he made enemies among the hardliners in the Soviet Union. His task was not made easier by President Eisenhower's secretary of state, John Foster Dulles, a man who said that Communism should be resisted at all times, even to the brink of war.

Yet Khruschev's support for better relations with the West did not stop him taking tough action to put down the rebellion in Hungary in 1956 (see below). He also told Western leaders, 'We will bury you'! Khruschev persuaded the Russians that nuclear war made it impossible to spread Communism by military means. They would have to do it peacefully, showing the rest of the world the advantages of living in a Communist society. He said there was more than one way of attaining this goal. He called it the 'different roads to socialism'. But Khruschev had many problems to solve at home in Russia. His attempt to increase food output, by ploughing up the virgin lands of Kazakhstan, failed to raise grain production to the levels needed. This led eventually to his downfall although the confrontation with Kennedy over Cuba (page 326) may also have made him lose face in the eyes of his rivals.

1 *Why do you think the word 'brinkmanship' was coined in the 1950s? What did it mean?*

2 *What did Khruschev mean by 'peaceful co-existence'?*

HUNGARY IN 1956

Khruschev's denunciation of Stalin had unforeseen consequences in Eastern Europe. In particular, it sent the wrong signals to Hungary where the repressive regime of the Communist dictator, Matyas Rakosi (page 305), aided by the brutality of the Hungarian secret police, had already stimulated

Angry Hungarians pull down a giant statue of Stalin in Budapest in 1956

Moderate prime minister, Imre Nagy. He was executed by the Communists in Hungary in 1958

unrest against the Government. Hungary's dissidents were further encouraged when Rakosi resigned in July 1956, under pressure from the Soviet Government. Khruschev thought a more liberal leader could satisfy the voices of dissent now being heard in Hungary.

But the move backfired. On 23 October 1956, thousands of Hungarians took to the streets of Budapest to protest against the presence of Soviet troops. They raised the Hungarian national flag on public buildings and confronted the authorities. Hundreds were killed in clashes with Soviet troops. The rioters seemed to have got their way when Imre Nagy was made prime minister the following day. Nagy had been prime minister from 1953–5 until Rakosi forced him out of office and expelled him from the Communist Party.

Nagy's return was greeted with great delight by the Hungarians. A mood of rejoicing led the crowds to smash the huge statue of Stalin in Budapest. This was no crime in Khruschev's eyes but it was only the beginning. The situation looked as if it could get out of control. Some Hungarians took the law into their own hands and revenged themselves on the hated secret police. Free speech flourished briefly. Nagy promised free elections.

Source A Tuesday, 23 October 1956

- We demand the immediate evacuation of all Soviet troops, in conformity with the provisions of the Treaty of Peace.
- A new Government must be constituted under the direction of Comrade Imre Nagy; all the criminal leaders of the Stalin–Rakosi era must be immediately relieved of their duties.
- The leadership must change. And Nagy shall be our leader.
- Imre Nagy to the Government. Rakosi into the Danube.

Demands of demonstrators in Budapest,
quoted by Tibor Meray in *Thirteen Days That Shook The Kremlin*,
translated by Howard L. Katzander, Thames and Hudson, 1958

Source B Wednesday, 24 October 1956

Government organizations have called for help from Soviet troops stationed in Hungary under the terms of the Warsaw Pact. Responding to the Government's appeal, Soviet troops will help in the restoration of order.

Radio Budapest, quoted in Tibor Meray, *Thirteen Days That Shook The Kremlin*,
translated by Howard L. Katzander, Thames and Hudson, 1958

Source C Wednesday, 31 October 1956

I speak to you once more, Hungarian brothers, from my heart. The revolutionary struggle in which you have been the heroes is won ... We have driven the band of Rakosi and Gero [a hardline Communist leader] from the country. They will answer for their crimes ... My dear friends today we have started negotiations for the withdrawal of Soviet troops from our country and for the abrogation of the obligations imposed on us by the Warsaw Pact ... Long live the Hungarian Republic, independent, free, and democratic! Long live Free Hungary!

Imre Nagy quoted in Tibor Meray, *Thirteen Days That Shook The Kremlin*,
translated by Howard L. Katzander, Thames and Hudson, 1958

Source D Sunday, 4 November 1956

05.20: This is Imre Nagy, President of the Council of Ministers of the Hungarian People's Republic, speaking. Today at dawn, Soviet forces launched an attack against the capital with the obvious purpose of overthrowing the legal Hungarian democratic Government. Our troops are fighting. The Government is at its post. I notify the people of our country and the entire world of these facts.

Radio broadcast quoted in Tibor Meray, *Thirteen Days That Shook The Kremlin*,
translated by Howard L. Katzander, Thames and Hudson, 1958

Source E Monday, 5 November 1956

Daily Mail

MORNING SPECIAL

NO. 18,833 TWOPENCE   FOR QUEEN AND COMMONWEALTH   MONDAY, NOVEMBER 5, 1956

A dying nation's last SOS. It reached Vienna from a Hungarian reporter. His full story is in Page 5

good bye we do not forget you   the russian are too near   good bye friends good bye friends, ,save ou souls

BUDAPEST CRUSHED—Red troops storm into Parliament

The MURDER OF HUNGARY

Comment
MONDAY, NOV. 5, 1956.

HUNGARIAN TRAGEDY

SIR ANTHONY EDEN spoke with calm confidence when he addressed his nation-wide audiences on television and radio.

In all his recent speeches, however, he has still failed to convince a large proportion of the country of the moral rightness of the intervention in the Egypt-Israel dispute.

This in itself would not be sufficient reason for stopping the operation if the PRIME MINISTER believed it to be right. His is the responsibility. His, therefore, must be the decision.

Yesterday the fast-moving events in the Middle East were overshadowed by something even more with supporting coun-

Nagy marched out at gunpoint

From JEFFREY BLYTH: On the Austro-Hungarian Frontier, Sunday Night

HUNGARY, the little country that dared to defy Russia, was murdered today. Russian troops struck at the freedom fighters all over the country. More than 1,000 tanks surrounded Budapest. Soviet soldiers stormed into the Parliament building after Premier Nagy had just broadcast to the world an agonised call for help.

They marched Mr. Nagy out at gun-point. He has been charged

GET OUT! IKE URGES BULGANIN

From NOEL CLARK : Washington, Sunday

PRESIDENT EISENHOWER today sent an urgent message to Marshal Bulganin, Soviet Premier, asking him to withdraw Soviet troops from Hungary.

Mr. Eisenhower expressed "shock and dismay" at the Russian attack on the Hungarian people. He urged that Hungary be given the right to choose her own Government.

He announced that he sent the message after an extraordinary Sunday meeting with his leading diplomatic and other advisers, as well as a personal 10-minute talk with the Secretary of State, Mr. Dulles.

And U.N. says 'Get out' too

AN overwhelming majority of the U.N. Assembly last night called on Russia to halt at once its armed attack on Hungary and to withdraw its troops from the country.

Mr. Dag Hammarskjold, U.N. Secretary-General, was asked to investigate the situation through his representatives and to report back as soon as possible.

Assembly debate—Page TWO.

Coast defences attacked

CYPRUS TROOPS BOARD THE INVASION SHIPS

From T. F. THOMPSON : Allied H.Q., Monday, 1 a.m.

TWELVE hours after some of the toughest units in the British and French armies embarked yesterday on the invasion fleet at a Cyprus port, Allied Headquarters announced this morning that coastal defences "well clear of Alexandria" were being attacked.

Bronzed Britons waved to tough French as long lines of men bristling with arms boarded merchant vessels and warships of the invasion fleet.

People at home may be split.

'Dag' plans police

From WILSON BROADBENT

Source F Monday, 5 November 1956

I saw streams of Hungarian refugees, walking in little groups along the road, carrying their worldly belongings on their backs, or on oxcarts, handcarts, bicycles, or wheelbarrows. The refugees, a look of sorrow and resignation on their faces, trudged in an unending stream to political asylum in Austria ...

[In the border town of Sopron]
We walked along and within two minutes I heard screams. Some men and women came running around the corner. 'They're here, they're here' they yelled. 'Four Russian tanks have entered the town'.

A sudden panic gripped everyone. We were swept along in a scurrying crowd of men, women, and children, some weeping, some screaming, some yelling senselessly ... Soon we heard them. The roar, screech, and rumble of tanks on concrete; then the first vehicle, an armoured car, round a corner. Three T-34 tanks followed it.

Peter Howard, Reuter's special correspondent, in the
Manchester Guardian, 5 November 1956

Source G Monday, 3 December 1956

The fascist *putsch* in Hungary is completely liquidated, thanks to the resolute action of the healthy forces of the Hungarian people ... [and] ... the Soviet Union, whose armed forces helped the Hungarian people in fighting the counter-revolution at the Hungarian Government's request.

Soviet delegate at the UN General Assembly

1 *Why did the Soviet delegate at the UN call it a 'fascist putsch'?*

2 *What did the demonstrators in Budapest want? How were their demands related to Khruschev's denunciation of Stalin?*

3 *Which source provides evidence which may explain why the Soviet Union decided to crush the Hungarian revolt and replace Imre Nagy as prime minister? What excuse did Khruschev have, if any, for intervening in Hungary? Was this excuse still valid on 4 November 1956?*

4 *Which of these sources is an original source? Which is an eyewitness account?*

In the street battles which followed the return of the Russian tanks, about 20 000 Hungarians were killed and many more were rounded up and imprisoned. Nagy was treacherously captured (he had been promised his freedom) and later executed. The new government, led by Janos Kadar (a former colleague of Nagy and ex-enemy of Rakosi), later introduced many reforms and helped, in fact, to liberalise Hungary. But it could not eradicate the disillusionment felt by many Communists in the West at the Soviet use of force to crush the uprising. Many left the Party in disgust.

THE BERLIN WALL

The East German Problem

The lesson of Hungary was not lost on the other leaders of the Eastern bloc countries. East Germany was losing thousands of its people every year as refugees fled across the border into West Germany. Living standards were much higher in the West, and improving. By contrast the East German Government was repressive. Its people had every reason to look with envy at the life style and freedoms of their fellow-Germans on the other side of the Iron Curtain.

Before 1961 it was relatively easy for an East German to cross over into West Germany, since there were many crossing points between East and West Berlin. The East German authorities began to find this an intolerable situation. The loss of thousands of skilled workers depleted their factories and offices, at the same time providing West Germany with the efficient and highly trained workforce it needed to sustain a booming economy.

The presence of West Berlin as a prosperous, democratic Western city in the middle of an Iron Curtain country had long been an embarrassment to the Russians as well as to the East Germans. In 1958 Khruschev proposed that the occupying powers should leave Berlin but this was rejected by the Western Allies.

For three years the issue simmered. Summit conferences, a visit by Khruschev to the United States and other signs of a thaw in East–West relations prevented Berlin becoming another crisis point. But in 1961 the flood of emigrants from East Germany (over 100 000 in six months) tried the patience of the East German Government for the last time.

The Wall

The Allies still refused to leave Berlin. So in August 1961 the East Germans closed the crossing points and erected a wall sealing off West Berlin from its twin in East Germany. The flood of refugees dwindled to a trickle. A number of East Berliners made daring escapes but many were killed by East German security troops.

The Allies protested. American tanks faced their Russian counterparts across the wall. But there was nothing else they could do, short of declaring war. There was nothing further the Russians could do, either, to get the Allies out of Berlin. Indeed when President Kennedy visited the city, in June 1963, he told the West Berliners:

> All free men, wherever they live, are citizens of Berlin. And therefore, as a free man, I take pride in the words, *Ich bin ein Berliner* [I am a Berliner].

President Kennedy examines the Berlin Wall in 1963

1 *Why did Kennedy say he was 'a Berliner'?*

2 *How was the building of the Berlin Wall seen by the West? Why was it looked on as part of the Cold War?*

THE CUBAN MISSILES CRISIS

The Cuban Revolution

Fidel Castro

On 2 December 1956, Fidel Castro, a young 30-year-old revolutionary, landed on the island of Cuba and began a two-year guerrilla war which led eventually to the overthrow of President Batista, Cuba's dictator. Castro formed a left-wing revolutionary government and announced many far-reaching, and much-needed, social and economic reforms. But these also included moves directed at American business activities in Cuba.

The Americans had a special interest in Cuba, since it was only 200 km or so off the coast of Florida. Near the eastern tip of the island they still had a large naval and air base at Guantanamo. Relations between the USA and Cuba deteriorated. The Americans broke off diplomatic relations and severed trade links. This pushed Castro into the Communist camp and he signed trade agreements with the Russians instead.

In secret, the United States Central Intelligence Agency (CIA) began to train supporters of President Batista, in preparation for an ill-fated landing at the Bay of Pigs in Cuba in April 1961. This fiasco humiliated the American Government. Worse, it forced Castro to look increasingly to the Soviet Union for support.

The Missile Sites

In the summer of 1962 American spies on Cuba saw Russian cargo ships unloading unusual objects. Cubans reported seeing long cigar-like objects on lorries. Russian engineers and other experts were also coming ashore in large numbers. What was going on? At that time the United States used special spy planes flying at high altitudes to take reconnaissance photographs of hostile territory. On Sunday, 14 October 1962 aerial photographs taken in the west of the island showed, unmistakably, that the Russians were building missile launching sites.

Aerial photograph showing a Soviet missile site on Cuba in 1962

Until this time American defence policy had been based on the assumption that the USA would always have at least 15 minutes warning of a Russian missile attack from land-based missiles in the Soviet Union. But Russian missiles on Cuba would give America's cities less than three minutes warning of an attack. Other reconnaissance photographs showed that the construction work in Cuba was proceeding rapidly and that a fleet of Russian cargo ships had been spotted in the Atlantic heading for Cuba.

The Blockade

President Kennedy talked with his advisers and generals for a week, debating what to do about the missile sites. The 'hawks' wanted to bomb the sites. But this would have meant killing Russian engineers and might have started the Third World War immediately. The 'doves' advocated caution. Kennedy opted instead for what was termed a 'measured response'. It allowed Khruschev to climb down without having to admit an outright defeat. The American navy and airforce would seal off Cuba. All ships would be searched. Any found carrying arms would be sent back to Russia.

US IMPOSES ARMS BLOCKADE ON CUBA
ON FINDING OFFENSIVE – MISSILE SITES;
KENNEDY READY FOR SOVIET SHOWDOWN

SHIPS MUST STOP	PRESIDENT GRAVE
Other Action Planned	Asserts Russians Lied
If Big Rockets Are	and Put Hemisphere
Not Dismantled	in Great Danger

New York Times, 23 October 1962

WE BLOCKADE CUBA WITH 40 WARSHIPS
JFK'S Orders: 'Search, And If Necessary,
Sink Any Arms Ship'

New York Mirror, 23 October 1962

These were the headlines which New Yorkers woke up to on Tuesday 23 October 1962. It was the start of the gravest crisis since the end of the Second World War. Many people feared the worst, that Kennedy really would sink Russian ships and that the threatened 'Soviet Showdown' would start the Third World War. Only this time it would be a nuclear conflict. Some pessimists left a CND demonstration in London and fled to Western Ireland!

---

1 *Why did Kennedy blockade Cuba? What was he afraid of?*

2 *What proof did the Americans have that the Russians had supplied Cuba with missiles?*

3 *What did Kennedy mean by a 'measured response'?*

4 *Why was it important to give Khruschev a method of climbing down without having to admit to an outright defeat?*

Tension

The two world leaders who faced each other across the Atlantic had been acclaimed as peace-makers. Khruschev of Russia had denounced his predecessor, Stalin, and made peace overtures to the West. It looked as if the Cold War might soon be over. People had talked of a 'thaw' in East–West relations. Just when everyone's hopes had been raised they seemed to sink overnight.

On Tuesday 23 October people throughout the world had to come to terms with the prospect of imminent nuclear war. If Khruschev did not back down there was no knowing what might happen. The anxiety would have been worse had they known the American missiles were primed and ready to fire at a second's notice. The Russian ships moved nearer to Cuba. Some were searched and passed through the Blockade. Others turned back. Khruschev had ordered the ships carrying missiles to return to base. But this did not solve the problem of the missiles already on the island.

Secret talks were held between the two superpowers. Khruschev wanted to trade an agreement on Cuban missile sites with one which stopped the Americans siting missiles in Turkey. Kennedy refused to agree. But he did promise there would be no attack on Cuba. In the end this was enough for Khruschev and on Sunday 28 October the crisis was over. The missiles would be removed under United Nations supervision. Kennedy paid a compliment to his adversary. It was 'an important contribution to peace', he said.

Soviet merchant ship carries missiles bound for Cuba in 1962

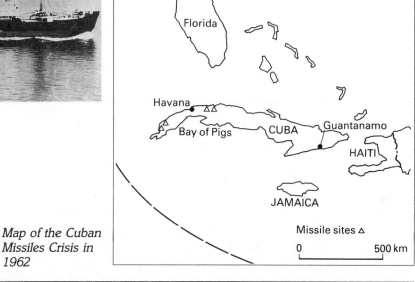

Map of the Cuban Missiles Crisis in 1962

Effects of the Crisis

- Firstly, it showed Khruschev and the Soviet Union that the United States would stand firm on a major issue and that it meant business.
- Secondly, the inability of the two superpowers to talk directly to one another at a time of great crisis led to the installation of a direct telephone link from the White House in Washington to the Kremlin in Moscow. This was called the hotline.
- Thirdly, it showed the United States that the Russians could be reasonable after all. Relations between East and West actually thawed because of the Cuban Missiles Crisis instead of getting worse. Russia had shied away from the prospect of a nuclear war. If this was the case, then negotiations on nuclear arms limitation might be fruitful.
- Fourthly, it gave Khruschev's enemies ammunition to fire at him in future. The Chinese, in particular, had nothing but contempt for him because he had climbed down.

---

1 *Was the Cuban Missiles Crisis necessary? Was there any other effective course of action which Kennedy could have taken to remove the threat from the Cuban missiles?*

2 *What good came out of the Crisis? Did it make nuclear war more or less likely in future?*

The Test Ban Treaty

In 1963 the two superpowers joined with other nations in signing the Test Ban Treaty banning nuclear tests in the atmosphere, in space or in the sea. Only nuclear explosions deep underground were permitted.

Five years later the Soviet Union, United States and United Kingdom signed the Non-Proliferation Treaty in 1968. This was designed to stop the spread of atomic weapons to other countries. People feared what might happen if every country had access to nuclear bombs.

In 1972 the Soviet Union and the United States began talks on limiting the actual numbers of missiles held by both sides. These were popularly known as the SALT (Strategic Arms Limitation Treaty) talks. Because there were other talks in 1978, the 1972 agreement was known as SALT 1. The SALT 2 agreement was signed but later suspended by the Americans after the Russians invaded Afghanistan in 1979.

THE VIETNAM WAR

French Indo-China

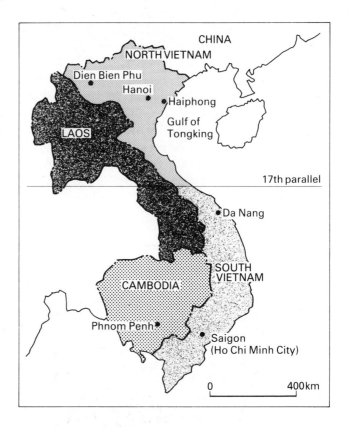

Map of the Vietnam War 1954–75

As you saw on page 262, French Indo-China was occupied by the Japanese during the War. The Vichy Government had little option but to agree to loan bases to the Japanese Army in 1941. But Communist guerrillas, led by Ho Chi Minh, harassed the Japanese forces so successfully, that after the War they felt strong enough to found the Democratic Republic of North Vietnam. The French returned and fought a long but fruitless war to regain control of their former colony. Despite assistance from the Americans they were unsuccessful. After a massive defeat at Dien Bien Phu in 1954 they gave up and the country was temporarily partitioned at the 17th parallel (17° North) between North and South Vietnam. The North became a Communist republic, based on Hanoi. The South became a republic under the right-wing dictator, Ngo Dinh Diem, based on Saigon. The peace conference at Geneva, where this was decided, stipulated that free elections should be held in 1956 throughout the country, since it was always intended that the two Vietnams would eventually merge as one.

American Advisers

Diem decided not to hold free elections, so Ho Chi Minh, who had expected to win them, trained guerrillas to harass the Government forces in the south. By the late 1950s these guerrillas (called Vietcong, meaning Vietnamese Communist) controlled large parts of South Vietnam.

President Eisenhower had used the domino theory to justify armed American support for the French in 1954. The domino theory stated that if one key country in a region turned Communist, the others would fall in turn like a set of dominoes, each one pushing over its neighbour. This policy was continued by President Kennedy to give help to the South Vietnamese in their fight against the Vietcong. By 1963 substantial numbers of American advisers, arms and equipment were involved in the civil war in South Vietnam. Unlike Berlin and West Germany, however, South Vietnam was no democracy. Diem was killed in a coup in 1963 and succeeded by a hardline army general called Nguyen Van Thieu.

The War Escalates

Lyndon B. Johnson became President of the United States at this time. Believing the Cold War theory, that Communism planned to control the world by stages, he escalated the war by sending in huge numbers of American servicemen to block the Vietcong advance. Johnson used an incident in the Gulf of Tongking as an excuse. Two American destroyers were said to have been fired upon by North Vietnamese torpedo boats. The United States Congress passed a special motion – the Tongking Gulf Resolution – which gave the President the right 'to take all necessary steps to repel the aggressor'. Now that Johnson had this approval, he widened the conflict by bombing the North Vietnamese cities of Hanoi and Haiphong.

But this did not halt the advance of the Vietcong. Instead, they launched a major campaign in 1968, the Tet Offensive. By this time there were over half a million American servicemen stationed in Vietnam, compared with the 50 000 or so who were there when Johnson became president in 1963.

The Protest Movement

Milwaukee, United States. The Vietnam War aroused so much opposition in the United States, many young protesters burnt the draft papers calling them up into the armed forces

Large numbers of American servicemen were killed in the fighting and this, together with the continued escalation of a war which seemed pointless, and none of America's business in the first place, led to riots and demonstrations throughout the United States. Students taunted Johnson:

> 'Hey! Hey! LBJ!
> How many kids did you kill today?'

Opposition to the war was so bitter that in 1970, four students at Kent State University, Ohio, were killed and many others wounded when National Guardsmen opened fire during a demonstration against US involvement in Vietnam and Cambodia.

Defeat

By now the United States was ready for peace talks. But the new President, Richard Nixon, first tried to bomb the North Vietnamese into submission. He escalated the war again by permitting American forces to attack the neighbouring countries of Laos and Cambodia, which were being used by North Vietnam to send supplies and reinforcements to the Vietcong. The position in the region was further complicated by a civil war in Cambodia between the Communist Khmer Rouge guerrillas backed by North Vietnam and the American-backed right-wing government of Lon Nol. In 1973 a cease fire was arranged in South Vietnam and most of the American troops withdrew. Two years later the North Vietnamese and Vietcong armies seized Saigon and the rest of South Vietnam. At the same time the Cambodian capital city of Phnom-Penh fell to the Khmer Rouge.

Results

- Thailand, Burma, Malaysia, and other neighbouring states, did not fall to the Communists, contrary to the expectations raised by the domino theory.
- Nor did the new Vietnam fit neatly into one large Communist empire stretching from East Berlin to Moscow, Peking, Phnom-Penh and Saigon (now renamed Ho Chi Minh City). Instead war broke out between Communist Cambodia (later renamed Kampuchea) and Communist Vietnam; and later still between Communist China and Communist Vietnam. It seemed clear that the driving force for the Communist guerrilla movements had as much to do with national rivalries as with Communism or Marxist theory.
- The American people felt entitled to know why vast resources had been spent, nearly 60 000 American lives lost and over 150 000 servicemen wounded, in a war which had been fought to stop Vietnam turning Communist. What had America gained from the war? In the eyes of many Americans it was the worst war in US history. Ever since, Congress has

been reluctant to endorse any military actions taken by the President which might involve America in a long drawn-out war against guerrillas. Vietnam has become a symbol of how *not* to combat aggression, just as Munich has become a warning against appeasement.

● America lost face with many nations when she withdrew her forces from Vietnam, thus hastening the fall of South Vietnam to the Communist North. But she had earlier been reviled throughout the world for intervening in what many Third World countries regarded as a civil war between rival groups. The Americans saw it differently – as part of a worldwide Communist conspiracy. Either way the Americans lost. Involvement in the Vietnam War cost the United States untold damage in prestige and loss of influence overseas.

---

1 *What was the domino theory?*

2 *What should have happened in South East Asia after 1975 according to the domino theory? What did happen?*

3 *Why were American forces involved in the Vietnam War? Was it for the same reasons as in Korea in 1950? If not, why not?*

4 *What did the United States achieve in Vietnam?*

THE THAW

Brezhnev

Leonid Brezhnev

When Khruschev was removed from office in 1964, his place as first secretary of the Communist Party was taken by Leonid Brezhnev. Brezhnev's policies were very similar to those pursued by Khruschev. He sought peaceful co-existence or *détente* between East and West. *Détente* is a French word, meaning release from tension. The Cold War had increased tension between East and West, so its opposite – the relaxation of tension – was called *détente*.

Both superpowers acknowledged that the other had areas of special interest. The United States claimed a special relationship with Western Europe, the Pacific and with North and South America. For his part Brezhnev was not prepared to see the USSR lose control over Eastern Europe or abandon its interests in the countries which bordered the Soviet Union. This was why Brezhnev organised the Warsaw Pact response to the liberal government of Alexander Dubček in Czechoslovakia in 1968 and why he planned the invasion of Afghanistan in 1979. He also suppressed opposition to the Soviet regime from within, imprisoning dissidents, as they were called.

Czechoslovakia in 1968

Prague, Czechoslovakia, August 1968. A Russian tank patrols the streets of Prague to the jeers and cat-calls of angry young Czechs

Klement Gottwald died in 1953 and was succeeded as leader of Czechoslovakia by a more liberal regime led by Antonin Zapotocky. But when Zapotocky died in 1957, he was succeeded as first secretary of the Czechoslovak Communist Party by Antonin Novotny, who later became president.

Novotny wanted no repetition of the Hungarian Uprising. But his repressive regime was not even in tune with the anti-Stalinist mood of the Soviet Union, let alone that of Hungary. Slowly he began to soften the harsher aspects of his policies. Like Khruschev he began a period of de-Stalinisation in Czechoslovakia. Attitudes to the Catholic Church softened. Liberal reforms were introduced. But the pace of change was not enough to satisfy many Czechs. Student demonstrations led the way in demanding fresh reforms. In 1968 Novotny was replaced as Czech leader by Alexander Dubček, the first secretary of the Communist Party of Slovakia, the south-eastern region of Czechoslovakia. Dubček introduced a number of important reforms, including free speech, the abolition of press censorship and greater political freedom. The Czechs called it 'socialism with a human face'. Corruption and bureaucratic delays were exposed by the media – on television, in the newspapers and on radio. The Czechs enjoyed their 'Prague Spring' but the accelerating liberalisation of Czechoslovakia alarmed the Russians and the leaders of the other Warsaw Pact countries. They reasoned with Dubček but he insisted on going ahead, while reassuring them that Czechoslovakia would remain within the Warsaw Pact.

This did not convince Brezhnev. On 20–1 August thousands of Soviet troops, backed by units from Bulgaria, East Germany, Hungary and Poland, entered Czechoslovakia and removed Dubček from office. There was no armed resistance by the Czech army and less than 100 people were killed. Nor were there the same reprisals by the Russians as in 1956 after the Hungarian uprising. Dubček was later released and not replaced as first secretary of the Czechoslovak Communist Party until 1969, although most of his reforms were abandoned. But the Warsaw Pact invasion of Czechoslovakia provoked a storm of criticism and Brezhnev could be said to have lost as much as he gained.

Results

- President Ceausescu refused to send Romanian troops to join the invading Warsaw Pact forces. Ever since, Romania has taken a more independent line than the other Communist countries of Eastern Europe.
- Albania did likewise and left the Warsaw Pact.
- China criticised the invasion, not because Mao Tse-tung approved of Dubček's reforms but because the Soviet Union used force to bring a fellow Communist state to heel. What could be done with Czechoslovakia could also be done with Communist China.
- Western nations and many Third World countries were appalled, since it was the equivalent of American and NATO forces invading Britain because they disapproved of the policies of a Labour Government.

---

1 *Why did the Warsaw Pact countries invade Czechoslovakia? What were they afraid of? Was it a successful intervention?*

2 *Compare Czechoslovakia in 1968 with Hungary in 1956. What were the similarities? What were the differences?*

Ostpolitik

Western leaders also played their part in *détente*. As you have seen, Germany was the battleground for much of the Cold War in the years between the Berlin Blockade and the Berlin Wall. Even here, the atmosphere between East and West visibly softened under the guiding hand of the German Social Democrat leader, Willy Brandt. Brandt had been an outstandingly successful mayor of West Berlin during the period when the Berlin Wall was built. In 1966 he became the West German foreign minister and German chancellor in 1969.

He decided to work for *détente* between East and West Germany, a policy which was known as *Ostpolitik* – meaning 'eastern policy'. The main results of this policy were, a) treaties with the Soviet Union and Poland agreeing boundaries and promising not to attack one another and, b) a lessening of tension between the two Germanies, with West Germany acknowledging the East German Government and accepting the reality of the Oder–Neisse line as the border between Poland and Germany in the east (see page 277).

The Helsinki Agreement

For a time, in the early 1970s, it looked as if *détente* could really work and that the superpowers might soon be able to reduce their stocks of arms. President Nixon visited Moscow in 1972 and 1974 while President Brezhnev visited Washington in 1973. At about this time, too, the Americans and Chinese began to bury their differences. President Nixon made a historic visit to Peking, in February 1972, to meet Mao Tse-tung and other Chinese leaders (see page 382).

In 1975 an international conference held in Helsinki was attended by leaders from 35 countries and they agreed on a number of measures designed to implement the spirit of *détente*. In particular the conference called on all participating nations, including the Soviet Union, to respect human rights, such as free speech. But when a group of Soviet dissidents formed the Helsinki Human Rights Group, to monitor Soviet progress on these issues, they were imprisoned by the Russians. This caused a fresh wave of bad feeling between East and West.

Afghanistan

Cartoon by Garland in the Daily Telegraph, *Thursday, 3 January 1980*

In 1979 the Soviet leaders were faced with the problem of what to do about Afghanistan, a Moslem country on their southern border which had turned Communist, but was threatened from within by tribesmen opposed to the regime. In December 1979 Soviet troops invaded Afghanistan and installed Babrak Karmal as the new Communist leader.

> Russian troops airlifted into Afghanistan deposed the country's leader Mr. Hafizullah Amin yesterday and installed in his place a new ruler with hard-line Communist credentials. Amin was removed from power after several thousand Russian troops and heavy armour arrived at Kabul airport . . . Radio Afghanistan announced that . . . Amin had been executed after a revolutionary trial had convicted him of crimes against the Afghan people.
>
> News report by Bruce Loudon in the *Daily Telegraph*, 28 December 1979

The rebel tribesmen who were hopelessly outnumbered retreated into the mountains and waged an effective guerrilla war which a large Russian force was unable to quell. To many outside observers, it looked as if

Brezhnev's intervention in Afghanistan was turning into a Russian Vietnam.

No one can say what really persuaded the Russians to react as they did. It seems likely they were worried about the possible effect the strict Islamic movements (which were anti-Communist) in neighbouring Pakistan and Iran might have on the predominantly Moslem people of Afghanistan (and also on the peoples of the neighbouring Socialist Soviet Republics of the Soviet Union, which were also largely Moslem).

The immediate effect of the invasion was a boycott of the 1980 Moscow Olympics by some Western nations, led by the USA. President Carter imposed a ban (called an embargo) on American grain sales to the Soviet Union. Like other Western leaders he was worried that the Soviet invasion might lead to further Soviet expansion in Central Asia, which would endanger Middle East oil supplies to the Western world.

---

1 *What was meant by 'détente'? Is it the same as 'peaceful co-existence'?*

2 *How did relations between the United States and the Soviet Union change in the 17 years between 1962 and 1979 after the Cuban Missiles crisis, compared with the 17 years before that crisis from 1945 to 1962? What were the successes and what were the failures?*

3 *Draw up a time chart for the Cold War from 1945–80.*

Solidarity

Lech Walesa

Poland with 35 million people is easily the largest of the Iron Curtain countries of eastern Europe (not including the USSR). In 1956 Khruschev allowed the Poles to select a liberal Communist, Wladyslaw Gomulka, as leader. He introduced many reforms including measures which kept most of the land in private hands instead of in collective farms, as in Russia. But even he couldn't stop food prices rising and, after a series of food riots, he resigned in 1970. His successors had little better luck and in the late 1970s there was considerable unrest in Poland.

In 1980 a series of strikes in the Polish port of Gdansk (formerly Danzig) led to the formation of a new and independent trade union, which the Polish workers called Solidarity. This was an astonishing departure for a Communist country, since strikes were usually forbidden.

Solidarity, which was led by Lech Walesa, caught the imagination of the Polish people and had the support of the Catholic Church. Strikes spread to many other industries, from coal mines to steel works. There could be no doubting the popular support the movement received.

Krakow, Poland. Demonstration by supporters of the banned Solidarity *Trade Union in June 1983*

At first the Polish Government made concessions (including the right to form trade unions). It introduced reforms under a new Communist leader Stanislaw Kania. When these failed to stem the growth of Solidarity and the movement to greater freedom, the Polish Communist Party called for sterner measures to deal with the crisis. The Soviet Government may well have had a hand in persuading the Polish Communists to replace Kania with another leader, General Jaruzelski.

In 1981 the more extreme Solidarity members demanded reforms which called into being the very existence of the Communist Party in Poland. Soviet army manoeuvres near the Polish border worried Western leaders, who thought it might be a prelude to a Soviet invasion of Poland. The West warned Brezhnev that any such move would harm East–West relations, despite Brezhnev's denial that any such move was contemplated.

Eventually General Jaruzelski banned Solidarity and placed its leaders in detention camps. He told the Poles, on 13 December 1981,

> Our country is on the edge of the abyss. Achievements of many generations, raised from the ashes, are collapsing into ruins. State structures no longer function. New blows are struck each day at our flickering economy.

Most of the leaders of Solidarity were later released, and the stricter laws relaxed, when the new Government felt it had the situation under control. The combination of the Soviet invasion of Afghanistan and the suppression of Solidarity in Poland had the effect, however, of bringing back the old atmosphere of mutual distrust and suspicion which characterised the Cold War in the days before *détente*.

US President Reagan later announced a massive increase in American spending on arms. This was matched by the Russians. When the NATO governments of Western Europe agreed to deploy the American cruise and Pershing missiles in 1983 the Russians retaliated by deploying their own medium-range missiles in Czechoslovakia and other Warsaw Pact countries.

FURTHER QUESTIONS AND EXERCISES

1 *Explain clearly what is, or was, meant by each of the following:*

   a) *the Iron Curtain*

   b) *the domino theory*

   c) *peaceful co-existence*

   d) *the Truman Doctrine*

   e) *détente*

   f) *Ostpolitik*

2 *Ask your older friends and relatives if they can recall the Cuban Missiles Crisis. How scared were they of the possibility of a nuclear war? Did they approve of Kennedy's actions at the time?*

3 *Write brief notes explaining when, why, and how the Russians were involved in the following crises:*

   a) *the Hungarian Uprising*

   b) *the Berlin Blockade*

   c) *the invasion of Czechoslovakia*

   d) *the invasion of Afghanistan*

4 *Write brief notes commenting on the part played by each of the following in the Cold War:*

   a) *Leonid Brezhnev*

   b) *John F. Kennedy*

   c) *Lyndon B. Johnson*

   d) *Willy Brandt*

   e) *Imre Nagy*

   f) *Alexander Dubček*

   g) *Harry S. Truman*

   h) *Nikita Khruschev*

   i) *Richard Nixon*

5 *Look at the map on page 304. Has the Iron Curtain moved any further west in the 40 or 50 years since the end of the War? How might, a) a Russian and b) an American, explain this fact?*

6 *The Berlin Blockade and the building of the Berlin Wall were two major flashpoints of the postwar period. Imagine you are a Berliner. Use information from the other chapters in this book to write an account of what it was like to live in Berlin through 22 years from the outbreak of war in 1939 to the Berlin Wall in 1961.*

Chapter Fifteen

The USA since 1945

INTRODUCTION

The assassination of President Kennedy in November 1963. The President, slumped down in his seat, leans towards his wife, Jacqueline Kennedy

DALLAS, Texas   23 November 1963

John Fitzgerald Kennedy, 46, the 34th President of the United States, died this afternoon within half-an-hour of being shot in the head as he drove through Dallas in an open car. He was on his way to make a speech at a political festival.

The shooting happened as the President's car drove through cheering crowds. Shots rang out and he slumped down in his seat.

Mrs. Jacqueline Kennedy, who was also in the car, jumped up and cried 'Oh, no!' She cradled her husband in her arms as the car sped to nearby Parkland Hospital. Police motor-cyclists, with sirens blaring, cleared a path through the crowds and the traffic.

At the hospital President Kennedy was given an immediate blood transfusion and a Roman Catholic priest was called to his bedside to administer the last rites. The President died 25 minutes after being shot.

Daily Telegraph, 24 November 1963

This was how Stephen Barber described the assassination of President Kennedy in the *Daily Telegraph* (London). Kennedy was young, virile, handsome and an inspiring speaker. Millions of Americans and tens of millions of non-Americans looked to him for leadership. It was later said that people throughout the world could remember exactly what they were doing when they heard the news of his assassination.

---

1 *Why?*

2 *Test this theory by asking your older friends and relatives what they can remember about the assassination. What did they think about Kennedy?*

Sadly, Kennedy's death was followed by other assassinations. The Black Civil Rights leader, Martin Luther King, and Bobby Kennedy, President Kennedy's talented younger brother, were both killed in 1968. Four university students were shot in 1970. They were demonstrating against the war in Vietnam, in which nearly 60 000 Americans lost their lives fighting to prevent Vietnam turning Communist, which it did anyway in 1975. Then in 1974, President Nixon was forced to resign over the Watergate Scandal, which put some of his closest advisers in prison. The United States, which under Truman, Eisenhower and Kennedy shone as a beacon of freedom and progress, suddenly looked shabby, lawless and vindictive.

BEFORE KENNEDY

Richest Nation on Earth

The World Trade Center, New York

In general, the economy of the United States prospered in the years after the Second World War, as it did at the end of the First World War. It was now the most advanced nation on Earth, had the most sophisticated technology, the greatest quantity of raw materials and foodstuffs, and the highest standard of living. Unlike the other major belligerents in the War (such as Russia, Germany and Japan) it suffered no extensive war damage, had no ruined cities to rebuild, nor millions of homeless to house. Many striking postwar innovations, such as computers, automation, jet aircraft, space technology and nuclear research, helped Americans to prosper. They included many of the people who were hit hardest by the Depression of the 1930s. Farmers mechanised their farms. Even the South witnessed an economic miracle as industries boomed in southern cities like Atlanta.

But these were troubled times as well as affluent times. Successive presidents turned their back on isolationism and intervened in foreign disputes, even when they only remotely threatened America or her allies. American involvement in Vietnam made many Americans look critically at the role their country was playing in world affairs.

President Truman

President Truman

Harry S. Truman became President when Roosevelt died in 1945. People thought him a modest, unassuming and rather insignificant man. But he made more important decisions than any other postwar president. Most of these decisions have been discussed in earlier chapters, such as the dropping of the atom bomb in 1945, Marshall Aid and the Truman Doctrine in 1947, the Berlin Blockade in 1948, the formation of NATO in 1949, the involvement in the Korean War in 1950, and the dismissal of General MacArthur in 1951. Truman did not flinch from making these decisions. He had a sign in his office in the White House which read 'The buck stops here'!

American presidents are often hampered (or restrained) by Congress if they seek to introduce controversial legislation. Congress has the power to overrule the president. Truman was a Democrat but this did not mean that every Democrat in the Senate and in the House of Representatives approved the measures he put before them. Unemployment, inflation and strikes were problems the American people faced immediately after the War. Labour troubles were so serious, Congress passed the Taft–Hartley Bill to curb the power of the trade unions in 1947, despite Truman's veto.

In the 1948 presidential election Truman was widely expected to lose. The *Chicago Daily Tribune* even printed a large headline 'DEWEY DEFEATS TRUMAN'! Instead he won with a comfortable majority. With Democratic majorities in both Houses of Congress, Truman had high hopes of pushing through his Fair Deal legislation in 1949. Some of these laws were approved, such as those guaranteeing farm prices, increasing welfare benefits and speeding up slum clearance. At the same time, Congress turned down Truman's attempt to repeal the Taft–Hartley Bill (one of his election promises). A national health insurance scheme and civil rights measures (designed to eliminate discrimination against Black Americans) were also defeated.

> 1 Why do you think Truman called his legislative programme the 'Fair Deal'? What was it designed to do?
>
> 2 How is the American system of Government different from that of the United Kingdom?

The Red Scare

The Cold War in Europe and the announcement of the Truman Doctrine (page 306) had unforeseen repercussions in America. Truman ordered that all Government employees should be vetted to check their loyalty to the State. Spy trials (notably that of a diplomat called Alger Hiss in 1948), Congressional investigations (such as the House of Representatives

Committee on Un-American Activities) and claims by the FBI (Federal Bureau of Investigation) that there were half a million Communists in the United States, began a witch hunt against Communism.

In 1950, a relatively unknown senator from Wisconsin, Joseph McCarthy, claimed that the State Department (the American foreign office) was riddled with Communists. In the next four years he was allowed to make a succession of wild accusations against his fellow Americans, accusing them of being part of a Red conspiracy to take over the United States.

This conspiracy, it was said, had helped the Communists to come to power in China. McCarthy's attacks were rarely supported by any evidence. To their discredit, many prominent Americans believed his accusations. They even sacked suspected employees and persecuted decent law-abiding citizens. These even included Hollywood film stars, scriptwriters and producers. In October 1953, Germany's Chancellor Adenauer told C.L. Sulzberger that he,

> agreed heartily with the objectives of the McCarthy investigations although he didn't agree with the methods. He thought Soviet espionage was magnificently organised and widespread and had to be dug out.
>
> C.L. Sulzberger, *A Long Row of Candles*, Macdonald, 1969

McCarthy eventually went too far when he attacked President Eisenhower and was censured by the US Senate. But the damage had been done. The whipping-up of antagonism to Communism forced American diplomats to take a tough line against the Soviet Union and China abroad. McCarthy even denounced Winston Churchill's Conservative Government in Britain for trading with Communist China!

---

1 *Why do you think Americans were prepared to take part in a witch hunt against Communism?*

2 *Why did McCarthyism involve Hollywood film stars and producers as well as civil servants and other Government officials? How could they harm America?*

President Eisenhower

President Eisenhower

In 1952 General Eisenhower was elected President. He was a likeable but rather dull man. His administration was generally moderate in tone but did little that was new. He disappointed right-wing supporters by not reversing earlier decisions on welfare legislation carried out under Roosevelt and Truman. Instead he carried through a number of measures of his own, improving welfare benefits, but failing to get Congress to approve a health insurance scheme. One of his main problems was what to do about a big drop in farm incomes. Production had increased so there were food surpluses and this meant lower prices. Under Eisenhower, some farmers were given Government assistance if they stopped growing crops on part of their land and left it as a conservation area. This was called a soil bank, since it would keep the land in reserve, yet help the soil to recover from the effects of many years of continuous farming.

CIVIL RIGHTS

Martin Luther King

In 1955 Mrs Rosa Parkes was arrested in Montgomery, Alabama, for the crime of not giving up her seat on a bus to a White man. The Black population was indignant and 26-year-old Martin Luther King, one of the city's Baptist ministers, helped to organise a successful Black boycott of the city's public transport system. A Federal Court later ruled that segregation on the buses was unconstitutional. In 1960, when four Black students were refused service in a restaurant in Greensboro, North Carolina, over 70 000 students, both Black and White, took part in organised sit-ins in Greensboro's shops and restaurants.

Slowly the tide turned in favour of the Civil Rights movement. The Supreme Court made a number of rulings, declaring that different forms of segregation and discrimination were unconstitutional. One of the earliest of these decisions came at the start of Eisenhower's Presidency.

The Supreme Court ruled, in 1954, that it was unconstitutional to segregate children in schools. Some southern states took steps to obey this

An armed policeman protects Black students at a former 'Whites Only' school in Kentucky

ruling, but many dragged their feet. Some openly defied the Supreme Court ruling, such as Governor Faubus of Arkansas, who used National Guardsmen to stop nine Black children enrolling at Central High School, Little Rock, in 1957.

Source A

A frightened 15-year-old Negro girl, Elizabeth Eckford, sought admission to the school. The troops [the locally-recruited state militia or National Guards] barred her way and now she had to go through the blocked-off street to the other exit, some 100 yards.

As the girl walked slowly toward the exit, the crowd surrounded her, jeered and yelled. From time to time several troops used their clubs to push the crowd back to prevent anyone from molesting her.

The *New York Times*, 4 September 1957

Eisenhower called up the entire state militia of Arkansas for Federal duty and sent paratroopers to escort the Black students into the school.

Source B

With police sirens wailing and headlights flashing, Army trucks loaded with soldiers roared into position. The soldiers represented about a quarter of the contingent of 1,000 crack troops of the division that was ordered to Little Rock by President Eisenhower to prevent mob riots and violence. Maj. Gen. Edwin A. Walker . . . issued a formal order to the people of Little Rock not to collect in crowds and to let Central High School be integrated peaceably . . . General Walker's mission is to make sure that no one frustrates Federal Court orders that nine Negro pupils be admitted to Central High School.

The *New York Times*, 25 September 1957

1 *How and why did the Arkansas state governor defy the ruling of the Supreme Court?*

2 *How did Eisenhower deal with the crisis?*

Civil rights was an issue throughout the 1950s and 1960s. Martin Luther King told an audience in 1963,

I have a dream that one day this nation will rise up and live out the true meaning of its creed: 'We hold these truths to be self-evident, that all men are created equal'.

He was quoting from the Declaration of Independence. In the Deep South at this time there were still White-only schools, White-only swimming pools and White-only seats on buses. Blacks were segregated from Whites and discriminated against in jobs, housing, the armed forces, even in church. Martin Luther King believed that Black Americans could get equality if they used peaceful, non-violent protests, like those used by Gandhi in India.

WASHINGTON   August 28 1963
More than 200,000 Americans, most of them Black but many of them White, demonstrated here today for a full and speedy program of civil rights and equal job opportunities. It was the greatest assembly for a redress of a grievance that this capital has ever seen ...

There was no violence to mar the demonstration. In fact, at times there was an air of hootenanny about it as groups of schoolchildren clapped hands and swung into the familiar freedom songs. But if the crowd was good natured, the underlying tone was one of dead seriousness. The emphasis was on 'freedom' and 'now'. At the same time the leaders emphasized, paradoxically but realistically, that the struggle was just beginning.

On Capitol Hill opinion was divided about the impact of the demonstration in stimulating Congressional action on civil rights legislation. But at the White House, President Kennedy declared that the cause of 20,000,000 Negroes had been advanced by the march ... The nation, the President said, 'can properly be proud of the demonstration that has occurred here today'.

E.W. Kenworthy, the *New York Times*, 29 August 1963

Dr Martin Luther King (centre) at a Civil Rights march in 1965, beneath the American and United Nations flags

---

1 *Why did 200 000 Americans demonstrate in Washington on 28 August 1963?*

2 *Who were they? What did they want and when did they want it? Who were they trying to persuade – the President, Congress or the people?*

Legislation

Civil Rights legislation slowly made progress in Congress, although southern opposition always made it difficult to make sweeping changes.

- 1957 [Eisenhower]: set up a Civil Rights Commission to investigate cases of discrimination against Blacks at elections.

- 1960 [Eisenhower]: protected Black voting rights in the southern states.

- 1964 [Johnson]: banned segregation and racial discrimination at elections, at work, and in hotels and shops. Kennedy first proposed this Bill but Congress delayed its passage for two years. It was only through Johnson's skill, as a former Senate leader, that it became law.

- 1965 [Johnson]: protected Black voters against discrimination.

- 1968 [Johnson]: made it illegal to discriminate against Blacks with regard to renting, selling or buying houses and most types of property.

Progress did not come fast enough for many militant Black Americans (such as the Black Panthers), oppressed by the poverty of the slums and often unemployed. They resented the failure of many states to implement the Civil Rights laws and obey the rulings of the Supreme Court. They thought Martin Luther King was too soft. 'We want Black power' they said.

Between 1965 and 1968 there were serious riots in the Black suburbs of over 100 American cities. About $200 million worth of damage was done in the Los Angeles suburb of Watts in 1965 alone, and 35 people were killed. President Johnson called it 'tragic and shocking' and told the rioters they could not obtain their rights 'through violence'. But the death toll continued. In 1967, 26 people died in Newark (near New York) and 43 in Detroit. In 1968, Martin Luther King was assassinated in Memphis, Tennessee. The nation was appalled. President Johnson said,

> Martin Luther King stands with our other American martyrs in the cause of freedom and justice. His death is a terrible tragedy.

By the 1970s Black Americans had achieved their goal of equality in the eyes of the law but there was still much racial discrimination in the North, as well as in the South.

---

1 *What did the Black Panthers have in common with Martin Luther King and his followers?*

2 *How did they differ?*

PRESIDENT KENNEDY

People throughout the world welcomed the election of President Kennedy in 1960. They saw him as an energetic, intelligent and courageous leader. He inspired thousands of young Americans to join the Peace Corps (volunteers working in Third World countries). Kennedy initiated a lot of much-needed legislation on civil rights, welfare measures for the poor and other social reforms. He called this the 'New Frontier'. But he had difficulty in getting these radical new proposals accepted by Congress. Many Americans were suspicious, as always, of anything which went against the national belief in self-help. It was Kennedy's successor, Lyndon Johnson, who actually managed to get Congress to pass these new laws.

You have seen in earlier chapters how Kennedy gained respect for his handling of the Cuban Missiles Crisis and the subsequent easing of tension between East and West – with the installation of a hotline between the White House and the Kremlin, and the Test Ban Treaty. On the debit side, he went ahead with the ill-advised and ill-fated attempt to overthrow Fidel Castro in the Bay of Pigs (see page 326). He escalated American involvement in the Vietnam war. Both ventures lowered American esteem in the eyes of the world.

John Fitzgerald Kennedy (1917–63)

John Fitzgerald Kennedy was born in 1917. He joined the American navy in the war and became a war hero in the Pacific, where he was wounded. In 1952 he was elected a senator for his home state of Massachusetts and eight years later was nominated as the Democratic candidate for the Presidency. At the time he was thought to have many disadvantages, being young (only 42), a member of one of America's top families, Catholic and a millionaire. But he narrowly defeated Richard Nixon, then the Republican Vice-President, with the promise of a new and better America.

He was killed in 1963 when a lone gunman, Lee Harvey Oswald, shot him with a marksman's rifle from the top of a building overlooking the route of the Presidential motorcade in Dallas, Texas.

AFTER KENNEDY

President Johnson

Lyndon B. Johnson became President the day Kennedy was assassinated. Although he had none of Kennedy's lustre he achieved much more because he was able to get Congress to work with him. His period as President saw the passage of many measures to improve the lot of the average American, such as the Civil Rights Acts of 1964, 1965 and 1968. Johnson earlier got Congress to approve the 1957 and 1960 Civil Rights Acts, when he was leader

President Johnson

of the Democratic majority in the US Senate. Since Congress can block the best laid plans of a president, or pass legislation in the face of a presidential veto, the wise president will try to ensure that the White House has many allies in Congress. Johnson had many friends in the Senate. He was skilled at getting Congress to approve controversial measures.

This is why he was able to secure the passage of the Medicare Bill in 1965, another measure originally proposed by President Kennedy. But this seemed like 'Socialism' to right-wing Americans. It helped to pay the costs incurred by senior citizens when in hospital or visiting a doctor.

Johnson wanted a 'Great Society'. He recognised that poverty could play no part in such a dream. He introduced other legislation designed to alleviate the lot of the poor American, such as a request to Congress for a grant of over $200 million to help the underprivileged people living in the Appalachian Mountain region. The Higher Education Act of 1965 provided Federal scholarships for students (contrary to American ideas of self-help). Other legislation raised minimum wages for the lowest paid workers. But President Johnson's concern for the underprivileged took place against a violent backcloth: the race riots (1965–8), assassinations (the two Kennedy brothers and Martin Luther King), the spiralling loss of life in Vietnam and violent student demonstrations.

President Nixon

The strength of the opposition to his policies persuaded Johnson against running for president for a second term. A Republican was elected in his place in 1968. The new president, Richard Nixon, was a Californian lawyer, who first achieved prominence as an anti-Communist member of the House of Representatives Committee on Un-American Activities in the 1940s, and later as a senator. In the 1950s he served eight years as Vice President under President Eisenhower. In 1960 he only just lost to Kennedy in the presidential election.

His years as President were marred by the war in Vietnam, but enhanced by the moves he took to reach agreement with both China and the Soviet Union. He also reaped the benefit of President Kennedy's pledge to put a man on the moon before the end of the decade.

He was re-elected President by a colossal margin in 1972 but fell from grace when Americans learned about the Watergate scandal. On 17 June 1972, five Republican activists were arrested after breaking into the Watergate Building in Washington. They were caught burgling the Democratic National Committee Headquarters there, hoping to find out the Democratic Party's election plans. A succession of presidential aides tried to cover up afterwards. Some resigned. Some were sent to prison. Was the President guilty as well? The scandal hardly ever left the front pages of the newspapers for over two years.

Mr Nixon swore he would never resign. But last Monday he was obliged to confess publicly that he had lied to his lawyers, the Congress and the public about his role in the plot to hush up the involvement of key members of his staff in the Watergate affair.

Previously he had always maintained that the first he knew of the Watergate cover-up was on March 21 last year. It then transpired from tape recordings of three conversations he had with his former Chief of Staff, Mr H.R. Haldeman, six days after the burglary, that he was indeed party to a plot to mislead Federal investigators looking into the affair by making out that it was part of a covert Central Intelligence Agency operation in the interests of national security.

Stephen Barber in the *Daily Telegraph*, Friday, 9 August 1974

---

1 *Was the Watergate burglary essential to Nixon's campaign?*

2 *Why did Nixon resign? Why was this a blow to America but a resounding triumph for American democracy?*

After Nixon

President Reagan

Gerald Ford became President when Nixon resigned. This was at a time when inflation and unemployment were causing serious problems in the United States in the wake of the 1973 energy crisis. As a Republican he stood little chance of being re-elected so soon after the Watergate scandal. It came as no real surprise when he was beaten in 1976 by Jimmy Carter, the former governor of Georgia.

Carter adopted a high moral tone in his work as President. He condemned the abuse of human rights in many countries throughout the world but was unable to solve America's economic problems back at home. His foreign policy was noteworthy for his striking achievement in persuading Israel and Egypt to make peace and his SALT 2 agreement with the Soviet Union. Unluckily he found himself powerless to free 52 American hostages when they were taken prisoner by Iranian Revolutionary Guards in 1979, and he had no effective answer when the Soviet Union invaded Afghanistan in December 1979. He was defeated in the 1980 presidential election by the former Hollywood film star, Ronald Reagan, a right-wing Republican.

FURTHER QUESTIONS AND EXERCISES

1 *Which American president after Roosevelt do you think achieved the greatest success, both at home and abroad?*

2 *Write briefly explaining each of the following:*

    a) McCarthyism   *b) Watergate*

c) the 'Fair Deal'

d) the 'New Frontier'

e) the 'Great Society'

f) the Peace Corps

g) Medicare

h) Black Power

i) Little Rock

3 Read the extract below. Who was 'he'? Why, when, and where was this meeting held? How 'militant' was the speaker? What did he and his supporters want? How effective was their campaign?

> 'I have a dream', he cried again and again . . . he was both militant and sad, and he sent the crowd away feeling that the long journey had been worthwhile.

4 President Kennedy promised much but fulfilled few of his campaign promises. His successor, President Johnson, promised less but achieved more. Why was this? Examine the records of both men. What were their successes and failures at home and abroad?

Chapter Sixteen

Unity in Europe

INTRODUCTION

Britain joins the European Community. Prime Minister Edward Heath signs the Treaty of Accession in Brussels in January 1972

In October 1943, Winston Churchill wrote a note to the foreign secretary, in which he listed the things he wanted to see accomplished after the War.

> We hold strongly to a system of a League of Nations which will include a Council of Europe, with an International Court and an armed Power capable of enforcing its decisions.

Seven years later he could point with satisfaction to the United Nations (1945), the Council of Europe (1949), the International Court of Justice (1945) and a United Nations force (in Korea, 1950).

Even at the height of the War, many Europeans looked forward to a postwar Europe which could unify nations rather than turn them into rivals. The exiled wartime governments in London of Belgium, the Netherlands and Luxembourg made a start when they agreed that after the War there would be a customs union between them – called *Benelux*. This came into effect in 1948. It abolished customs duties on all goods passing between the three member states. Optimists saw it as a first stage towards the creation of a European Federation – a union of different governments (like the United States or the Union of Socialist Soviet Republics).

---

1 *Why was the customs union in the Low Countries called Benelux?*

2 *What are the benefits of a customs union to foreign travellers?*

3 *Give an example of a federal government, a) in Western Europe and b) in the Commonwealth.*

POSTWAR GERMANY

Recovery

The recovery of Germany was crucial to the postwar prosperity of Europe and the eventual creation of a thriving European Community. But in 1947 things looked bleak to the Germans. Food was desperately short, there was a flourishing black market and people preferred to barter goods rather than use the existing paper currency.

Something had to be done. Marshall Aid seemed to be one solution but the Russians would not hear of it being used to help Germany. A new system of currency was badly needed but the Russians would not agree to this either. The three Western Allies (Britain, France and the United States) decided to go ahead on their own. The introduction of the new currency, the Deutschemark, was seen by the Russians as a challenge. They began the Berlin Blockade in retaliation. The Allied action and the chain of events it set off put Germany on the road to recovery.

- It gave them a reliable currency they could trust.
- It provided them with the financial aid they needed to put industry back on its feet once more.
- It reassured them, through the Berlin Airlift and the formation of NATO, that Germany would not be deserted if attacked by the Soviet Union.
- It gave them the opportunity, at last, to form a democratic government.

The first postwar German Parliament was elected in 1949 with Dr Adenauer as chancellor. It was the first free election since 1933. Konrad Adenauer had an impeccable record as an opponent of Hitler. He had been dismissed as mayor of Cologne and was later sent to a concentration camp. West Germany became an independent, sovereign nation on 5 May 1955. The Federal Republic of Western Germany was now on equal terms with the other countries of Western Europe.

Wirtschaftswunder

Berlin in ruins after Allied bombing raids during the War

Berlin in 1963

By 1955 West Germany was already making a remarkable recovery from the ruinous effects of the War. Exactly why German industry should have prospered so swiftly is hard to say. German workers worked hard, there were few strikes and pay rises were kept to a minimum, but the same could also be said of other less prosperous countries at this time. Few of these had to start from scratch as in Germany. Not only were many German factories in ruins at the end of the war, but Russian demands for war reparations stripped many works of their plant and machinery.

As a result, Germany's new factories were equipped with the very latest technology, while their competitors made do with older, less efficient machines. German businesses ploughed back their profits and spare cash to expand their works and factories and instal the latest machinery. By 1960 people were talking about the *Wirtschaftswunder* – the 'economic miracle'. Germany was now the richest country in Europe.

1 *Why did the restoration of cities like Berlin help to stimulate the recovery of German industries after the War?*

2 *What advantages did the new factories have over their predecessors?*

3 *What advantages did Germany's new industries have compared with industries in Britain which had not been badly damaged in the War?*

4 *What incentives were there for German factory workers in the years immediately after the War?*

EUROPEAN UNITY

The Council of Europe

Winston Churchill's hope in 1943, and his plea in 1946 at Zurich for 'a kind of United States of Europe', began to bear fruit in 1949 when the three Benelux countries, France, the United Kingdom, the Irish Republic, Italy, Denmark, Norway and Sweden formed the Council of Europe. Austria, West Germany, Greece, Iceland and Turkey joined later in the 1950s. By 1984 the Council included almost all the countries of Western Europe. It meets in Strasbourg in France. Representatives appointed by their national parliaments meet three times a year as the European Assembly. Foreign ministers, who form a Committee of Ministers, meet about twice a year.

The Council was set up to safeguard Europe's heritage, to strive for greater unity, and to preserve human rights (such as freedom of speech). In 1950 it approved the European Convention on Human Rights and authorised the formation of a Commission to implement this Convention. A European Court of Human Rights was set up in 1959 to decide cases where people complained that their basic human rights had been violated.

The European Court of Human Rights in session

EFTA

The European Free Trade Association (EFTA) came into being in 1959 when the countries of the Organisation for European Economic Co-operation (OEEC) tried unsuccessfully to link up with the European Economic Community (EEC). The OEEC had originally been founded to administer Marshall Aid (page 308). The seven original EFTA members were Austria, Denmark, Norway, Portugal, Sweden, Switzerland and the United Kingdom. They were later joined by Iceland and Finland. Denmark and the UK withdrew when they joined the EEC in 1973. The main work of EFTA has been to remove tariff barriers on industrial goods. It differs from the European Community in that its aims are almost entirely commercial. It seeks free trade within EFTA and promotes world trade in general and European trade in particular.

COMECON

COMECON or the Council for Mutual Economic Assistance (see page 308) was originally founded in 1949 as a response to Marshall Aid and the formation of the OEEC in 1947. It was Russia's way of providing economic assistance for the Communist countries of Eastern Europe. Since then it has developed into a much larger organisation. It aims to further trade between member nations and to assist the planned development of national economies. A large number of commissions have been formed to develop industries such as iron and steel, food production, and the peaceful use of atomic energy.

The six original members (USSR, Bulgaria, Czechoslovakia, Hungary, Poland and Romania) were joined by Albania in 1949 (resigned in 1961), East Germany (1950), Mongolia (1962), Cuba (1972) and Vietnam (1978). Interestingly, China did not become a member, nor did Yugoslavia.

> **1** *What is meant by free trade?*
> **2** *How does the Council of Europe differ from, a) EFTA and b) COMECON?*
> **3** *How does EFTA differ from COMECON?*

THE EUROPEAN COMMUNITY
Origins of the Common Market

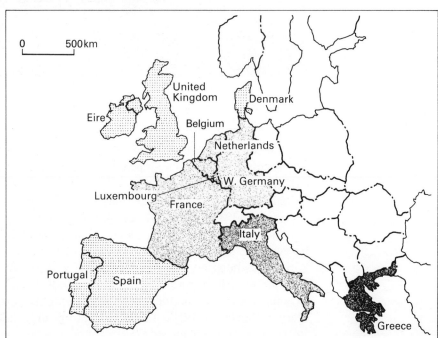

Map of the European Community in 1989

Jean Monnet

Robert Schuman

The Council of Europe was a notable attempt to provide a place where leading Europeans could meet to discuss ways of ensuring that freedom, human rights and the European heritage would be preserved for the benefit of future generations. But it was not the 'United States of Europe' which Churchill had talked about in 1946.

This was also the dream of two Frenchmen, Robert Schuman and Jean Monnet. They thought that the best way to bring about such a union was through economic co-operation. This is why they drew up the Schuman Plan in 1950. It proposed, initially, to make industry more efficient in Western Europe by establishing a common policy on coal, iron and steel.

> By the pooling of basic production and the establishment of a new High Authority whose decisions will be binding on France, Germany and the countries that join them, this proposal will lay the first concrete foundations of the European Federation which is indispensable to the maintenance of peace.
>
> *The Schuman Plan* (drafted by Jean Monnet), 1950

Six countries (Belgium, France, Germany, Italy, Luxembourg and the Netherlands) accepted the plan and signed the Treaty of Paris to bring it into being on 18 April 1951. This created the European Coal and Steel Community, or ECSC. It removed restrictions on trade between member countries in coal, iron ore and steel. The Community was given the task of planning the future growth of these basic industries. In 1953, Jean Monnet made a speech at a joint meeting between members of the Council of Europe and the ECSC. He said that the ECSC was the start of a 'united Europe'. But, as you will see in the sources which follow, these proposals were viewed, at first, with suspicion in Britain.

Source A

> Our Community is an open Community. We want other countries to join on an equal footing with us ... to give up the divisions of the past and, by pooling their coal and steel production, to ensure the establishment of common bases for economic development as the first stage towards the European federation ...
>
> When I think that Frenchmen, Germans, Belgians, Dutchmen, Italians and Luxemburgers will all follow common rules and, in doing so, will view their common problem in the same light and that, as a result, their behaviour towards one another will have fundamentally changed, I realise that definite progress has been made in relations between the countries and men of Europe.
>
> Speech by Jean Monnet at Strasbourg on 22 June 1953.
> Quoted in *Readings in Western Civilization: Twentieth-Century Europe*,
> edited by J.W. Boyer and J. Goldstein, University of Chicago Press, 1987

Source B

Eden [a leading Conservative cabinet minister] felt himself out of the European swim. He became, and the Foreign Office under him became, sincerely but implacably opposed to the whole European concept, to Strasbourg and all it stood for. He once said to me, 'Association, not participation. Association is as far as I'm prepared to go in any European connection'.

Lord Boothby quoted in Alan Thompson, The Day before Yesterday, Panther, 1971

Source C

We never had any great drive towards Europe in the early 1950s . . . If we had, of course, we wouldn't have had the difficulties we later had with de Gaulle or with France, as we would have come in on the ground floor.

Lord Butler (another leading Conservative cabinet minister)
quoted in Alan Thompson, The Day before Yesterday, Panther, 1971

Source D

After the Schuman declaration, Jean Monnet and myself went to London to explain the proposal to the British [Labour] government . . . I am not sure that Bevin [Foreign Secretary] and Cripps [Chancellor of the Exchequer] had a precise understanding of what we meant by 'community'. They certainly hated the idea of having an organization which would have powers in some instances above the national governments. I think that was the crux of the decision.

Etienne Hirsch, quoted in Alan Thompson, The Day before Yesterday, Panther, 1971

Source E

The uniting of Europe is a necessity for the prosperity of Europeans and for the peace of the whole world . . . the Coal and Steel Community appears to me to be the most hopeful and constructive development so far toward the economic and political integration of Europe.

US President Dwight Eisenhower quoted by Jean Monnet in his speech at Strasbourg
(see Source A above)

---

1 *Why were Britain's leading politicians opposed to the idea of joining the European Coal and Steel Community?*

2 *Why did Eisenhower welcome the formation of the ECSC?*

3 *What natural advantage did the six member nations of the ECSC have compared with Great Britain and Ireland?*

4 *How did Jean Monnet see the ECSC changing relationships between the six member countries of the European Coal and Steel Community?*

The Treaty of Rome

The ECSC was so successful that the member countries could see no good reason why the same idea should not be applied to every item of trade, not merely the raw materials of heavy industry. This is why they signed the Treaty of Rome on 25 March 1957. It set up the European Economic Community (EEC). The Treaty of Rome had four main objectives. These were, a) to promote unity among the peoples of the Community, b) to generate social and economic progress, c) to preserve and maintain peace and liberty, d) to improve living standards and working conditions.

Article 3 of the Treaty of Rome listed the activities of the Community.

- The removal of customs duties, and restrictions as to quantity, in regard to the import and export of goods.
- The establishment of a common customs tariff and a common trading policy towards non-EEC countries.
- The removal of obstacles to the free movement of people, services and money.
- A common agricultural policy.
- A common transport policy.
- A European Social Fund to improve the possibilities of employment for workers and to contribute to the raising of their standard of living.
- A European Investment Bank to facilitate the economic expansion of the Community through the creation of new resources.
- The association of overseas countries and territories with the Community with a view to increasing trade and to pursuing jointly their effort towards economic and social development.

---

1 *How was the EEC different from the ECSC?*

2 *What did the founders of the EEC hope to achieve in the end?*

3 *What did they mean by a 'common agricultural policy' and a 'common transport policy'? How could these help the EEC achieve its aims?*

The EEC, or Common Market as it was usually called, was highly successful. It made it much easier for the six member nations to export to, and import from, each other. Trade boomed and the industries of the EEC countries prospered. At the same time the member nations founded Euratom to research into, and encourage the peaceful uses of atomic energy. In 1958 the European Investment Bank came into being to finance major projects.

The EEC Expands

The United Kingdom was originally invited to join the ECSC (and EEC) but declined because many British politicians feared the consequences of putting control of the British economy, and ultimately many other aspects of government, in the hands of a supranational organisation (i.e. a body representing several different countries). They did not want to surrender any of the power of Parliament to a higher power – the European Community. They disliked the idea that European laws might take precedence over British laws. In addition many were worried about the effect that Common Market membership would have on Britain's trade with the countries of the Commonwealth. Many of these were wholly or partly dependent on Britain as the main market for their goods.

However, the undoubted success of the Common Market and the growing independence of the Commonwealth nations left the United Kingdom isolated. Harold Macmillan's Conservative Government decided to apply for membership of the EEC in 1961 (together with three of Great Britain's main trading partners in Europe – the Irish Republic, Denmark and Norway). This change of heart was welcomed by five of the six members of the EEC but not by France. Talks broke down in 1963 when President de Gaulle of France vetoed the British application. He gave his reasons:

> England is insular, maritime, linked by trade, markets and food supply to very different and often very distant islands. She is essentially an industrial and commercial nation, and her agriculture is relatively unimportant . . . how can England, as she is, be brought within . . . the Common Market.

Cartoon by Vicky in 1961

"HE SAYS HE WANTS TO JOIN—ON HIS OWN TERMS . . ."

- He thought the entry of the United Kingdom would upset the agreements which had already been accepted by the six founder members of the EEC.
- He didn't think the British had their hearts set on a united Europe, since their strong and intimate links with both the Commonwealth nations and the United States meant that Europe might well take third place in Britain's priorities.
- In any case, he thought that Britain had a weak economy and would weaken rather than strengthen the EEC.

A further attempt by Britain's Labour Government (led by Harold Wilson) to join the EEC failed again in 1967. In the same year the three different communities (ECSC, EEC and Euratom) merged to form the European Community.

---

1 *Why did the UK want to join the EEC in the 1960s but not in the 1950s?*

2 *How did the fact that Great Britain is an island affect the question of Britain's entry into the EEC?*

3 *Why did President de Gaulle veto Britain's application to join? In the light of subsequent events, was he right or wrong?*

4 *Why did the other five members want Britain to join the EEC? What advantages would that have brought to the Community?*

5 *Identify Macmillan, Adenauer and de Gaulle in the cartoon. What was its point? How did Vicky see Britain's application to join the EEC?*

The Enlarged Community

When de Gaulle retired in 1969, the new French President (Georges Pompidou) offered no objection when the other five members of the EEC invited Britain, Denmark, the Irish Republic and Norway to renew their applications. This was after a summit meeting of the European Community leaders at the Hague, in December 1969, made the crucial decision to expand membership even if this weakened the Community. However, the people of Norway voted in 1972 against joining the Common Market. So, in 1973, *The Six* became *The Nine*. The United Kingdom, the Irish Republic and Denmark became part of the new Europe and Edward Heath, the British Conservative prime minister, signed the Treaty of Accession in Brussels in January 1972 (see photograph on page 352).

There was a lot of opposition to UK membership of the Common Market both from the Left and the Right. This is why the new Labour Government held a national referendum in 1975 asking the people to vote on whether they wanted to stay in the Common Market or not. They did, by a majority of two to one.

1 *Why was a national referendum held in Britain in 1975?*

2 *What are the arguments for and against having a national referendum on an important issue?*

Recognition of the special trading relationship of the former colonial powers to their ex-colonies was established when the Yaounde Convention made special arrangements for 18 French-speaking countries of Africa. This was enlarged to 46 and later 57 countries under the terms of the Lome Convention in 1975 when it brought in the former countries of the British Empire as well. This helped the developing countries of Africa to sell their goods more easily to the countries of the European Community. In 1981 Greece became the tenth member of the Community. Spain and Portugal joined later in 1986.

How the Community Works

The European Parliament in session in 1988

Like the United Nations, or indeed the government of any democratic state, the European Community is organised so that it has:

- An assembly (the European Parliament) which meets in Strasbourg and is representative of the people of the Community as a whole. The 518 MPs are directly elected by their constituents. They are not selected by their national parliaments (as is the case with the Council of Europe).
- An executive committee (the Council of Ministers) to make decisions. Each country takes it in turn to have its leader serve a term of six months as president of the Council of Ministers.
- A civil service (the European Commission) to run the day to day business of the Community and to prepare new laws and regulations. Seventeen commissioners, two each from France, Germany, Italy, Spain and the UK, and one each from the other seven member nations run the Commission. It has its headquarters in the Berlaymont Building in Brussels.
- A law court in Luxembourg (the European Court of Justice) to hear cases which infringe the laws of the Community.

The most important change made by the Six in 1957 was their decision that all tariffs and duties were to be phased out over a period of about 11 years. This meant that goods traded inside the Common Market were to be free of customs duties. Goods imported from outside the EEC had to pay a common import duty or tariff of about 6 per cent.

The Common Agricultural Policy

Article 38 of the Treaty of Rome stated that, 'The common market shall extend to agriculture and trade in agricultural products'. In other words, it was agreed that there should be no trade barriers on farm products sold within the Community, but that tariffs (taxes) should be imposed on agricultural products from outside the Community to stop them undercutting the prices which European farmers expected to get for their produce.

In 1962 the EEC decided that the Community could best help its farmers if it guaranteed minimum prices for their produce, no matter how cheaply these products could be purchased from abroad. Community grants were to be used to help farmers modernise their farms. Special schemes would help farmers in difficult areas, such as hill farms. This Common Agricultural Policy (CAP) was successful in protecting European farmers from competition from America where grain was cheaper to grow, but it also created serious problems for the Community.

This was because the Community's farmers knew they could sell their crops and livestock products at a fixed price. There was nothing to discourage them from growing as much as they could. As a result the Community began to pile up huge surpluses of food which it had to buy at the fixed prices. It paid out more and more cash to farmers for surpluses it didn't want! The Community had to find a way of dealing with the huge butter, cheese and grain 'mountains' and the large wine and milk 'lakes' which accumulated as a result of the CAP. It also had to find a way of cutting down the rapid growth in the cost of the CAP, since it was taking too high a proportion of the Community's annual budget. In the early 1980s, the British Government held up Community business by insisting that the other nine countries solve these financial problems first without calling on member states to pay higher contributions to the annual budget.

European butter mountain in July 1984. It was later sold off cheaply to the Soviet Union

> **1** *What was the point of selling the butter cheaply to the Russians? Why wasn't it sold cheaply, instead, to needy people in the European Community, such as pensioners or the unemployed?*
>
> **2** *The CAP works because people in the Community pay taxes to keep food prices high enough to make farming worthwhile. Why do opponents say the consumer pays twice for food? What might happen to the countryside if the CAP collapsed?*

Achievements of the Community

On balance there seems little reason to doubt that the European Community has been a success. But by the early 1980s little real progress had been made towards a United States of Europe. The European Parliament had little authority and insufficient power to alter decisions or formulate policy. The Council of Ministers spent much of its time squabbling about finance. The high hopes many people had, of the Community as a rival to the USA and the USSR, had not yet been fulfilled. But there were some achievements.

- Bitter wartime enemies were now friends.
- Many barriers to movement between countries had been removed, such as abolition of customs duties, common regulations (e.g. Value Added Tax), abolition of restrictions on people seeking work in the different countries of the Community.
- Trade had increased, bringing prosperity to the members of the Community. In particular, the Common Agricultural Policy, for all its faults, had kept food prices steady and prevented thousands of farmers from going out of business.

Headquarters of the European Community in Brussels. The Berlaymont Building is built in the shape of a cross

- The Community had also fought for equal pay for men and women. Member countries had harmonised some of their laws so that people throughout the Community enjoyed similar standards (e.g. Britain changed over to the metric system and to a decimal currency). Scientific and technological research was stimulated through joint projects.
- On several major world issues, such as the Middle East, the president of the Council of Ministers had been able to speak for the Community as a whole.

POSTWAR FRANCE

The humiliation of defeat in 1940 and the subsequent formation of a Vichy Government, subservient to Hitler, helped to strengthen General de Gaulle's determination to make France strong once again. Yet in the years immediately after the war France saw a return to the pre-war history of weak coalition governments.

A disastrous war in French Indo-China (see page 330), and a long and unsuccessful war in Algeria against the FLN guerrillas, further undermined French confidence in its politicians. But the postwar years also saw a steady growth in the French economy and the rebuilding of her industries. In particular, the EEC played an important part in France's new prosperity. The inability of the politicians to settle the Algerian crisis eventually brought de Gaulle back to power in 1958. When he died in 1970 he left France one of the strongest powers in Europe, with a thriving economy and a stable political system.

Under the earlier Fourth Republic (1947–59) there were 24 different governments. President de Gaulle persuaded the French people to accept a new system of democracy in which the president assumed a more important role than that of the prime minister. In the next 30 years (1959–88) there were only four presidents: de Gaulle (1959–69), Pompidou (1969–74), d'Estaing (1974–81) and Mitterand (1981 onwards).

Charles de Gaulle (1890–1970)

Charles de Gaulle was born in 1890 and joined the French army, serving in the First World War and later rising to the rank of general. He escaped to Britain after 1940, where he became leader of the Free French.

He became Head of State in the Provisional Government of 1944 but resigned in 1946. Twelve years later he returned as Prime Minister and served as President for ten years – a period made noteworthy by his determination to make France great and prosperous again. He made France an independent nuclear power, resolved the Algerian crisis and took a distinctive and independent line in foreign policy.

FURTHER QUESTIONS AND EXERCISES

1 *Explain simply what each of the following is or was. Who or what did it involve and why?*

    a) *Benelux*   f) *COMECON*

    b) *the Schuman Plan*   g) *CAP*

    c) *the Council of Europe*   h) *EEC*

    d) *ECSC*   i) *EFTA*

    e) *the OEEC*

Conservative and Labour politicians fight for the same cause

2 *What was that cause? Why did Left and Right share the same platform? When do you think this meeting was held? What was the subject of the meeting? When did people in Britain get the chance to 'say "No"'? What was their verdict then?*

3 *Explain the different steps which the countries of western Europe took to achieve greater political and economic unity after 1945.*

Chapter Seventeen

The Chinese Revolution

INTRODUCTION

Source A

Mao Tse-tung proclaims the People's Republic of China. A Chinese artist's impression of the ceremony in Peking on 1 October 1949

Source B

FIGHT FOR POWER AS MAO DIES
Chinese weep in the streets

By NIGEL WADE
The Daily Telegraph's Peking Correspondent, who is the
only British newspaper staff reporter based in China.

China's 800 million people, a quarter of the world's population, will stand to attention for three minutes a week tomorrow in mourning for Chairman Mao Tse-tung who died yesterday aged 82.

Peking accepted with quiet sorrow the announcement of the death of the god-like symbol of the Chinese Communist Revolution.

Two opposing political factions and a group of powerful military commanders must now decide who will lead the nation ...

Several hundred mourners, some sobbing openly, gathered in the Square of Heavenly Peace within minutes of the announcement. A uniformed soldier pulled his field car over to the kerb, opened the door and wept uncontrollably into a light blue handkerchief. People dabbed at their eyes as they walked or cycled along . . . The red flag of China was soon flying at half mast on buildings across the city. People standing around the flagpole in the square stared at the flag and a huge portrait of Mao on the wall of the Forbidden City.

The *Daily Telegraph*, 10 September 1976

---

1 *How did the artist depict the Proclamation of the Chinese People's Republic on 1 October 1949? What type of historical source is this?*

2 *For how many years was Mao Tse-tung the leader of China? Which US presidents took office during that time?*

3 *How do you account for the reaction of the Chinese people to the news of Mao's death? What was its significance to the rest of the world?*

4 *What did Nigel Wade mean when he called Mao 'the god-like symbol of the Chinese Communist Revolution'?*

5 *What type of historical evidence is Source B?*

For nearly 50 years Mao led the Chinese Revolution. He made many grave mistakes but few can doubt his success. In 1976 China had a strong unified government. This was something Chiang Kai-shek and Sun Yat-sen had been unable to achieve. By any standards, China was an industrial and agricultural giant. Already it ranked alongside the United States and the Soviet Union in the production of coal and grain.

THE CIVIL WAR

The Japanese Surrender

Although Mao Tse-tung's Communists and Chiang Kai-shek's Kuomintang were allies during the war against Japan, they distrusted each other. Neither made much of a dent in the Japanese front line during the war, although the Red Army did infiltrate Japanese lines throughout China, destroying war materials and ambushing units of the Japanese army.

By August 1945, the Communists controlled much of the countryside but the Japanese garrisons held on to the cities in the east. On 6 August the first atom bomb was dropped on Hiroshima. The Soviet Union entered the war, two days later, on 8 August. Within two more days the Soviet Red Army was 200 km deep inside Japanese-held Manchuria. On 11 August Chiang Kai-shek ordered the Chinese Red Army to halt its operations. At the same time, however, he ordered the Kuomintang 'to push forward without the slightest relaxation'. Mao Tse-tung reacted sharply to this blatant attempt by the

Nationalists to extend their control over China at the Red Army's expense. On 13 August, he told the Chinese Communist Party,

> As for the reactionaries in China, it is up to us to organize the people to overthrow them. Everything reactionary is the same; if you don't hit it, it won't fall. It is like sweeping the floor; where the broom does not reach, the dust never vanishes of itself ... Chiang Kai-shek wants to launch a country-wide civil war and his policy is set; we must be prepared for this!

> Mao Tse-tung, *Selected Works*, Foreign Languages Press, Peking, 1961

The Allies, however, ordered the Japanese forces to surrender to the Kuomintang not to the Communists. Chiang Kai-shek was helped in this by the Americans. They used their ships and aircraft to ferry half a million Kuomintang troops to different parts of China to accept the Japanese surrender, but not to Manchuria which by now was held by the Russians. Mao's guerrillas, who controlled much of the countryside in the rest of China, responded to Chiang's moves by cutting Kuomintang lines of communications between the cities.

On 28 August 1945, Mao Tse-tung began peace talks with Chiang Kai-shek in Chungking. But they broke down on 11 October and the civil war erupted once more. The Americans sent General Marshall to negotiate a truce (January 1946) between the sides but it only lasted six months.

The Russians left Manchuria in 1946 but, before Chiang Kai-shek could reclaim it for the Nationalists, Mao's guerrillas had seized much of the Japanese military equipment which was left behind. In addition, they strengthened their support in the mountains and villages and were able to stop the Kuomintang armies advancing into northern Manchuria.

Chiang Kai-shek

Victory for the Red Army

Chiang Kai-shek (and most Americans) assumed that the much larger Kuomintang army, equipped with aeroplanes, was bound to defeat Mao Tse-tung whose Red Army lacked aircraft. But despite American aid, the Kuomintang forces were soon on the defensive. Chiang Kai-shek had difficulty in co-ordinating his forces and was hampered by the inefficiency of corrupt officials and the incompetence of his generals. The Communists avoided open conflict, used guerrilla tactics to harass the enemy, and continued to build up their strength among the peasants.

Early in 1948, Lin Piao, the Red Army commander, led a brilliant offensive which drove the Kuomintang forces in Manchuria into the two main Manchurian cities of Mukden and Changchun. In October 1948, Lin Piao cut off the links between the 300 000 Kuomintang soldiers trapped in Manchuria and those in the rest of China. On 20 October he seized Changchun and then captured Mukden at the end of the month.

It was the beginning of the end for Chiang Kai-shek, The Red Army had overwhelmed a huge Kuomintang army and taken 300 000 soldiers prisoner. It had also seized control of the rich industrial and grain-growing region of Manchuria. The victory meant that 400 000 crack Red Army troops were ready to march into the rest of China.

In November-December they fought and won the crucial battle of Huai Hai north of Nanking. They captured Peking in January 1949 and advanced to the banks of the Yangtze. The Nationalists tried desperately to negotiate with the Communists but war broke out once more. The Red Army crossed the Yangtze, captured Nanking on 24 April and Shanghai a month later.

Communist forces crossing the Yangtze-kiang on 20 April 1949

The southern city of Canton fell six months later and the remnants of Chiang Kai-shek's Nationalists were forced out of China, most of them going to the island of Taiwan, off the Chinese coast. In Peking, on 1 October 1949, Mao Tse-tung was able at long last to read the official proclamation announcing the new People's Republic of China (see picture on page 367).

China's involvement in the Korean War in 1950 prevented the Red Army from following up this victory by invading Taiwan. The United States, at war with Chinese troops in Korea, was no longer prepared to take a semi-neutral stand in the conflict between Chiang Kai-shek and Mao Tse-tung. American warships patrolled the seas and the American Government stepped up military aid to the Taiwan Government.

1 *How has the Chinese artist depicted the crossing of the Yangtze? Is this a realistic picture? Or is it propaganda?*

2 *How did Chiang Kai-shek try to take advantage of the Japanese surrender in August 1945? How was he assisted by the United States?*

3 *How did the Soviet invasion of Manchuria on 8 August 1945 help Mao to win the Civil War?*

4 *Why did Chiang Kai-shek and the Nationalists (who controlled the air) lose the Civil War to Mao Tse-tung and the Communists?*

THE PEOPLE'S REPUBLIC

Foreign Relations

Mao now had the problem of bringing Communism to a vast country with over 600 million people and a land area of nearly 10 million square kilometres – almost as big as the United States. It was a formidable task. It was not made any easier when many foreign governments refused to recognise (accept) the People's Republic as the legitimate government of China. However, the Soviet Union did so, on 2 October 1949. This action was soon followed by other countries as well, such as the United Kingdom in 1950. But France only did so in 1964 and the United States waited until 1978.

The Soviet Union offered substantial material support and signed a 30-year treaty of 'friendship, alliance and mutual assistance' on 15 February 1950. As a result thousands of Soviet engineers, agricultural scientists and other technicians and experts went to China to help Mao rebuild a country which had been shattered by war.

American hostility to the Communist regime and friendship for the Kuomintang continued. This was at the time of the Red Scare in the United States (see page 342) when politicians and diplomats could not afford to be thought 'soft' on Communism. The Korean War did nothing to reassure China when General MacArthur drove the North Korean forces back to the Chinese border. For its part, the US Government suspected the Chinese of having encouraged the North Korean aggression in the first place.

Tensions were also heightened when Chinese forces invaded Tibet in October 1950 and later occupied the whole of that region in 1959. Because it was a relatively uninhabited mountainous region, the boundaries between the countries in that area were not clearly marked. The Chinese claimed territory from Burma (the Wa district which was ceded to China in 1960) and the Aksai region of Kashmir (which later led to a border war with India in 1962).

Land Reform

Mao Tse-tung's immediate problem was to reform the system by which the peasants held land. In the past, rich landlords had often extorted high rents from their tenant farmers. Some were even accused of torturing and killing peasants. Many poor peasant families had starved. One peasant on a commune near Peking told a Western visitor,

> By the time I was ten, five of my brothers and sisters had died of starvation and exposure.

At first the Communist authorities told the peasants to set up tribunals to punish the landlords and to redistribute the land, giving everyone an equal share. Many of the richer peasants and the landlords were executed or imprisoned when they resisted the forcible seizure of their land.

A landlord faces his accusers in 1949

1 *What does the look on the principal accuser's face suggest to you?*

2 *Imagine you are an eyewitness to this event. Use the photograph to give you the information you need to write a news report along similar lines to Nigel Wade's report on the death of Mao on page 367.*

Providing the peasants with small farms was not Communism, of course. So in 1953 the Communist authorities began to persuade groups of peasants to co-operate with one another. They stressed the benefits that mutual aid could bring. This was only a short step from the next stage – the introduction of collective farms. The main difference was that under collectivisation the peasants became employees not landowners. Collective farming made sense because sharing out the land among China's huge population would have left each family with only a small holding on which to grow crops. Collective farming enabled the peasants to pool their resources.

Stalin's reforms of 1928 also provided Mao with another way of reshaping China – the Five Year Plan. The first of these was introduced in 1953 and, like Stalin's 1928 Plan, was designed to put most of China's effort into the development of heavy industry, improving power supplies and building and maintaining railways.

A Hundred Flowers

Mao Tse-tung believed in the idea of a permanent revolution. He didn't want to see Party officials becoming complacent, settling down into routines and losing touch with the peasants and workers of China. Needless to say, this approach was often resented by many members of the Chinese Communist Party, who, like most bureaucrats, preferred a settled existence. Complaints had already been made about the high-handed behaviour of some Party workers. In 1956 Mao initiated a campaign to let the people challenge the work and attitudes of Party officials. He told them,

Let a hundred flowers blossom and a hundred schools of thought compete.

In February 1957 he explained,

Marxists should not be afraid of criticism from any quarter . . . Will it do to ban such ideas and deny them any opportunity for expression. Certainly not . . . You may ban the expression of wrong ideas, but the ideas will still be there . . . it is only by employing the method of discussion, criticism and reasoning that we can really foster ideas and overcome wrong ones and that we can really settle issues.

Quoted in Charles Meyer and Ian Allen, *Source Materials in Chinese History*,
Frederick Warne, 1970

But the 'hundred flowers' campaign back-fired. Mao and his colleagues were surprised at the scale of the response and alarmed at the strength of the opposition. The 'hundred flowers' policy was quickly abandoned. Some critics even suggest it may have been a trap to lure enemies of the system into the open!

> **1** What did Mao Tse-tung mean by his celebrated phrase 'Let a hundred flowers blossom'? Was this the same as allowing the Chinese people free speech?
>
> **2** What did Mao have in mind when he talked of 'permanent revolution'? What advantages did he think this could bring to China?

THE GREAT LEAP FORWARD

The Communes

Mao had another plan to revitalise China and strengthen the grip of the Party on the countryside. This was 'The Great Leap Forward' of 1958. Progress under the first Five Year Plan (1953–8) had been disappointing. The new second Five Year Plan would take a great leap forward to bring a new form of Communism to the countryside and to the towns.

This is why the collective farms were merged into super-collectives, called communes, which were not only responsible for growing farm produce but also for building dams, weaving cloth, and running many other local industries as well, even smelting iron.

The communes were groups of 50 to 60 villages, each with a combined population, on average, of about 20 000 to 30 000 people. By the end of 1960 there were about 25 000 of these communes throughout China. Some were even as large as 70 000 or 80 000 people.

Each commune was divided into brigades and each brigade into work units. These brigades were run by committees of the workers themselves and given the responsibility of determining what crops should be grown and when.

Each commune was also expected to build its own schools, hospitals, stores and machine shops (where machinery could be repaired). It was expected to try to become self-sufficient for most of its needs, in addition to food. Dams were to be built for irrigation purposes, using local stones and clay as raw materials and the manual labour of thousands of peasants to build them, instead of using trucks and machinery. A visitor wrote,

> Monumental ant heaps were busy on the sites of future reservoirs. Endless lines of blue-clad men and women were filing up mountainsides like some unnatural stream changing its course. In the background, scattered all over the fields, multitudes of people were moving around with two buckets hanging from their shoulder poles.
>
> Tibor Mendes, *China and Her Shadow*, 1962

The emphasis was on peasants helping each other to rebuild the economy, not expecting the initiative to come from the Government – the new landlord. But the idea of the communes had not been properly thought out and the Great Leap Forward ran into trouble. Prime Minister Chou En-lai told an Indian Agricultural Mission in Peking that he doubted whether large co-operatives were always more efficient than small ones. Making them larger could 'lead to a lack of initiative on the part of individual workers and working teams'.

Albert Belhomme, an American living in China, described the effect that the Great Leap Forward had on industry. He said that party officials put output before safety and common sense. For instance, they insisted that output from a paper-making machine be increased by speeding up the belt. Instead of 90 metres of paper per minute, they raised it to 200 metres per minute but the bearings packed up, the belt slipped and the machine was put out of production until spare parts could be fitted! Backyard iron furnaces were encouraged in an effort to increase iron and steel production. But this diverted workers from their other jobs. Many people were badly burned. It proved a disastrous failure since the quality of the iron produced in these home-made furnaces was poor and unsuitable for conversion into steel.

The people were told to exterminate vermin: rats, mosquitoes, flies and sparrows. But when they got rid of the sparrows 'we began to notice something strange . . . there were millions of these goddam bugs about a half-inch long falling into your hair and down your neck'.

The Tachai commune depicted on a Chinese poster by Chang Yi-ching. Tachai was a symbol to the Chinese of what could be achieved through co-operative farming. Twenty years earlier, Tachai had been a backward, poorly-farmed district. Co-operative intensive farming transformed it. Like the Stakhanovite movement in Russia (page 126), it was held up to the Chinese as a model commune. 'IN AGRICULTURE LEARN FROM TACHAI'

1 *How has the artist depicted the Tachai commune? Is this a realistic painting or is it propaganda?*

2 *What does it tell you about a commune? Where did the people live? How did they cultivate the land? What problems had they overcome? What was their main crop?*

3 *Why were other communes told to learn from Tachai? How has the poster been designed to put over this message?*

4 *Why did the Chinese place great emphasis on human labour during the Great Leap Forward?*

5 *Why did Mao want a 'Great Leap Forward' instead of slow, but steady progress? Why did the 'Leap' fail?*

Paper Tigers

To make matters worse, many of the technical experts returned to Russia and the Soviet Union cut its aid programme to China. This was because the Chinese leaders had accused the Russians (led by Khruschev – see page 319) of revisionism in tampering with Marxist–Leninist ideas. The Russians, for their part, distrusted Mao Tse-tung's insistence that the mainspring for the Chinese Revolution must come from the peasants, rather than from the urban working class of the orthodox Marxist belief.

The Chinese disapproved of Khruschev's attack on Stalin in 1956 and opposed Russia's desire for 'peaceful co-existence' with the West. Nor did Mao Tse-tung take the threat of nuclear war as reason for abandoning Marxist–Leninist principles. As early as August 1946 he told an American journalist,

> The atom bomb is a paper tiger which the US reactionaries use to scare people. It looks terrible, but in fact it isn't. Of course, the atom bomb is a weapon of mass slaughter, but the outcome of a war is decided by the people, not by one or two new types of weapon.

> Mao Tse-tung, *Selected Works*, Foreign Languages Press, Peking, 1961

On 1 December 1958, he repeated the idea. Although reactionary forces might act like 'real tigers' and inflict terrible losses in the short-term, they would be defeated in the end. It cost the Chinese people,

> tens of millions of lives before the victory in 1949. Look! Were these not living tigers, iron tigers, real tigers? But in the end they changed into paper tigers, dead tigers, bean-curd tigers. These are historical facts.

> Mao Tse-tung, *Selected Works*, Foreign Languages Press, Peking, 1961

1 *When Mao was reported as having described the atom bomb as a 'paper tiger', people in Britain thought he was bluffing and that he had no conception of the destruction a nuclear explosion could cause. Was this true? What did he mean by 'paper tigers'? Who did he think would triumph in the end? What were the 'historical facts'?*

Setback

Unhappily for Mao these tensions coincided with two extremely poor harvests. Food production fell sharply and millions of Chinese came close to starvation. Nor did industrial output improve at anything like the rate demanded by the Five Year Plan. The Great Leap Forward was modified and the Chinese reverted to less radical ways of increasing output. The larger communes were reduced in size and greater concentration on food production, not industry, was made their top priority.

Mao was unrepentant. He thought the exercise had shaken up the Communist Party and taught the country 'a lesson'. But the failure of the Great Leap Forward seriously damaged his position in China. His opponents were growing in number and were so successful they put Liu Shao-chi in his place as Chairman of the People's Republic, although Mao, nonetheless, retained the top post of Chairman of the Chinese Communist Party.

Liu Shao-chi was now the likely successor to Mao Tse-tung. He wanted to emphasise the role that industrial workers could have in bringing Communism to China. He was backed by many city officials, thinkers, writers and lecturers. But Mao Tse-tung always took the view that real power in China, unlike the Soviet Union, lay in the hands of the peasants.

THE CULTURAL REVOLUTION
Our Glorious Helmsman
Source A

Chinese poster published in 1973 depicting the 'Great Proletarian Cultural Revolution'. Red Guards are shown gathering in the Square of Heavenly Peace in Peking to hear Chairman Mao

Source B

Today our glorious leader, our glorious commander, our glorious helmsman Chairman Mao, together with a million revolutionary masses from Peking and the entire country, in the capital of our glorious motherland, on the heroic T'ien An Men Square [The Square of Heavenly Peace], convened a great rally in celebration of the great proletarian cultural revolution . . .

Chairman Mao, Lin Piao, and other comrades appeared on the T'ien An Men ramparts to the strains of the tune 'The East is Red'. At this point the masses throughout the square rose with great clamour. Countless hands only holding red copies of *The Sayings of Mao Tse-tung* stretched up towards the T'ien An Men ramparts. A million fiery hearts flew out to Chairman Mao. A million eyes gleaming with revolutionary pride gazed up at Chairman Mao.

People's Daily, 18 August 1966, translated by Orville Schell,
in *China Readings: Communist China*, edited by Schurman & Schell, Penguin, 1968

Source C

'Big character' posters in Peking

Source D

A Chinese official told an American journalist about his experiences during Mao Tse-tung's Cultural Revolution (1965–8):

'First of all', he said, 'you can't imagine how exciting it all was. Every morning, you came to your office. You could hardly wait to get there to see what was new, to see what the new posters said . . .

You never knew when you yourself might be attacked. Often you and your comrades would make up a Big Character poster attacking someone in the morning, and in the afternoon another poster would denounce that of the morning. It was a continuous fever. Everyone was swept up in it.

There were meetings in the Tien-an Men. Something was happening all the time.' . . .

Officials, party members, bureaucrats, members of the party apparatus were sent to live in the country to work with their hands, to 'cleanse their thought', to get back to Marxist and Maoist fundamentals. Everyone went . . . They built their own huts with crude brick or baked mud walls. They broke ground, planted crops, irrigated the land. They worked to exhaustion and suffered freezing cold in winter and the blazing-oven heat of China's summer.

'It was a wonderful experience', the official said. 'It was the great experience of my life . . . Now I know what life in China means.'

To Peking – And Beyond, by Harrison E. Salisbury, Arrow Books, 1973

A Chinese girl told a European visitor that the wall posters meant 'we can now write about things that have been forbidden for twenty years'.

---

1 *Why were they called 'Big Character' posters? Why were they put up on walls? Why were the Chinese excited by this type of political activity? How did it stimulate discussion? Did it allow the Chinese free speech?*

2 *What was the 'Great Proletarian Cultural Revolution'? Who was it against? How were the aims of the Cultural Revolution carried out? What happened to Party officials? How was this movement related to Mao's other ideas of 'permanent revolution', 'the hundred flowers' and 'the Great Leap Forward'?*

3 *In what ways was the attitude of the Chinese to Mao Tse-tung similar to or different from that of the Russians and Stalin (see page 124) or the Germans and Hitler (see page 103)?*

4 *What are the shortcomings of Sources A and B as historical evidence? How do they differ from the way in which the media would cover a similar event in Britain or the United States?*

The Red Guards

Mao Tse-tung had decided to overthrow Liu Shao-chi – 'The number-one person in the Party taking the capitalist road' – and to 'purify' the Party and the Government. 'False thinkers' were to be weeded out – those who put their own interests and those of officials and city workers before the peasants and the Party. Mao's supporters urged the young people of China to go back to the basic principles of the Communist Party. They formed the Red Guards from hundreds of thousands of university, college and high school students. They used propaganda to carry the message of the Cultural Revolution across China. It was designed to give fresh impetus to Chinese

Communism and to question the beliefs of philosophers and intellectuals. It was to be a revolution of the peasants and workers although the Red Guards Congress in Peking on 22 February 1967 did allow some exceptions:

> Students of non-working-people family origin [the middle classes] who have deep feeling for Chairman Mao and a proletarian revolutionary spirit . . . can also be enrolled.

Gangs of youths stormed the offices of Party officials, commune headquarters, schools and universities, denouncing and humiliating their seniors and sending many of them to work on the land. Students made their lecturers and professors wear dunce's hats and hung placards round their necks denouncing them as capitalists or as middle-class. Red Guards were to be seen everywhere, travelling by lorry, van or bus, attending mass rallies and hanging on to Mao's words with religious zeal and rapt attention. They even attacked the staff of foreign embassies. In August 1967, Red Guards threw petrol bombs at the British Mission in Peking and kicked men and women staff as they fled from the burning building.

All Red Guards, without exception, carried a little red book containing the thoughts of Chairman Mao. These were committed to memory, chanted by enthusiastic crowds and read out to workers in the fields. At the Red Guards Congress on 22 February 1967 they declared their faith:

> We, the Red Guards, pledge to be thorough-going proletarian revolutionaries . . . Whoever dares to oppose Chairman Mao, to oppose Mao Tse-tung's thought, and foster revisionism in China, no matter how high his position, how senior his service and how great his renown, we will resolutely rebel against him, and we will rebel to the end! We must always keep New China bright red and smash the dream of imperialists and modern revisionists to bring about a 'peaceful evolution'.
>
> *Peking Review*, 10 March 1967, quoted in Charles Meyer and Ian Allen, *Source Materials in Chinese History*, Frederick Warne, 1970

In October 1968 Liu Shao-chi was dismissed from his posts, following thousands of others who had been justly or unjustly purged. But the Cultural Revolution got out of hand. Red Guards fought pitched battles with peasants and many people were killed. Mao had to tell the Red Guard leaders, on 27 July 1968,

> You have let me down and, moreover, you have disappointed the workers, peasants, and soldiers of China.

He used the Red Army under Marshal Lin Piao to curb their power and China went back to normal once more.

Red Guards humiliate a number of Chinese accused of being counter-revolutionaries

1 *What is happening in the photograph?*

2 *How are the Chinese officials being humiliated? Why was the humiliation of officials made part of the Cultural Revolution?*

3 *How did the Red Guards let down Mao? Was it their fault?*

4 *How do you account for the undoubted popularity of the Red Guard movement with young people? What were many young people doing in the United States at this time?*

5 *Did the Red Guards believe in free speech? If not, why not?*

FOREIGN RELATIONS

The Soviet Union

By now relations with the Soviet Union had fallen to their lowest point yet. The reason this time had less to do with Marxism and more to do with Nationalism. The Chinese claimed a border zone in Siberia which had been acquired by Russia in the days of the Czars. In 1969 Chinese and Russian troops even exchanged fire along the Ussuri River on the border between the two countries.

After the Cultural Revolution Marshal Lin Piao was made heir-apparent to Mao. But, in a curious incident in 1971, he was killed in an air crash while escaping to the Soviet Union, after attempting to seize power.

Fear of Soviet intentions made the Chinese leaders rethink their policy on defence. Who were China's friends and who were her enemies? China was now a nuclear power, having successfully tested an atomic bomb in 1964 and a hydrogen bomb in 1967.

The United States

Instead of approaching the United States directly, the Chinese let it be known they would welcome a visit by an American table tennis team! This unexpected gesture of friendship led to President Nixon's widely publicised visit in 1972 when he met Mao Tse-tung, Chou En-lai and many other Chinese leaders. Tension between the two countries lessened and trade links multiplied.

US President Richard Nixon greeting Chairman Mao Tse-tung in Peking, on his visit to China in 1972

---

1 *Why did Nixon visit China? What had the United States to gain from establishing friendly relations with Mao after 23 years of hatred between the two sides?*

2 *Why did Mao agree to a visit from the US President? What had China to gain from such a meeting?*

In 1976, Mao Tse-tung died. In the same year two of Mao's oldest colleagues, Chou En-lai and Chu Teh, also died. Who would be China's new leaders and what would be their relations with the rest of the world?

AFTER MAO
Teng Hsiao-ping

Teng Hsiao-ping

In 1976 Hua Kuo-feng became first the prime minister (when Chou En-lai died) and then Party Chairman (when Mao died). The influence of the Cultural Revolution was still much in evidence in China. For instance, Chou En-lai's deputy prime minister, Teng Hsiao-ping, was purged and sacked from all his posts in the Government and in the Party at this time.

But a year later Teng Hsiao-ping was restored to power and by 1984 had become China's new leader. His policies were still those of a convinced Communist, but he was also a pragmatist. This means someone who is usually more concerned to make sure something works, rather than insisting that everything be done exactly according to a set of existing principles.

The Responsibility System

This was well illustrated when the Chinese introduced the Responsibility System in the early 1980s. Although the commune system worked well, it had the disadvantage of not giving workers and peasants an incentive to work to their maximum capacity. It was easy for hard workers to feel they were supporting the lazy workers as well.

Under the commune system the peasants had been given small plots of land, to grow vegetables and rear pigs and poultry. These provided a small income to supplement the wages paid by the commune. Now, under the Responsibility System, the peasants were given the responsibility of planning and cultivating their own individual holdings under the overall supervision of the commune's committees.

---

1 *What are the advantages and disadvantages of the Responsibility System?*

2 *What do you think the reaction of the Red Guards would have been in 1967 to Teng Hsiao-ping's reforms? Where are the Red Guards today?*

FURTHER QUESTIONS AND EXERCISES

1 *Which event in recent Chinese history is depicted in this poster? When did it occur? What was its purpose? What part did Mao Tse-tung play at this time? What are the people in the picture carrying? What was the significance of this at that time?*

2 *Write short notes explaining the circumstances which led to each of the undermentioned events or happenings in recent Chinese history. What was their effect on China and on the Chinese people?*

a) 'Let a hundred flowers blossom'

b) 'the Great Leap Forward'

c) the break with the Soviet Union

d) 'the Responsibility System'

3 *Why did Chiang Kai-shek lose control of China after 1945? Outline and explain the events which led to his exile to Taiwan.*

4 *Many people say that Mao Tse-tung was probably the greatest leader of the twentieth century. When he was born in 1893, China was ruled by Emperors. How did this son of a peasant become the leader of over a quarter of the world's population by the time he was 56?*

Chapter Eighteen
Imperialism and Decolonisation

INTRODUCTION

The wind of change is blowing through the continent. And this tide of national consciousness which is now arising in Africa is a political fact and we must accept it as such.

The British prime minister, Harold Macmillan, used these famous words when he addressed the South African parliament in 1960.

> **1** What was the 'wind of change'? Why did Macmillan call it a 'tide' as well as a 'wind'? What was he suggesting?
>
> **2** Why did he choose to say this to the South African parliament?

The pace of change in Africa was indeed rapid. In 1955 the independent countries in Africa could be counted on the fingers of one hand: South Africa, Liberia, Libya, Egypt and Ethiopia. In the next ten years (by 1965) 33 other African states gained their independence from colonial rulers and formed their own governments. Ten years later still (by 1975) only three countries had yet to gain that freedom.

Some gained independence the hard way, through revolution, terrorism and guerrilla warfare. Others came by it peacefully, without conflict and without acrimony.

Midnight, 5 March 1957. Prime minister Kwame Nkrumah of Ghana celebrates the arrival of independence

IMPERIALISM

The Empire Builders

In 1900, Imperialism, Colonialism and Imperialist were not words to be ashamed of. On the contrary. Most people in Britain were very proud of the British Empire, by far the largest in the world. France had the second largest empire, while King Leopold II of Belgium ruled an African colony (the Belgian Congo) 80 times larger than Belgium itself. Portugal, Spain, Germany and Italy also had overseas colonies while Russia had expanded its frontiers into Central Asia towards India and the Far East. Many motives fired the enthusiasm of the empire-builders:

- Missionaries and legislators wanted to stamp out 'evils', such as slavery, 'barbaric' punishments, sacrifices and 'heathen' rites. They thought they knew what was best and what was 'right' for other people.
- Politicians wanted colonies because empires brought greatness to a nation. They made people patriotic and gave them national pride.
- Industrialists wanted raw materials for industry, such as sugar cane, cocoa for chocolate, palm oil for soap and margarine, gold, diamonds, tin, jute for sacking, cotton and rubber.
- Businesses wanted to grow and sell tropical fruits and plants, such as bananas, coconuts and tea which could not be grown at home.

The British Empire after the First World War

- Investors thought that money could be made by exploiting the natural resources of the colonies. Rich people could invest their wealth there, and watch it multiply.
- The armed forces sought overseas military bases and coastal fuelling stations to supply the navy.
- Adventurous spirits were prepared to settle in the tropics with the aim of farming in Kenya, mining in the Congo or growing tea in Ceylon (Sri Lanka).

By 1914 the British Empire controlled 32 million square kilometres and the destinies of 400 million people. The French Empire, smaller but still massive, had 10 million square kilometres and 60 million people.

---

1 *Why did people say the sun never set on the British Empire? What did they mean by this? Why did they say it?*

2 *At home, in Europe, laws protected people's right to own property. Why, then, did the Imperialists seize land in the colonies without paying for it and without the agreement of the people living there? What assumptions did they make about those people?*

The Statute of Westminster

When Britain declared war on Germany in 1914, she did so in the name of the Empire as well, involving countries, such as Australia, in a European war of little concern to the people of those lands. The start of the Second World War was different. Britain made no automatic declaration of war then, though in practice the Dominions rose valiantly to the occasion. What had happened was simply, that at the Imperial Conference in 1926, the United Kingdom and the Dominions (Canada, Australia, New Zealand, South Africa, Newfoundland and the Irish Free State) agreed they were all:

> autonomous (self-governing) Communities, equal in status, in no way subordinate one to another in any aspect of their domestic or external affairs, though united by a common allegiance to the Crown, and free association as members of the British Commonwealth of Nations.

This is still the accepted definition of a member of the Commonwealth (the word 'British' was dropped in the mid-1950s). But 'common allegiance to the Crown' no longer applies, since more than 20 of the Commonwealth countries are republics.

The principles enunciated at the 1926 Imperial Conference were put into English law in 1931 in the Statute of Westminster. But it only applied to the 'White' Dominions before 1939. Other parts of the Empire had a different status. Most of these were colonies, run by colonial officials controlled from London. The only major exception was India, with its provincial governments and long history of resistance to British rule.

Colonialism

Some of the colonial administrators, such as Lord Lugard in Nigeria (British) and Louis Lyautey in Morocco (French) were skilled and well-meaning rulers. They brought discipline and prosperity to the territories they governed. But other officials were petty, corrupt, power-mad and often contemptuous of races, skin colours, languages, traditions and religions which were different from their own.

At the end of the First World War, a British journalist feared the effects on Africa, not of European Imperialism as such, but of Western civilisation. He said it would reduce the 'varied and picturesque and stimulating' African way of life 'to a dull routine of endless toil'.

> What the partial occupation of his soil by the White man has failed to do; what the mapping out of European political 'spheres of influence' has failed to do; what the Maxim [machine-gun] and the rifle, the slave gang, labour in the bowels of the earth and the lash, have failed to do; what imported measles, smallpox and syphilis have failed to do; whatever the overseas slave trade failed to do, the power of modern capitalistic exploitation, assisted by modern engines of destruction, may yet succeed in accomplishing.
>
> Edward Morel, *The Black Man's Burden*, National Labour Press, 1920

---

1 *What would have happened if Africa had been ignored by the West and left unexplored, never colonised, and undeveloped? How would this affect everyday life today in Britain?*

2 *How would it have affected Africa? Did colonisation bring more benefits than it did disadvantages, or the reverse? Was it right to bring benefits to Africa (e.g. Western medicine, crop sprays, fertilisers) but harm as well (such as guns and Western diseases)?*

The Seeds of Independence

In 1942 Churchill boasted that he had 'not become the King's First Minister in order to preside over the liquidation of the British Empire'. In fact he had no choice. It was not the intention of his Soviet or American allies to fight to preserve an empire. Indeed, when Churchill and Roosevelt signed the Atlantic Charter in 1941, they acknowledged

> the right of all peoples to choose the form of government under which they wish to live; and they wish to see sovereign rights and self-government restored to those who have been forcibly deprived of them.

If this meant anything at all, it clearly gave the peoples of India and of other countries (such as Kenya) the right to choose their own governments and to have their right to self-government restored to them.

Churchill had opposed the granting of independence to India before 1939. But the war changed his mind. He promised in 1940 that India would decide her own constitution after the War. In 1942 he told the King that all the political parties had agreed that India would be given its independence then.

The War also put ideas of freedom in the heads of the Commonwealth soldiers who helped to free France and liberate Rangoon.

> Men who had fought side by side with European troops, had shared the same hardships and experiences, and had found that bullets did not discriminate between Black and White, found it difficult on returning home to understand why they were no longer equals. If they had fought an enemy who wanted to dominate other nationalities then there were conditions back home which demanded similar action against foreigners who dominated the African people in the land of their birth.
>
> P.C. Mazicana and I.J. Johnstone, *Zimbabwe Epic*, Harare National Archive, 1982

An Asian army showed what could be done when the Japanese humiliated the might of the British Empire at Singapore, taking 130 000 soldiers prisoner. Some Nationalists, such as the Indonesians, hailed the invading Japanese as liberators and a small minority even joined the Japanese armed forces. The Indian National Army, founded by the Indian Nationalist leader, Subhas Chandra Bose, fought against the Allied forces in Burma.

After the War it was only a matter of time before people in colonies throughout the world sought and gained their independence. But the Nationalists faced a long struggle, since many Europeans had invested huge sums of money in the colonies. Influential people opposed the idea of granting independence to people they thought unfit to rule. Others were more receptive. In the House of Commons on 20 December 1946, the British Labour prime minister, Clement Attlee, said

> We do not desire to retain within the Commonwealth and Empire any unwilling peoples. It is for the people of Burma to decide their own future.

Many of the Nationalists who demanded independence, had been educated at European universities. There they had been taught the virtues of democracy, such as freedom of speech, freedom to vote and freedom to choose a government. People like Jomo Kenyatta of Kenya and Kwame Nkrumah of Ghana, who both went to the London School of Economics, Julius Nyerere of Tanzania who studied at Edinburgh, and Lee Kuan Yew of Singapore and Pandit Nehru of India who both went to Cambridge, saw no reason why they should not enjoy the same basic freedoms in their own countries as in Britain.

1 *How did the Second World War help the peoples of Africa and Asia who sought independence from colonial rule?*

2 *You are a Nationalist. A European puts these arguments to you, saying the colony is not ready for independence. How do you reply?*

    a) *Most of the people are poor and illiterate. How can you expect them to vote sensibly? They are not ready yet for democracy.*

    b) *You and other Nationalist leaders have little or no experience of politics or government. You are not ready yet to take control.*

    c) *If Western experts leave, the country will be ruined.*

    d) *If the colony is given its independence now, civil war will break out between the different tribal or religious groups. There will be terrible bloodshed.*

    e) *All the advantages of Western civilisation – justice, fair play, democracy, Christianity, education – will be lost.*

DECOLONISATION IN ASIA

Decolonisation is the name given to the process by which the former colonies of the great European empires were given up and their peoples granted independence. Sometimes this process was achieved only after a long and hard-fought guerrilla war (as in Algeria and Zimbabwe). In other cases it came about as the result of peaceful negotiation.

Progress in India

The British authorities made a genuine attempt to bring the benefits of Western technology to India in the late nineteenth century. By 1919, there were over 60 000 km of railway line in India – twice the length of the railway system in Britain and nearly as long as that of Russia. Hospitals, clinics, schools and universities had been opened. Indian students, like Gandhi and Nehru, could study in Britain as well as in India. But there was still enormous poverty and there were frequent famines despite the new dams, irrigation schemes and modern factories.

Material progress was one thing but many Indians also wanted a say in their country's future. This is why the Indian National Congress was founded by moderates in 1885. They were proud of the new India but resented the fact that many senior government posts went to Europeans not Indians. They wanted partnership with the British. Indians should be able to take an active and important part in the government of their own country.

This approach did not satisfy Indian activists who resented British rule and wanted to see rapid progress towards independence. They were not prepared to wait. Terrorist attacks and assassinations in the early years of the twentieth century showed the extent of their discontent.

The Amritsar Massacre

This discontent reached a new peak in 1919 after the Amritsar Massacre. Mohandas Gandhi, a lawyer who had worked in South Africa, had organised an ingenious campaign of protest against a new law which gave the British authorities the power to detain agitators for up to two years without putting them on trial. Instead of using violence, Gandhi told his supporters to follow a policy of passive resistance or civil disobedience. In this way he hoped to bring the routine government of India to a halt. But in Amritsar the authorities panicked and arrested three Indian leaders. Rioters took to the streets in retaliation. Five Europeans were murdered and a woman missionary was badly beaten in the street. A number of Indians were killed when the local authorities attempted to quell the riot. In desperation the British Deputy Commissioner asked General Dyer to send troops 'to restore order in Amritsar and to use all force necessary'.

Source A

Amritsar on the morning following the riots [11 April 1919] was like a ghost city. The deserted streets were littered with debris and several of the buildings were gutted shells; others were still smouldering. The shops and bazaars were closed and a sullen and subdued population was making preparations for the burial and burning of the dead.

Alfred Draper, *Amritsar*, Cassell, 1981

Source B

General Dyer

General Dyer, giving evidence, said in April last he was in command of the 45th Brigade at Jullundur, and in response to a request for help from Amritsar on April 10 he sent 100 British and 200 Indian soldiers to that city . . .

On the morning of the 13th [April 1919] he decided to go into the city and issue a proclamation warning the people against assembling together, and if they did so they were liable to be dispersed by force of arms. At 12.40 he heard that a meeting was to be held in the evening at Jalliamwalla Bagh. He immediately marched off with a striking force consisting of 25 British rifles, 25 Indian rifles, 40 Gurkhas armed with kukris, and two armoured cars.

As far as he could remember he reached Jalliamwalla Bagh about 5.15. When he arrived on the scene he proceeded through the narrow entrance on to the high ground and deployed his men on the right and left. Within 30 seconds he ordered fire to be opened. The meeting was then going on and a man was addressing it. At the time of firing he estimated the crowd at 5,000, but later on he heard that it was a good deal more . . . His object was to disperse the crowd, and he was going to fire until they were dispersed. The witness added 'In my view the situation at Amritsar was a serious one indeed, and communications I received from the neighbourhood were indicative of a serious rising. . . . I looked upon the crowd as rebels, and I considered it was my duty to fire and fire well. There was no other course. I looked upon it as a duty, a very horrible duty.'

Report of the Official Indian Government Inquiry in the *Daily Telegraph*, 15 December 1919

Source C

I had to shoot. I had thirty seconds to make up my mind what action to take and I did it. Every Englishman I have met in India has approved my act, horrible as it was. What would have happened if I had not shot? I and my little force would have been swept away like chaff and then what would have happened?

General Dyer quoted in the *Daily Mail*, 4 May 1920

In fact the Jalliamwalla Bagh was very confined and the crowd had difficulty in escaping through its narrow exits. Dyer did not give them chance to escape. Instead his soldiers fired 1650 rounds of ammunition into the crowd, killing at least 379 people, and wounding over 1000 others. Six days later he issued an order forcing Indians to crawl along the ground if they wanted to use a street where the lady missionary had been beaten. He flogged six Indian youths in the street even though he had no evidence they had committed the crime. These actions were strongly condemned and Dyer was forced to resign from the Army three months later.

Source D

The action taken by General Dyer has been described by others as having saved the situation in the Punjab and having averted a rebellion on a scale similar to the Mutiny. It does not, however, appear to us possible to draw this conclusion, particularly in view of the fact that it is not proved that a conspiracy to overthrow the British power had been formed prior to the outbreak.

Report of the Official Indian Government Inquiry, quoted in Alfred Draper, *Amritsar*, Cassell, 1981

Source E

There was no conspiracy to overthrow the Government of the Punjab. The arrest and deportation of the three Indian leaders was the direct cause of the hysteria in Amritsar ... The Jalliamwalla Bagh massacre was a calculated piece of inhumanity towards utterly innocent and unarmed men, including children and unparalleled for its ferocity in the history of modern British administration.

Report of the Inquiry by the Indian National Congress, quoted in Alfred Draper, *Amritsar*, Cassell, 1981

Winston Churchill and many other liberal British politicians were horrified. Edwin Montagu, the Secretary of State for India, condemned General Dyer's actions in the House of Commons.

Source F

Once you are entitled to have regard neither to the intentions nor to the conduct of a particular gathering, but to shoot and to go on shooting with all the horrors that were involved in order to teach somebody else a lesson, you are embarking on terrorism to which there is no end.

House of Commons debate, 8 July 1920, quoted in Alfred Draper, *Amritsar*, Cassell, 1981

But the British in India, as well as many people in Britain itself (including a leading British judge and the House of Lords), approved. Supporters subscribed £26 000 (worth about £400 000 today) to a fund set up to help General Dyer in his enforced retirement. The message this approval conveyed was not lost on India. The Amritsar Massacre and the support for General Dyer changed the way in which Indians looked on the British administration. Until then, most had been prepared to co-operate. Now they wanted India for themselves. They did not want partnership. They did not want compromise. They wanted independence. Gandhi became an outstanding national leader, using strikingly effective methods of protest to bring India's fight for independence to international attention.

1 *Which soldiers carried out the order to fire? What does this tell you about the Indian Army at that time? How would the situation have changed if these soldiers had disobeyed the order to fire? What would have happened to the soldiers?*

2 *General Dyer said his intention was to make the crowd disperse. Why was it unable to do so? Which evidence tells us that General Dyer should have been aware of this fact?*

3 *What evidence is there that General Dyer went far beyond the bounds of duty in order to maintain law and order in Amritsar?*

4 *Which of the sources quoted in B to F is most likely to be free from any bias?*

5 *What reservations have to be made when examining the evidence of someone directly involved as a participant? Is there any hint in Source B that General Dyer misled the Inquiry in any way?*

6 *What different reasons were given to explain why General Dyer ordered his soldiers to fire? How do the sources differ in their interpretation of the General's actions? Are Dyer's own statements consistent with each other? What reasons did Edwin Montagu give for the Massacre? What arguments did the two Inquiries consider? What reason for the Massacre was given by the Indian National Congress? Who was in the best position to know? What do you think happened? Write an explanatory account of the Massacre summing up the evidence.*

7 *What would have been your reaction, as an Indian, to news of the Massacre in 1919?*

Gandhi

The Mahatma Gandhi

Gandhi was imprisoned several times in the 1920s and 1930s but the British authorities found no effective way to counter his policy of passive resistance. He became a symbol of resistance to the British Empire and an example to subject peoples in other countries as well. His unique form of protest gained the sympathy and support of people throughout the world. He was even applauded by unemployed Lancashire cotton workers whose mills had closed down partly as a result of his call to Indians to spin and weave their own cotton clothes instead of buying British textiles. He told the Indian people to boycott the British and have nothing to do with them. He even organised a protest against the law which stopped Indians making their own salt (to avoid paying taxes to the British authorities).

Source A

A FRANKENSTEIN OF THE EAST

Punch, *12 March 1930*

Gandhi "Remember — no violence; just disobedience."
Genie "And what if I disobey *you*?"

Source B

In the presence of an enormous crowd of about 100,000 people lining the road for a distance of four miles (6.4 km), amid a swelling chorus of 'Long live Gandhi!', Mr.Gandhi set out this morning to open the campaign for Independence. It was 6.30 when he left at the head of the pilgrimage to the coast where Civil Disobedience to the salt-manufacturing laws is to begin. Wealthy Hindus and impoverished labourers vied in hailing the Mahatma ('Great Soul') and as the procession slowly moved along, the crowds showered upon him coins, currency notes, flowers and saffron.

Daily News & Chronicle, 13 March 1930

Source C

As the throng drew near the salt pans they commenced chanting the revolutionary slogan, *Inquilab zindabad*, intoning the two words over and over . . . Suddenly, at a word of command, scores of native police rushed upon the advancing marchers and rained blows on their heads with their steel-shod *lathis*. Not one of the marchers even raised an arm to fend off the blows . . . There was no fight, no struggle; the marchers simply walked forward until struck down. There were no outcries, only groans after they fell.

Webb Miller, *I Found No Peace*, Gollancz, 1937

Source D

All hope of reconciling India with the British Empire is lost for ever. I can understand any government's taking people into custody and punishing them for breaches of the law, but I cannot understand how any government that calls itself civilised could deal as savagely and brutally with non-violent, unresisting men as the British have this morning.

V.J. Patel (a leader of the Protest Movement) after watching the events recorded in Source C, in Webb Miller, *I Found No Peace*, Gollancz, 1937

---

1 *Which of the Sources A, B, C and D do you think was sympathetic to Gandhi's methods and policies?*

2 *What was the 'Frankenstein of the East'? Why 'Frankenstein'? What was the point of the cartoon? Was the comment justified?*

3 *How did the British authorities make it easy for Gandhi to get massive backing for his policies? Which Indians supported him?*

Independence

Some progress towards Indian independence was made before the War, with the granting of a limited form of self-government to the provinces. But these were dominated by the Hindu majority. The Moslems, who formed a very substantial minority, were worried what would happen if India later became independent with a Hindu-dominated government. Thei. leader, Mohammed Ali Jinnah, demanded that when independence came, it should take the form of partition – with two governments, Hindu India and Moslem Pakistan.

Mohammed Ali Jinnah After the war the British Labour Government speeded up moves to make India an independent nation. They tried to get the two sides to agree to a system of government which would allow India to remain as one country. But the situation in India deteriorated when riots broke out. Thousands were killed when Moslems and Hindus fought each other in the streets of Calcutta.

Rioters stoning trams in the streets of Calcutta in April 1947

Partition

The British Viceroy in India, Lord Mountbatten, advised that the immediate granting of independence was the only way to avoid further bloodshed and the possibility of full scale civil war. The British Government agreed and on 15 August 1947 Moslem Pakistan and Hindu India became independent. The Viceroy's solution was to divide the country into three parts. The major part of the sub-continent which was largely, but not exclusively, Hindu, became India. The largely Moslem communities of the north-west and north-east, 1600 km apart, became West and East Pakistan respectively.

Instead of an orderly planned progression to independence, however, partition only made matters worse. Millions of Moslems were stranded in India. Millions of Hindus were isolated inside Pakistan, to say nothing of the Sikhs, Parsees and other substantial religious minorities who lived in both countries. The bloodshed continued. There were massacres on both sides of the frontiers. Long streams of refugees crossed the borders in both directions. Half a million people may have died in the killings. The worst incident occurred when 1200 Moslem refugees were slaughtered by religious extremists when their train stopped at Amritsar on 24 September 1947. Gandhi, the man of peace, was appalled and openly deplored the violence; but was himself assassinated by a Hindu fanatic in 1948.

1 Why did Britain grant independence to the Indian sub-continent in a hurry in 1947?

2 What problems did independence bring to India and Pakistan?

India and Pakistan

Relations between India and Pakistan were never very good in the years immediately following independence. They fought border wars over the disputed territory of Kashmir in 1948 and again in 1965. Kashmir had a Hindu ruler but the Kashmiris included many Moslems who wanted to become part of Pakistan, not India. India was led for much of the period after independence by members of the Nehru family. Pandit Nehru led the country vigorously from 1947 to 1964, gaining a world reputation as a statesman and peace-maker. Two years later, his daughter, Mrs Indira Gandhi, took over as prime minister and led India from 1966 to 1977 and again from 1980 until she was assassinated by extremists in 1984. She was immediately succeeded as prime minister by her son, Rajiv Gandhi.

Pakistan, too, has had prime ministers drawn from the same family – Zulfikar Ali Bhutto from 1971 to 1977 and his daughter Benazir Bhutto in 1988. But Pakistan's history since independence has been troubled. General Mohammed Ayub Khan took control in October 1958 and for much of the next 30 years Pakistan was ruled by military dictators.

In 1971, East Pakistan attempted to break away from West Pakistan. President Yahya Khan sent troops to crush the rebellion in the east, but this action precipitated a brief war with India. It ended with the creation of the new state of Bangladesh, led by Sheik Mujibur Rahman. Pakistan reverted to democratic rule and Zulfikar Ali Bhutto became prime minister. Six years later he was overthrown in a military coup led by General Mohammed Zia ul-Haq and was later tried and executed. General Zia was himself assassinated in 1988. At the election later the same year, Benazir Bhutto became Pakistan's new prime minister.

South East Asia

The granting of independence to India and Pakistan was followed in 1948 with the creation of the independent states of Ceylon (later Sri Lanka) and Burma. In the Dutch East Indies, the Indonesian Nationalist Party was active before the war but its leaders were suppressed by the Dutch. When the Japanese invaded the islands in 1942 they were welcomed by the Nationalists as liberators. After the Japanese surrendered and before the Dutch could return to reclaim their colony, Achmad Sukarno declared Indonesia an independent republic. A bitter war followed, which ended in 1949 when UN intervention secured Indonesian independence.

Nationalist movements in the French colony of Indo-China before the war were led by Ho Chi Minh, a veteran revolutionary. They gained prominence during the Japanese occupation between 1941 and 1945. Instead of regarding the Japanese as liberators, Ho Chi Minh organised a successful campaign by Viet-Minh guerrillas against the invaders. At the end of the War Ho Chi Minh founded the independent republic of Vietnam centred on Hanoi in the north (see page 330). When the French returned to reclaim their

Ho Chi Minh

colony they tried to make Ho Chi Minh's Vietnam part of Indo-China once more. A bitter war of independence followed which ended after the French defeat at Dien Bien Phu (1954) and later with the reunification of Vietnam in 1975 (page 332).

British settlements on the Malay Peninsula were also overrun by the Japanese when they fought their way through the jungle to Singapore. After the war the British successfully reclaimed these territories and formed them into a Federation. In 1948, Communist guerrillas began a ten-year war against the British occupying forces. Although the guerrillas were defeated, the agitation they created during the 'Emergency' stimulated more general demands for independence and this was granted in 1957. Six years later the Federation joined Sabah and Sarawak (north Borneo) and Singapore to form the federation of Malaysia in 1963. Singapore left two years later when her largely Chinese population found it impossible to reconcile its differences with the Malays.

Supplying British troops during the Emergency in Malaya

DECOLONISATION IN AFRICA
Gaining Independence

Julius Nyerere of Tanzania

As you have seen the 'wind of change' blew rapidly through Africa in the 1950s and 1960s. Some countries like the British colonies of **The Gold Coast (Ghana), Nigeria, Uganda, Tanganyika (Tanzania – with Zanzibar)** and **Northern Rhodesia (Zambia)** were able to follow the constitutional path – mainly peaceful protests, civil disobedience and a stage-by-stage progression through elections and local self-government to full independence.

Others used force. Violent confrontation between guerrillas and settlers was a feature of the war of independence in many territories, such as **Kenya** where the Kikuyu tribe joined the Mau-Mau to fight against British rule in the 1950s. They swore a secret oath of loyalty promising not to betray their country, making a vow 'to kill for our soil', and accepting the consequences willingly,

> If I am called on to shed my blood for it I shall obey and I shall never surrender.

Kenneth Kaunda of Zambia

In **Southern Rhodesia (Zimbabwe)**, Joshua Nkomo and Robert Mugabe led Black guerrilla attacks in the 1970s on the White settlers and forces controlled by Ian Smith's White government. Smith had earlier declared Rhodesia independent of Britain in 1965. This was called UDI (unilateral declaration of independence) and was never accepted by the British Government.

In **Algeria** the FLN (National Liberation Front) fought an eight-year war against the French. In **Angola** several different guerrilla groups fought against the Portuguese from 1961 to 1974. Other long guerrilla wars were fought by FRELIMO guerrillas against the Portuguese in **Mozambique** and by SWAPO guerrillas against South Africa in **Namibia**.

When independence came it was usually celebrated with fireworks, parades, church services, the lowering and raising of flags, and military bands playing the new national anthem. The Governor of Nigeria commented that the raising of the Nigerian flag, while the new Nigerian anthem was being played, affected the new Nigerian prime minister so much that

Robert Mugabe of Zimbabwe

> tears were running down his face when I turned and shook him by the hand and congratulated him.

President Kwame Nkrumah of Ghana told his audience on Ghana's Independence Day on 7 March 1957 (see photograph on page 385)

> We part from the former Imperial power, Great Britain, with the warmest feelings of friendship and goodwill . . . instead of that feeling of bitterness which is often born of colonial struggle, we enter on our independence in association with Great Britain and with good relations unimpaired.
>
> Kwame Nkrumah, *I Speak of Freedom*, Panaf Books, 1973

Kwame Nkrumah of Ghana

In some cases the granting of independence brought civil war, often with foreign interference, as in Angola where Cuban, South African and White mercenary soldiers were involved. In 1960 the Belgians, like the British in India, were pressured into granting independence in a hurry to the **Congo (Zaire)**. In the chaos which followed, the prime minister, Patrice Lumumba, was murdered and the richest province, Katanga, claimed independence from the rest of the country. UN forces intervened and eventually helped to restore order. The Congo, like many other newly-independent states, was later taken over by the army, under its leader General Mobutu.

After Independence

The independent nations of Africa have had a varied history since independence. Some, such as Zambia, Kenya, Tanzania and Malawi, have enjoyed the benefit of stable government and the rule of the same president for many years. Other nations, such as Ghana and Nigeria, have witnessed a number of military coups. Ghana's first President, Kwame Nkrumah (see page 399), was deposed in 1966 only nine years after independence. A bloody civil war in 1967–70 cost thousands of lives after the leader of the Ibo people of neighbouring Nigeria, Colonel Ojukwu, announced in May 1967 that the Eastern region of Nigeria had seceded from the Nigerian Federation and would be known in future as Biafra. As always, it was the ordinary people who suffered. Thousands of Biafran children died in the famine which accompanied the Civil War.

Civil wars have also been fought in Chad, Mauritania, the Sudan, Ethiopia, Somalia and Uganda. Some of these countries, too, have suffered terrible famines as a consequence, such as in Somalia, Ethiopia and the Sudan. Cruel dictators have ruled in some countries, like Idi Amin in Uganda and the 'Emperor' Bokassa in the Central African Republic. Even the two countries which were already independent, Ethiopia and Liberia, have seen their rulers overthrown by military coups.

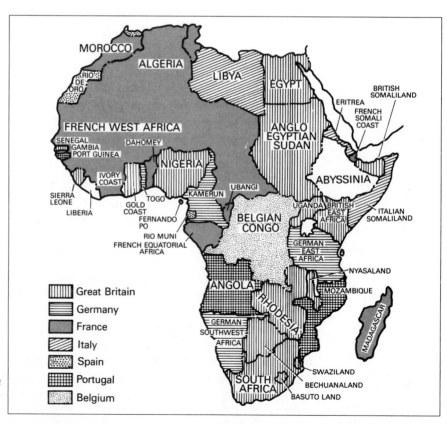

Map of Africa showing the European empires in Africa in 1914

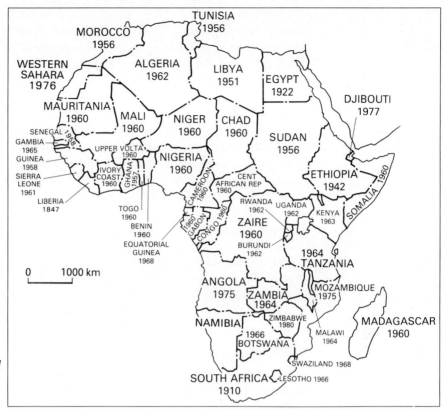

Map showing how Africa was decolonised after the Second World War

1 Which years were crucial in the decolonisation of Africa?

2 Which European powers were among a) the first and b) the last, to grant independence to their African colonies?

3 Make a list of the three or four most important events in Russian history in the years immediately following the March 1917 Revolution. Which African countries have seen a similar pattern of events since gaining independence? Why?

Apartheid

In general the most violent independence movements have been in countries where there are, or were, large numbers of European settlers (such as in Kenya, Zimbabwe and Algeria). After independence many settlers stayed behind and co-operated with the new governments. In South Africa the White population forms a substantial minority (roughly one person in every five). This White, Afrikaaner-dominated minority gained independence for South Africa (as a Dominion within the British Commonwealth) as long ago as 1910, after fighting a bitter war of independence in 1899–1902. White South Africa prospered because the country had valuable minerals (gold, diamonds and coal) and a large Black population to provide the cheap labour needed by the country's mines, factories, farms, businesses and homes.

The Blacks did not have the vote. Many Black workers lived in compounds owned by the mining companies. Although they were often better educated and better off than Africans in other parts of the continent, they were not free. After the Second World War the Blacks in South Africa shared the same aspirations as Africans throughout the continent. But things got worse, not better. In 1948 Daniel Malan's Nationalist Party introduced the policy of apartheid to the country. Apartheid means 'keeping apart'. It was implemented by segregating Whites from Blacks, Asians and Coloureds. Schools, ambulances, buses, beaches and even hospitals were reserved for Whites or Non-Whites only.

> Why is it that in this courtroom I face a White magistrate, am confronted by a White prosecutor, and escorted into the dock by a White orderly? Can anyone honestly and seriously suggest that in this type of atmosphere the scales of justice are evenly balanced?
>
> Nelson Mandela in court in 1962. Quoted in *Apartheid The Facts*, International Defence and Aid Fund for Southern Africa, 1983

In 1959 the ruling Nationalist Party introduced a new plan – of creating independent Black homelands for the peoples of different tribal groups. Those who spoke the Xhosa language were to belong to the Transkei. These new homelands were designated as self-governing independent republics, or *Bantustans*. The Transkei became the first of these independent homelands in 1976 but was not recognised as such by foreign governments.

The Sharpeville Massacre, 1960

In practice most Black people continued to live and work outside their homelands because this was the only place where they could find work. Without these Black workers the South African gold and coal mines, the farms, transport system and the whole economy would have ground to a halt. Apartheid was also accompanied by much-resented laws, such as those introduced by Dr Hendrik Verwoerd's Government which required Blacks, but not Whites, to carry pass books.

> Shooting by South African police on the first day of a campaign by Africans against the pass laws which require them to carry identity cards today ended in the deaths of 63 men, women and children. A further 191 were wounded.
>
> The worst outbreak was in the African township of Sharpeville, near Vereeniging, Witwatersrand, where the Treaty ending the Boer War was signed. Seventy-five White police, besieged in the police station, fired on thousands of demonstrators, killing 56 and wounding 162 . . . Anger over the pass system, which insists that every African carries a pass and renders him liable to imprisonment if caught moving from his prescribed locality to another in search of work, is long pent up. The alternative of freedom of movement, however, might produce mass descents on cities without prospect of work.
>
> *Daily Telegraph*, 22 March 1960

Apartheid was the reason why South Africa left the Commonwealth in 1961 and why few countries developed close links with it in the years which followed. The United Nations tried repeatedly, but unsuccessfully, to force the South African Government to change its policies.

The African National Congress played the leading role in opposing apartheid in South Africa. In 1964, Nelson Mandela, its outstanding leader, and other ANC activists were sentenced to life imprisonment.

In the years since then, the demonstrations have become more vocal and more violent. Increasingly, bomb attacks and killings have reflected the strength of the opposition to the race laws. In 1976, over 700 Africans were killed in riots in Soweto and other towns protesting against Government moves to teach Afrikaans as the official language in Black schools.

---

1 *The Blacks in South Africa heavily outnumber the Whites. Why, then, has South Africa got a White government and not a Black government like neighbouring Zimbabwe and Zambia?*

2 *Why has support for the African National Congress gained in strength since 1960?*

3 *What was the immediate cause of the Sharpeville Massacre? When was that cause eliminated? What other racial policies have changed since 1980? Why?*

DECOLONISATION IN THE MIDDLE EAST

Zionism

Israel also gained its independence shortly after the War, when the British left Palestine in 1948. This led immediately to war with the surrounding Arab nations. Since then Israel has fought three other major wars (see below) and many other campaigns, clashes and skirmishes with her Arab neighbours. The origins of this unhappy state of affairs go back to the founding of Zionism, to the promises made by Britain in 1915–17, and to the Jewish settlement of Palestine in the inter-war years.

Zionism is the name given to the movement, initiated by European Jews in the late nineteenth century, to establish a homeland for the Jewish people. The Jews originally lived in Palestine but were expelled by the Romans in AD 70. By the late nineteenth century many of them lived in western Russia (which then included Poland). Most Jews at that time thought they had been assimilated into the communities where they lived. They didn't think of themselves as a separate people. It was just that they had their own religion and traditions. But racial prejudice (highlighted by the Dreyfus case in France), and the pogroms (persecution of Russian and Polish Jews) in the 1880s, convinced some Jews that the only safe and adequate solution lay in the creation of an independent Jewish state. Since the Holy Land was the original home of the Jews, 2000 years earlier, the Zionists wanted to make Palestine their homeland in the twentieth century as well (Zion was the name given to the people of Israel in the Bible). Palestine, like most of the Middle East, was mainly inhabited by Arabs whose religion was Islam not Judaism. But Palestine in 1900 was not an Arab state. It was part of the Ottoman Empire and remained under Turkish control until it was captured by British forces in 1917–18. The Turks let Jewish settlers buy land there, as you can see from Sources A and B.

Source A

From a letter dated 2 August 1909:
Palestine was a decent country then [in Roman times], and could so easily be made so again. The sooner the Jews farm it all the better: their colonies are bright spots in a desert.

The Letters of T.E. Lawrence, edited by David Garnett, Cape, 1938

Source B

When war broke out there were some fifty Jewish colonies in Palestine, owning between them 110,000 acres [44 500 hectares] of land on which dwelt 15,000 Jews. They were for the most part agricultural settlements ... Some date back forty years and more, though the majority of them were founded within the last twenty years through the generosity of Sir Moses Montefiore, Baron Edmond de Rothschild, and other wealthy Jews. Land was purchased and Jews from all parts of Europe were encouraged to settle on it ... They have opened agricultural schools, improved the cereals, vines, olives and citrus fruits, and shown farmers what the land could produce.

Harold Shepstone, *The Graphic*, 21 August 1920

Jewish settlements in Palestine before 1914

Turkey entered the war against the Allies in November 1914. Britain struck back by enlisting the help of Arab leaders, promising them independence when the Turks were expelled from the Middle East.

Source C

From a letter, dated 24 October 1915, written by Sir Henry McMahon, then High Commissioner for Egypt, to the Grand Sherif Hussein of Mecca

> Subject to the above modifications, Great Britain is prepared to recognise and support the independence of the Arabs in all the regions within the limits demanded by the Sherif of Mecca ...
> When the situation admits, Great Britain will give to the Arabs her advice and will assist them to establish what may appear to be the most suitable forms of government in those various territories.

Printed in *Keesing's Contemporary Archives 1937–40*

The 'limits demanded by the Sherif of Mecca' were bounded by Latitude 37°N in the north, Persia (Iran) in the east, the Indian Ocean in the south (but not Aden) and the Red Sea and Mediterranean Sea in the west. Sir Henry's 'modifications' excluded land 'to the west of Damascus' which 'cannot be said to be purely Arab'. The Grand Sherif later insisted on the inclusion of the province of Beirut (which included much of Palestine) but Sir Henry did not commit himself.

The British also made a promise to the Zionists, hoping to gain support from American Zionists for the war effort.

Source D

From a letter, dated 2 November 1917, asking Lord Rothschild to bring this Declaration to the attention of the Zionist Federation

His Majesty's Government views with favour the establishment in Palestine of a National Home for the Jewish people, and will use their best endeavours to facilitate the achievement of this object, it being clearly understood that nothing shall be done which may prejudice the civil and religious rights of existing non-Jewish communities in Palestine, or the rights and political status enjoyed by Jews in any other country.

SIGNED: A.J. Balfour (British foreign secretary), 2 November 1917

1 *What is Zionism? What was the extent of Zionist settlement in Palestine by 1914?*

2 *How and why had Jews been able to settle in Moslem Palestine? Was there any reason why Jews should not have settled in Palestine provided they paid for their land?*

3 *How did Lawrence describe Palestine in 1909? How do you think the Zionist settlers turned their colonies into 'bright spots'?*

4 *Look at an atlas map. Did Britain promise Sherif Hussein that Palestine would become an independent Arab State after the War?*

5 *What was the Balfour Declaration? Did it promise to make the whole of Palestine the Jewish 'National Home' or to establish a 'National Home' within Palestine? What difference does this make?*

6 *People have argued that the promises in Sources C and D contradict each other. Do you agree or disagree? State your reasons.*

Between the Wars

Soon after the War, at a conference in San Remo (25 April 1920) Britain's Mandate over Palestine was confirmed. Zionists welcomed the decision. One of them said

With one foot already in the Holy Land, we shall now enter Palestine with firm steps, declaring 'Here we are; here we remain'.

This was because the League of Nations Mandate specifically referred to the Jewish claim to Palestine 'and the ground for reconstituting their national home in that country'. The British authorities encouraged Jewish settlers to continue setting up communal farm settlements (kibbutzim) like those begun when Palestine was part of the Turkish Empire. As a result, the ratio of Jews to Arabs increased. It grew from less than one in ten in 1920 to one in three in 1940. Increasingly, the Arab peoples of Palestine and the Middle East saw these Jewish settlements as a threat to their own existence. There were serious clashes between the two sides in 1929 (when 100 Arabs and 100 Jews were killed) and again in 1936. Arab nationalists mobilised Arab opinion against the Jews by organising demonstrations and strikes. The principal Arab leader was the Grand Mufti of Jerusalem. He told Webb Miller, an American journalist,

Source A

We affirm that we are merely seeking our just rights and safeguarding our national existence. We demand the fulfilment of the clear promises which the British gave the Arabs in 1915 regarding the independence of Arab territories, including Palestine. Our principal grievances at present are, first, agricultural land is being increasingly acquired by Jews, leaving the Arabs homeless or on restricted land insufficient for them. Second, abnormal Jewish immigration has caused widespread unemployment of Arabs.

He claimed that the British Government was prejudiced in favour of the Jews.

Palestine has been Arab for more than thirteen centuries and there is no way of reconciling the divergences between the Arabs and the Zionists . . . Palestine is sacred to all Moslems and particularly to the Arabs. We demand nothing more than the liberty to be independent in our own homeland. The policy of establishing a National Home for the Jews in Palestine will be fruitless because the Arabs and other Moslem countries will co-operate to oppose this policy.

The Grand Mufti of Jerusalem, quoted in Webb Miller, *I Found No Peace*, Gollancz, 1937

But Miller heard a different story when he met the Secretary of the Zionist Organization of America. He learned that

Source B

Ever since their second dispersion from Palestine in the year 70, the Jewish people have made their return to Palestine an integral part of their national aspirations . . . By the end of 1935 the Jewish population of the country was approximately 400,000, having been 12,000 in 1868, 59,000 in 1919, and 163,000 in 1928. With the return of this great mass of Jews into Palestine a new economic and cultural life has been created. The Jews returning to the soil have proved their ability at farming. They have rehabilitated the ancient Hebrew language and made it an instrument for daily usage. In recent years, particularly as a result of the large number of German refugees, the Jews have expanded the economic and industrial life of the country so that Palestine today manufactures and produces virtually all the products of a modern country . . . Responsible Jewish leadership has repeatedly affirmed its desire to co-operate whole-heartedly with the Arabs of Palestine . . . Some 275,000 Arabs have entered Palestine since 1922, as against 250,000 Jews who entered during the same period.

Morris Margulies, Secretary of the Zionist Organisation of America,
quoted in Webb Miller, *I Found No Peace*, Gollancz, 1937

1 *Was the Grand Mufti correct in using the words 'clear promises' to describe the British undertakings about Palestine in 1915?*

2 *Draw a graph to show the growth of Jewish settlement in Palestine by 1935. Was it sudden or steady growth?*

3 *Who do you think had a greater claim to Palestine in the 1930s, a) the Jews who wanted to reclaim the land from which their ancestors had been expelled 'in the year 70', or, b) the Arabs who claimed to have lived there 'for more than thirteen centuries'?*

4 *Sum up the arguments put forward by the Zionists and the Arabs in the 1930s. Having heard these arguments, what arrangements would you have made in order to grant independence to Palestine?*

Partition

The difficulty of reconciling the differences between the two peoples made the British authorities think seriously of partition in 1937 but the report of the Peel Commission which recommended this step was rejected by most Jews and Arabs. This left the British authorities pleasing neither side. Britain was torn between the humane wish to accommodate Jews fleeing from tyranny in Europe and the desire to placate the Arabs whose homeland it had been for hundreds of years.

Source A

Having reached the conclusion that the Arab–Jewish differences are irreconcilable, as shown by the history of the past 17 years, and that the present mandatory system provides no solution of Palestinian problems, its termination is recommended in favour of the establishment of a Jewish and an Arab State with the Holy Places of Jerusalem, Nazareth and Bethlehem coming under a new and permanent British Mandate.

Summary of the Peel Commission Report, July 1937,
in *Keesing's Contemporary Archives 1937–40*

Source B

JEWISH
STATE

ARAB
STATE

BRITISH
MANDATE

INTERNATIONAL
BOUNDARY

SYRIA

Safad

SEA of
GALILEE

Acre

HAIFA

Nazareth

Samakh

Jenin

Beisan

Tulkarm

NABLUS

TRANS
JORDANIA

RIVER JORDAN

JAFFA

Lydda

Jericho

JERUSALEM

Al Majdal

Bethlehem

Hebron

DEAD
SEA

GAZA

MEDITERRANEAN
SEA

*Map of the proposed
partition of Palestine,
July 1937, from
Keesing's
Contemporary
Archives*

Source C

Whatever criticisms may be levelled against partition it does offer the
greatest possible measure of justice to the two nations of Palestine.

The Times, July 1937

Source D

the proposed partition offers little or no hope of eliminating or even
lessening the effects in Palestine of those forces, internal and external,
which according to the Commission have made Zionist–Arab peace
impossible.

New York Times, July 1937

Source E

Zionists will resist these conclusions obstinately and energetically.

The Zionist newspaper *Haolam*, July 1937

Source F

an obstruction to Arab unity, depriving the Arabs of their country and coast, driving them to the hills and creating minorities.

The Arab newspaper *Lewa*, July 1937

---

1 *Why did the Peel Commission propose to partition Palestine?*

2 *Why did the Arabs reject partition?*

3 *Compare the map of the proposed Jewish State in 1937 with an atlas map of modern Israel. What are the principal differences?*

In November 1938, the British Government abandoned plans to partition Palestine. Instead, it held a conference in London, early in 1939. Both Arabs and Jews were represented. But they failed to agree. By this time an ugly civil war seemed imminent in Palestine. There were nearly a thousand murders between August 1938 and July 1939. Sabotage, bomb attacks and armed robberies were common. Official statistics revealed the extent of the conflict: 'Jews killed by rebels 236: Arabs killed by rebels 435'.

In May 1939, the British Government decided to impose its own solution. It rejected the notion of a Jewish State (based on Zionist interpretations of the Balfour Declaration). Equally, it dismissed the Arab argument that McMahon had promised to turn Palestine into an Arab State. Instead it proposed to create 'within ten years'

an independent Palestine State, one in which Arabs and Jews shall share authority in government in such a way that the essential interests of each are secured.

Arabs and Jews would share in government to ensure that the essential interests of each community were safeguarded. Britain would

allow such Jewish immigration during the next five years as will bring the Jewish population to about one-third of the whole. This will allow the admission of 75,000 immigrants in the next five years . . . Measures will be taken to stop illegal immigration . . . After the five years are up no further Jewish immigration will be permitted 'unless the Arabs of Palestine are prepared to acquiesce in it'.

Keesing's Contemporary Archives 1937–40

---

1 *Why was the proposal unacceptable to the Arabs?*

2 *Why were Zionists bitterly opposed to the plan? What did the future hold for them? Why did the extremists among them turn to terrorism?*

3 *Why do you think this proposal was eventually abandoned?*

After the War

The problem of Palestine became almost insoluble after the War when thousands of Jews fled from a Europe where their relatives had been systematically put to death in Nazi concentration camps. The British authorities, under pressure from the Arab world (who threatened Britain's oil supplies), and fearing another explosive civil war, refused them entry. The United States exerted pressure in the other direction and demanded that 100 000 displaced Jews from Europe be allowed to enter Palestine at once. At the same time, Jewish terrorist groups (the Stern Gang and Irgun) tried to force the British out of Palestine with bomb attacks and killings.

Source A

THE WANDERING JEW

Cartoon by Vicky in the News Chronicle, *20 September 1945*

NO PROMISED LAND

Source B

Irgun poster explaining why 91 people (including several Jews) were killed and 46 injured when the King David Hotel in Jerusalem was blown up by Zionist terrorists on 22 July 1946:

Yesterday at 12.05 p.m. soldiers of the Irgun Zvai Leumi attacked the central building of the British power of occupation in Palestine ... The tragedy which happened in the offices of the government is not the guilt of the Jewish soldiers who have received orders to spare human lives and they fulfilled that order. But this tragedy came through the fault of the British tyrants who played with human life on the advice of the military experts who said that they would be able to disarm the bombs and therefore there was no need for evacuation.

Thurston Clarke, *By Blood and Fire*, Hutchinson, 1981

Source C

Then for reasons which will never be understood by me . . . the British . . . forcibly caged and returned to Germany the 4500 refugees who had come to Palestine aboard the *Haganah* ship *Exodus 1947* . . . If I live to be a hundred, I shall never erase from my mind the gruesome picture of hundreds of British soldiers in full combat dress, bearing and using clubs, pistols and grenades against the wretched refugees on the *Exodus*, 400 of whom were pregnant women determined to give birth to their babies in Palestine.

Mrs Golda Meir [Israeli prime minister 1969–74], *My Life*, Weidenfeld and Nicolson, 1975

---

1 *Why did Britain's refusal to accept refugee ships like this antagonise Jews throughout the world? Was Britain justified in doing this?*

2 *Why do you think many Jews were bitterly opposed to the tactics of Irgun and the Stern Gang? Was this terrorism or patriotism?*

3 *What was the point of the cartoon? Who were the 'wandering Jews'? Where had they come from?*

After two British sergeants were hanged by the Irgun group, anti-Semitism increased sharply in Britain and many politicians told the Government to let the warring Jews and Arabs solve the problem on their own. Winston Churchill told an audience of Conservatives in 1947,

Nearly one hundred thousand British soldiers have been kept in Palestine, and £30 million or £40 million a year of our hard-earned money has been cast away there . . . No British interest is involved in our retention of the Palestine Mandate. For nearly thirty years we have done our best to carry out an honourable and self-imposed task. A year ago, I urged the Government to give notice to the United Nations that we could and would bear the burden of insults and injuries no longer.

Quoted in Eric Silver, *Begin: A Biography*, Weidenfeld and Nicolson, 1984

Britain's Labour Government needed no advice. The United Nations was told that Britain was relinquishing its Mandate. It was up to the UN to come up with a solution.

The United Nations General Assembly approved yesterday a proposal to partition Palestine into two states, one Arab and the other Jewish that are to become independent by Oct. 1 [1948] ... Andrei A. Gromyko [Soviet Union] and Herschel V. Johnson [United States] both urged the Assembly yesterday not to agree to further delay but to vote for partition at once.

Thomas J. Hamilton in the *New York Times*, 30 November 1947

Moshe Dayan

The Israelis were delighted. Mrs Golda Meir, a future Israeli prime minister, said there were 'hundreds of people, British soldiers among them, holding hands, singing and dancing'. Moshe Dayan, an Israeli general, said

It was night time. I took the children from their beds and we joined the rest of the village in festive dancing in the community hall ... I felt in my bones the victory of Judaism, which for two thousand years of exile from the Land of Israel had withstood persecutions, the Spanish Inquisition, pogroms, anti-Jewish decrees, restrictions, and the mass slaughter by the Nazis in our own generation.

Moshe Dayan, *Story of My Life*, Weidenfeld and Nicolson, 1976

Independence

But the rejoicing was shortlived as you can see from these sources:

Source A

The Arab states refused to accept the U.N. Decision and announced that they would make war on the Jewish state ... For the next five and a half months, the country was ravaged by violence. Arab attacks on Jewish rural settlements, towns, and inter-urban transport mounted daily. The British government, announcing that it would relinquish the Mandate on May 15, did little to stop them. Order gave way to anarchy.

Moshe Dayan, *Story of My Life*, Weidenfeld and Nicolson, 1976

Source B

There had been atrocities on both sides ... the Irgun massacred an estimated 110 Arab civilians at Dir Yassin in April (That horrible act is still shrouded in mystery: the Irgun claimed there was a battle; Arab survivors claimed as many as 254 dead). Reports of the massacre started something of a stampede out of Arab Jerusalem; Arab radio dwelt endlessly on tales of Jewish cruelty, while Jewish radio exaggerated Jewish strength. A few days after Dir Yassin, 77 Jewish doctors, nurses, and students were murdered on the road to Mt. Scopus's Hadassah Hospital.

Bernard Avishai, *The Tragedy of Zionism*, Farrar, Straus & Giroux, 1985

Source C

9 April 1948: On that day one of the most barbaric crimes was committed against the 775 inhabitants of the village of Deir Yassine, near Jerusalem. At 3.45 in the morning, Zionist aeroplanes dropped 7 shells on the village: the Zionist forces, backed up by 15 tanks and intense mortar fire, surrounded the village, killing and murdering 254 innocent and unarmed people. Among the dead there was an old man of 90 years, Haj Ismail Atiyeh, and an 18-month-old baby who was found dead at the breast of its mother, her throat slit as well. The mutilated bodies of the victims were then thrown into one of the village wells.

Youssef Al-Khatib, *Agenda Palestinien 1972* (translated from the French), Les Editions Palestine, published in Syria, 1972

Source D

The tragic trouble about Deir Yassin was that the Arabs were stronger than us. They had more rifles, more ammunition, and they fought from house to house.

Senior Irgun officer quoted in Eric Silver, *Begin: A Biography*, Weidenfeld and Nicolson, 1984

Source E

It [Dir Yassin] was a massacre in hot blood, it was not pre-planned. It was an outburst from below with no one to control it. Groups of men went from house to house looting and shooting, shooting and looting. You could hear the cries from within the houses of Arab women, Arab elders, Arab kids. I tried to find the commanders, but I did not succeed. I tried to shout and hold them, but they took no notice. Their eyes were glazed. It was as if they were drugged, mentally poisoned, in ecstasy.

Meir Pa'il (a Jewish Army intelligence officer), quoted in Eric Silver, *Begin: A Biography*, Weidenfeld and Nicolson, 1984

---

1 *Which of these sources is an eyewitness account? Which of these sources is biased in one direction or the other? Give an example of bias. Is the use of the word 'massacre' an example of bias?*

2 *What disagreement on fact is there between Sources C and D? Which source do you believe? Why?*

3 *Write an impartial account of the incident at Dir Yassin.*

4 *What was the Palestinian Arab reaction to Dir Yassin?*

The British Mandate over Palestine ended, as promised, on 14 May 1948 and the Palestinian Jews, under their leader David Ben-Gurion, immediately proclaimed the state of Israel.

The following day, 15 May 1948, the Arab armies of Jordan, Iraq, Syria, Lebanon and Egypt attacked Israel. But the Israelis had prepared for the conflict. With their superior equipment and training and the financial support of American Jews they not only held on to the land awarded to them under the UN partition plan, they seized other territory which made their country less fragmented than before (see map on page 418).

It is estimated that over 700 000 Arabs fled from the parts of Palestine threatened by the advancing Israelis. This created a massive problem. The Palestinian refugees, housed in temporary camps, had hoped to return to Palestine when the Arab armies conquered Israel. Now they found, to their cost, that they were the homeless ones, not the Jews. The refugee camps lacked basic facilities. They soon became the breeding places of disease and training grounds for the *fedayeen*, or 'freedom-fighters'. One group called Al Fatah (led by Yasser Arafat) later united with other groups to form the PLO (Palestine Liberation Organisation).

They were supported by Israel's Arab neighbours who licked their wounds and prepared for the next war. Egypt, by far the largest state in terms of population, posed the biggest threat. A young, charismatic army officer, Colonel Gamal Abdel Nasser, seized power there in 1954. Nasser was ambitious. He persuaded the British to withdraw their troops from the Suez Canal zone which they had 'protected' ever since 1882.

The Suez Crisis

The British troops left Egypt on 6 June 1956. Nasser was elected President on 23 June. He promised the Egyptians he would build a new dam across the Nile, the Aswan High Dam, which would provide electricity to power new industries and supply enough water to let farmers cultivate vast new tracts of desert. On 19 July 1956, the United States (annoyed because Nasser was negotiating with the Soviet Union) withdrew its offer of a loan to Egypt to build the dam. The British Government did likewise the next day. This was a savage blow to Nasser's pride.

Source A   26 July 1956

President Nasser tells cheering crowds: 'We shall build the High Dam we want. We are determined. The Canal Company takes £35 million a year. Today, Citizens, the Suez Canal is nationalised! This decree is now law!'

Although Egypt was prepared to pay compensation, Nasser's action in nationalising the Anglo–French Suez Canal infuriated the British and French governments.

Source B   31 July 1956

Egypt's action in nationalising the Canal company has been received with too much excitement in Britain and France . . . In our view, nothing illegal has occurred. Where is the Suez Canal? In Egypt. What land does it cross? Egyptian land. By whom was the Canal built? By Arabs, the inhabitants of Egypt.

Nikita Khruschev (Soviet leader), quoted in the Daily Express, 1 August 1956

Source C   1 August 1956

Britain is ready to go it alone. Britain is determined to stand for no more trouble in the Suez Canal. That is the explanation behind yesterday's decision by the Cabinet to order full naval and military preparations for the occupation of the Canal should it prove necessary.

Daily Express, 1 August 1956

In fact, nothing happened for nearly three months. People in Britain accused Eden of inaction.

> The grand old Anthony Eden
> He had ten thousand men
> He marched them up to the top of the hill
> And marched them down again.

However, according to the Israeli commander, General Moshe Dayan, a secret meeting was held at Sèvres, near Paris, on 22 October, between senior British, French and Israeli leaders. Moshe Dayan claimed that they agreed on a secret plan of campaign:

- Israel to start military action against Egypt
- Franco–British ultimatum to be issued to Egypt and Israel demanding their withdrawal from the Canal area
- Egyptian airfields to be bombed after the expiry of the ultimatum.

Source D   22–4 October 1956

Selwyn Lloyd [British foreign secretary] was not shocked. He did not even seem surprised at my plan. He simply urged that our military action not be a small-scale encounter but a 'real act of war', otherwise there would be no justification for the British ultimatum and Britain would appear in the eyes of the world as an aggressor.

Moshe Dayan, Story of My Life, Weidenfeld and Nicolson, 1976

On 29 October 1956, Israel launched a sudden attack on Egypt. It went according to plan. France and Britain immediately used it as the pretext to attack Egypt. They said they were sending in troops to protect the canal even though the fighting between Egypt and Israel was nowhere near the canal zone. They gave Israel and Egypt 12 hours to withdraw their troops from the zone. On 31 October, hardly waiting for a reply, British bombers attacked Egyptian airfields near Cairo and Suez. They were immediately condemned for this action by the United Nations, the Soviet Union, the United States, the Commonwealth and the British Labour Party.

Source E 31 October 1956

How can they have done such a thing with the whole of world opinion against us passes my comprehension. We shall now be accused of exploiting the crime of the Jews in invading Sinai in order to resume control of the Canal. To do this we have sacrificed our principles and practically destroyed UNO and the Charter. We are in danger of being denounced as aggressors.

Harold Nicolson, *Diaries and letters 1945–62*, edited by Nigel Nicolson, Collins, 1968

Britain and France vetoed a US resolution in the Security Council and sent in troops. But international pressure forced them to climb down.

Source F 7 November 1956

Well! That really is a fiasco! I experienced shameful relief when I heard of the cease-fire, but I fear that we have not heard the end of the story by a long chalk (whatever that may be). Eden has failed all along the line. The Canal will now be blocked for weeks: Nasser is regarded as a hero and a martyr: our oil supplies will be cut for two months at least: we have shown that we have not a friend in the world: our reputation is tarnished: and in the end, at the first serious threat from Bulganin [Soviet prime minister], we have had to climb down.

Harold Nicolson, *Diaries and letters 1945–62*, edited by Nigel Nicolson, Collins, 1968

On 23 November, Eden agreed to withdraw his forces under financial pressure from the United States and veiled threats of force from the Soviet Union. United Nations troops were sent in to keep the peace between Israel and Egypt. Nasser got his canal back and eventually his dam (with the aid of a Russian loan and Russian technology). Eden resigned as prime minister on 9 January 1957 on the grounds of ill health.

1 *Why did Nasser nationalise the Suez Canal? Who supported this action and on what grounds? Why did Britain and France intervene? Why did they back down? What had Israel to gain by attacking Egypt? Who won in the end?*

2 *Why was Harold Nicolson shocked? What had 'they' done? Who were 'they'? What was 'such a thing'? What did he see as the likely consequences of the Suez Crisis? What was the 'fiasco'? What do you think his reaction would have been had he seen Source D?*

3 *Ask your older friends and relatives if they can tell you what they thought at the time of the Suez Crisis in 1956. What did they think of Nasser, Eden, the Anglo-French intervention, the UN, USA, etc.?*

4 *How do you think the Israelis reacted to Selwyn Lloyd's reported fear that Britain might 'appear in the eyes of the world as an aggressor'?*

5 *What sort of policy did the leaders of Britain and France think they could still pursue in 1956? Why were they opposed by both the Soviet Union and the United States?*

The Six Day War

After the Suez War, President Nasser turned increasingly to the Soviet Union for help. By the mid 1960s, Israel was ringed by hostile forces. At one stage Egypt and Syria even united to form the United Arab Republic (1958–61). Egypt's increasingly aggressive stance alerted the Israelis to the likelihood of a new war. This seemed imminent when Nasser told U Thant to remove the UN peace-keeping force from the border zone between Egypt and Israel, on 18 May 1967. He followed this by closing the Gulf of Aqaba to Israeli ships. This cut off Israel's access to the Red Sea and the Indian Ocean from her port of Eilat. Israel reacted by calling up her army. On 5 June, without warning and without a declaration of war, Israeli planes left Israel and destroyed

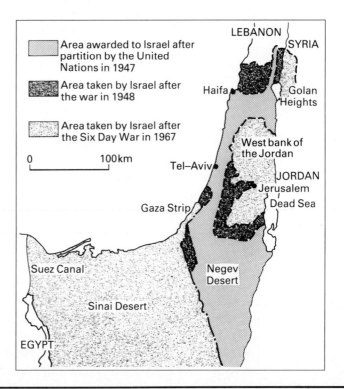

Map of Israel's conquests 1948–67

Arab fighters and bombers on the ground at airfields throughout the Middle East. The Israeli Army launched a massive attack on several fronts. It seized the whole of the Sinai Peninsula (to protect the Gulf of Aqaba shipping route), occupied the west bank of the Jordan and captured Jerusalem and the Golan Heights in Syria.

The UN Security Council (Soviet Union, United States, United Kingdom and France included) demanded that Israel withdraw from these territories, at the same time asking the Arab nations to respect Israel's right to exist as an independent nation. Neither side was prepared to do this.

---

1 *What disadvantages were there for Israel in the original partition of Palestine in 1947?*

2 *How did Israel's frontiers change after the wars in 1948 and 1967?*

3 *What has happened to the lands seized by Israel in 1967?*

The Yom Kippur War

Israel's prime minister, Mrs Golda Meir

During the next six years, the Arab countries re-equipped their armed forces, mainly with Soviet help. The PLO (see page 415) stepped up its campaign against Israeli targets. In September 1970 it hijacked three Western airliners. It blew one up, a jumbo jet, at Cairo. Then it flew the other two to Jordan where they, too, were blown up, together with a British airliner. This had been hijacked after a woman terrorist, Leila Khaled, was captured after failing to hijack an Israeli airliner over London. The hijackers took their hostages to a hiding place and demanded the release of Arab prisoners in exchange. The Western governments agreed to do this. The operation was counter-productive for the PLO, however, since the government of Jordan took immediate action to curb their activities and expelled the PLO from Jordan.

In 1973, it was the turn of the Arabs to catch the Israelis off guard. On Saturday 6 October most Israelis were busy observing Yom Kippur (the Day of Atonement). This is the holiest day of the Jewish year. But Egyptian tanks broke the peace. They crossed the Suez Canal and advanced across the Sinai Peninsula towards Israel. Simultaneously, Syrian forces launched an attack on the Golan Heights. Once again Israel's commanders lived up to their reputation for military daring. Their troops crossed the Suez Canal and trapped the Egyptian Third Army. The United Nations arranged a cease fire and a UN peace-keeping force patrolled the borders once more.

The Oil Weapon

The Yom Kippur War caused much heart-searching in Israel. Over 2 000 soldiers had been killed. The Arab armies had acquitted themselves well.

Israel couldn't count on a swift military victory in future. Nor could she count on continuing political support from the West. The Arabs had discovered a powerful new weapon. As oil producers they exerted pressure on the West to end the conflict by doubling oil prices, cutting oil production and banning oil exports to the Netherlands and to the United States (in retaliation for a massive US airlift of weapons which had re-supplied the Israeli forces).

The resulting oil crisis had dramatic side effects. The rise in oil prices caused a steep rise in inflation and a huge rise in unemployment in the industrial countries. It caused petrol rationing in many countries. It also made the cost of essential fertilisers prohibitively expensive in Third World countries as well as vastly increasing the price they paid for essential oil and petrol.

Camp David

Egyptian President Sadat (right), Israeli Premier Menachem Begin (left) and US President Carter (centre) at Camp David, 1979

The high cost of the war also affected the Egyptians. The Egyptian President, Anwar Sadat (who succeeded Nasser in 1970), took the courageous step of suggesting peace talks with Israel. These negotiations at Camp David (near Washington DC) produced a peace agreement which was signed on 26 March 1979. It ended the long on-and-off conflict between Israel and her largest neighbour, Egypt. Israel agreed to withdraw from the Sinai Peninsula and to return to the pre-1967 frontier with Egypt. At the time, the Camp David Agreement offered hope that peace might come at last to the Middle East. In no other part of the world has the likelihood of conflict seemed greater than in the countries surrounding Israel.

In 1979 American hostages were seized in Iran, soon after the Ayatollah Khomeini replaced the Shah as leader and brought the Islamic Revolution to Iran. The Islamic Revolution is the name given to the resurgence of Moslem feeling in some of the countries of the Middle East. Countries like Pakistan and Iran re-introduced traditional Islamic laws, many of them prescribing grave penalties, such as flogging and stoning, for serious offences. In Iran the fervour was stimulated by Moslem leaders called Mullahs and by the very militant Revolutionary Guards. In 1980 war broke out between Iraq and Iran. In 1981 Sadat was assassinated. In 1982 Israel invaded the Lebanon.

FURTHER QUESTIONS AND EXERCISES

German cartoon

Cartoon drawn by Illingworth in the 1950s

Cartoon drawn in the 1960s by Vicky for the Evening Standard

"LOOK! I'M SAVING WHITE CIVILISATION..."

Dutch cartoon drawn in the 1970s. The four leaders on the right are from Germany, France, the USA and the UK

1   *Look at these cartoons. For each drawing, write down the name of the event and the year or (approximate year) to which it refers? Identify the people involved and write brief notes explaining the point of each cartoon. Outline and explain the course of events both before and after. What was their significance?*

2 *Was European Imperialism harmful or beneficial to Africa? What do you think? Discuss this with your friends. Draw up a table, like the one below, comparing the arguments for and the arguments against.*

Beneficial to Africa	Harmful to Africa
Explorers and settlers gave the peoples of Africa the benefits of a great civilisation, with its customs, languages, Christian religion, medicine and sophisticated way of life.	*Africa already had its own languages, laws, governments, religions, and traditions long before the Europeans came. It was wrong of the Europeans to assume that theirs was a superior civilisation.*

3 *Write brief notes to explain the significance of each of the following in the history of Imperialism (a–d) and the Middle East (e–h):*

a) passive resistance

b) apartheid

c) Nationalism

d) religious conflict

e) the Balfour Declaration

f) Zionism

g) the Suez Crisis

h) the Yom Kippur War.

4 *What do you understand by the term* decolonisation? *Use recent examples from different continents to illustrate your answer.*

5 *Describe the struggle for independence in India. Why was Britain reluctant to grant independence at first but over-anxious to settle the question in 1947? What were the consequences of that decision?*

6 *Why do you think the Suez Crisis is often seen as a major turning point for both Britain and France? What happened in the next few years to change the relationship both nations had, a) with the rest of Europe and b) with the peoples of their empires?*

Index

Acknowledgements

The author and publishers are grateful to the following for supplying and giving permission to reproduce illustrative material: Associated Newspapers, p 250; Associated Newspapers/Centre for Study of Cartoons, University of Canterbury, pp 308, 360, 411, 422T; Berendt, p 422B; Bildarchiv Preussischer Kulturbesitz, pp 137B, 252B; Britain/Israel Public Affairs Centre, pp 413, 419; British Library, pp 49, 235, 237, 243, 391, 421T; Bundesarchiv, p 74; Camera Press, p 366; Jean-Loup Charmet, p 151; the Commission of the European Communities, pp 355, 357T & B, 362, 364; *Daily Telegraph*, p 336; René Dazy, pp 138T, 147, 150; John Hillelson/Marc Ribaud, p 372; Hulton Picture Library, pp 3, 22B, 66, 73, 121B, 124, 138B, 142, 143, 146, 153, 157, 162, 170, 227, 229, 245, 255, 270, 306, 337, 369, 382, 394T; Intervention Board, p 363; David King Collection, p 118; Kladderadatsch, p 204; Labour Party Library, p 145; Landesbildstelle, Berlin, p 354R; Lords Gallery, p 51; Magnum/Rene Burri, p 180; Mail Newspapers plc, pp 323, 421B; The Mansell Collection Ltd, pp 5, 18, 24, 25, 29, 30, 48, 64, 76, 79, 99L & R, 121T, 123B, 159, 173, 176, 203, 215, 238; Moro, Rome, p 71; Museo del Prado (© DACS 1989), p 231; National Library of Ireland, p 140; Novosti, pp 17, 22T, 26, 32, 114, 125; Popperfoto, pp 19, 54, 58, 59, 65, 69, 97, 101, 123T, 164, 167, 193, 194, 226, 228, 239, 252T, 254, 257, 267, 273, 280, 282, 302, 307, 311, 319, 321T & B, 326T & B, 328L, 331, 333, 334, 338, 340, 341, 342, 343, 344, 346, 348, 349, 352, 354L, 365, 395, 396, 397, 398T & B, 399M & B, 402, 415, 420; Roger-Viollet, p 184; School of Slavonic and East European Studies, pp 111, 314; Society for Anglo-Chinese Understanding Ltd, pp 195, 378, 383; Society for Cultural Relations with the USSR, p 107; Suddeutscher Verlag, p 137T; Topham, pp 186, 189, 367, 381, 385; Trustees of the Imperial War Museum, pp 13, 39, 276, 278; United Nations, pp 205, 209, 285, 288, 291, 292, 295T & B, 300; United States Information Service, p 350; US Navy, p 262; World Health Organization, p 296; Zambia High Commission, p 399T.

Every attempt has been made to contact copyright holders, but we apologise if any have been overlooked.